HTML5

2nd Edition

the missing manual®

The book that should have been in the box®

Matthew MacDonald

O'REILLY®

Beijing | Cambridge | Farnham | Köln | Sebastopol | Tokyo

HTML5: The Missing Manual, 2nd Edition

by Matthew MacDonald

Published by O'Reilly Media, Inc.,
1005 Gravenstein Highway North, Sebastopol, CA 95472.

O'Reilly books may be purchased for educational, business, or sales promotional use. Online editions are also available for most titles (*http://my.safaribooksonline.com*). For more information, contact our corporate/institutional sales department: (800) 998-9938 or *corporate@oreilly.com*.

August 2011:   First Edition.
December 2013:   Second Edition

Revision History for the Second Edition:

2013-12-09   First release

See *http://oreil.ly/html5tmm_2e* for release details.

ISBN-13: 978-1-4493-6326-0

[LSI]

Contents

The Missing Credits . . . . **vii**

Introduction . . . . **xi**

Part One: Modern Markup

CHAPTER 1: **Introducing HTML5** **3**

The Story of HTML5. 3
Three Key Principles of HTML5 7
Your First Look at HTML5 Markup. 10
A Closer Look at HTML5 Syntax 16
HTML5's Element Family. 21
Using HTML5 Today. 26

CHAPTER 2: **Structuring Pages with Semantic Elements** **37**

Introducing the Semantic Elements 38
Retrofitting a Traditional HTML Page 39
Browser Compatibility for the Semantic Elements 51
Designing a Site with the Semantic Elements. 53
The HTML5 Outlining System. 65

CHAPTER 3: **Writing More Meaningful Markup** **75**

The Semantic Elements Revisited. 76
Other Standards That Boost Semantics. 82
A Practical Example: Retrofitting an "About Me" Page 88
How Search Engines Use Metadata 93

CHAPTER 4: **Building Better Web Forms** **103**

Understanding Forms 104
Revamping a Traditional HTML Form. .105
Validation: Stopping Errors. 112
Browser Support for Web Forms and Validation. 119
New Types of Input 123
New Elements 130
An HTML Editor in a Web Page 136

Part Two: Video, Graphics, and Glitz

CHAPTER 5: **Audio and Video** **143**
The Evolution of Web Video...144
Introducing HTML5 Audio and Video...............................145
Understanding the HTML5 Media Formats 149
Fallbacks: How to Please Every Browser 154
Controlling Your Player with JavaScript...........................160
Video Captions 169

CHAPTER 6: **Fancy Fonts and Effects with CSS3** **177**
Using CSS3 Today...178
Building Better Boxes 184
Creating Effects with Transitions.....................................195
Web Fonts 206

CHAPTER 7: **Responsive Web Design with CSS3** **221**
Responsive Design: The Basics 222
Adapting Your Layout with Media Queries 231

CHAPTER 8: **Basic Drawing with the Canvas** **245**
Getting Started with the Canvas......................................246
Building a Basic Paint Program 263
Browser Compatibility for the Canvas 271

CHAPTER 9: **Advanced Canvas: Interactivity and Animation** **275**
Other Things You Can Draw on the Canvas.......................275
Shadows and Fancy Fills...281
Making Your Shapes Interactive 293
Animating the Canvas 300
A Practical Example: The Maze Game 307

Part Three: Building Web Apps

CHAPTER 10: **Storing Your Data** **319**
Web Storage Basics..320
Deeper into Web Storage 326
Reading Files...332
IndexedDB: A Database Engine in a Browser 340

CHAPTER 11: **Running Offline** **355**
Caching Files with a Manifest...356
Practical Caching Techniques 366

CHAPTER 12: **Communicating with the Web Server** **375**
   Sending Messages to the Web Server 376
   Server-Sent Events. 386
   Web Sockets 393

CHAPTER 13: **Geolocation, Web Workers, and History Management** . . . **401**
   Geolocation. 402
   Web Workers. 414
   History Management 425

Part Four: **Appendixes**

APPENDIX A: **Essential CSS** **435**
   Adding Styles to a Web Page. 435
   The Anatomy of a Style Sheet 436
   Slightly More Advanced Style Sheets. 440
   A Style Sheet Tour 445

APPENDIX B: **JavaScript: The Brains of Your Page** **451**
   How a Web Page Uses JavaScript. 452
   A Few Language Essentials 459
   Interacting with the Page 470

   Index. **477**

The Missing Credits

ABOUT THE AUTHOR

 Matthew MacDonald is a science and technology writer with well over a dozen books to his name. Web novices can tiptoe out onto the Internet with him in *Creating a Website: The Missing Manual*. Office geeks can crunch the numbers in *Excel 2013: The Missing Manual*. And human beings of all description can discover just how strange they really are in the quirky handbooks *Your Brain: The Missing Manual* and *Your Body: The Missing Manual*.

ABOUT THE CREATIVE TEAM

Nan Barber (editor) has been working on the Missing Manual series since its inception. She lives in Massachusetts with her husband and various Apple and Android devices. Email: *nanbarber@oreilly.com*.

Kristen Brown (production editor) is a graduate of the publishing program at Emerson College. She lives in the Boston area with her husband and their large collection of books and board games. Email: *kristen@oreilly.com*.

Kara Ebrahim (conversion) lives, works, and plays in Cambridge, MA. She loves graphic design and all things outdoors. Email: *kebrahim@oreilly.com*.

Julie Van Keuren (proofreader) quit her newspaper job in 2006 to move to Montana and live the freelancing dream. She and her husband (who is living the novel-writing dream) have two sons. Email: *little_media@yahoo.com*.

Julie Hawks (indexer) is a teacher and eternal student. She can be found wandering about with a camera in hand. Email: *juliehawks@gmail.com*.

Shelley Powers (technical reviewer) is a former HTML5 working group member and author of several O'Reilly books. Website: *http://burningbird.net*.

Darrell Heath (technical reviewer) is a freelance web/print designer and web developer from Newfoundland and Labrador, Canada, with a background in Information Technology and visual arts. He has authored weekly tutorial content for NAPP, *Layers* magazine, and Planet Photoshop, and in his spare time offers design- and technology-related tips through his blog at *www.heathrowe.com/blog*. Email: *darrell@heathrowe.com*.

ACKNOWLEDGEMENTS

No author could complete a book without a small army of helpful individuals. I'm deeply indebted to the whole Missing Manual team, especially my editor Nan Barber, who never seemed fazed by the shifting sands of HTML5; and expert tech reviewers Shelley Powers and Darrell Heath, who helped spot rogue errors and offered consistently good advice. And, as always, I'm also deeply indebted to numerous others who've toiled behind the scenes indexing pages, drawing figures, and proofreading the final copy.

Finally, for the parts of my life that exist outside this book, I'd like to thank all my family members. They include my parents, Nora and Paul; my extended parents, Razia and Hamid; my wife, Faria; and my daughters, Maya, Brenna, and Aisha. Thanks, everyone!

—Matthew MacDonald

THE MISSING MANUAL SERIES

Missing Manuals are witty, superbly written guides to computer products that don't come with printed manuals (which is just about all of them). Each book features a handcrafted index; cross-references to specific pages (not just chapters); and RepKover, a detached-spine binding that lets the book lie perfectly flat without the assistance of weights or cinder blocks.

Recent and upcoming titles include:

Access 2013: The Missing Manual by Matthew MacDonald

Adobe Edge Animate: The Missing Manual by Chris Grover

Buying a Home: The Missing Manual by Nancy Conner

Creating a Website: The Missing Manual, Third Edition by Matthew MacDonald

CSS3: The Missing Manual, Third Edition by David Sawyer McFarland

David Pogue's Digital Photography: The Missing Manual by David Pogue

Dreamweaver CS6: The Missing Manual by David Sawyer McFarland

Dreamweaver CC: The Missing Manual by David Sawyer McFarland and Chris Grover

Excel 2013: The Missing Manual by Matthew MacDonald

FileMaker Pro 12: The Missing Manual by Susan Prosser and Stuart Gripman

Flash CS6: The Missing Manual by Chris Grover

Galaxy Tab: The Missing Manual by Preston Gralla

Google+: The Missing Manual by Kevin Purdy

iMovie '11 & iDVD: The Missing Manual by David Pogue and Aaron Miller

iPad: The Missing Manual, Sixth Edition by J.D. Biersdorfer *iPhone: The Missing Manual, Fifth Edition* by David Pogue

iPhone App Development: The Missing Manual by Craig Hockenberry

iPhoto '11: The Missing Manual by David Pogue and Lesa Snider

iPod: The Missing Manual, Eleventh Edition by J.D. Biersdorfer and David Pogue

JavaScript & jQuery: The Missing Manual, Second Edition by David Sawyer McFarland

Kindle Fire HD: The Missing Manual by Peter Meyers

Living Green: The Missing Manual by Nancy Conner

Microsoft Project 2013: The Missing Manual by Bonnie Biafore

Motorola Xoom: The Missing Manual by Preston Gralla

Netbooks: The Missing Manual by J.D. Biersdorfer

NOOK HD: The Missing Manual by Preston Gralla

Office 2011 for Macintosh: The Missing Manual by Chris Grover

Office 2013: The Missing Manual by Nancy Conner and Matthew MacDonald

OS X Mountain Lion: The Missing Manual by David Pogue

OS X Mavericks: The Missing Manual by David Pogue

Personal Investing: The Missing Manual by Bonnie Biafore

Photoshop CS6: The Missing Manual by Lesa Snider

Photoshop CC: The Missing Manual by Lesa Snider

Photoshop Elements 12: The Missing Manual by Barbara Brundage

PHP & MySQL: The Missing Manual, Second Edition by Brett McLaughlin

QuickBooks 2013: The Missing Manual by Bonnie Biafore

Switching to the Mac: The Missing Manual, Mountain Lion Edition by David Pogue

Switching to the Mac: The Missing Manual, Mavericks Edition by David Pogue

Windows 8.1: The Missing Manual by David Pogue

WordPress: The Missing Manual by Matthew MacDonald

Your Body: The Missing Manual by Matthew MacDonald

Your Brain: The Missing Manual by Matthew MacDonald

Your Money: The Missing Manual by J.D. Roth

For a full list of all Missing Manuals in print, go to *www.missingmanuals.com/library. html.*

Introduction

A t first glance, you might assume that HTML5 is the fifth version of the HTML web page–writing language. But the real story is a whole lot messier.

HTML5 is a rebel. It was dreamt up by a loose group of freethinkers who weren't in charge of the official HTML standard. It allows page-writing practices that were banned a decade ago. It spends thousands of words painstakingly telling browser makers how to deal with markup mistakes, rather than rejecting them outright. It finally makes video playback possible without a browser plug-in like Flash. And it introduces an avalanche of JavaScript-fueled features that can give web pages some of the rich, interactive capabilities of traditional desktop software.

Understanding HTML5 is no small feat. One stumbling block is that people use the word *HTML5* to refer to a dozen or more separate standards. (As you'll learn, this problem is the result of HTML5's evolution. It began as a single standard and was later broken into more manageable pieces.) In fact, HTML5 has come to mean "HTML5 and all its related standards" or, even more broadly, "the next generation of web-page-writing technologies." That's the version of HTML5 that you'll explore in this book: everything from the HTML5 core language to a few new features lumped in with HTML5 even though they were *never* a part of the standard.

The second challenge of HTML5 is browser support. Different browsers support HTML5 to different degrees. The most notable laggard is Internet Explorer 8, which supports very little HTML5 and is still found on one out of every 20 web-surfing computers. (At least it was at the time of this writing. Page 30 explains how you can get the latest browser usage statistics.) Fortunately, there are workarounds that can bridge the browser support gaps—some easy, and some ugly. In this book, you'll learn a bit of both on your quest to use HTML5 in your web pages *today*.

Despite the challenges HTML5 presents, there's one fact that no one disputes—*HTML5 is the future*. Huge software companies like Apple, Google, and Microsoft have lent it support, and the W3C (World Wide Web Consortium) has given up its work on XHTML to formalize and endorse it. With this book, you too can join the party and use HTML5 to create cool pages like the one shown in Figure I-1.

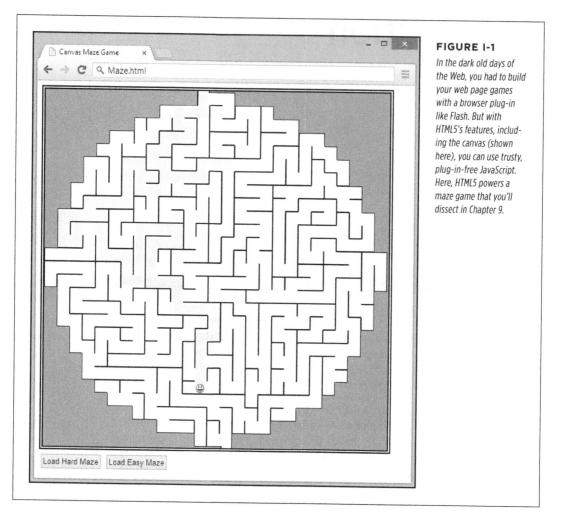

FIGURE I-1

In the dark old days of the Web, you had to build your web page games with a browser plug-in like Flash. But with HTML5's features, including the canvas (shown here), you can use trusty, plug-in-free JavaScript. Here, HTML5 powers a maze game that you'll dissect in Chapter 9.

What You Need to Get Started

This book covers HTML5, the latest and greatest version of the HTML standard. And while you don't need to be a markup master to read it, you *do* need some previous web design experience. Here's the official rundown:

- **Web page writing.** This book assumes you've written at least a few web pages before (or at the very least, you understand how to use HTML elements to structure content into headings, paragraphs, and lists). If you're new to web design, you're better off with a gentler introduction, like my own *Creating a Website: The Missing Manual, Third Edition*. (But don't worry; you won't be trapped in the past, as all the examples in the third edition of *Creating a Website* are valid HTML5 documents.)

- **Style sheet experience.** No modern website is possible without CSS—the Cascading Style Sheet standard—which supplies the layout and formatting for web pages. To follow along in this book, you should know the basics of style sheets: how to create them, what goes inside, and how to attach one to a page. If you're a bit hazy on the subject, you can catch up in Appendix A, "Essential CSS." But if you need more help, or if you just want to sharpen your CSS skills to make truly cool layouts and styles, check out a supplementary book like *CSS3: The Missing Manual* by David Sawyer McFarland.

- **JavaScript experience.** No, you don't need JavaScript to create an HTML5 page. However, you do need JavaScript if you want to use many of HTML5's most powerful features, like drawing on a canvas or talking to a web server. If you have a smattering of programming experience but don't know much about JavaScript, then Appendix B, "JavaScript: The Brains of Your Page" can help you get up to speed. But if the idea of writing code sounds about as comfortable as crawling into bed with an escaped python, then you'll either end up skipping a lot of material in this book, or you'll need to fill in the gaps with a book like *JavaScript & jQuery: The Missing Manual* by David Sawyer McFarland.

Writing HTML5

You can write HTML5 pages using the same software you use to write HTML pages. That can be as simple as a lowly text editor, like Notepad (on Windows) or TextEdit (on Mac). Many current design tools, like Adobe Dreamweaver and Microsoft Visual Studio, have templates that let you quickly create new HTML5 documents. However, the basic structure of an HTML5 page is so simple that you can use any web editor to create one, even if it wasn't specifically designed for HTML5.

> **NOTE** And, of course, it doesn't matter whether you do your surfing and web page creation on a Windows PC or the latest MacBook Pro—HTML5 pays no attention to what operating system you use.

Viewing HTML5

You'll get support for most HTML5 features in the latest version of any modern browser, including the mobile browsers than run on Apple and Android devices. As long as your browser is up to date, HTML5 will perform beautifully—and you'll be able to try out the examples in this book.

Currently, no browser supports *every* last detail of HTML5, in part because HTML5 is really a collection of interrelated standards. Google Chrome generally leads the browser race in HTML5 support, with Firefox and Opera in close pursuit. Safari lags the pack a bit, and Internet Explorer trails still further behind. The real problem lies in the old copies of Internet Explorer that can't be updated because they're running on creaky operating systems like Windows Vista or Windows XP (which is still chugging away on a fifth of the world's desktop computers). Page 26 has a closer look at this problem and some advice on how to deal with it.

When Will HTML5 Be Ready?

The short answer is "now." Even the despised Internet Explorer 6, which is 10 years old and chock-full of website-breaking quirks, can display basic HTML5 documents. That's because the HTML5 standard was intentionally created in a way that embraces and extends traditional HTML.

The more detailed answer is "it depends." As you've already learned, HTML5 is a collection of different standards with different degrees of browser support. So although every web developer can switch over to HTML5 documents today (and many big sites, like Google, YouTube, and Wikipedia, already have), it may be some time before it's safe to use all of HTML5's fancy new features—at least without adding some sort of fallback mechanism for less-enlightened browsers.

> **NOTE** Before encouraging you to use a new HTML5 feature, this book clearly indicates that feature's current level of browser support. Of course, browser versions change relatively quickly, so you'll want to perform your own up-to-date research before you embrace any feature that might cause problems. The website *http://caniuse.com* lets you look up specific features and tells you exactly which browser versions support them. (You'll learn more about this useful tool on page 27.)

As a standards-minded developer, you also might be interested in knowing how far the various standards are in their journey toward official status. This is complicated by the fact that the people who dreamt up HTML5 have a slightly subversive philosophy, and they often point out that what browsers support is more important than what the official standard says. In other words, you can go ahead and use everything that you want right now, if you can get it to work. But web developers, big companies, governments, and other organizations often take their cues about whether a language is ready to use by looking at the status of its standard.

At this writing, the HTML5 language is in the *candidate recommendation* stage, which means the standard is largely settled but browser makers are still polishing up their HTML5 implementations. The next and final stage is for the standard to become a full *recommendation*, and HTML5 is expected to hit that landmark in late 2014. In the meantime, the W3C has already published a *working draft* of the next version of the standard, which it calls HTML 5.1. (For more help making sense of all the different versions, see the box on the next page.)

The Difference Between HTML5 and HTML 5.1

Is there another new version of HTML? And what's with the inconsistent spacing?

As you'll learn in Chapter 1, HTML5 has gone through two sets of hands. This process has left a few quirks behind, including a slightly schizophrenic versioning system.

The people who originally created HTML5—the members of WHATWG, which you'll meet on page 5—aren't much interested in version numbers. They consider HTML5 to be a living language. They encourage web developers to pay attention to browser support, rather than worry about exact version numbers.

However, the WHATWG passed HTML5 to the official web standard-keepers—the W3C—so they could finalize it. The W3C is a more careful, methodical organization. The folks there wanted a way to separate their initial publication of the HTML5 standard from the slightly tweaked and cleaned up successors that were sure to follow. Thus, the W3C decided to name the first release of the HTML5 standard HTML 5.0 (note the space). The second release will be HTML 5.1, followed by a third release called HTML 5.2. Confusingly enough, all these versions are still considered to be HTML5.

Incidentally, the later iterations of the HTML5 standard aren't likely to add major changes. Instead, new features will turn up in separate, complementary specifications. This way, small groups of people can quickly develop new, useful HTML5 features without needing to wait for an entirely new revision of the language.

■ About the Outline

This book crams a comprehensive HTML5 tutorial into 13 chapters. Here's what you'll find:

Part One: Meet the New Language

- Chapter 1 explains how HTML turned into HTML5. You'll meet your first HTML5 document, see how the language has changed, and take a look at browser support.

- Chapter 2 tackles HTML5's *semantic elements*—a group of elements that can inject meaning into your markup. Used properly, this extra information can help browsers, screen readers, web design tools, and search engines work smarter.

- Chapter 3 goes deeper into the world of semantics with add-on standards like *microdata*. And while it may seem a bit theoretical, there's a fat prize for the web developers who understand it best: better, more detailed listings in search engines like Google.

- Chapter 4 explores HTML5's changes to the web form elements—the text boxes, lists, checkboxes, and other widgets that you use to collect information from your visitors. HTML5 adds a few frills and some basic tools for catching data-entry errors.

Part Two: Video, Graphics, and Glitz

- Chapter 5 hits one of HTML5's most exciting features: its support for audio and video playback. You'll learn how to survive Web Video Codec Wars to create playback pages that work in every browser, and you'll even see how to create your own customized player.

- Chapter 6 introduces the latest version of the CSS3 standard, which complements HTML5 nicely. You'll learn how to jazz up your text with fancy fonts and add eye-catching effects with transitions and animation.

- Chapter 7 explores CSS3 media queries. You'll learn how to use them to create responsive designs—website layouts that seamlessly adapt themselves to different mobile devices.

- Chapter 8 introduces the two-dimensional drawing surface called the *canvas*. You'll learn how to paint it with shapes, pictures, and text, and even build a basic drawing program (with a healthy dose of JavaScript code).

- Chapter 9 pumps up your canvas skills. You'll learn about shadows and fancy patterns, along with more ambitious canvas techniques like clickable, interactive shapes and animation.

Part Three: Building Web Apps

- Chapter 10 covers the web storage feature that lets you store small bits of information on the visitor's computer. You'll also learn about ways to process a user-selected file in your web page JavaScript code, rather than on the web server.

- Chapter 11 explores the HTML5 caching feature that can let a browser keep running a web page, even if it loses the web connection.

- Chapter 12 dips into the challenging world of web server communication. You'll start with the time-honored XMLHttpRequest object, which lets your JavaScript code contact the web server and ask for information. Then you'll move on to two newer features: server-side events and the more ambitious web sockets.

- Chapter 13 covers three miscellaneous features that address challenges in modern web applications. First, you'll see how geolocation can pin down a visitor's position. Next, you'll use web workers to run time-consuming tasks in the background. Finally, you'll learn about the browser history feature, which lets you sync up the web page URL to the current state of the page.

There are also two appendixes that can help you catch up with the fundamentals you need to master HTML5. Appendix A, "Essential CSS," gives a stripped-down summary of CSS; Appendix B, "JavaScript: The Brains of Your Page" gives a concise overview of JavaScript.

■ About the Online Resources

As the owner of a Missing Manual, you've got more than just a book to read. Online, you'll find example files as well as tips, articles, and maybe even a video or two. You can also communicate with the Missing Manual team and tell us what you love (or hate) about the book. Head over to *www.missingmanuals.com*, or go directly to one of the following sections.

The Missing CD

This book doesn't have a CD pasted inside the back cover, but you're not missing out on anything. Go to *http://missingmanuals.com/cds/html5tmm2e* to download the web page examples discussed and demonstrated in this book. And so you don't wear down your fingers typing long web addresses, the Missing CD page offers a list of clickable links to the websites mentioned in each chapter.

> **TIP** If you're looking for a specific example, here's a quick way to find it: Look at the corresponding figure in this book. The file name is usually visible at the end of the text in the web browser's address box. For example, if you see the file path *c:\HTML5\Chapter01\SuperSimpleHTML5.html* (Figure 1-1), you'll know that the corresponding example file is *SuperSimpleHTML5.html*.

The Try-Out Site

There's another way to use the examples: on the example site at *www.prosetech.com/html5*. There you'll find live versions of every example from this book, which you can run in your browser. This convenience just might save you a few headaches, because HTML5 includes several features that require the involvement of a real web server. (If you're running web pages from the hard drive on your personal computer, these features may develop mysterious quirks or stop working altogether.) By using the live site, you can see how an example is supposed to work before you download the page and start experimenting on your own.

> **NOTE** Don't worry—when you come across an HTML5 feature that needs web server hosting, this book will warn you.

Registration

If you register this book at oreilly.com (*www.oreilly.com*), you'll be eligible for special offers—like discounts on future editions of *HTML5: The Missing Manual*. Registering takes only a few clicks. Type *http://tinyurl.com/registerbook* into your browser to hop directly to the Registration page.

Feedback

Got questions? Need more information? Fancy yourself a book reviewer? On our Feedback page, you can get expert answers to questions that come to you while reading, share your thoughts on this Missing Manual, and find groups of folks who share your interest in creating their own sites.

To have your say, go to *www.missingmanuals.com/feedback*.

Errata

To keep this book as up to date and accurate as possible, each time we print more copies, we'll make any confirmed corrections you suggest. We also note such changes on the book's website, so you can mark important corrections into your own copy of the book, if you like. Go to *http://tinyurl.com/html52e-mm* to report an error and view existing corrections.

◼ Safari® Books Online

Safari® Books Online is an on-demand digital library that lets you search over 7,500 technology books and videos.

With a subscription, you can read any page and watch any video from our library. Access new titles before they're available in print. Copy and paste code samples, organize your favorites, download chapters, bookmark key sections, create notes, print out pages, and benefit from tons of other time-saving features.

O'Reilly Media has uploaded this book to the Safari Books Online service. To have full digital access to this book and others on similar topics from O'Reilly and other publishers, sign up for free at *http://my.safaribooksonline.com*.

Modern Markup

CHAPTER 1:
Introducing HTML5

CHAPTER 2:
Structuring Pages with Semantic Elements

CHAPTER 3:
Writing More Meaningful Markup

CHAPTER 4:
Building Better Web Forms

Introducing HTML5

If HTML were a movie, HTML5 would be its surprise twist. HTML wasn't meant to survive into the 21st century. The official web standards organization, the W3C (short for World Wide Web Consortium), left HTML for dead way back in 1998. The W3C pinned its future plans on a specification called XHTML, which it intended to be HTML's cleaned-up, modernized successor. But XHTML stumbled, and a group of disenfranchised rebels resuscitated HTML, laying the groundwork for the features that you'll explore in this book.

In this chapter, you'll get the scoop on why HTML died and how it came back to life. You'll learn about HTML5's philosophy and features, and you'll consider the thorny issue of browser support. You'll also get your first look at an authentic HTML5 document.

■ The Story of HTML5

The basic idea behind HTML—that you use *elements* to structure your content—hasn't changed since the Web's earliest days. In fact, even the oldest web pages still work perfectly in the most modern web browsers.

Being old and successful also carries some risks—namely, that everyone wants to replace you. In 1998, the W3C stopped working on HTML and attempted to improve it with an XML-powered successor called XHTML 1.0.

XHTML 1.0: Getting Strict

XHTML has most of the same syntax conventions as HTML, but it enforces stricter rules. Much of the sloppy markup that traditional HTML permitted just isn't acceptable in XHTML.

For example, suppose you want to italicize the last word in a heading, like so:

```
<h1>The Life of a <i>Duck</i></h1>
```

And you accidentally swap the final two tags:

```
<h1>The Life of a <i>Duck</h1></i>
```

When a browser encounters this slightly messed-up markup, it can figure out what you really want. It italicizes the last word without even a polite complaint. However, the mismatched tags break XHTML's official rules. If you plug your page into an XHTML validator (or use a web design tool like Dreamweaver), you'll get a warning that points out your mistake. From a web design point of view, XHTML's strictness is helpful in that it lets you catch minor mistakes that might cause inconsistent results on different browsers (or might cause bigger problems when you edit and enhance the page).

At first, XHTML was a success story. Professional web developers, frustrated with browser quirks and the anything-goes state of web design, flocked to XHTML. Along the way, they were forced to adopt better habits and give up a few of HTML's half-baked formatting features. However, many of XHTML's imagined benefits—like interoperability with XML tools, easier page processing for automated programs, portability to mobile platforms, and extensibility of the XHTML language itself—never came to pass.

Still, XHTML became the standard for most serious web designers. And while everyone seemed pretty happy, there was one dirty secret: Although browsers understood XHTML markup, they didn't enforce the strict error-checking that the standard required. That means a page could break the rules of XHTML, and the browsers wouldn't blink twice. In fact, there was nothing to stop a web developer from throwing together a mess of sloppy markup and old-fashioned HTML content and calling it an XHTML page. There wasn't a single browser on the planet that would complain. And *that* made the people in charge of the XHTML standard deeply uncomfortable.

XHTML 2: The Unexpected Failure

XHTML 2 was supposed to provide a solution to this sloppiness. It was set to tighten up the error-handling rules, forcing browsers to reject invalid XHTML 2 pages. XHTML 2 also threw out many of the quirks and conventions that originated with HTML. For example, the system of numbered headings (<h1>, <h2>, <h3>, and so on) was superseded by a new <h> element, whose significance depended on its position in a web page. Similarly, the <a> element was eclipsed by a feature that let web developers transform any element into a link, and the <img> element lost its alt attribute in favor of a new way to supply alternate content.

These changes were typical of XHTML 2. In theory, they made for cleaner, more logical markup. In practice, the changes forced web designers to alter the way they wrote web pages (to say nothing of updating the web pages they already had), and added no new features to make all that work worthwhile. XHTML 2 even dumped a few well-worn elements that some web designers still loved, like <b> for bold text, <i> for italics, and <iframe> for embedding one web page inside another.

But perhaps the worst problem was the glacial pace of change. Development on XHTML 2 dragged on for five years, and developer enthusiasm slowly leaked away.

HTML5: Back from the Dead

At about the same time—starting in 2004—a group of people started looking at the future of the Web from a different angle. Instead of trying to sort out what was wrong (or just "philosophically impure") in HTML, they focused on what was missing, in terms of the things web developers wanted to get done.

After all, HTML began its life as a tool for displaying documents. With the addition of JavaScript, it had morphed into a system for developing web applications, like search engines, ecommerce stores, mapping tools, email clients, and a whole lot more. And while a crafty web application can do a lot of impressive things, it isn't easy to create one. Most web apps rely on a soup of handwritten JavaScript, one or more popular JavaScript toolkits, and a code module that runs on the web server. It's a challenge to get all these pieces to interact consistently on different browsers. Even when you get it to work, you need to mind the duct tape and staples that hold everything together.

The people creating browsers were particularly concerned about this situation. So a group of forward-thinking individuals from Opera Software (the creators of the Opera browser) and the Mozilla Foundation (the creators of Firefox) lobbied to get XHTML to introduce more developer-oriented features. When they failed, Opera, Mozilla, and Apple formed the loosely knit WHATWG (Web Hypertext Application Technology Working Group) to think of new solutions.

The WHATWG wasn't out to replace HTML, but to *extend* it in a seamless, backward-compatible way. The earliest version of its work had two add-on specifications called Web Applications 1.0 and Web Forms 2.0. Eventually, these standards evolved into HTML5.

NOTE The number 5 in the HTML5 specification name is supposed to indicate that the standard picks up where HTML left off (that's HTML version 4.01, which predates XHTML). Of course, this isn't really accurate, because HTML5 supports everything that's happened to web pages in the decade since HTML 4.01 was released, including strict XHTML-style syntax (if you choose to use it) and a slew of JavaScript innovations. However, the name still makes a clear point: HTML5 may support the *conventions* of XHTML, but it enforces the *rules* of HTML.

By 2007, the WHATWG camp had captured the attention of web developers everywhere. After some painful reflection, the W3C decided to disband the group that was working on XHTML 2 and work on formalizing the HTML5 standard instead. At this point, the original HTML5 was broken into more manageable pieces, and many of the features that had originally been called HTML5 became separate standards (for more, see the box on this page).

> **TIP** You can read the official W3C version of the HTML5 standard at *www.w3.org/TR/html5*.

What Does HTML5 Include?

HTML5 is really a web of interrelated standards. This approach is both good and bad. It's good because the browsers can quickly implement mature features while others continue to evolve. It's bad because it forces web page writers to worry about checking whether a browser supports each feature they want to use. You'll learn some painful and not-so-painful techniques for doing so in this book.

Here are the major feature categories that fall under the umbrella of HTML5:

- **Core HTML5.** This part of HTML5 makes up the official W3C version of the specification. It includes the new semantic elements (Chapter 2 and Chapter 3), new and enhanced web form widgets (Chapter 4), audio and video support (Chapter 5), and the canvas for drawing with JavaScript (Chapter 8 and Chapter 9).

- **Features that were once HTML5.** These features sprang from the original HTML5 specification as prepared by the WHATWG. Most of these are specifications for features that require JavaScript and support rich web applications. The most significant include local data storage (Chapter 10), offline applications (Chapter 11), and messaging (Chapter 12), but you'll learn about several more in this book.

- **Features that are sometimes called HTML5.** These are next-generation features that are often lumped together with HTML5, even though they weren't ever a part of the HTML5 standard. This category includes CSS3 (Chapter 6 and Chapter 7) and geolocation (Chapter 13).

Even the W3C is blurring the boundaries between the "real" HTML5 (what's actually in the standard) and the "marketing" version (which includes everything that's part of HTML5 and many complementary specifications). For example, the official W3C logo website (*www.w3.org/html/logo*) encourages you to generate HTML5 logos that promote CSS3 and SVG—two standards that were under development well before HTML5 appeared.

HTML: The Living Language

The switch from the W3C to the WHATWG and back to the W3C again has led to a rather unusual arrangement. Technically, the W3C is in charge of determining what is and isn't official HTML5. But at the same time, the WHATWG continues its work dreaming up future HTML features. Only now, they no longer refer to their work as HTML5. They simply call it HTML, explaining that HTML will continue as a *living language*.

Because HTML is a living language, an HTML page will never become obsolete and stop working. HTML pages will never use a version number (even in the doctype), and web developers will never need to "upgrade" their markup from one version to another to get it to work on new browsers. By the same token, new features may be added to HTML at any time.

When web developers hear about this plan, their first reaction is usually unmitigated horror. After all, who wants to deal with a world of wildly variable standards support, where developers need to pick and choose the features they use based on the likelihood that these features will be supported? However, on reflection, most web developers come to a grudging realization: For better or for worse, this is exactly the way browsers have worked since the dawn of the Web.

As explained earlier, today's browsers are happy with any mishmash of supported features. You can take a state-of-the-art XHTML page and add something as scandalously backward as the `<marquee>` element (an obsolete feature for creating scrolling text), and no browser will complain. Similarly, browsers have well-known holes in their support for even the oldest standards. For example, browser makers started implementing CSS3 before CSS2 support was finished, and many CSS2 features were later dropped. The only difference is that now HTML5 makes the "living language" status official. Still, it's no small irony that just as HTML is embarking on a new, innovative chapter, it has finally returned full circle to its roots.

TIP To see the current, evolving draft of HTML that includes the stuff called HTML5 and a small but ever-evolving set of new, unsupported features, go to *http://whatwg.org/html*.

Three Key Principles of HTML5

By this point, you're probably eager to get going with a real HTML5 page. But first, it's worth climbing into the minds of the people who built HTML5. Once you understand the philosophy behind the language, the quirks, complexities, and occasional headaches that you'll encounter in this book will make a whole lot more sense.

1. Don't Break the Web

"Don't break the Web" means that a standard shouldn't introduce changes that make other people's web pages stop working. Fortunately, this kind of wreckage rarely happens.

"Don't break the Web" *also* means that a standard shouldn't casually change the rules, and in the process make perfectly good current-day web pages to be obsolete (even if they still happen to work). For example, XHTML 2 broke the Web because it demanded an immediate, dramatic shift in the way web pages were written. Yes, old pages would still work—thanks to the backward compatibility that's built into browsers. But if you wanted to prepare for the future and keep your website up to date, you'd be forced to waste countless hours correcting the "mistakes" that XHTML 2 had banned.

HTML5 has a different viewpoint. Everything that was valid before HTML5 remains valid in HTML5. In fact, everything that was valid in HTML 4.01 also remains valid in HTML5.

> **NOTE** Unlike previous standards, HTML5 doesn't just tell browser makers what to support—it also documents and formalizes the way they *already work*. Because the HTML5 standard documents reality, rather than just setting out a bunch of ideal rules, it may become the best-supported web standard ever.

How HTML5 Handles Obsolete Elements

Because HTML5 supports all of HTML, it supports many features that are considered obsolete. These include formatting elements like <font>, despised special-effect elements like <blink> and <marquee>, and the awkward system of HTML frames.

This open-mindedness is a point of confusion for many HTML5 apprentices. On the one hand, HTML5 should by all rights ban these outdated elements, which haven't appeared in an official specification for years (if ever). On the other hand, modern browsers still quietly support these elements, and HTML5 is supposed to reflect how web browsers really work. So what's a standard to do?

To solve this problem, the HTML5 specification has two separate parts. The first part—which is what you'll consider in this book—targets web developers. Developers need to avoid the bad habits and discarded elements of the past. You can make sure you're following this part of the HTML5 standard by using an HTML5 validator.

The second, much longer part of the HTML5 specification targets browser makers. Browsers need to support everything that's ever existed in HTML, for backward compatibility. Ideally, the HTML5 standard should have enough information that someone could build a browser from scratch and make it completely compatible with the modern browsers of today, whether it was processing new or old markup. This part of the standard tells browsers how to deal with obsolete elements that are officially discouraged but still supported.

Incidentally, the HTML5 specification also formalizes how browsers should deal with a variety of errors (for example, missing or mismatched tags). This point is important, because it ensures that a flawed page will work the same on different browsers, even when it comes to subtle issues like the way a page is modeled in the DOM (that's the Document Object Model, the tree of in-memory objects that represents the page and is made available to JavaScript code). To create this long, tedious part of the standard, the creators of HTML5 performed exhaustive tests on modern browsers to figure out their undocumented error-handling behavior. Then, they wrote it down.

2. Pave the Cowpaths

A cowpath is the rough, heavily trodden track that gets people from one point to another. A cowpath exists because it's being used. It might not be the best possible way to move around, but at some point it was the most practical working solution.

HTML5 standardizes these unofficial (but widely used) techniques. It may not be as neat as laying down a nicely paved expressway with a brand-new approach, but it has a better chance of succeeding. That's because switching over to new techniques may be beyond the ability or interest of the average website designer. And worse, new techniques may not work for visitors who are using older browsers. XHTML 2 tried to drive people off the cowpaths, and it failed miserably.

The "pave the cowpaths" approach also requires some compromises. Sometimes it means embracing a widely supported but poorly designed feature. One example is HTML5's drag-and-drop ability (page 337), which is based entirely on the behavior Microsoft created for IE 5. Although this drag-and-drop feature is now supported in all browsers, it's universally loathed for being clumsy and overly complicated. This magnanimousness has led some web designers to complain that "HTML5 not only encourages bad behavior, it defines it."

3. Be Practical

This principle is simple: Changes should have a practical purpose. And the more demanding the change, the bigger the payoff needs to be. Web developers may prefer nicely designed, consistent, quirk-free standards, but that isn't a good enough reason to change a language that's already been used to create several billion pages. Of course, it's still up to someone to decide whose concerns are the most important. A good clue is to look at what web pages are already doing—or trying to do.

For example, the world's third most popular website (at the time of this writing) is YouTube. But because HTML had no real video features before HTML5, YouTube has had to rely on the Flash browser plug-in. This solution works surprisingly well because the Flash plug-in is present on virtually all web-connected computers. However, there are occasional exceptions, like locked-down corporate computers that don't allow Flash, or mobile devices that don't support it (like the iPhone, iPad, and Kindle). And no matter how many computers have Flash, there's a good case for extending the HTML standard so it directly supports one of the most fundamental ways people use web pages today—to watch video.

There's a similar motivation behind HTML5's drive to add more interactive features—drag-and-drop support, editable HTML content, two-dimensional drawing on a canvas, and so on. You don't need to look far to find web pages that use all of these features right now, some with plug-ins like Adobe Flash and Microsoft Silverlight, and others with JavaScript libraries or (more laboriously) with pages of custom-written JavaScript code. So why not add official support to the HTML standard and make sure these features work consistently on all browsers? That's what HTML5 sets out to do.

■ Your First Look at HTML5 Markup

Here's one of the simplest HTML5 documents you can create:

```
<!DOCTYPE html>
<title>A Tiny HTML Document</title>
<p>Let's rock the browser, HTML5 style.</p>
```

It starts with the HTML5 doctype (a special code that's explained on page 11), followed by a title, and then followed by some content. In this case, the content is a single paragraph of text.

You already know what this looks like in a browser, but if you need reassuring, check out Figure 1-1.

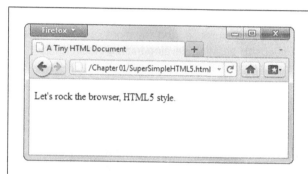

FIGURE 1-1

This super-simple HTML5 document holds a single line of text.

You can pare down this document a bit more. For example, the HTML5 standard doesn't really require the final `</p>` tag, since browsers know to close all open elements at the end of the document (and the HTML5 standard makes this behavior official). However, shortcuts like these create confusing markup and can lead to unexpected mistakes.

The HTML5 standard also lets you omit the `<title>` element if the title information is provided in another way. For example, if you're sending an HTML document in an email message, you could put the title in the title of the email message and put the rest of the markup—the doctype and the content—into the body of the message. But this is obviously a specialized scenario.

More commonly, you'll want to flesh out this bare-bones HTML5 document. Most web developers agree that using the traditional <head> and <body> sections can prevent confusion, by cleanly separating the information about your page (the head) and its actual content (the body). This structure is particularly useful when you start adding scripts, style sheets, and meta elements.

```
<!DOCTYPE html>
<head>
  <title>A Tiny HTML Document</title>
</head>
<body>
  <p>Let's rock the browser, HTML5 style.</p>
</body>
```

As always, the indenting (at the beginning of lines three and six) is purely optional. This example uses it to make the structure of the page easier to see at first glance.

Finally, you can choose to wrap the entire document (not including the doctype) in the traditional `<html>` element. Here's what that looks like:

```
<!DOCTYPE html>
<html>
<head>
  <title>A Tiny HTML Document</title>
</head>
<body>
  <p>Let's rock the browser, HTML5 style.</p>
</body>
</html>
```

Up until HTML5, every version of the official HTML specification had demanded that you use the `<html>` element, despite the fact that it has no effect on browsers. However, HTML5 makes this detail completely optional.

NOTE The use of the `<html>`, `<head>`, and `<body>` elements is simply a matter of style. You can leave them out and your page will work perfectly well, even on old browsers that don't know a thing about HTML5. In fact, the browser will automatically assume these details. So if you use JavaScript to peek at the DOM (the set of programming objects that represents your page), you'll find objects for the `<html>`, `<head>`, and `<body>` elements, even if you didn't add them yourself.

Currently, this example is somewhere between the simplest possible HTML5 document and the fleshed-out starting point of a practical HTML5 web page. In the following sections, you'll fill in the rest of what you need and dig a little deeper into the markup.

The HTML5 Doctype

The first line of every HTML5 document is a special code called the *doctype*. The doctype clearly indicates the standard that was used to write the document markup that follows. Here's how a page announces that it adheres to the HTML5 standard:

```
<!DOCTYPE html>
```

The first thing you'll notice about the HTML5 doctype is its striking simplicity. Compare it, for example, to the ungainly doctype that web developers need when using XHTML 1.0 strict:

```
<!DOCTYPE html PUBLIC "-//W3C//DTD XHTML 1.0 Strict//EN"
   "http://www.w3.org/TR/xhtml1/DTD/xhtml1-strict.dtd">
```

Even professional web developers were forced to copy and paste the XHTML doctype from one document to another. But the HTML5 doctype is short and snappy, so you won't have much trouble typing it by hand.

The HTML5 doctype is also notable for the fact that it doesn't include the official specification version (that's the *5* in HTML5). Instead, the doctype simply indicates that the page is HTML, which is in keeping with the new vision of HTML5 as a living language (page 6). When new features are added to the HTML language, they're automatically available in your page, without requiring you to edit the doctype.

All of this raises a good question—if HTML5 is a living language, why does your web page require any doctype at all?

The answer is that the doctype remains for historical reasons. Without a doctype, most browsers (including Internet Explorer and Firefox) will lapse into *quirks mode*. In this mode, they'll attempt to render pages according to the slightly buggy rules that they used in older versions. The problem is that one browser's quirks mode differs from the next, so pages designed for one browser are likely to get inconsistently sized fonts, scrambled layouts, and other glitches on another browser.

When you add a doctype, the browser recognizes that you want to use the stricter *standards mode*, which ensures that the web page is displayed with consistent formatting and layout on every modern browser. The browser doesn't even care *which* doctype you use (with just a few exceptions). Instead, it simply checks that you have *some* doctype. The HTML5 doctype is simply the shortest valid doctype, so it always triggers standards mode.

TIP The HTML5 doctype triggers standards mode on all browsers that have a standards mode, including browsers that don't know anything about HTML5. For that reason, you can use the HTML5 doctype now, in all your pages, even if you need to hold off on some of HTML5's less-supported features.

Although the doctype is primarily intended to tell web browsers what to do, other agents can also check it. This includes HTML5 validators, search engines, design tools, and other human beings when they're trying to figure out what flavor of markup you've chosen for your page.

Character Encoding

The *character encoding* is the standard that tells a computer how to convert your text into a sequence of bytes when it's stored in a file—and how to convert it back again when the file is opened. For historical reasons, there are many different character encodings in the world. Today, virtually all English websites use an encoding called UTF-8, which is compact, fast, and supports all the non-English characters you'll ever need.

Often, the web server that hosts your pages is configured to tell browsers that it's serving out pages with a certain kind of encoding. However, because you can't be sure that your web server will take this step (unless you own the server), and because browsers can run into an obscure security issue when they attempt to guess a page's encoding, you should always add encoding information to your markup.

HTML5 makes that easy to do. All you need to do is add the <meta> element shown below at the very beginning of your <head> section (or right after the doctype, if you don't define the <head> element):

```
<head>
  <meta charset="utf-8">
  <title>A Tiny HTML Document</title>
</head>
```

Design tools like Dreamweaver add this detail automatically when you create a new page. They also make sure that your files are being saved with UTF encoding. However, if you're using an ordinary text editor, you may need to take an extra step to make sure your files are being saved correctly. For example, when editing an HTML file in Notepad (on Windows), in the Save As dialog box, you must choose UTF-8 from the Encoding list (at bottom). In TextEdit (on Mac), in the Save As dialog box, you need to first choose Format→Make Plain Text to make sure the program saves your page as an ordinary text file, and then choose "Unicode (UTF-8)" from the Plain Text Encoding pop-up menu.

The Language

It's considered good style to indicate your web page's *natural language*. This information is occasionally useful to other people—for example, search engines can use it to filter search results so they include only pages that match the searcher's language.

To specify the language of some content, you use the lang attribute on any element, along with the appropriate language code. That's *en* for plain English, but you can find more exotic language codes at *http://tinyurl.com/l-codes*.

The easiest way to add language information to your web page is to use the <html> element with the lang attribute:

```
<html lang="en">
```

This detail can also help screen readers if a page has text from multiple languages. In this situation, you use the lang attribute to indicate the language of different sections of your document; for example, by applying it to different <div> elements that wrap different content. Screen readers can then determine which sections to read aloud.

Adding a Style Sheet

Virtually every web page in a properly designed, professional website uses CSS style sheets. You specify the style sheets you want to use by adding <link> elements to the <head> section of an HTML5 document, like this:

```
<head>
  <meta charset="utf-8">
  <title>A Tiny HTML Document</title>
  <link href="styles.css" rel="stylesheet">
</head>
```

This method is more or less the same way you attach style sheets to a traditional HTML document, but slightly simpler.

> **NOTE** Because CSS is the only style sheet language around, there's no need to add the type="text/css" attribute that web pages used to require.

Adding JavaScript

JavaScript started its life as a way to add frivolous glitter and glamour to web pages. Today, JavaScript is less about user interface frills and more about novel web applications, including super-advanced email clients, word processors, and mapping engines that run right in the browser.

You add JavaScript to an HTML5 page in much the same way that you add it to a traditional HTML page. Here's an example that references an external file with JavaScript code:

```
<head>
  <meta charset="utf-8">
  <title>A Tiny HTML Document</title>
  <script src="scripts.js"></script>
</head>
```

There's no need to include the language="JavaScript" attribute. The browser assumes you want JavaScript unless you specify otherwise—and because JavaScript is the only HTML scripting language with broad support, you never will. However, you *do* still need to remember the closing </script> tag, even when referring to an external JavaScript file. If you leave it out or attempt to shorten your markup using the empty element syntax, your page won't work.

If you spend a lot of time testing your JavaScript-powered pages in Internet Explorer, you may also want to add a special comment called the *mark of the Web* to your <head> section, right after the character encoding. It looks like this:

```
<head>
  <meta charset="utf-8">
  <!-- saved from url=(0014)about:internet -->
  <title>A Tiny HTML Document</title>
  <script src="scripts.js"></script>
</head>
```

This comment tells Internet Explorer to treat the page as though it has been down-loaded from a remote website. Otherwise, IE switches into a special locked-down mode, pops up a security warning in a message bar, and won't run any JavaScript code until you explicitly click "Allow blocked content."

All other browsers ignore the "mark of the Web" comment and use the same security settings for remote websites and local files.

The Final Product

If you've followed these steps, you'll have an HTML5 document that looks something like this:

```
<!DOCTYPE html>
<html lang="en">
<head>
  <meta charset="utf-8">
  <title>A Tiny HTML Document</title>
  <link href="styles.css" rel="stylesheet">
  <script src="scripts.js"></script>
</head>

<body>
  <p>Let's rock the browser, HTML5 style.</p>
</body>
</html>
```

Although it's no longer the shortest possible HTML5 document, it's a reasonable starting point for any web page you want to build. And while this example seems wildly dull, don't worry—in the next chapter, you'll step up to a real-life page that's full of carefully laid-out content, and all wrapped up in CSS.

> **NOTE** All the HTML5 syntax you've learned about in this section—the new doctype, the meta element for character encoding, the language information, and the style sheet and JavaScript references, work in browsers both new and old. That's because they rely on defaults and built-in error-correcting practices that all browsers use.

A Closer Look at HTML5 Syntax

As you've already learned, HTML5 loosens some of the rules. That's because the creators of HTML5 wanted the language to more closely reflect web browser reality—in other words, they wanted to narrow the gap between "web pages that work" and "web pages that are considered valid, according to the standard." In the next section, you'll take a closer look at how the rules have changed.

NOTE There are still plenty of obsolete practices that browsers support but that the HTML5 standard strictly discourages. For help catching these in your own web pages, you'll need an HTML5 validator (page 17).

The Loosened Rules

In your first walk through an HTML5 document, you discovered that HTML5 makes the `<html>`, `<head>`, and `<body>` elements optional (although they can still be pretty useful). But HTML5's relaxed attitude doesn't stop there.

HTML5 ignores capitalization, letting you write markup like the following:

```
<P>Capital and lowercase letters <EM>don't matter</eM> in tag names.</p>.
```

HTML5 also lets you omit the closing slash from a *void element*—that's an element with no nested content, like an `<img>` (image), a `<br>` (line break), or an `<hr>` (horizontal line). Here are three equivalent ways to add a line break:

```
I cannot<br />
move backward<br>
or forward.<br/>
I am caught
```

HTML5 also changes the rules for attributes. Attribute values don't need quotation marks anymore, as long as the value doesn't include a restricted character (typically >, =, or a space). Here's an example of an `<img>` element that takes advantage of this ability:

```
<img alt="Horsehead Nebula" src=Horsehead01.jpg>
```

Attributes with no values are also allowed. So while XHTML required the somewhat redundant syntax to put a checkbox in the checked state...

```
<input type="checkbox" checked="checked" />
```

...you can now revive the shorter HTML 4.01 tradition of including the attribute name on its own.

```
<input type="checkbox" checked>
```

What's particularly disturbing to some people isn't the fact that HTML5 allows these things. It's the fact that inconsistent developers can casually switch back and forth between the stricter and the looser styles, even using both in the same document. In reality, though, XHTML permitted the same kind of inconsistency. In both cases, good style is the responsibility of the web designer, and the browser tolerates whatever you can throw at it.

Here's a quick summary of what constitutes good HTML5 style—and what conventions the examples in this book follow, even if they don't have to:

- **Including the optional <html>, <body>, and <head> elements.** The <html> element is a handy place to define the page's natural language (page 13); and the <body> and <head> elements help to keep page content separate from the other page details.

- **Using lowercase tags (like <p> instead of <P>).** They're not necessary, but they're far more common, easier to type (because you don't need the Shift key), and not nearly as shouty.

- **Using quotation marks around attribute values.** The quotation marks are there for a reason—to protect you from mistakes that are all too easy to make. Without quotation marks, one invalid character can break your whole page.

On the other hand, there are some old conventions that this book ignores (and you can, too). The examples in this book don't close empty elements, because most developers don't bother to add the extra slash (/) when they switch to HTML5. Similarly, there's no reason to favor the long attribute form when the attribute name and the attribute value are the same.

HTML5 Validation

HTML5's new, relaxed style may suit you fine. Or, the very thought that there could be inconsistent, error-ridden markup hiding behind a perfectly happy browser may be enough to keep you up at night. If you fall into the latter camp, you'll be happy to know that a validation tool can hunt down markup that doesn't conform to the recommended standards of HTML5, even if it doesn't faze a browser.

Here are some potential problems that a validator can catch:

- Missing mandatory elements (for example, the <title> element)

- A start tag without a matching end tag

- Incorrectly nested tags

- Tags with missing attributes (for example, an <img> element without the src attribute)

- Elements or content in the wrong place (for example, text that's placed directly in the <head> section)

Web design tools like Dreamweaver often have their own validators. But if you don't want the cost or complexity of a professional web editor, you can get the same information from an online validation tool. Here's how to use the popular validator provided by the W3C standards organization:

1. **In your web browser, go to** *http://validator.w3.org* **(Figure 1-2).**

   The W3C validator gives you three choices, represented by three separate tabs: "Validate by URI" (for a page that's already online), "Validate by File Upload" (for a page that's stored in a file on your computer), and "Validate by Direct Input" (for a bunch of markup you type in yourself).

2. **Click the tab you want, and supply your HTML content.**

   - **Validate by URI** lets you validate an existing web page. You just need to type the page's URL in the Address box (for example, *http://www.MySloppySite.com/FlawedPage.html*).

   - **Validate by File Upload** lets you upload any file from your computer. First, click the Browse button (in Chrome, click Choose File). In the Open dialog box, select your HTML file and then click Open.

   - **Validate by Direct Input** lets you validate any markup—you just need to type it into a large box. The easiest way to use this option is to copy the markup from your text editor and paste it into the box on the W3C validation page.

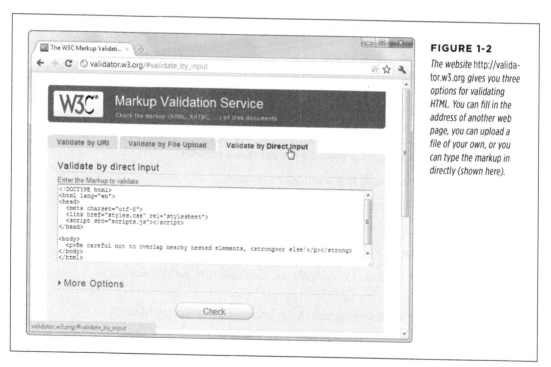

FIGURE 1-2

The website http://validator.w3.org gives you three options for validating HTML. You can fill in the address of another web page, you can upload a file of your own, or you can type the markup in directly (shown here).

Before continuing, you can click More Options to change some settings, but you probably won't. It's best to let the validator automatically detect the document type—that way, the validator will use the doctype specified in your web page. Similarly, use automatic detection for the character set unless you have an HTML page that's written in another language and the validator has trouble determining the correct character set.

3. **Click the Check button.**

   This click sends your HTML page to the W3C validator. After a brief delay, the report appears. You'll see whether your document passed the validation check and, if it failed, what errors the validator detected (see Figure 1-3).

NOTE Even in a perfectly valid HTML document, you may get a few harmless warnings, including that the character encoding was determined automatically and that the HTML5 validation service is considered to be an experimental, not-fully-finished feature.

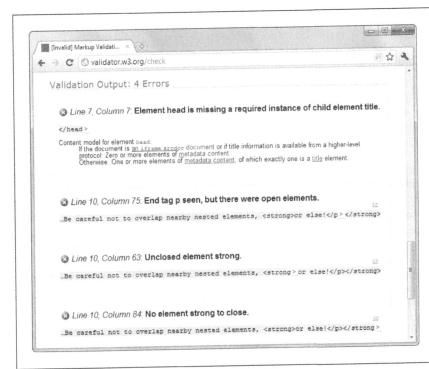

FIGURE 1-3

The validator has discovered four errors in this document that stem from two mistakes. First, the page is missing the mandatory <title> element. Second, it closes the <p> element before closing the <strong> element that's nested inside. (To solve this problem, you would replace </p></strong> with </strong></p>.) Incidentally, this document is still close enough to being correct that all browsers will display it properly.

The Return of XHTML

As you've already learned, HTML5 spells the end for the previous king of the Web—XHTML. However, reality isn't quite that simple, and XHTML fans don't need to give up all the things they loved about the past generation of markup languages.

First, remember that XHTML syntax lives on. The rules that XHTML enforced either remain as guidelines (for example, nesting elements correctly) or are still supported as optional conventions (for example, including the trailing slash on empty elements).

But what if you want to *enforce* the XHTML syntax rules? Maybe you're worried that you (or the people you work with) will inadvertently slip into the looser conventions of ordinary HTML. To stop that from happening, you need to use XHTML5—a less common standard that is essentially HTML5 with the XML-based restrictions slapped on top.

To turn an HTML5 document into an XHTML5 document, you need to explicitly add the XHTML namespace to the <html> element, close every element, make sure you use lowercase tags, and so on. Here's an example of a web page that takes all these steps:

```
<!DOCTYPE html>
<html lang="en" xmlns="http://www.w3.org/1999/xhtml">
<head>
  <meta charset="utf-8"/>
  <title>A Tiny HTML Document</title>
  <link href="styles.css" rel="stylesheet"/>
  <script src="scripts.js"></script>
</head>

<body>
  <p>Let's rock the browser, XHTML5 style.</p>
</body>
</html>
```

Now you can use an XHTML5 validator to get stricter error checking that enforces the old-style XHTML rules. The standard W3C validator won't do it, but the validator at *http://validator.w3.org/nu* will, provided you click the Options button and choose XHTML5 from the Preset list. You also need to choose the "Be lax about content-type" option, unless you're using the direct input approach and pasting your markup into a text box.

By following these steps, you can create and validate an XHTML document. However, *browsers* will still process your page as an HTML5 document—one that just happens to have an XML inferiority complex. They won't attempt to apply any extra rules.

If you want to go XHTML5 all the way, you need to configure your web server to serve your page with the MIME type application/xhtml+xml or application/xml, instead of the standard text/html. (See page 152 for the lowdown on MIME types.) But before you call your web hosting company, be warned that this change will prevent your page from being displayed by any version of Internet Explorer before IE 9. For that reason, true XHTML5 is an immediate deal-breaker in the browser.

Incidentally, browsers that do support XHTML5 deal with it differently from ordinary HTML5. They attempt to process the page as an XML document, and if that process fails (because you've left a mistake behind), the browser gives up on the rest of the document.

Bottom line? For the vast majority of web developers, from ordinary people to serious pros, XHTML5 isn't worth the hassle. The only exceptions are developers who have a specific XML-related goal in mind; for example, developers who want to manipulate the content in their pages with XML-related standards like XQuery and XPath.

TIP If you're curious, you can trick your browser into switching into XHTML mode. Just rename your file so that it ends with .xhtml or .xht. Then open it from your hard drive. Most browsers (including Firefox, Chrome, and IE 9 or later) will act as though you downloaded the page from a web server with an XML MIME type. If there's a minor error in the page, the browser window will show a partially processed page (IE), an XML error message (Firefox), or a combination of the two (Chrome).

■ HTML5's Element Family

So far, this chapter has focused on the changes to HTML5's syntax. But more important are the additions, subtractions, and changes to the *elements* that HTML supports. In the following sections, you'll get an overview of how they've changed.

Added Elements

In the following chapters, you'll spend most of your time learning about new elements—ingredients that haven't existed in web pages up until now. Table 1-1 has a preview of what's in store (and where you can read more about it).

TABLE 1-1 *New HTML5 elements*

CATEGORY	ELEMENTS	DISCUSSED IN...
Semantic elements for structuring a page	`<article>`, `<aside>`, `<figcaption>`, `<figure>`, `<footer>`, `<header>`, `<nav>`, `<section>`, `<details>`, `<summary>`	Chapter 2
Semantic elements for text	`<mark>`, `<time>`, `<wbr>` (previously supported, but now an official part of the language)	Chapter 3
Web forms and interactivity	`<input>` (not new, but has many new subtypes) `<datalist>`, `<keygen>`, `<meter>`, `<progress>`, `<command>`, `<menu>`, `<output>`	Chapter 4
Audio, video, and plug-ins	`<audio>`, `<video>`, `<source>`, `<embed>` (previously supported, but now an official part of the language)	Chapter 5
Canvas	`<canvas>`	Chapter 8
Non-English language support	`<bdo>`, `<rp>`, `<rt>`, `<ruby>`	HTML5 specification at *http://dev.w3.org/html5/ markup*

Removed Elements

Although HTML5 adds new elements, it also boots a few out of the official family. These elements will keep working in browsers, but any decent HTML5 validator will smoke them out of their hiding places and complain loudly.

Most obviously, HTML5 keeps the philosophy (first cooked up with XHTML) that *presentational elements* are not welcome in the language. Presentational elements are elements that are simply there to add formatting to web pages, and even the greenest web designer knows that's a job for style sheets. Rejects include elements that professional developers haven't use in years (like <big>, <center>, <font>, <tt>, and <strike>). HTML's presentational attributes died the same death, so there's no reason to rehash them all here.

Additionally, HTML5 kicks more sand on the grave where web developers buried the HTML frames feature. When it was first created, HTML frames seemed like a great way to show multiple web pages in a single browser window. But now, frames are better known as an accessibility nightmare because they cause problems with search engines, assistive software, and mobile devices. Interestingly, the <iframe> element—which lets developers put one page inside another—squeaks through. That's because web applications use the <iframe> for a range of integration tasks, like incorporating YouTube windows, ads, and Google search boxes in a web page.

A few more elements were kicked out because they were redundant or the cause of common mistakes, including <acronym> (use <abbr> instead) and <applet> (because <object> is preferred). But the vast majority of the element family lives on in HTML5.

> **NOTE** For those keeping count, HTML5 includes a family of just over 100 elements. Out of these, almost 30 are new and about 10 are significantly changed. You can browse the list of elements (and review which ones are new or changed) at *http://dev.w3.org/html5/markup*.

Adapted Elements

HTML5 has another odd trick: Sometimes it adapts an old feature to a new purpose. For example, consider the <small> element, which fell out of favor as a clumsy way to shrink the font size of a block of text—a task more properly done with style sheets. But unlike the discarded <big> element, HTML5 keeps the <small> element, with a change. Now, the <small> element represents "small print"—for example, the legalese that no one wants you to read at the bottom of a contract:

```
<small>The creators of this site will not be held liable for any injuries that
may result from unsupervised unicycle racing.</small>
```

Text inside the <small> element is still displayed as it always was, using a smaller font size, unless you override that setting with a style sheet.

Another changed element is <hr> (short for horizontal rule), which draws a separating line between sections. In HTML5, <hr> represents a thematic break—for example, a transition to another topic. The default formatting stays, but now a new meaning applies.

Similarly, <s> (for struck text), isn't just about crossing out words anymore—it now represents text that is no longer accurate or relevant, and has been "struck" from the document. Both of these changes are subtler than the <small> element's shift in meaning, because they capture ways that the <hr> and <s> elements are commonly used in traditional HTML.

■ BOLD AND ITALIC FORMATTING

The most important adapted elements are the ones for bold and italic formatting. Two of HTML's most commonly used elements—that's <b> for bold and <i> for italics—were partially replaced when the first version of XHTML introduced the look-alike <strong> and <em> elements. The idea was to stop looking at things from a formatting point of view (bold and italics), and instead substitute elements that had a real logical meaning (strong importance or stressed emphasis). The idea made a fair bit of sense, but the <b> and <i> tags lived on as shorter and more familiar alternatives to the XHTML fix.

HTML5 takes another crack at solving the problem. Rather than trying to force developers away from <b> and <i>, it assigns new meaning to both elements. The idea is to allow all four elements to coexist in a respectable HTML5 document. The result is the somewhat confusing set of guidelines listed here:

- Use **<strong>** for text that has *strong importance*. This is text that needs to stand out from its surroundings.

- Use **<b>** for text that should be presented in bold but doesn't have greater importance than the rest of your text. This could include keywords, product names, and anything else that would be bold in print.

- Use **<em>** for text that has *emphatic stress*—in other words, text that would have a different inflection if read out loud.

- Use **<i>** for text that should be presented in italics but doesn't have extra emphasis. This could include foreign words, technical terms, and anything else that you'd set in italics in print.

And here's a snippet of markup that uses all four of these elements in the appropriate way:

```
<strong>Breaking news!</strong> There's a sale on <i>leche quemada</i> candy
at the <b>El Azul</b> restaurant. Don't delay, because when the last candy
is gone, it's <em>gone</em>.
```

In the browser, the text looks like this:

> **Breaking news!** There's a sale on *leche quemada* candy at the **El Azul** restaurant. Don't delay, because when the last candy is gone, it's *gone*.

Some web developers will follow HTML's well-intentioned rules, while others just stick with the most familiar elements for bold and italic formatting.

Tweaked Elements

HTML5 also shifts the rules of a few elements. Usually, these changes are minor details that only HTML wonks will notice, but occasionally they have deeper effects. One example is the rarely used <address> element, which is not suitable (despite the name) for postal addresses. Instead, the <address> element has the narrow purpose of providing contact information for the creator of the HTML document, usually as an email address or website link:

```
Our website is managed by:
<address>
<a href="mailto:jsolo@mysite.com">John Solo</a>,
<a href="mailto:lcheng@mysite.com">Lisa Cheng</a>, and
<a href="mailto:rpavane@mysite.com">Ryan Pavane</a>.
</address>
```

The <cite> element has also changed. It can still be used to cite some work (for example, a story, article, or television show), like this:

```
<p>Charles Dickens wrote <cite>A Tale of Two Cities</cite>.</p>
```

However, it's not acceptable to use <cite> to mark up a person's name. This restriction has turned out to be surprisingly controversial, because this usage was allowed before. Several guru-level web developers are on record urging people to disregard the new <cite> rule, which is a bit odd, because you can spend a lifetime editing web pages without ever stumbling across the <cite> element in real life.

A more significant tweak affects the <a> element for creating links. Past versions of HTML have allowed the <a> element to hold clickable text or a clickable image. In HTML5, the <a> element allows anything and everything, which means it's perfectly acceptable to stuff entire paragraphs in there, along with lists, images, and so on. (If you do, you'll see that all the text inside becomes blue and underlined, and all the images inside sport blue borders.) Web browsers have supported this behavior for years, but it's only HTML5 that makes it an official, albeit not terribly useful, part of the HTML standard.

There are also some tweaks that don't work yet—in any browser. For example, the `<ol>` element (for ordered lists) now gets a reversed attribute, which you can set to count backward (either toward 1, or toward whatever starting value you set with the start attribute), but currently there are only two browsers that recognize this setting—Chrome and Safari.

You'll learn about a few more tweaks as you make your way through this book.

Standardized Elements

HTML5 also adds supports for a few elements that were supported but weren't officially welcome in the HTML or XHTML language. One of the best-known examples is `<embed>`, which is used all over the Web as an all-purpose way to shoehorn a plug-in into a page.

A more exotic example is `<wbr>`, which indicates an optional word break—in other words, a place where the browser can split a line if the word is too long to fit in its container:

```
<p>Many linguists remain unconvinced that
<b>supercali<wbr>fragilistic<wbr>expialidocious</b> is indeed a word.</p>
```

The `<wbr>` element is useful when you have long names (sometimes seen in programming terminology) in small places, like table cells or tiny boxes. Even if the browser supports `<wbr>`, it will break the word only if it doesn't fit in the available space. In the previous example, that means the browser may render the word in one of the following ways:

> Many linguists remain unconvinced that **supercalifragilisticexpialidocious** is indeed a word.

> Many linguists remain unconvinced that **supercalifragilistic expialidocious** is indeed a word.

> Many linguists remain unconvinced that **supercali fragilistic expialidocious** is indeed a word.

The <wbr> element has a natural similarity to the <nobr> element, which prevents text from wrapping no matter how narrow the available space. However, HTML5 considers <nobr> obsolete and advises all self-respecting web developers to avoid using it. Instead, you can get the same effect by adding the white-space property to your style sheet and setting it to nowrap.

Using HTML5 Today

Before you commit to HTML5, you need to know how well it works with the browsers your visitors are likely to use. After all, the last thing any web developer wants is a shiny new page that collapses into a muddle of scrambled markup and script errors when it meets a vintage browser.

In a moment, you'll learn how to research specific HTML5 features to find out which browsers support them, and examine browser usage statistics to find out what portion of your audience meets the bar. But before digging into the fine details, here's a broad overview of the current state of HTML5 support:

- If your visitors use the popular Google Chrome or Mozilla Firefox, they'll be fine. Not only have both browsers supported the bulk of HTML5 for several years, but they're also designed to update themselves automatically. That means you're unlikely to find an old version of Chrome or Firefox in the wild.

- If your visitors use Safari or Opera, you're probably still on safe ground. Once again, these browsers have had good HTML5 support for several years, and old versions are rarely seen.

- If your visitors use tablet computers or smartphones, you may face some limitations with certain features, as you'll learn throughout this book. However, the mobile browsers on all of today's web-enabled gadgets were created with HTML5 in mind. That means your pages are in for maybe a few hiccups, not a horror show.

- If your visitors use an older version of Internet Explorer—that is, any version before IE 10—most HTML5 features *won't* work. Here's where the headaches come in. Old versions of Windows are still common, and they typically include old versions of Internet Explorer. Even worse, many old versions of Windows don't let their users upgrade to a modern, HTML5-capable version of IE. Windows Vista, for example, is limited to IE 9. The mind-bogglingly old (but still popular) Windows XP is stuck with IE 8.

No, it's not Microsoft's diabolical plan to break the Web—it's just that newer versions of IE were designed with newer computer hardware in mind. This new software simply won't work on old machines. But people with old versions of Windows can use an alternative browser like Firefox, although they may not know how to install it or may not be allowed to make such changes to a company computer.

NOTE Although really old versions of Internet Explorer—like IE 6 and IE 7—have finally disappeared from the scene, the problematic IE 8 and IE 9 still account for over 10 percent of all Web traffic (at the time of this writing). And because it's never OK to force one in ten website visitors to suffer, you'll need to think about workarounds for most HTML5 features—at least for the immediate future.

UP TO SPEED

Dealing with Old Browsers

For the next few years, some of your visitors' browsers won't support all the HTML5 features you want to use. That's a fact of life. But it doesn't need to prevent you from using these features, if you're willing to put in a bit more work. There are two basic strategies you can use:

- **Degrade gracefully.** Sometimes, when a feature doesn't work, it's not a showstopper. For example, HTML5's new <video> element has a fallback mechanism that lets you supply something else to older browsers, like a video player that uses the Flash plug-in. (Supplying an error message is somewhat rude, and definitely not an example of degrading gracefully.) Your page can also degrade gracefully by ignoring nonessential frills, like some of the web form features (like placeholder text) and some of the formatting properties from CSS3 (like rounded corners and drop shadows). Or, you can write your own JavaScript

code that checks whether the current browser supports a feature you want to use (using a tool like Modernizr). If the browser fails the test, your code can show different content or use a less glamorous approach.

- **Use a JavaScript workaround.** Many of HTML5's new features are inspired by the stuff web developers are already doing the hard way. Thus, it should come as no surprise that you can duplicate many of HTML5's features using a good JavaScript library (or, in the worst-case scenario, by writing a whackload of your own custom JavaScript). Creating JavaScript workarounds can be a lot of work, but there are hundreds of good (and not-so-good) workarounds available free on the Web, which you can drop into your pages when needed. The more elaborate ones are called polyfills (page 35).

How to Find the Browser Requirements for Any HTML5 Feature

The people who have the final word on how much HTML5 you use are the browser vendors. If they don't support a feature, there's not much point in attempting to use it, no matter what the standard says. Today, there are four or five major browsers (not including the mobile variants that run on web-connected devices like smartphones and tablets). A single web developer has no chance of testing each prospective feature on every browser—not to mention evaluating support in older versions that are still widely used.

Fortunately, there's an ingenious website named "Can I use" that can help you out. It details the HTML5 support found in *every* mainstream browser. Best of all, it lets you focus on exactly the features you need. Here's how it works:

1. **Point your browser to *http://caniuse.com.***

   The main page has a bunch of links grouped into categories, like CSS, HTML5, and so on.

2. Choose the feature you want to study.

The quickest way to find a feature is to type its name into the Search box near the top of the page.

Or, you can browse to the feature by clicking one of the links on the front page. The HTML5 group has a set of links that are considered part of the core HTML5 standard; the JS API group has links for JavaScript-powered features that began as part of HTML5 but have since been split off; the CSS group has links for the styling features that are part of CSS3; and so on.

> **TIP** If you want, you can view the support tables for every feature in a group, all at once. Click the group title (like HTML5 or JS API), which is itself a link.

3. Examine your results (Figure 1-4).

Each feature table shows a grid of different browser versions. The tables indicate support with the color of the cell, which can be red (no support), bright green (full support), olive green (partial support), or gray (undetermined, usually because this version of the browser is still under development and the feature hasn't been added yet).

4. Optionally, choose different browsers to put under the microscope.

Ordinarily, the support table includes the most recent versions of the most popular browsers. However, you can tweak the table so it includes support information for other browsers that may be important to you—say, the aging IE 7 or a specialized mobile browser like Firefox for Android.

To choose which browsers appear in the tables, start by clicking the "Show options" link above the table. A list of browsers appears, and you can choose the browsers you want by adding a checkmark next to their names. You can also tweak the "Versions shown" slider, which acts as a kind of popularity threshold—lower it to include older browser versions that are used less frequently.

Alternatively, click the "Show all versions" link in the top-left corner of the table to see *all* the browser compatibility information that "Can I use" has in its database. But be warned that you'll get an immense table that stretches back to the dark days of Firefox 2 and IE 5.5.

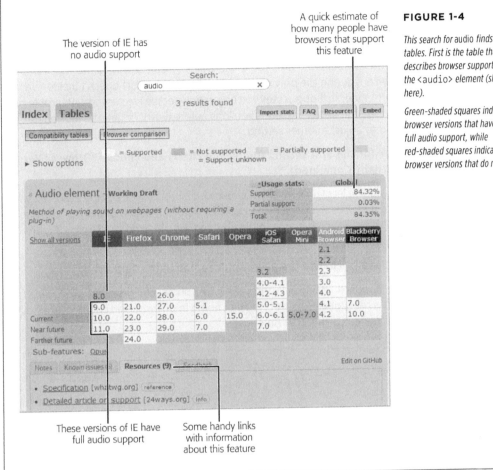

FIGURE 1-4

The version of IE has
no audio support

A quick estimate of
how many people have
browsers that support
this feature

*This search for audio finds two
tables. First is the table that
describes browser support for
the <audio> element (shown
here).*

*Green-shaded squares indicate
browser versions that have
full audio support, while
red-shaded squares indicate
browser versions that do not.*

These versions of IE have
full audio support

Some handy links
with information
about this feature

How to Find Out Which Browsers Are on the Web

How do you know *which* browser versions you need to worry about? Browser adoption statistics can tell you what portion of your audience has a browser that supports the features you plan to use. One good place to get an overall snapshot of all the browsers on the Web is GlobalStats, a popular tracking site. Here's how to use it:

1. **Browse to *http://gs.statcounter.com*.**

   On the GlobalStats site, you'll see a line graph showing the most popular browsers during the previous year. However, this chart doesn't include version information, so it doesn't tell you how many people are surfing with problematic versions of Internet Explorer (versions before IE 10). To get this information, you need to adjust another setting.

2. **Look for the Stat setting (under the chart) and choose "Browser Version (Partially Combined)."**

   This choice lets you consider not just which browsers are being used, but which *versions* of each browser. The partial combining tells GlobalStats to group together browsers that are rapidly updated, like Chrome and Firefox (Figure 1-5), so your chart isn't cluttered with dozens of extra lines.

3. **Optionally, change the geographic region in the Region box.**

   The standard setting is Worldwide, which shows browser statistics culled from across the globe. However, you can home in on a specific country (like Bolivia) or continent (like North America).

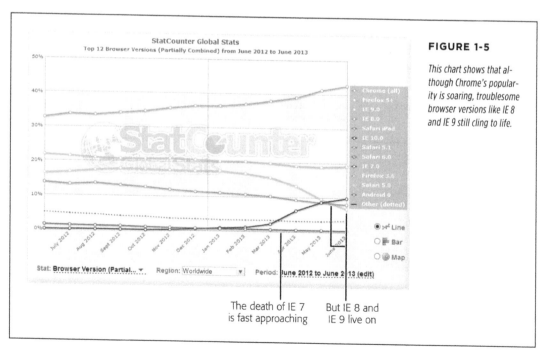

FIGURE 1-5

This chart shows that although Chrome's popularity is soaring, troublesome browser versions like IE 8 and IE 9 still cling to life.

The death of IE 7 is fast approaching

But IE 8 and IE 9 live on

4. **Optionally, click the text next to the Period setting to pick a different date range.**

   You'll usually see the browser usage trends for an entire year, but you can choose to focus on a smaller range, like the past three months.

5. **Optionally, change the chart type using the option buttons that are just to the right of the chart box.**

   Choose the Line option to see a line chart that shows the trend in browser adoption over time. Choose Bar to see a bar chart that shows a snapshot of the current situation. Or, choose Map to see a color-coded map that shows the countries where different browsers reign supreme.

GlobalStats compiles its statistics daily using tracking code that's present on millions of websites. And while that's a large number of pages and a huge amount of data, it's still just a small fraction of the total Web, which means you can't necessarily assume that your website visitors will use the same browsers.

Furthermore, browser-share results change depending on the web surfer's country and the type of website. For example, in Germany, Firefox is the top browser with over 40 percent of web surfers. And on the TechCrunch website (a popular news site for computer nerds), old versions of Internet Explorer are a rarity. So if you want to design a website that works for your peeps, it's worth reviewing the web statistics generated by your own pages. (And if you aren't already using a web tracking service for your site, check out the top-tier and completely free Google Analytics at *www.google.com/analytics*.)

Feature Detection with Modernizr

Feature detection is one strategy for dealing with features that aren't supported by all the browsers that hit up your site. The typical pattern is this: Your page loads and runs a snippet of JavaScript code to check whether a specific feature is available. You can then warn the user (the weakest option), fall back to a slightly less impressive version of your page (better), or implement a workaround that replicates the HTML5 feature you wanted to use (best).

Unfortunately, because HTML5 is, at its heart, a loose collection of related standards, there's no single HTML5 support test. Instead, you need dozens of different tests to check for dozens of different features—and sometimes even to check if a specific *part* of a feature is supported, which gets ugly fast.

Checking for support usually involves looking for a property on a programming object, or creating an object and trying to use it a certain way. But think twice before you write this sort of feature-testing code, because it's so easy to do it badly. For example, your feature-testing code might fail on certain browsers for some obscure reason or another, or quickly become out of date. Instead, consider using Modernizr (*http://modernizr.com*), a small, constantly updated tool that tests the support of a wide range of HTML5 and related features. It also has a cool trick for implementing fallback support when you're using new CSS3 features, which you'll see on page 180.

Here's how to use Modernizr in one of your web pages:

1. **Visit the Modernizr download page at *http://modernizr.com/download*.**

   Look for the "Development version" link, which points to the latest all-in-one JavaScript file for Modernizr.

2. **Right click the "Development version" link and choose "Save link as" or "Save target as."**

   Both commands are the same thing—the wording just depends on the browser you're using.

3. **Choose a place on your computer to save the file, and click Save.**

   The JavaScript file has the name *modernizr-latest.js*, unless you pick something different.

4. **When you're ready to use Modernizr, place that file in the same folder as your web page.**

   Or, place it in a subfolder and modify the path in the JavaScript reference accordingly.

5. **Add a reference to the JavaScript file in your web page's <head> section.**

   Here's an example of what your markup might look like, assuming the *modernizr-latest.js* file is in the same folder as your web page:

   ```
   <head>
     <meta charset="utf-8">
     <title>HTML5 Feature Detection</title>
     <script src="modernizr-latest.js"></script>
     ...
   </head>
   ```

   Now, when your page loads, the Modernizr script runs. It tests for a couple of dozen new features in mere milliseconds, and then creates a JavaScript object called modernizr that contains the results. You can test the properties of this object to check the browser's support for a specific feature.

   TIP For the full list of features that Modernizr tests, and for the JavaScript code that you need to examine each one, refer to the documentation at *http://modernizr.com/docs*.

6. **Write some script code that tests for the feature you want and then carries out the appropriate action.**

   For example, here's how you might test whether Modernizr supports the HTML5 drag-and-drop feature, and show the result in the page:

```
<!DOCTYPE html>
<html lang="en">
<head>
  <meta charset="utf-8">
  <title>HTML5 Feature Detection</title>
  <script src="modernizr-latest.js"></script>
</head>

<body>
  <p>The verdict is... <span id="result"></span></p>

  <script>
// Find the element on the page (named result) where you can show
// the results.
var result = document.getElementById("result");
if (Modernizr.draganddrop) {
    result.innerHTML = "Rejoice! Your browser supports drag-and-drop.";
}
else {
    result.innerHTML = "Your feeble browser doesn't support drag-and-drop.";
}
  </script>
</body>

</html>
```

Figure 1-6 shows the result.

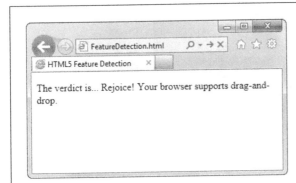

FIGURE 1-6

Although this example shows the right way to test for features, it shows a less-than-ideal approach for dealing with them. Instead of telling your website visitor about a missing feature, it's far, far better to implement some sort of workaround (even if it's not as neat or fully featured as the HTML5 equivalent) or to simply ignore the problem altogether (if the missing feature is a minor frill that's not necessary for the visitor to enjoy the page).

TIP This example uses basic and time-honored JavaScript techniques—looking up an element by ID and changing its content. If you find it a bit perplexing, you can brush up with the JavaScript review in Appendix B, "JavaScript: The Brains of Your Page."

The full Modernizr script is a bit bulky. It's intended for testing purposes while you're still working on your website. Once you've finished development and you're ready to go live, you can create a slimmed-down version of the Modernizr script that tests only for the features you need. To do so, go to the download page at *http://modernizr.com/download*. But this time, instead of using the "Development version" link, peruse the checkboxes below. Click the ones that correspond to the features you need to detect. Finally, click the Generate button to create your own custom Modernizr version, and then click the Download button to save it on your computer (Figure 1-7).

FIGURE 1-7

You're about to download a custom build of Modernizr that can detect support for the HTML5 canvas, the canvas text feature, and HTML5 video. This build of Modernizr won't be able to check for other features.

Feature "Filling" with Polyfills

Modernizr helps you spot the holes in browser support. It alerts you when a feature won't work. However, it doesn't do anything to patch these problems. That's where *polyfills* come in. Basically, polyfills are a hodgepodge collection of techniques for filling the gaps in HTML5 support on aging browsers. The word *polyfills* is borrowed from the product polyfiller, a compound that's used to fill in drywall holes before painting (also known as spackling paste). In HTML5, the ideal polyfill is one you can drop into a page without any extra work. It takes care of backward compatibility in a seamless, unobtrusive way, so you can work with pure HTML5 while someone else worries about the workarounds.

But polyfills aren't perfect. Some rely on other technologies that may be only partly supported. For example, one polyfill allows you to emulate the HTML5 canvas on old versions of Internet Explorer using the Silverlight plug-in. But if the web visitor isn't willing or able to install Silverlight, then you need to fall back on something else. Other polyfills may have fewer features than the real HTML5 feature, or poorer performance.

Occasionally, this book will point you to a potential polyfill. If you want more information, you can find the closest thing there is to a comprehensive catalog of HTML5 polyfills on GitHub at *http://tinyurl.com/polyfill*. But be warned—polyfills differ greatly in quality, performance, and support.

TIP Remember, it's not enough to simply know that a polyfill exists for a given HTML5 feature. You must test it and check how well it works on various old browsers *before* you risk incorporating the corresponding feature into your website.

With tools like browser statistics, feature detection, and polyfills, you're ready to think in depth about integrating HTML5 features into your own web pages. In the next chapter, you'll take the first step, with some HTML5 elements that can function in browsers both new and old.

Structuring Pages with Semantic Elements

Over the two decades that the Web's been around, websites have changed dramatically. But the greatest surprise isn't how much the Web has changed, but how well ancient HTML elements have held up. In fact, web developers use the same set of elements to build today's modern sites that they used to build their predecessors 10 years ago.

One element in particular—the humble <div> (or *division*)—is the cornerstone of nearly every modern web page. Using <div> elements, you can carve an HTML document into headers, side panels, navigation bars, and more. Add a healthy pinch of CSS formatting, and you can turn these sections into bordered boxes or shaded columns, and place each one exactly where it belongs.

This <div>-and-style technique is straightforward, powerful, and flexible, but it's not *transparent*. When you look at someone else's markup, you have to put some effort into figuring out what each <div> represents and how the whole page fits together. To make sense of it all, you need to jump back and forth among the markup, the style sheet, and the displayed page in the browser. And you'll face this confusion every time you crack open anyone else's halfway-sophisticated page, even though you're probably using the same design techniques in your own websites.

This situation got people thinking. What if there was a way to replace <div> with something better? Something that worked like <div>, but conveyed a bit more meaning. Something that might help separate the sidebars from the headers and the ad bars from the menus. HTML5 fulfills this dream with a set of new elements for structuring pages.

TIP If your CSS skills are so rusty that you need a tetanus shot before you can crack open a style sheet, then you're not quite ready for this chapter. Fortunately, Appendix A, "Essential CSS," has a condensed introduction that covers the fundamentals.

Introducing the Semantic Elements

To improve the structure of your web pages, you need HTML5's *semantic elements.* These elements give extra meaning to the content they enclose. For example, the new `<time>` element flags a valid date or time in your web page. Here's an example of the `<time>` element at its very simplest:

```
Registration begins on <time>2014-11-25</time>.
```

And this is what someone sees when viewing the page:

Registration begins on 2014-11-25.

The important thing to understand is that the `<time>` element doesn't have any built-in formatting. In fact, the web page reader has no way of knowing that there's an extra element wrapping the date. You can add your own formatting to the `<time>` element using a style sheet, but by default, the text inside a `<time>` element is indistinguishable from ordinary text.

The `<time>` element is designed to wrap a single piece of information. However, most of HTML5's semantic elements are designed to identify larger sections of content. For example, the `<nav>` element identifies a set of navigation links. The `<footer>` element wraps the footer that sits at the bottom of a page. And so on, for a dozen (or so) new elements.

NOTE Although semantic elements are the least showy of HTML5's new features, they're one of the largest. In fact, the majority of the new elements in HTML5 are semantic elements.

All the semantic elements share a distinguishing feature: They don't really do anything. By contrast, the `<video>` element, for example, embeds a fully capable video player in your page (page 147). So why bother using all these new elements that don't change the way your web page looks?

There are several good reasons:

- **Easier editing and maintenance.** It can be difficult to interpret the markup in a traditional HTML page. To understand the overall layout and the significance of various sections, you'll often need to scour a web page's style sheet. But by using HTML5's semantic elements, you provide extra structural information in the markup. That makes your life easier when you need to edit the page months later, and it's even more important if someone else needs to revise your work.

- **Accessibility.** One of the key themes of modern web design is making *accessible* pages—that is, pages that people can navigate using screen readers and other assistive tools. Accessibility tools that understand HTML5 can provide a far better browsing experience for disabled visitors. (For just one example, imagine how a screen reader can home in on the <nav> sections to quickly find the navigation links for a website.)

> **TIP** To learn more about the best practices for web accessibility, you can visit the WAI (Web Accessibility Initiative) website at *www.w3.org/WAI*. Or, to get a quick look at what life is like behind a screen reader (and to learn why properly arranged headings are so important), check out the YouTube video at *http://tinyurl.com/6bu4pe*.

- **Search-engine optimization.** Search engines like Google use powerful *search bots*—automated programs that crawl the Web and fetch every page they can— to scan your content and index it in their search databases. The better Google understands your site, the better the chance that it can match a web searcher's query to your content, and the better the chance that your website will turn up in someone's search results. Search bots already check for some of HTML5's semantic elements to glean more information about the pages they're indexing.

- **Future features.** New browsers and web editing tools are sure to take advantage of semantic elements. For example, a browser could provide an outline that lets visitors jump to the appropriate section in a page. (In fact, Chrome already has a plug-in that does exactly that—see page 65.) Similarly, web design tools can include features that let you build or edit navigation menus by managing the content you've placed in the <nav> section.

The bottom line is this: If you can apply the semantic elements correctly, you can create cleaner, clearer pages that are ready for the next wave of browsers and web tools. But if your brain is still tied up with the old-fashioned practices of traditional HTML, the future may pass you by.

Retrofitting a Traditional HTML Page

The easiest way to introduce yourself to the new semantic elements—and to learn how to use them to structure a page—is to take a classic HTML document and inject it with some HTML5 goodness. Figure 2-1 shows the first example you'll tackle. It's a simple, standalone web page that holds an article, although other types of content (like a blog posting, a product description, or a short story) would work equally well.

> **TIP** You can view or download the example in Figure 2-1 from the try-out site at *http://prosetech.com/html5*, along with all the examples for this chapter. Start with *ApocalypsePage_Original.html* if you'd like to try to remodel the HTML yourself, or *ApocalypsePage_Revised.html* if you want to jump straight to the HTML5-improved final product.

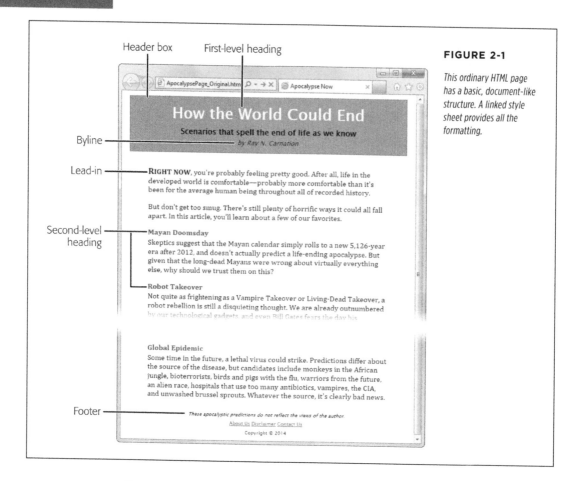

FIGURE 2-1

This ordinary HTML page has a basic, document-like structure. A linked style sheet provides all the formatting.

Page Structure the Old Way

There are a number of ways to format a page like the one shown in Figure 2-1. Happily, this example uses HTML best practices, which means the markup doesn't have a lick of formatting logic. There are no bold or italic elements, no inline styles, and certainly nothing as hideous as the obsolete <font> element. Instead, it's a neatly formatted document that's bound to an external style sheet.

Here's a shortened version of the markup, which highlights where the document plugs into its style sheet:

```
<div class="Header">
  <h1>How the World Could End</h1>
  <p class="Teaser">Scenarios that spell the end of life as we know it</p>
  <p class="Byline">by Ray N. Carnation</p>
</div>

<div class="Content">
  <p><span class="LeadIn">Right now</span>, you're probably ...</p>
  <p>...</p>

  <h2>Mayan Doomsday</h2>
  <p>Skeptics suggest ...</p>
  ...
</div>

<div class="Footer">
  <p class="Disclaimer">These apocalyptic predictions ...</p>
  <p>
    <a href="AboutUs.html">About Us</a>
    ...
  </p>
  <p>Copyright © 2014</p>
</div>
```

UP TO SPEED

What Are These Dots (...)?

This book can't show you the full markup for every example—at least not without expanding itself to 12,000 pages and wiping out an entire old-growth forest. But it *can* show you basic structure of a page and all its important elements. To do that, many of the examples in this book use an ellipsis (a series of three dots) to show where some content has been left out.

For example, consider the markup shown above on this page. It includes the full body of the page shown in Figure 2-2, but it leaves out the full text of most paragraphs, most of the article after the "Mayan Doomsday" heading, and the full list of links in the footer. But, as you know, you can pore over every detail by examining the sample files for this chapter on the try-out site (*http://prosetech.com/html5*).

In a well-written, traditional HTML page (like this one), most of the work is farmed out to the style sheet using the <div> and <span> containers. The <span> lets you format snippets of text inside another element. The <div> allows you to format entire sections of content, and it establishes the overall structure of the page (Figure 2-2).

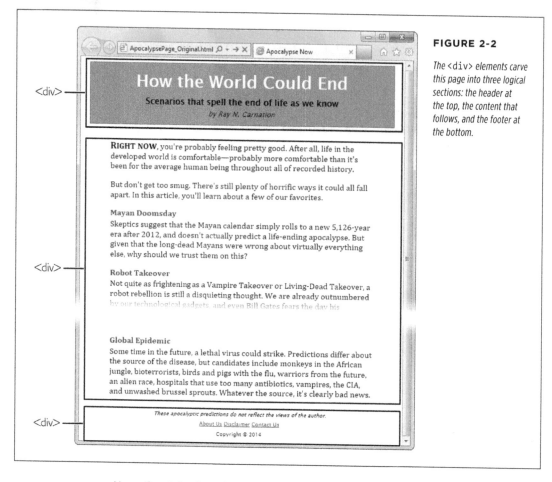

FIGURE 2-2

The <div> elements carve this page into three logical sections: the header at the top, the content that follows, and the footer at the bottom.

Here, the style sheet formatting tasks are simple. The entire page is given a maximum width (800 pixels) to prevent really long text lines on widescreen monitors. The header is put in a bordered blue box. The content is padded on either side, and the footer is centered at the bottom of the page.

Thanks to the <div>, formatting is easy. For example, the *ApocalypsePage_Original. css* style sheet uses the following rules to format the header box and the content inside:

```
/* Format the <div> that represents the header (as a blue, bordered box). */
.Header {
  background-color: #7695FE;
  border: thin #336699 solid;
  padding: 10px;
```

```
    margin: 10px;
    text-align: center;
  }


  /* Format any <h1> headings in the header <div> (that's the article title). */
  .Header h1 {
    margin: 0px;
    color: white;
    font-size: xx-large;
  }


  /* Format the subtitle in the header <div>. */
  .Header .Teaser {
    margin: 0px;
    font-weight: bold;
  }


  /* Format the byline in the header <div>. */
  .Header .Byline {
    font-style: italic;
    font-size: small;
    margin: 0px;
  }
```

You'll notice that this example makes good use of contextual selectors (page 441). For example, it uses the selector .Header h1 to format all <h1> elements in the header box.

> **TIP** This example is also described in the CSS review in Appendix A, "Essential CSS." If you'd like to take a detailed walk through the style sheet rules that format each section, flip to page 445.

Page Structure with HTML5

The <div> element is still a staple of web design. It's a straightforward, all-purpose container that you can use to apply formatting anywhere you want in a web page. The limitation of the <div> is that it doesn't provide any information about the page. When you (or a browser, or a design tool, or a screen reader, or a search bot) come across a <div>, you know that you've found a separate section of the page, but you don't know the purpose of that section.

To improve this situation in HTML5, you can replace some of your <div> elements with more descriptive semantic elements. The semantic elements behave exactly like <div> elements: They group a block of markup, they don't do anything on their own, and they give you a styling hook that lets you apply formatting. However, they also give your page a little more semantic smarts.

Here's a quick revision of the article shown in Figure 2-1. It removes two <div> elements and adds two semantic elements from HTML5: <header> and <footer>.

```
<header class="Header">
  <h1>How the World Could End</h1>
  <p class="Teaser">Scenarios that spell the end of life as we know it</p>
  <p class="Byline">by Ray N. Carnation</p>
</header>

<div class="Content">
  <p><span class="LeadIn">Right now</span>, you're probably ...</p>
  <p>...</p>

  <h2>Mayan Doomsday</h2>
  <p>Skeptics suggest ...</p>
  ...
</div>

<footer class="Footer">
  <p class="Disclaimer">These apocalyptic predictions ...</p>
  <p>
    <a href="AboutUs.html">About Us</a>
    ...
  </p>
  <p>Copyright © 2014</p>
</footer>
```

In this example, the <header> and <footer> elements take the place of the <div> elements that were there before. Web developers who are revising a large website might start by wrapping the existing <div> elements in the appropriate HTML5 semantic elements.

You'll also notice that the <header> and <footer> elements in this example still use the same class names. This way, you don't need to change the original style sheet. Thanks to the class names, the style sheet rules that used to format the <div> elements now format the <header> and <footer> elements.

However, you might feel that the class names seem a bit redundant. If so, you can leave them out, like this:

```
<header>
  <h1>How the World Could End</h1>
  <p class="Teaser">Scenarios that spell the end of life as we know it</p>
  <p class="Byline">by Ray N. Carnation</p>
</header>
```

To make this work, you need to alter your style sheet rules so they apply themselves by element name. This works for the header and footer, because the current page has just a single <header> element and a single <footer> element.

Here's the revised style sheet that applies its formatting to the <header> element:

```
/* Format the <header> (as a blue, bordered box.) */
header {
  ...
}

/* Format any <h1> headings in the <header> (that's the article title). */
header h1 {
  ...
}

/* Format the subtitle in the <header>. */
header .Teaser {
  ...
}

/* Format the byline in the <header>. */
header .Byline {
  ...
}
```

Both approaches are equally valid. As with many design decisions in HTML5, there are plenty of discussions but no hard rules.

You'll notice that the <div> section for the content remains. This is perfectly acceptable, as HTML5 web pages often contain a mix of semantic elements and the more generic <div> containers. Because there's no HTML5 "content" element, an ordinary <div> still makes sense.

> **NOTE** Left to its own devices, this web page won't display correctly on versions of Internet Explorer before IE 9. To fix this issue, you need the simple workaround discussed on page 51. But first, check out a few more semantic elements that can enhance your pages.

Finally, there's one more element worth adding to this example. HTML5 includes an <article> element that represents a complete, self-contained piece of content, like a blog posting or a news story. The <article> element includes the whole shebang, including the title, author byline, and main content. Once you add the <article> element to the page, you get this structure:

```
<article>
  <header>
    <h1>How the World Could End</h1>
    ...
  </header>
```

```
<div class="Content">
  <p><span class="LeadIn">Right now</span>, you're probably ...</p>
  <p>...</p>
  <h2>Mayan Doomsday</h2>
  <p>Skeptics suggest ...</p>
  ...
</div>
</article>

<footer>
  <p class="Disclaimer">These apocalyptic predictions ...</p>
  ...
</footer>
```

Figure 2-3 shows the final structure.

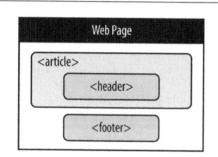

FIGURE 2-3

After the redesign, the page uses three of HTML5's semantic elements. If the old structure said, "Here is a page with three sections," then the new structure says, "Here is an article with a header, on a page with a footer."

Although the web page still looks the same in the browser, there's a fair bit of extra information lurking behind the scenes. For example, a search bot that stops by your site can quickly find your page's content (that's your article) and the title of that content (that's the header). It won't pay as much attention to the footer.

> **NOTE** Sometimes articles are split over several web pages. The current consensus of webheads is that each part of the article should be wrapped in its own `<article>` element, even though it's not complete and self-contained. This messy compromise is just one of many that occur when semantics meet the practical, presentational considerations of the Web.

Adding a Figure with `<figure>`

Plenty of pages have images. But the concept of a *figure* is a bit different. The HTML5 specification suggests that you think of them much like figures in a book—in other words, a picture that's separate from the text, yet referred to in the text.

Generally, you let figures *float*, which means you put them in the nearest convenient spot alongside your text, rather than lock them in place next to a specific word or element. Often, figures have captions that float with them.

The following example shows some HTML markup that adds a figure to the apocalyptic article. It also includes the paragraph that immediately precedes the figure and the one that follows it, so you can see exactly where the figure is placed in the markup.

```
<p><span class="LeadIn">Right now</span>, you're probably ...</p>
<div class="FloatFigure">

  <img src="human_skull.jpg" alt="Human skull">
  <p>Will you be the last person standing if one of these apocalyptic
  scenarios plays out?</p>
</div>
```

```
<p>But don't get too smug ...</p>
```

This markup assumes that you've created a style sheet rule that positions the figure (and sets margins, controls the formatting of the caption text, and optionally draws a border around it). Here's an example:

```
/* Format the floating figure box. */
.FloatFigure {
  float: left;
  margin-left: 0px;
  margin-top: 0px;
  margin-right: 20px;
  margin-bottom: 0px;
}
```

```
/* Format the figure caption text. */
.FloatFigure p {
  max-width: 200px;
  font-size: small;
  font-style: italic;
  margin-bottom: 5px;
}
```

Figure 2-4 shows this example at work.

If you've created this sort of figure before, you'll be interested to know that HTML5 provides new semantic elements that are tailor-made for this pattern. Instead of using a boring <div> to hold the figure box, you use a <figure> element. And if you have any caption text, you put that in a <figcaption> element inside the <figure>:

```
<figure class="FloatFigure">
   <img src="human_skull.jpg" alt="Human skull">
   <figcaption>Will you be the last person standing if one of these
   apocalyptic scenarios plays out?</figcaption>
</figure>
```

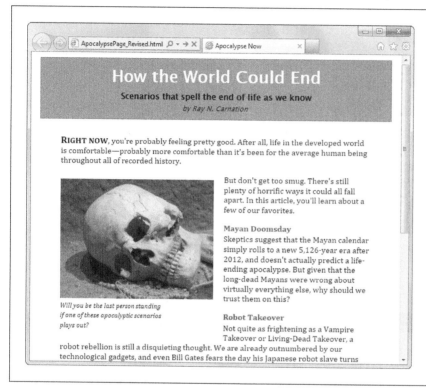

FIGURE 2-4

Now a figure graces the article. In the markup, it's defined just after the first paragraph, so it floats to the left of the following text. Notice that the width of the caption is limited, to create a nice, packed paragraph.

Of course it's still up to you to use a style sheet to position and format your figure box. In this example, you need to change the style rule selector that targets the caption text. Right now it uses `.FloatFigure p`, but the revised example requires `.FloatFigure figcaption`.

> **TIP** In this example, the `<figure>` element still gets its formatting based on its class name (FloatFigure), not its element type. That's because you're likely to format figures in more than one way. For example, you might have figures that float on the left, figures that float on the right, ones that need different margin or caption settings, and so on. To preserve this sort of flexibility, it makes sense to format your figures with classes.

In the browser, the figure still looks the same. The difference is that the purpose of your figure markup is now perfectly clear. (Incidentally, `<figcaption>` isn't limited to holding text—you can use any HTML elements that make sense. Other possibilities include links and tiny icons.)

Finally, it's worth noting that in some cases the figure caption may include a complete description of the image, rendering the alt text redundant. In this situation, you can remove the `alt` attribute from the `<img>` element:

```
<figure class="FloatFigure">
    <img src="human_skull.jpg">
    <figcaption>A human skull lies on the sand</figcaption>
</figure>
```

Just make sure you don't set the alternate text with an empty string, because that means your image is purely presentational and screen readers should avoid it altogether.

Adding a Sidebar with <aside>

The new `<aside>` element represents content that is tangentially related to the text that surrounds it. For example, you can use an `<aside>` in the same way you use a sidebar in print—to introduce a related topic or to expand on a point that's raised in the main document. (See, for instance, the box at the bottom of page 50.) The `<aside>` element also makes sense if you need somewhere to stash a block of ads, some related content links, or even a pull-quote like the one shown in Figure 2-5.

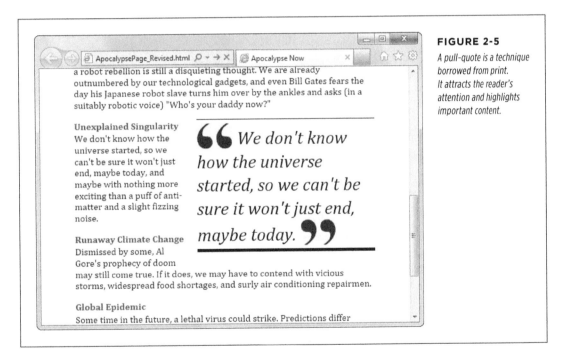

FIGURE 2-5

A pull-quote is a technique borrowed from print. It attracts the reader's attention and highlights important content.

You can easily create this effect with the well-worn `<div>` element, but the `<aside>` element gives you a more meaningful way to mark up the same content:

```
<p>... (in a suitably robotic voice) "Who's your daddy now?"</p>
```

```
<aside class="PullQuote">
    <img src="quotes_start.png" alt="Quote">
```

```
We don't know how the universe started, so we can't be sure it won't
just end, maybe today.
<img src="quotes_end.png" alt="End quote">
</aside>

<h2>Unexplained Singularity</h2>
```

This time, the style sheet rule floats the pull-quote to the right. Here are the styling details, just in case you're curious:

```css
.PullQuote {
  float: right;
  max-width: 300px;
  border-top: thin black solid;
  border-bottom: thick black solid;
  font-size: 30px;
  line-height: 130%;
  font-style: italic;
  padding-top: 5px;
  padding-bottom: 5px;
  margin-left: 15px;
  margin-bottom: 10px;
}

.PullQuote img {
  vertical-align: bottom;
}
```

UP TO SPEED

How the Semantic Elements Were Chosen

Before inventing HTML5, its creators took a long look at the current crop of web pages. And they didn't just browse through their favorite sites; instead, they reviewed the Google-crunched statistics for over a *billion* web pages. (You can see the results of this remarkable survey at *http://tinyurl.com/state-of-the-web.*)

The Google survey analyzed the markup and compiled a list of the class names web authors were using in their pages. Their idea was that the class name might betray the purpose of the element and give a valuable clue about the way people were structuring pages. For example, if everyone has a <div> element that uses a class named header, then it's logical to assume everyone is putting headers at the tops of their web pages.

The first thing that Google found is that the vast majority of pages didn't use class names (or style sheets at all). Next, they compiled a short list of the most commonly used class names. Some of the most popular names were footer, header, title, menu, nav—which correspond well to HTML5's new semantic elements <footer>, <header>, and <nav>. A few others suggest possible semantic elements that haven't been created yet, like search and copyright.

In other words, the Web is awash with the same basic designs—for example, pages with headers, footers, sidebars, and navigation menus. But everyone has a slightly different way of doing more or less the same thing. From this realization, it's just a small leap to decide that the HTML language could be expanded with a few new elements that capture the semantics of what everyone is already doing. And this is exactly the insight that inspired HTML5's semantic elements.

◼ Browser Compatibility for the Semantic Elements

So far, this exercise has been a lot of fun. But the best-structured page is useless if it won't work on older browsers.

Fortunately, HTML5's semantic elements are broadly supported on all modern browsers. It's almost impossible to find a version of Chrome, Firefox, Safari, or Opera that doesn't recognize them. The chief stumbling block is any version of Internet Explorer before IE 9, including the still-kicking IE 8.

Fortunately, this is one missing feature that's easy to patch up. After all, the semantic elements don't actually do anything. To support them, a browser simply needs to treat them like an ordinary `<div>` element. And to make that happen, all you need to do is fiddle with their styles, as described in the following sections. Do that, and you'll be rewarded with super-reliable semantic elements that work with any browser that's been released in the last 10 years.

> **NOTE** If you're already using Modernizr (page 31), your pages are automatically immunized against semantic element issues, and you can safely skip the following discussion. But if you aren't using Modernizr, or if you're curious about how this fix works, read on.

Styling the Semantic Elements

When a browser meets an element it doesn't recognize, it treats it as an inline element. Most of HTML5's semantic elements (including all the ones you've seen in this chapter, except `<time>`) are *block* elements, which means the browser is supposed to render them on a separate line, with a little bit of space between them and the preceding and following elements.

Web browsers that don't recognize the HTML5 elements won't know to display some of them as block elements, so they're likely to end up in a clumped-together mess. To fix this problem, you simply need to add a new rule to your style sheet. Here's a super-rule that applies block display formatting to the nine HTML5 elements that need it in one step:

```
article, aside, figure, figcaption, footer, header, main, nav, section,
summary {
  display: block;
}
```

This style sheet rule won't have any effect for browsers that already recognize HTML5, because the `display` property is already set to `block`. And it won't affect any style rules you already use to format these elements. They will still apply *in addition* to this rule.

Using the HTML5 Shiv

That technique described in the previous section is enough to solve compatibility issues in most browsers, but "most" doesn't include Internet Explorer 8 and older. Old versions of IE introduce a second challenge: They refuse to apply style sheet formatting to elements they don't recognize. Fortunately, there is a workaround: You can trick IE into recognizing a foreign element by registering it with a JavaScript command. For example, here's a script block that gives IE the ability to recognize and style the <header> element:

```
<script>
  document.createElement('header')
</script>
```

Rather than write this sort of code yourself, you can find a ready-made script that does it for you. You simply need to add a reference to it in the <head> section of your page, like this:

```
<head>
  <title>...</title>
  <script src="http://html5shim.googlecode.com/svn/trunk/html5.js"></script>
  ...
<head>
```

This code grabs the script from the *html5shim.googlecode.com* web server and runs it before the browser starts processing the rest of the page. This script uses the JavaScript described above to create all the new HTML5 elements and goes one step further, by dynamically applying the styles described on page 51, to make sure the new elements display as proper block elements. The only remaining task is for you to use the elements and add your own style sheet rules to format them.

Incidentally, the *html5.js* script code is conditional—it runs only if it detects that you're running an old version of Internet Explorer. But if you want to avoid the overhead of requesting the JavaScript file at all, you can make the script reference conditional, like so:

```
<!--[if lt IE 9]>
  <script src="http://html5shim.googlecode.com/svn/trunk/html5.js"></script>
<![endif]-->
```

That way, other browsers (and IE 9 or later) will ignore this instruction, saving your page a few milliseconds of time.

> **TIP** The previous example uses the HTML5 shiv straight from Google's code-hosting site. However, you can download your own copy from *http://tinyurl.com/the-shiv* and place it alongside your web pages. Just modify the script reference to point to the location where you upload the script file.

Finally, it's worth pointing out that if you test a web page on your own computer (rather than uploading it to a web server), Internet Explorer automatically places the page in restricted mode. That means you'll see the infamous IE security bar at the top of the page, warning you that Internet Explorer has disabled all your scripts, including the HTML5 shiv. To run it, you need to explicitly click the security bar and choose to allow active content.

This problem disappears once you upload the page to a website, but it can be a hassle when testing your work. The solution is to add the "mark of the Web" comment to the beginning of your web page, as described on page 14.

Modernizr: An All-in-One Fix

There's one excellent alternate solution to the semantic styling problem: Use Modernizr (page 31). It has the HTML5 shiv built in, which means there's no need for you to fiddle with style rules or to include a reference to the *html5.js* script. So if you're already using Modernizr to test for feature support, consider the problem solved.

Designing a Site with the Semantic Elements

Adding the semantic elements to a simple, document-like page is easy. Adding them to a complete website isn't any harder, but it does raise a whole lot more questions. And because HTML5 is essentially virgin territory, there are a small number of settled conventions (but a large number of legitimate disagreements). That means when you have a choice between two markup approaches, and the HTML5 standard says they're both perfectly acceptable, it's up to you to decide which one makes the most sense for your content.

Figure 2-6 shows the more ambitious example that you'll consider next.

Deeper into Headers

There are two similar, but subtly different, ways to use the <header> element. First, you can use it to title some content. Second, you can use it to title your web page. Sometimes, these two tasks overlap (as with the single article example shown in Figure 2-1). But other times, you'll have a web page with both a page header and one or more pieces of headered content. Figure 2-6 is this sort of example.

What makes this situation a bit trickier is that the conventions for using the <header> element change based on its role. If you're dealing with content, you probably won't use a header unless you need it. And you need it only if you're creating a "fat" header. That is, one that includes the title and some other content—for example, a summary, the publication date, an author byline, an image, or subtopic links. Here's an example:

```
<header>
    <h1>How the World Could End</h1>
    <p class="Tagline">Scenarios that spell the end of life as we know it</p>
    <p class="Byline">by Ray N. Carnation</p>
</header>
```

FIGURE 2-6

Here, the single-page article you considered previously has been placed in a complete content-based website. A site header caps the page; the content is underneath; and a sidebar on the left provides navigation controls, "About Us" information, and an image ad.

However, when people create a header for a website, they almost always wrap it in a <header> element, even if there's nothing there but a title in a big CSS-formatted box. After all, it's a major design point of your website, and who knows when you might need to crack it open and add something new?

Here's the takeaway: Pages can have more than one <header> element (and they often will), even though these headers play different roles on the page.

The apocalyptic site (Figure 2-6) uses the <header> element for the website header and another <header> element for the article title. The <header> that caps the website holds a banner image, which combines graphical text and a picture:

```
<header class="SiteHeader">
  <img src="site_logo.png" alt="Apocalypse Today">
  <h1 style="display:none">Apocalypse Today</h1>
</header>
```

Turning a Web Page into a Website

Figure 2-6 shows a single page from a fictional website.

In a real website, you'd have the same layout (and the same side panel) on *dozens* of different pages or more. The only thing that would change as the visitor clicks around the page is the main page content—in this case, the article.

HTML5 doesn't have any special magic for turning web pages into websites. Instead, you need to use the same tricks and technologies that web developers rely on in traditional HTML:

- **Server-side frameworks.** The idea is simple: When a browser requests a page, the web server assembles the pieces, including the common elements (like a navigation bar) and the content. This approach is by far the most common, and it's the only way to go on big, professional websites. Countless different technologies implement this approach in different ways, from web programming platforms like ASP.NET and PHP to content management systems like Drupal and WordPress.

- **Page templates.** Some high-powered web page editors (like Adobe Dreamweaver and Microsoft Visual Studio) include a page template feature. You begin by creating a template that defines the structure of your web pages and includes the repeating content you want to appear on every page (like the header and the sidebar). Then you use that template to create all your site pages. Here's the neat part: When you update the template, your web page editor automatically updates all the pages that use it.

Of course, you're free to use either technique, so this book focuses on the final result: the pasted-together markup that forms a complete page and is shown in the web browser.

Right away, you'll notice that this header adds a detail that you don't see on the page: an <h1> heading that duplicates the content that's in the picture. However, an inline style setting hides this heading.

This example raises a clear question: What's the point of adding a heading that you can't see? There are actually several reasons. First, all <header> elements require some level of heading inside, just to satisfy the rules of HTML5. Second, this design makes the page more accessible for people who are navigating it with screen readers, because they'll often jump from one heading to the next without listening to the content in between. And third, it establishes a heading structure that you can use in the rest of the page. That's a fancy way of saying that if you start with an <h1> for your website header, you may decide to use <h2> elements to title the other sections of the page (like "Articles" and "About Us" in the sidebar). For more about this design decision, see the box on page 56.

NOTE Of course, you could simplify your life by creating an ordinary text header. (And if you want fancy fonts, the CSS3 web font feature, described on page 206, can help you out.) But for the many web pages that put the title in a picture, the hidden heading trick is the next best solution.

The Heading Structure of a Site

Is it acceptable to have more than one level-1 heading on a page? Is it a good idea?

According to the official rules of HTML, you can have as many level-1 headings as you want. However, website creators often strive to have just a single level-1 heading per page, because it makes for a more accessible site—because people using screen readers might miss a level-1 heading as they skip from one level-2 heading to the next. There's also a school of webmaster thought that says every page should have exactly one level-1 heading, which is unique across the entire website and clearly tells search engines what content awaits.

The example in Figure 2-6 uses this style. The "Apocalypse Today" heading that tops the site is the only <h1> on the page. The other sections on the page, like "Articles" and "About Us" in the sidebar, use level-2 headings. The article title also uses a level-2 heading. (With a little bit of extra planning, you could vary the text of the level-1 heading to match the current article—after all, this heading isn't actually visible,

and it could help the page match more focused queries in a search engine like Google.)

But there are other, equally valid approaches. For example, you could use level-1 headings to title each major section of your page, including the sidebar, the article, and so on.

Or, you could give the website a level-1 site heading and put level-2 headings in the sidebar (as in the current example) but make the article title into a second level-1 heading. This works fine in HTML5, because of its new outlining system. As you'll learn on page 65, some elements, including <article>, are treated as separate sections, with their own distinct outlines. So it makes perfect sense for these sections to start the heading hierarchy over again with a brand new <h1>. (However, HTML5 says it's fine to start with a different heading level, too.)

In short, there's no clear answer about how to structure your website. It seems likely that the "multiple <h1>" approach will become increasingly popular as HTML5 conquers the Web. But for now, many web developers are sticking with the "single <h1>" approach to keep screen readers happy.

Navigation Links with <nav>

The most interesting new feature in the apocalyptic website is the sidebar on the left, which provides the website's navigation, some extra information, and an image ad. (Typically, you'd throw in a block of JavaScript that fetches a randomly chosen ad using a service like Google AdSense. But this example just hard-codes a picture to stand in for that.)

In a traditional HTML website, you'd wrap the whole sidebar in a <div>. In HTML5, you almost always rely on two more specific elements: <aside> and <nav>.

The <aside> element is a bit like the <header> element in that it has a subtle, slightly stretchable meaning. You can use it to mark up a piece of related content, as you did with the pull-quote on page 49. Or, you can also use it to designate an entirely separate section of the page—one that's offset from the main flow.

The <nav> element wraps a block of links. These links may point to topics on the current page, or to other pages on the website. Most pages will have multiple <nav> sections in them. But not all links need a <nav> section—instead, it's generally reserved for the largest and most important navigational sections on a page. For example, if you have a list of articles (as in Figure 2-6), you definitely need a <nav> section. But if you have just a couple of links at the bottom of the page with licensing and contact information, a full-blown <nav> isn't necessary.

With these two elements in mind, it's a good time to try a practice exercise. First, review the sidebar in Figure 2-6. Next, sketch out on a piece of paper how you would mark up the structure of this content. Then, read on to find out the best possible solution.

In fact, there are at least two reasonably good ways to structure this sidebar, as shown in Figure 2-7.

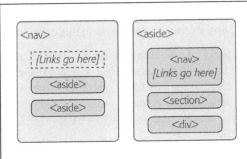

FIGURE 2-7

Left: You can think of the entire side panel as a navigation bar, with some other content wedged in. In this case, the whole panel can be a <nav>, *and the other content sections require an* <aside> *(because they aren't related to the sidebar's main content, the links).*

Right: Alternatively, consider the entire side panel to be a separate web page section that serves several purposes. In this case, the sidebar becomes an <aside> *while the navigational content inside is wrapped in a* <nav>.

The apocalyptic site uses the second approach (Figure 2-7, right). That's because the sidebar seems to serve several purposes, with none clearly being dominant. But if you have a lengthy and complex navigational section (like a collapsible menu) followed by a short bit of content, the first approach just might make more sense.

Here's the markup that shapes the sidebar, dividing it into three sections:

```
<aside class="NavSidebar">
  <nav>
    <h2>Articles</h2>
    <ul>
      <li><a href="...">How The World Could End</a></li>
      <li><a href="...">Would Aliens Enslave or Eradicate Us?</a></li>
      ...
    </ul>
  </nav>

  <section>
    <h2>About Us</h2>
    <p>Apocalypse Today is a world leader in conspiracy theories ..."
    </p>
  </section>
```

```
<div>
  <img src="ad.jpg" alt="Luckies cigarette ad: it's toasted">
</div>
</aside>
```

Here are the key points:

- **The title sections ("Articles" and "About Us") are level-2 headings.** That way, they are clearly subordinate to the level-1 website heading, which makes the page more accessible to screen readers.

- **The links are marked up in an unordered list using the `<ul>` and `<li>` elements.** Website designers agree that a list is the best, most accessible way to deal with a series of links. However, you may need to use style sheet rules to remove the indent (as done here) and the bullets (not done in this example).

- **The "About Us" section is wrapped in a `<section>` element.** That's because there's no other semantic element that suits this content. A `<section>` is slightly more specific than a `<div>`—it's suitable for any block of content that starts with a heading. If there were a more specific element to use (for example, a hypothetical `<about>` element), that would be preferable to a basic `<section>`, but there isn't.

- **The image ad is wrapped in a `<div>`.** The `<section>` element is appropriate only for content that starts with a title, and the image section doesn't have a heading. (Although if it did—say, "A Word from Our Sponsors"—a `<section>` element would be the better choice.) Technically, it's not necessary to put any other element around the image, but the `<div>` makes it easier to separate this section, style it, and throw in some JavaScript code that manipulates it, if necessary.

There are also some details that this sidebar *doesn't* have but many others do. For example, complex sidebars may start with a `<header>` and end with a `<footer>`. They may also include multiple `<nav>` sections—for example, one for a list of archived content, one with a list of late-breaking news, one with a blogroll or list of related sites, and so on. For an example, check out the sidebar of a typical blog, which is packed full of sections, many of which are navigational.

The style sheet rules you use to format the `<aside>` sidebar are the same as the ones you'd use to format a traditional `<div>` sidebar. They place the sidebar in the correct spot, using absolute positioning, and set some formatting details, like padding and background color:

```
aside.NavSidebar
{
  position: absolute;
  top: 179px;
  left: 0px;
  padding: 5px 15px 0px 15px;
  width: 203px;
```

```
    min-height: 1500px;
    background-color:#eee;
    font-size: small;
}
```

This rule is followed by contextual style sheet rules that format the <h2>, <ul>, <li>, and <img> elements in the sidebar. (As always, you can get the sample code from *http://prosetech.com/html5*, and peruse the complete style sheet.)

Now that you understand how the sidebar is put together, you'll understand how it fits into the layout of the entire page, as shown in Figure 2-8.

NOTE As you've learned, the <nav> is often found on its own, or in an <aside>. There's one more common place for it to crop up: in the <header> element that tops a web page.

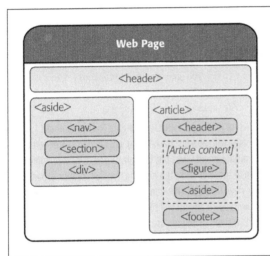

FIGURE 2-8

Here are all the semantic elements that you'll find in the apocalyptic web page shown in Figure 2-6.

Deeper into Sections

As you've already learned, the <section> is the semantic element of last resort. If you have a titled block of content, and the other semantic elements aren't appropriate, then the <section> element is generally a better choice than <div>.

So what goes in a typical section? Depending on your perspective, the <section> element is either a flexible tool that fits many needs, or a loose and baggy monster with no clear identity. That's because sections play a variety of different web page roles. They can mark up any of the following:

- Small blocks of content that are displayed alongside the main page, like the "About Us" paragraph in the apocalyptic website.

- Self-contained content that can't really be described as an article, like a customer billing record or a product listing.

- Groups of content—for example, a collection of articles on a news site.

- A *portion* of a longer document. For example, in the apocalyptic article, you could mark up each separate end-of-the-world scenario as a distinct section. Sometimes you'll use sections in this way to ensure a correct outline for your document, as explained in the next section.

The last two items in the list are the most surprising. Many web developers find it's a bit of a stretch to use the same element to deal with a small fragment of an article and an entire group of articles. Some think that HTML5 should have at least two different elements to deal with these different scenarios. But the creators of HTML5 decided to keep things simple (by limiting the number of new elements) while making the new elements as flexible and practical as possible.

There's one last consideration. The `<section>` element also has an effect on a web page's outline, which is the concept you'll explore on page 65.

GEM IN THE ROUGH

Collapsible Boxes with <details> and <summary>

You've no doubt seen collapsible boxes on the Web—sections of content that you can show or hide by clicking a heading. Collapsible boxes are one of the easiest feats to pull off with basic JavaScript. You simply need to react when the heading is clicked, and then change a style setting to hide your box:

```
var box = document.
getElementById("myBox");
box.style.display = "none";
```

And then back again to make it reappear:

```
var box = document.
getElementById("myBox");
box.style.display = "block";
```

Interestingly, HTML5 adds two semantic elements that aim to make this behavior automatic. The idea is that you wrap your collapsible section in a `<details>` element and wrap the heading inside in a `<summary>` element. The final result is something like this:

```
<details>
  <summary>Section #1</summary>
```

```
  <p>If you can see this content, the
  section is expanded</p>
</details>
```

Browsers that support these elements (currently, that's just Chrome), will show just the heading, possibly with some sort of visual adornment (like a tiny triangle icon next to the heading). Then, if the user clicks the heading, the full content expands into view. Browsers that don't support the `<details>` and `<summary>` elements will show the full content right from the start, without giving the user any way to collapse it.

The `<details>` and `<summary>` elements are controversial. Many web developers feel that they aren't really semantic, because they're more about visual style than logical structure.

For now, it's best to avoid the `<details>` and `<summary>` elements because they have such poor browser support. Although you could write a workaround that uses JavaScript on browsers that don't support them, writing this workaround is more effort than just using a few lines of JavaScript to perform the collapsing on your own, on any browser.

Deeper into Footers

HTML5 and fat headers were meant for each other. Not only can you stuff in subtitles and bylines, but you can also add images, navigational sections (with the <nav> element), and virtually anything else that belongs at the top of your page.

Oddly, HTML5 isn't as accommodating when it comes to footers. The footer is supposed to be limited to a few basic details about the website's copyright, authorship, legal restrictions, and links. Footers aren't supposed to hold long lists of links, important pieces of content, or extraneous details like ads, social media buttons, and website widgets.

This raises a question: What should you do if your website design calls for a fat footer? After all, fat footers are wildly popular in website design right now (see Figure 2-9 for an example). They incorporate a number of fancy techniques, sometimes including the following:

- **Fixed positioning**, so the footer is always attached to the bottom of the browser window, no matter where the visitor scrolls (as with the example in Figure 2-9).

- **A close button**, so the visitor can close the footer and reclaim the space after reading the content (as with the example in Figure 2-9). To make this work, you use a simple piece of JavaScript that hides the element that wraps the footer (like the code shown in the box on page 60).

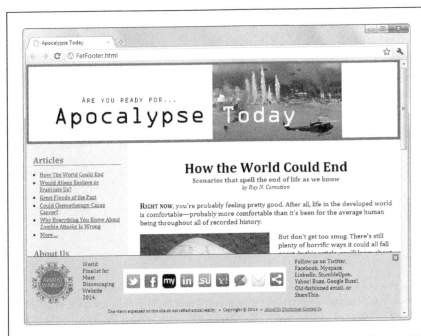

FIGURE 2-9

This absurdly fat footer is stuffed with garish extras, like an award picture and social media buttons. It uses fixed positioning to lock itself to the bottom of the browser window, like a toolbar. Fortunately, this footer has one redeeming quality: the close button in the top-right corner that lets anyone banish it from view.

- **A partially transparent background**, so you can see the page content *through* the footer. This setup works well if the footer is advertising breaking news or an important disclaimer, and it's usually used in conjunction with a close button.

- **Animation**, so the footer springs or slides into view. (For an example, see the related-article box that pops up when you reach the bottom of an article at *www.nytimes.com*.)

If your site includes this sort of footer, you have a choice. The simple approach is to disregard the rules. This approach is not as terrible as it sounds, because other website developers are sure to commit the same mistake, and over time the official rules may be loosened, allowing fancier footers. But if you want to be on the right side of the standard right now, you need to adjust your markup. Fortunately, it's not too difficult.

The trick is to split the standard footer details from the extras. In the browser, these can appear to be a single footer, but in the markup, they won't all belong to the <footer> element. For example, here's the structure of the fat footer in Figure 2-9:

```
<div id="FatFooter">
  <!-- Fat footer content goes here. -->
  <img onclick="CloseBox()" src="close_icon.png" class="CloseButton">
  ...
  <footer>
    <!-- Standard footer content goes here. -->
    <p>The views expressed on this site do not ... </p>
  </footer>
</div>
```

The outer <div> has no semantic meaning. Instead, it's a convenient package that bundles the extra "fat" content with the bare-bones footer details. It also lets you apply the style sheet formatting rule that locks the fat footer into place:

```
#FatFooter {
  position: fixed;
  bottom: 0px;
  height: 145px;
  width: 100%;
  background: #ECD672;
  border-top: thin solid black;
  font-size: small;
}
```

> **NOTE** In this example, the style sheet rule applies its formatting by ID name (using the #FatFooter selector) rather than by class name (for example, using a .FatFooter selector). That's because the fat footer already needs a unique ID, so the JavaScript code can find it and hide it when someone clicks the close button. It makes more sense to use this unique ID in the style sheet than to add a class name for the same purpose.

You could also choose to put the footer in an `<aside>` element, to clearly indicate that the footer content is a separate section, and tangentially related to the rest of the content on the page. Here's what that structure looks like:

```
<div id="FatFooter">
 <aside>
    <!-- Fat footer content goes here. -->
    <img onclick="CloseBox()" src="close_icon.png" class="CloseButton">
    ...
 </aside>

 <footer>
    <!-- Standard footer content goes here. -->
    <p>The views expressed on this site do not ... </p>
 </footer>
</div>
```

The important detail here is that the `<footer>` is not placed inside the `<aside>` element. That's because the `<footer>` doesn't apply to the `<aside>` but to the entire website. Similarly, if you have a `<footer>` that applies to some piece of content, your `<footer>` needs to be placed inside the element that wraps that content.

> **NOTE** The rules and guidelines for the proper use of HTML5's semantic elements are still evolving. Questions about the proper way to mark up large, complex sites stir ferocious debate in the HTML community. The best advice is this: If something doesn't seem true to your content, don't do it. Or you can discuss it online, where you can get feedback from dozens of super-smart HTML gurus. (One particularly good site is *http://html5doctor.com*, where you can see these ongoing debates unfolding in the comments section of most articles.)

Identifying the Main Content with <main>

HTML5 includes a sometimes-overlooked `<main>` element that identifies a web page's primary content. In the apocalypse site, for example, the main content is the entire article, not including the website header, sidebar, or footer. You should strongly consider using it on your own pages.

A properly applied `<main>` element wraps the `<article>` element precisely. Here's how it looks in the apocalypse page:

```
<!DOCTYPE html>
<html lang="en">
<head>
  ...
</head>

<body>
  <header>
     ...
  </header>
```

```
<aside>
    ...
</aside>

<main>
  <article>
    ...
  </article>
</main>
<footer>
    ...
</footer>
</body>
</html>
```

You can't put the <main> element inside the <article> element (or in any other semantic element). That's because the <main> element is meant to hold the page's full main content. It's *not* meant to indicate a portion of important content inside your document. For the same reason, unlike the other semantic elements, the <main> element can be used only *once* in a page.

At first glance, the <main> element doesn't seem terribly useful. However, it can be important for screen readers, because it lets them skip over extraneous material—like website headers, navigation menus, ads, sidebars, and so on—to get to the real content. And although the <main> element clings to the <article> element in this example, that's not necessarily the case in a more complex page. For example, if you created a page that lists multiple article summaries, each one wrapped in an <article> element, the <main> element would wrap the complete list of <article> elements, like this:

```
<main>
  <article>
    ...
  </article>

  <article>
    ...
  </article>

  <article>
    ...
  </article>

    ...
</main>
```

Here, the distinction is clear—each `<article>` represents a self-contained piece of content, but the main content of the page is the full set of articles.

It's appropriate to use the `<main>` element on any type of page, even if that page doesn't include an article. For example, if you build a game or an app, the main content is the bunch of markup that creates that game or app. You can use the `<main>` element to wrap the whole shebang, not including outside details like headers and footers.

> **NOTE** The `<main>` element is a relative newcomer. It was introduced in the slightly tweaked version of the HTML5 standard called HTML 5.1 (page xv).

The HTML5 Outlining System

HTML5 defines a set of rules that dictate how you can create a *document outline* for any web page. A web page's outline could come in handy in a lot of ways. For example, a browser could let you jump from one part of an outline to another. A design tool could let you rearrange sections by dragging and dropping them in an outline view. A search engine could use the outline to build a better page preview, and screen readers could benefit the most of all, by using outlines to guide users with vision difficulties through a deeply nested hierarchy of sections and subsections.

However, none of these scenarios is real yet, because—except for the small set of developer tools you'll consider in the next section—almost no one uses HTML5 outlines today.

> **NOTE** It's hard to get excited about a feature that doesn't affect the way the page is presented in a browser and isn't used by other tools. However, it's still a good idea to review the outline of your web pages (or at least the outline of a typical page from your website) to make sure that its structure makes sense and that you aren't breaking any HTML5 rules.

How to View an Outline

To understand outlines, you can simply take a look at the outlines your own pages produce. Right now, no browser implements the rules of HTML5 outlines (or gives you a way to peek at one). However, there are several tools that fill the gap:

- **Online HTML outliner.** Visit *http://gsnedders.html5.org/outliner* and tell the outliner which page you want to outline. As with the HTML5 validator you used in Chapter 1 (page 17), you can submit the page you want to outline in any of three ways: by uploading a file from your computer, by supplying a URL, or by pasting the markup into a text box.

- **Chrome extension.** You can use the h5o plug-in to analyze the outlines of pages when you view them in Chrome. Install it at *http://code.google.com/p/ h5o* and then surf to an HTML5 page somewhere on the Web (sadly, h5o doesn't work with files that are stored on your computer). An outline icon appears in the address bar, which reveals the structure of the page when clicked (Figure 2-10). The h5o page also provides a *bookmarklet* (a piece of JavaScript code that you can add to your web browser's bookmark list) which lets you display page outlines in Firefox and Internet Explorer, albeit with a few quirks.

- **Opera extension.** There's an Opera version of the h5o Chrome extension. Get it at *http://tinyurl.com/3k3ecdy.*

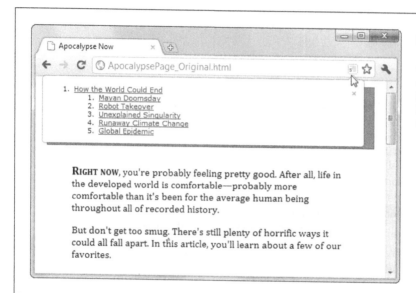

FIGURE 2-10

When you visit an HTML5 page with the Chrome h5o extension installed, an outline icon appears in the address bar. Click the icon to pop open a window with the full page outline.

Basic Outlines

To visualize the outline of your web page, imagine it stripped of all content except for the text in a numbered heading element (<h1>, <h2>, <h3>, and so on). Then, indent those headings based on their place in your markup, so more deeply nested headings are indented more in the outline.

For example, consider the apocalypse article in its initial, pre-HTML5 state:

```
<body>
  <div class="Header">
    <h1>How the World Could End</h1>
    ...
  </div>
  ...
  <h2>Mayan Doomsday</h2>
  ...
```

```
  <h2>Robot Takeover</h2>
  ...
  <h2>Unexplained Singularity</h2>
  ...
  <h2>Runaway Climate Change</h2>
  ...
  <h2>Global Epidemic</h2>
  ...
  <div class="Footer">
    ...
  </div>
</body>
```

This simple structure leads to an outline like this:

1. How the World Could End

      1. Mayan Doomsday

      2. Robot Takeover

      3. Unexplained Singularity

      4. Runaway Climate Change

      5. Global Epidemic

Two levels of headings (<h1> and <h2>) create a two-level outline. This scheme is similar to the outline features in many word processing programs—for example, you can see much the same thing in Microsoft Word's Navigation pane.

On the other hand, markup like this:

```
  <h1>Level-1 Heading</h1>
  <h2>Level-2 Heading</h2>
  <h2>Level-2 Heading</h2>
  <h3>Level-3 Heading</h3>
  <h2>Level-2 Heading</h2>
```

Gets an outline like this:

1. Level-1 Heading

      1. Level-2 Heading

      2. Level-2 Heading

            1. Level-3 Heading

      3. Level-2 Heading

Again, there are no surprises.

Finally, the outline algorithm is smart enough to ignore skipped levels. For example, if you write this slightly wobbly markup, which skips from <h1> directly to <h3>:

```
<h1>Level-1 Heading</h1>
<h2>Level-2 Heading</h2>
<h1>Level-1 Heading</h1>
<h3>Level-3 Heading</h3>
<h2>Level-2 Heading</h2>
```

You get this outline:

1. Level-1 Heading

    1. Level-2 Heading

2. Level-1 Heading

    1. Level-3 Heading

    2. Level-2 Heading

Now the level-3 heading has level-2 status in the outline, based on its position in the document. This might seem like one of those automatic error corrections browsers love to make, but it actually serves a practical purpose. In some situations, a web page may be assembled out of separate pieces—for example, it might contain a copy of an article that's published elsewhere. In this case, the heading levels of the embedded content might not line up perfectly with the rest of the web page. But because the outlining algorithm smooths these differences out, it's unlikely to be a problem.

Sectioning Elements

Sectioning elements are the ones that create a new, nested outline inside your page: <article>, <aside>, <nav>, and <section>. To understand how sectioning elements work, imagine a page that contains two <article> elements. Because <article> is a sectioning element, this page has (at least) three outlines—the outline of the overall page and one nested outline for each article.

To get a better grasp of this situation, consider the structure of the apocalypse article, after it's been revised with HTML5:

```
<body>
  <article>
    <header>
      <h1>How the World Could End</h1>
      ...
    </header>

    <div class="Content">
      ...
      <h2>Mayan Doomsday</h2>
      ...
```

```
    <h2>Robot Takeover</h2>
    ...
    <h2>Unexplained Singularity</h2>
    ...
    <h2>Runaway Climate Change</h2>
    ...
    <h2>Global Epidemic</h2>
      ...
    </div>
  </article>

  <footer>
    ...
  </footer>
</body>
```

Plug this into an outline viewer like *http://gsnedders.html5.org/outliner*, and you'll
see this:

1. *Untitled Section*

    1. How the World Could End

        1. Mayan Doomsday

        2. Robot Takeover

        3. Unexplained Singularity

        4. Runaway Climate Change

        5. Global Epidemic

Here, the outline starts with an untitled section, which is the root <body> element.
The <article> element starts a new, nested outline, which contains a single <h1>
and several <h2> elements.

Sometimes, the "Untitled Section" note indicates a mistake. Although it's considered
acceptable for <aside> and <nav> elements to exist without titles, the same leniency
isn't usually given to <article> or <section> elements. In the previous example,
the untitled section is the main section for the page, which belongs to the <body>
element. Because the page contains a single article, there's no reason for the page
to have a separate heading, and you can ignore this quirk.

Now consider what happens with a more complex example, like the apocalypse
site with the navigation sidebar (page 54). Put that through an outliner, and you'll
get this outline:

1. *Apocalypse Today*

    1. *Untitled Section*

        1. Articles

        2. About Us

    2. How the World Could End

        1. Mayan Doomsday

        2. Robot Takeover

        3. *Untitled Section*

        4. Unexplained Singularity

        5. Runaway Climate Change

        6. Global Epidemic

Here, there are two sectioning elements, and two nested outlines: one for the sidebar and one for the article. There are also two untitled sections, both of which are legitimate. The first is the `<aside>` element for the sidebar, and the second is the `<aside>` element that represents the pull-quote in the article.

> **NOTE** In addition to sectioning elements, some elements are called *section roots*. These elements aren't just branches of an existing outline; they start a new outline of their own that doesn't appear in the main outline of the containing page. The `<body>` element that contains your web page content is a sectioning root, which makes sense. But HTML5 also considers the following elements to be sectioning roots: `<blockquote>`, `<td>`, `<fieldset>`, `<figure>`, and `<details>`.

Solving an Outline Problem

So far, you've looked at the examples in this chapter and seen the outlines they generated. And so far, the outlines have made perfect sense. But sometimes, a problem can occur. For example, imagine you create a document with this structure:

```
<body>
  <article>
    <h1>Natural Wonders to Visit Before You Die</h1>
    ...
    <h2>In North America</h2>
    ...
    <h3>The Grand Canyon</h3>
    ...
    <h3>Yellowstone National Park</h3>
    ...
    <h2>In the Rest of the World</h2>
    ...
    <aside>...</aside>
```

```
...
    <h3>Galapagos Islands</h3>
    ...
    <h3>The Swiss Alps</h3>
    ...
    </article>
</body>
```

How Sectioning Elements Help Complex Pages

Sectioning is a great help with *syndication* and *aggregation*—two examples of the fine art of taking content from one web page and injecting it into another.

For example, imagine you have a web page that includes excerpts from several articles, all of which are drawn from other sites. Now imagine that this page has a deeply nested structure of headings, and somewhere inside—let's say under an <h4> heading—there's an article with content pulled from another web page.

In traditional HTML, you'd like the first heading in this content to use the <h5> element, because it's nested under an <h4>. But this article was originally developed to be placed somewhere else, on a different page, with less nesting, so it probably starts with an <h2> or an <h1>. The page would still work, but its hierarchy would be scrambled, and the page could be more difficult for screen readers, search engines, and other software to process.

In HTML5, this page isn't a problem. As long as you wrap the nested article in an <article> element, the extracted content becomes part of its own nested outline. That outline can start with any heading—it doesn't matter. What matters is its position in the containing document. So if the <article> element falls after an <h4>, then the first level of heading in that article behaves like a logical <h5>, the second level acts like a logical <h6>, and so on.

The conclusion is this: HTML5 has a logical outline system that makes it easier to combine documents. In this outline system, the position of your headings becomes more important, and the exact level of each heading becomes less significant—making it harder to shoot yourself in the foot.

You probably expect an outline like this:

1. *Untitled Section for the <body>*

    1. Natural Wonders to Visit Before You Die

        1. In North America

            1. The Grand Canyon

            2. Yellowstone National Park

        2. In the Rest of the World

        3. *Untitled Section for the <aside>*

            1. Galapagos Islands

            2. The Swiss Alps

But the outline you actually get is this:

1. *Untitled Section for the <body>*

   1. Natural Wonders to Visit Before You Die

      1. In North America

         1. The Grand Canyon

         2. Yellowstone National Park

      2. In the Rest of the World

      3. *Untitled Section for the <aside>*

      4. Galapagos Islands

      5. The Swiss Alps

Somehow, the addition of the <aside> after the <h2> throws off the following <h3> elements, making them have the same logical level as the <h2>. This clearly isn't what you want.

To solve this problem, you first need to understand that the HTML5 outline system automatically creates a new section every time it finds a numbered heading element (like <h1>, <h2>, <h3>, and so on), *unless* that element is already at the top of a section.

In this example, the outline system doesn't do anything to the initial <h1> element, because it's at the top of the <article> section. But the outline algorithm does create new sections for the <h2> and <h3> elements that follow. It's as though you wrote this markup:

```
<body>
  <article>
    <h1>Natural Wonders to Visit Before You Die</h1>
    ...
    <section>
      <h2>In North America</h2>
      ...
      <section>
        <h3>The Grand Canyon</h3>
        ...
      </section>
      <section>
        <h3>Yellowstone National Park</h3>
        ...
      </section>
    </section>
```

```
  <section>
    <h2>In the Rest of the World</h2>

    ...
  </section>
  <aside>...</aside>

  ...
  <section>
  <h3>Galapagos Islands</h3>

    ...
  </section>
  <section>
    <h3>The Swiss Alps</h3>

    ...
  </section>
</article>
</body>
```

Most of the time, these automatically created sections aren't a problem. In fact, they're usually an asset, because they make sure incorrectly numbered headings are still placed in the right outline level. The cost for this convenience is an occasional glitch, like the one shown here.

As you can see in this listing, everything goes right at first. The top <h1> is left alone (because it's in an <article> already), there's a subsection created for the first <h2>, then a subsection for each <h3> inside, and so on. The problem starts when the outline algorithm runs into the <aside> element. It sees this as a cue to close the current section, which means that when the sections are created for the following <h3> elements, they're at the same logical level as the <h2> elements before.

To correct this problem, you need to take control of the sections and subsections by defining some yourself. In this example, the goal is to prevent the second <h2> section from being closed too early, which you can do by defining it explicitly in the markup:

```
<body>
  <article>
    <h1>Natural Wonders to Visit Before You Die</h1>

    ...
    <h2>In North America</h2>

    ...
    <h3>The Grand Canyon</h3>

    ...
    <h3>Yellowstone National Park</h3>

    ...
    <section>
      <h2>In the Rest of the World</h2>

      ...
      <aside>...</aside>

      ...
```

```
      <h3>Galapagos Islands</h3>
      ...
      <h3>The Swiss Alps</h3>
      ...
    </section>
  </article>
</body>
```

Now, the outline algorithm doesn't need to create an automatic section for the second `<h2>`, and so there's no risk of it closing the section when it stumbles across the `<aside>`. Although you could define the section for every heading in this document, there's no need to clutter your markup, as this single change fixes the problem.

> **NOTE** Another solution is to replace the `<aside>` with a `<div>`. The `<div>` is not a sectioning element, so it won't cause a section to close unexpectedly.

Using the `<aside>` element doesn't always cause this problem. The earlier article examples used the `<aside>` element for a pull-quote but worked fine, because the `<aside>` fell between two `<h2>` elements. But if you carelessly plunk a sectioning element between two different heading levels, you should check your outline to make sure it still makes sense.

> **TIP** If the whole outline concept seems overwhelmingly theoretical, don't worry. Truthfully, it's a subtle concept that many web developers will ignore (at least for now). The best approach is to think of the HTML5 outlining system as a quality assurance tool that can help you out. If you review your pages in an outline generator (like one of the tools listed on page 65), you can catch mistakes that may indicate other problems and make sure that you're using the semantic elements correctly.

Writing More Meaningful Markup

I n the previous chapter, you met HTML5's semantic elements. With their help, you can give your pages a clean, logical structure and prepare for a future of super-smart browsers, search engines, and assistive devices.

But you haven't reached the end of the semantic story yet. Semantics are all about adding *meaning* to your markup, and there are several types of information you can inject. In Chapter 2, semantics were all about *page structure*—you used them to explain the purpose of large blocks of content and entire sections of your layout. But semantics can also include *text-level information*, which you add to explain much smaller pieces of content. You can use text-level semantics to point out important types of information that would otherwise be lost in a sea of web page content, like names, addresses, event listings, products, recipes, restaurant reviews, and so on. Then this content can be extracted and used by a host of different services—everything from nifty browser plug-ins to specialized search engines.

In this chapter, you'll start by returning to the small set of semantic elements that are built into the HTML5 language. You'll learn about a few text-level semantic elements that you can use today, effortlessly. Next, you'll look at the companion standards that tackle text-level semantics head-on. That means digging into *microdata*, which began its life as part of the original HTML5 specification but now lives on as a separate, still-evolving standard managed by the W3C. Using microdata, you'll learn how to enrich your pages and juice up your web search listings.

▇ The Semantic Elements Revisited

There's a reason you began your exploration into semantics with the page structure elements (see Table 3-1 for a recap). Quite simply, page structure is an easy challenge. That's because the vast majority of websites use a small set of common design elements (headers, footers, sidebars, and menus) to create layouts that are—for all their cosmetic differences—very similar.

TABLE 3-1 *Semantic elements for page structure*

ELEMENT	DESCRIPTION
`<article>`	Represents whatever you think of as an article—a section of self-contained content like a newspaper article, a forum post, or a blog entry (not including frills like comments or the author bio).
`<aside>`	Represents a complete chunk of content that's separate from the main page content. For example, it makes sense to use `<aside>` to create a sidebar with related content or links next to a main article.
`<figure>` and `<figcaption>`	Represents a figure. The `<figcaption>` element wraps the caption text, and the `<figure>` element wraps the `<figcaption>` and the `<img>` element for the picture itself. The goal is to indicate the association between an image and its caption.
`<footer>`	Represents the footer at the bottom of the page. This is a tiny chunk of content that may include small print, a copyright notice, and a brief set of links (for example, "About Us" or "Get Support").
`<header>`	Represents an enhanced heading that includes a standard HTML heading and extra content. The extra content might include a logo, a byline, or a set of navigation links for the content that follows.
`<nav>`	Represents a significant collection of links on a page. These links may point to topics on the current page or to other pages on the website. In fact, it's not unusual to have a page with multiple `<nav>` sections.
`<section>`	Represents a section of a document or a group of documents. The `<section>` is an all-purpose container with a single rule: The content it holds should begin with a heading. Use `<section>` only if the other semantic elements (for example, `<article>` and `<aside>`) don't apply.
`<main>`	Represents the main content of the page—all of it. For example, `<main>` might wrap an `<article>` element but leave out site-wide headers, footers, and sidebars. The `<main>` element is a new addition to the HTML 5.1 revision of HTML5 (page xv).

Text-level semantics are a tougher nut to crack. That's because people use a huge number of different types of content. If HTML5 set out to create an element for every sort of information you might add to a page, the language would be swimming in a mess of elements. Complicating the problem is the fact that structured information is also made of smaller pieces that can be assembled in different ways. For example, even an ordinary postal address would require a handful of elements (like <address>, <name>, <street>, <postalcode>, <country>, and so on) before anyone could use it in a page.

HTML5 takes a two-pronged approach. First, it adds a very small number of text-level semantic elements. But second, and more importantly, HTML5 supports a separate microdata standard, which gives people an extensible way to define any sort of information they want and then flag it in their pages. You'll cover both of these topics in this chapter. First up are three new text-level semantic elements: <time>, <output>, and <mark>.

Dates and Times with <time>

Date and time information appears frequently in web pages. For example, it turns up at the end of most blog postings. Unfortunately, there's no standardized way to tag dates, so there's no easy way for other programs (like search engines) to extract them without guessing. The <time> element solves this problem. It allows you to mark up a date, time, or combined date and time. Here's an example:

```
The party starts <time>2014-03-21</time>.
```

NOTE It may seem a little counterintuitive to have a <time> element wrapping a date (with no time), but that's just one of the quirks of HTML5. A more sensible element name would be <datetime>, but that isn't what they chose.

The <time> element performs two roles. First, it indicates where a date or time value is in your markup. Second, it provides that date or time value in a form that any software program can understand. The previous example meets the second requirement using the universal date format, which includes a four-digit year, a two-digit month, and a two-digit day, in that order, with each piece separated by a dash. In other words, the format follows this pattern:

```
YYYY-MM-DD
```

However, it's perfectly acceptable to present the date in a different way to the person reading your web page. In fact, you can use whatever text you want, as long as you supply the computer-readable universal date with the datetime attribute, like this:

```
The party starts <time datetime="2014-03-21">March 21<sup>st</sup></time>.
```

Which looks like this in the browser:

The party starts March 21st.

The `<time>` element has similar rules about times, which you supply in this format:

```
HH:MM
```

That's a two-digit hour (using a 24-hour clock), followed by a two-digit number of minutes, like this:

```
Parties start every night at <time datetime="16:30">4:30 p.m.</time>.
```

Finally, you can specify a time on a specific date by combining these two standards. Just put the date first, followed by a space, and then the time information.

```
The party starts <time datetime="2014-03-21 16:30">March 21<sup>st</sup>
at 4:30 p.m.</time>.
```

> **NOTE** Originally, the `<time>` element required a slightly different format to combine date and time information. Instead of separating the two components with a space, you had to separate them with an uppercase *T* (for *time*), as in 2014-03-21T16:30. This format is still acceptable, so you may encounter it while perusing other people's web pages.

When combining dates and times, you may choose to tack a time zone offset on the end. For example, New York is in the Eastern time zone, which is known as UTC-5:00. (You can figure out your time zone at *http://en.wikipedia.org/wiki/Time_zone*.) To indicate 4:30 p.m. in New York, you'd use this markup:

```
The party starts <time datetime="2014-03-21 16:30-05:00">March 21<sup>st</sup>
at 4:30 p.m.</time>.
```

This way, the people reading your page get the time in the format they expect, while search bots and other bits of software get an unambiguous datetime value that they can process.

The `<time>` element also supports a pubdate attribute. You should use this if your date corresponds to the publication date of the current content (for example, the `<article>` in which the `<time>` is placed). Here's an example:

```
Published on <time datetime="2014-03-21" pubdate>March 31, 2014</time>.
```

> **NOTE** Because the `<time>` element is purely informational and doesn't have any associated formatting, you can use it with any browser. There are no compatibility issues to worry about. But if you want to style the `<time>` element, you need the Internet Explorer workaround described on page 51.

JavaScript Calculations with `<output>`

HTML5 includes one semantic element that's designed to make certain types of JavaScript-powered pages a bit clearer—the `<output>` element. It's nothing more than a placeholder that your code can use to show a piece of calculated information.

For example, imagine you create a page like the one shown in Figure 3-1. This figure lets the user enter some information. A script then takes this information, performs a calculation, and displays the result just underneath.

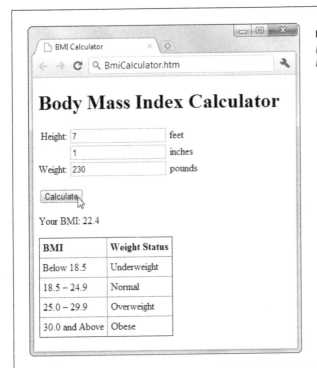

FIGURE 3-1

It's a time-honored web design pattern. Type some numbers, click a button, and let the page give you the answer.

The usual way of dealing with this is to assign a unique ID to the placeholder, so the JavaScript code can find it when it performs the calculation. Typically, web developers use the <span> element, which works perfectly but doesn't provide any specific meaning:

```
<p>Your BMI: <span id="result"></span></p>
```

Here's the more meaningful version you'd use in HTML5:

```
<p>Your BMI: <output id="result"></output></p>
```

The actual JavaScript code doesn't need any changes, because it looks up the element by name and doesn't care about the element type:

```
var resultElement = document.getElementById("result");
```

NOTE Before you use <output>, make sure you've included the Internet Explorer workaround described on page 51. Otherwise, the element won't be accessible in JavaScript on old versions of Internet Explorer (IE 8 and earlier).

Often, this sort of page has its controls inside a `<form>` element. In this example, that's the three text boxes where people can type in information:

```
<form action="#" id="bmiCalculator">
  <label for="feet inches">Height:</label>
  <input name="feet"> feet<br>
  <input name="inches"> inches<br>

  <label for="pounds">Weight:</label>
  <input name="pounds"> pounds<br><br>
  ...
</form>
```

If you want to make your `<output>` element look even smarter, you can add the `form` attribute (which indicates the ID of the form that has the related controls) and the `for` attribute (which lists the IDs of the related controls, separated by spaces). Here's an example:

```
<p>Your BMI: <output id="result" form="bmiCalculator" for="feet inches pounds">
</output></p>
```

These attributes don't actually do anything, other than convey information about where your `<output>` element gets its goods. But they will earn you some serious semantic brownie points. And if other people need to edit your page, these attributes could help them sort out how it works.

> **TIP** If you're a bit hazy about forms, you'll learn more in Chapter 4. If you know more about Esperanto than JavaScript, you can brush up on the programming language in Appendix B, "JavaScript: The Brains of Your Page." And if you want to try this page out for yourself, you can find the complete example at *http://prosetech.com/html5*.

Highlighted Text with <mark>

The `<mark>` element represents a section of text that's highlighted for reference. It's particularly appropriate when you're quoting someone else's text and you want to bring attention to something:

```
<p>In 2009, Facebook made a bold grab to own everyone's content,
<em>forever</em>. This is the text they put in their terms of service:</p>
<blockquote>You hereby grant Facebook an <mark>irrevocable, perpetual,
non-exclusive, transferable, fully paid, worldwide license</mark> (with the
right to sublicense) to <mark>use, copy, publish</mark>, stream, store,
retain, publicly perform or display, transmit, scan, reformat, modify, edit,
frame, translate, excerpt, adapt, create derivative works and distribute
(through multiple tiers), <mark>any user content you post</mark>
...
</blockquote>
```

The text in a <mark> element gets the yellow background shown in Figure 3-2.

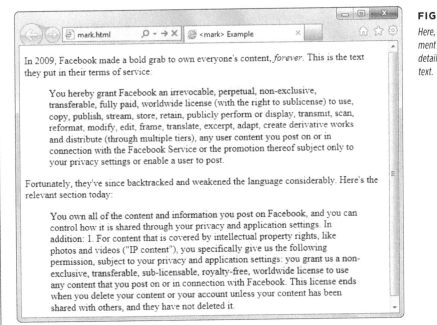

FIGURE 3-2

Here, the <mark> element highlights important details in a block of quoted text.

You can also use <mark> to flag important content or keywords, as search engines do when showing matching text in your search results, or to mark up document changes, in combination with <del> (for deleted text) and <ins> (for inserted text).

Truthfully, the <mark> element is a bit of a misfit. The HTML5 specification considers it to be a semantic element, but it plays a presentational role that's arguably more important. By default, marked-up text is highlighted with a bright yellow background (Figure 3-2), although you can apply your own style sheet rules to use a different formatting effect.

TIP The <mark> element isn't really about formatting. After all, there are lots of ways to make text stand out in a web page. Instead, you should use <mark> (coupled with any CSS formatting you like) when it's semantically appropriate. A good rule of thumb is to use <mark> to draw attention to ordinary text that has *become* important, either because of the discussion that frames it, or because of the task the user is performing.

Even if you stick with the default yellow-background formatting, you should add a style sheet fallback for browsers that don't support HTML5. Here's the sort of style rule you need:

```
mark {
  background-color: yellow;
  color: black;
}
```

You'll also need the Internet Explorer workaround described on page 51 to make the <mark> element style-able in old versions of IE.

Other Standards That Boost Semantics

At this point, it's probably occurring to you that there are a lot of potential semantic elements that HTML *doesn't* have. Sure, you can flag dates and highlighted text, but what about other common bits of information, like names, addresses, business listings, product descriptions, personal profiles, and so on? HTML5 deliberately doesn't wade into this arena, because its creators didn't want to bog the language down with dozens of specialized elements that would suit some people but leave others bored and unimpressed. To really get to the next level with semantics, you need to broaden your search beyond the core HTML5 language, and consider a few standards that can work with your web pages.

Semantically smart markup isn't a new idea. In fact, way back when HTML5 was still just a fantasy in WHATWG editor Ian Hickson's head, there were plenty of web developers clamoring for ways to make their markup more meaningful. Their goals weren't always the same—some wanted to boost accessibility, some were planning to do data mining, and others just wanted to dial up the cool factor on their resumés. But none of them could find what they wanted in the standard HTML language which is why several new specifications sprung up to fill the gap.

In the following sections, you'll learn about no fewer than *four* of these standards. First, you'll get the scoop on ARIA, a standard that's all about improving accessibility for screen readers. Then, you'll take a peek at three competing approaches for describing different types of content, whether it's contact details, addresses, business listings, or just about anything else you can fit between the tags of an HTML page.

ARIA (Accessible Rich Internet Applications)

ARIA is a developing standard that lets you supply extra information for screen readers through attributes on any HTML element. For example, ARIA introduces the role attribute, which indicates the purpose of a given element. For example, if you have a <div> that represents a header:

```
<div class="header">
```

You can announce that fact to screen readers by setting the ARIA role attribute to banner:

```
<div class="header" role="banner">
```

Of course, you learned last chapter that HTML5 also gives you a more meaningful way to mark up headers. So what you really should use is something like this:

```
<header role="banner">
```

This example demonstrates two important facts. First, ARIA requires you to use one of a short list of recommended role names. (For the full list, refer to the appropriate section of the specification at *http://tinyurl.com/roles-aria*.) Second, parts of ARIA overlap the new HTML5 semantic elements—which makes sense, because ARIA pre-dates HTML5. But the overlap isn't complete. For example, some role names duplicate HTML5 (like banner and article), while others go further (like toolbar and search).

ARIA also adds two attributes that work with HTML forms. The aria-required attribute in a text box indicates that the user needs to enter a value. The aria-invalid attribute in a text box indicates that the current value isn't right. These attributes are helpful, because screen readers are likely to miss the visual cues that sighted users rely on, like an asterisk next to a missing field, or a flashing red error icon.

In order to apply ARIA properly, you need to learn the standard and spend some time reviewing your markup. Web developers are divided over whether it's a worthwhile investment, given that the standard is still developing and that HTML5 provides some of the same benefits with less trouble. However, if you want to create a truly accessible website today, you need to use both, because newer screen readers support ARIA but not yet HTML5.

NOTE For more information about ARIA (fully known as WAI-ARIA, because it was developed by the Web Accessibility Initiative group), you can read the specification at *www.w3.org/TR/wai-aria*.

RDFa (Resource Description Framework)

RDFa is a standard for embedding detailed metadata into your web documents using attributes. RDFa has a significant advantage: Unlike the other approaches discussed in this chapter, it's a stable, settled standard. RDFa also has two significant drawbacks. First, RDFa was originally designed for XHTML, not HTML5. It's a matter of debate how well the stricter, more elaborate RDFa syntax meshes with the more freewheeling philosophy of HTML5. Second, RDFa is complicated. Markup that's augmented with RDFa metadata is significantly longer and more cumbersome than ordinary HTML. And because of its complexity, RDFa is also more likely to contain errors—three times more likely, according to a recent Google web page survey.

RDFa isn't discussed in this chapter, although you will dig into its close HTML5 relative, microdata, on page 85. But if you prefer to learn more about RDFa, you can get a solid introduction on Wikipedia at *http://en.wikipedia.org/wiki/RDFa*, or you can visit the Google Rich Snippets page described later (page 94), which has RDFa versions of all its examples.

Microformats

Microformats are a simple, streamlined approach to putting metadata in your pages. Microformats don't attempt to be any sort of official standard. Instead, they're a loose collection of agreed-upon conventions that let pages share structured information without requiring the complexities of something like RDFa. This approach has given microformats tremendous success, and a recent web survey found that when a page has some sort of rich metadata, it's microformats 70 percent of the time.

Microformats work in an interesting way—they piggyback on the class attribute that's usually used for styling. You mark up your data using certain standardized style names, depending on the type of data. Then, another program can read your markup, extract the data, and check the attributes to figure out what everything means.

For example, you can use the hCard microformat to represent the contact details for a person, company, organization, or place. The first step is to add a root element that has the right class name. For hCard, the class name is vcard. (Usually, the class name matches the name of the microformat. The name vcard was chosen for historical reasons, because hCards are based on a much older format called Versitcard.)

Here's an example of a <div> that's ready to hold contact details using the hCard microformat:

```
<div class="vcard">
</div>
```

Inside this root element, you supply the contact information. Each detail must be wrapped in a separate element and marked up with the correct class name, as defined by the microformat you're using. For example, in an hCard you can use the fn class to flag a person's full name and the url class for that person's home page:

```
<div class="vcard">
  <h3 class="fn">Mike Rowe</h3>
  You can see Mike Rowe's website at
  <a class="url" href="http://www.magicsemantics.com">www.magicsemantics.com
  </a>
</div>
```

When you use class names for a microformat, you don't need to create matching styles in your style sheet. In the example above, that means that you don't need to write style rules for the vcard, fn, or url classes. Instead, the class names are put to a different use—advertising your data as a nicely structured, meaningful chunk of content.

> **NOTE** Before you can mark up any data, you need to choose the microformat you want to use. There are only a few dozen microformats in widespread use, and most are still being tweaked and revised. You can see what's available and read detailed usage information about each microformat at *http://microformats.org/wiki*. To learn more about hCard, surf straight to *http://microformats.org/wiki/hCard*.

Once you've worked your way around hCard, you'll have no trouble understanding hCalendar, the world's second-most-popular microformat. Using hCalendar, you can mark up appointments, meetings, holidays, product releases, store openings, and so on. Just wrap the event listing in an element with the class name vevent. Inside, you need at least two pieces of information: the start date (marked up with the dt-start class) and a description (marked up with the summary class). You can also choose from a variety of optional attributes described at *http://microformats.org/wiki/hCalendar*, including an ending date or duration, a location, and a URL with more details. Here's an example:

```
<div class="vevent">
  <h2 class="summary">Web Developer Clam Bake</h2>
  <p>I'm hosting a party!</p>
  <p>It's
  <span class="dtstart" title="2014-10-25 13:30">Tuesday, October 25,
  1:30PM</span>
  at the <span class="location">Deep Sea Hotel, San Francisco, CA</span></p>
</div>
```

Based on the popularity of microformats, you might assume that the battle for the Semantic Web is settled. But not so fast—there are several caveats. First, the vast majority of pages have no rich semantic data at all. Second, most of the pages that have adopted microformats use them for just two purposes: contact information and event listings. So although microformats aren't going anywhere soon, there's still plenty of space for the competition. Third, the climate is beginning to shift to the more flexible but still lesser-known *microdata* specification. It seems increasingly likely that microformats were an interim stopping point on the way to the more sophisticated microdata standard, which is described in the next section.

Microdata

Microdata is a third take at solving the challenge of semantic markup. It began life as part of the HTML5 specification and later split into its own developing standard at *http://dev.w3.org/html5/md*. Microdata uses an approach that's similar to RDFa's, but simpler. Unlike microformats, microdata uses its own attributes and doesn't risk colliding with style sheet rules (or confusing the heck out of other web developers). This design means microdata is more logical, as well as easier to adapt for your own custom languages. But it also comes at the cost of brevity—microdata-enriched markup can bloat up a bit more than microformat-enriched markup.

Recently, microdata received a big boost when Microsoft, Google, Yahoo, and Yandex (Russia's largest search engine) teamed up to create a microdata-cataloguing site called *http://schema.org*. Here you'll find examples of all sorts of different microdata formats, including Person and Event (which echo the popular hCard and hEvent microformats) and more specialized types for marking up businesses, restaurants, reviews, products, books, movies, recipes, TV shows, bus stops, tourist attractions, medical conditions, medications, and more. Right now, only search engines pay any attention to this information, but their traffic-driving, web-shaping clout is undeniable. (You'll see how search engines use this sort of information starting on page 94.)

> **NOTE** It now seems possible that microdata just might catch on as the Goldilocks standard for metadata—a specification that's more flexible than microformats but not quite as complex as RDFa.

To begin a microdata section, you add the `itemscope` and `itemtype` attributes to any element (although a `<div>` makes a logical container, if you don't have one already). The `itemscope` attribute indicates that you're starting a new chunk of semantic content. The `itemtype` attribute indicates the specific type of data you're encoding:

```
<div itemscope itemtype="http://schema.org/Person">
</div>
```

To identify the data type, you use a predetermined, unique piece of text called an *XML namespace*. In this example, the XML namespace is *http://schema.org/Person*, which is a standardized microdata format for encoding contact details, as discussed in the box below.

UP TO SPEED

Understanding Microdata Namespaces

Every microdata format needs a namespace. Technically, the namespace identifies the *vocabulary* your microdata uses. For example, the namespace *http://schema.org/Person* indicates that this section of markup uses the Person vocabulary. You can go cross-eyed exploring dozens of microdata vocabularies at *http://schema.org* (see Figure 3-3).

XML namespaces are often URLs. Sometimes, you can even find a description of the corresponding data type by typing the URL into your web browser (as you can with the *http://schema.org/Person* data format). However, XML namespaces don't *need* to correlate to real web locations, and they don't need to be URLs at all. It just depends on what the developer chose when creating the format. The advantage of a URL is

that it can incorporate a domain name belonging to a person or organization. This way, the namespace is more likely to be unique—no one else will create a different data format that shares the same namespace name and confuses everyone.

If a namespace begins with *http://schema.org*, it's an official vocabulary endorsed by the search engine dream team of Microsoft, Google, Yahoo, and Yandex. So if you use that vocabulary, you can be confident that the search engines of the world will understand what you're doing. If a namespace begins with *http://data-vocabulary.org*, it's using a slightly older set of microdata vocabularies. Most search engines will still understand your markup, but it's better to stick with the times and find an equivalent vocabulary at *http://schema.org*.

Once you have the container element, you're ready to move on to the next step. Inside your container element, you use the `itemprop` attribute to capture the important bits of information. The basic approach is the same as it was for microformats—you use a recognized `itemprop` name, and other pieces of software can grab the information from the associated elements.

Here's a microdata-fied version of the hCard microformat you saw earlier:

```
<div itemscope itemtype="http://schema.org/Person">
  <h3 itemprop="name">Mike Rowe</h3>
  You can see Mike Rowe's website at
  <a itemprop="url" href="http://www.magicsemantics.com">www.magicsemantics.
  com</a>
</div>
```

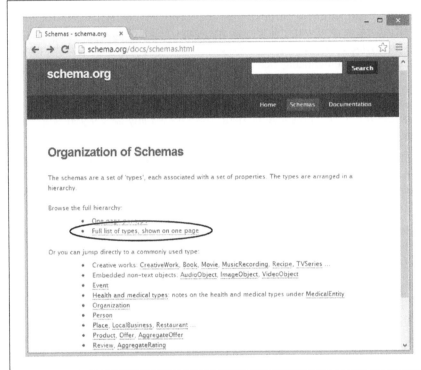

FIGURE 3-3

To find a microdata vocabulary that suits your information, there are few better starting points than the http://schema.org/docs/schemas.html page. Click a link to jump straight to the definition of a common vocabulary, like Person, Organization, or Event. Or, browse through the sprawling catalog by clicking the "Full list of types" link.

The most significant difference between microdata and microformats is that microdata uses the `itemprop` attribute to mark up elements instead of the `class` attribute.

NOTE Since microdata uses its own `itemscope`, `itemtype`, and `itemprop` attributes, rather than the `class` attribute, there's no chance you'll confuse your semantic markup with your style sheet formatting.

There are plenty of additional details you can mark up using the Person vocabulary. Common choices include postal and email address, telephone number, birth date, photo, job title, organization name, gender, nationality, and so on. For the full list of possible properties, refer to *http://schema.org/Person*.

> **NOTE** The three standards for rich semantic data—RDFa, microdata, and microformats—all share broad similarities. They aren't quite compatible, but the markup is similar enough that the skills you pick up learning one system are mostly applicable to the others.

◼ A Practical Example: Retrofitting an "About Me" Page

So far, you've learned about the basic structure of two semantic staples: microformats and microdata. Armed with this knowledge, you could look up a new microformat (from *http://microformats.org*) or microdata vocabulary (from *http://schema.org*) and start writing semantically rich markup.

However, life doesn't usually unfold this way—at least not for most web developers. Instead, you'll often need to take a web page that already has all the data it needs and retrofit the page with semantic data. This task is fairly easy if you keep a few points in mind:

- Often, you'll have important data mixed in with content that you want to ignore. In this case, you can add new elements around each piece of information you want to capture. Use a <div> if you want a block-level element or a <span> if you want to get a piece of inline content.

- Don't worry about the order of your information. As long as you use the right class names (for a microformat) or property names (for microdata), you can arrange your markup however you wish.

- If you're supplying a picture, you can use the <img> element. If you're supplying a link, you can use the <a> element. The rest of the time, you'll usually be marking up ordinary text.

Here's a typical example. Imagine you start with an "About Me" page (Figure 3-4) that has content like this:

```
<h1>About Me</h1>

<img src="face.jpg" alt="Mike's Face">
<p>This website is the work of <b>Mike Rowe Formatte</b>.
His friends know him as <b>The Big M</b>.</p>

<p>You can contact him where he works, at
The Magic Semantic Company (phone
641-545-0234 and ask for Mike) or email mike-f@magicsemantics.com.</p>

<p>Or, visit Mike on the job at:<br>
42 Jordan Gordon Street, 6th Floor<br>
San Francisco, CA 94105<br>
USA<br>
```

```
<a href="http://www.magicsemantics.com">www.magicsemantics.com</a>
</p>
```

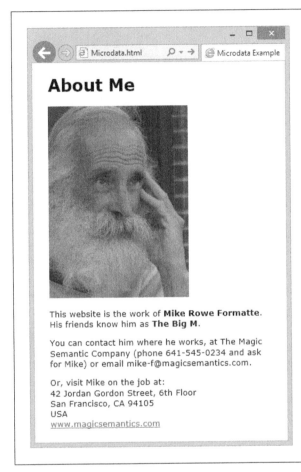

FIGURE 3-4

This "About Me" page includes the website author's contact details, before adding any microdata.

Clearly, this is a good fit for the familiar Person vocabulary (detailed at *http://schema.org/Person*). Here's a first attempt at weaving microdata around the key details in the "About Me" page. The newly inserted bits of microdata are emphasized with bold lettering:

```
<h1>About Me</h1>

<div itemscope itemtype="http://schema.org/Person">
  <img itemprop="image" src="face.jpg" alt="Mike's Face">
  <p>This website is the work of
  <span itemprop="jobTitle" style="display:none">Web Developer</span>
  <b itemprop="name">Mike Rowe Formatte</b>.
  His friends know him as <b itemprop="additionalname">The Big M</b>.</p>
```

```
<p>You can contact him where he works, at
The Magic Semantic Company</span> (phone
<span itemprop="telephone">641-545-0234</span> and ask for Mike)
 or email <span itemprop="email">mike-f@magicsemantics.com</span>.</p>

<p>Or, visit Mike on the job at:<br>
42 Jordan Gordon Street, 6th Floor<br>
San Francisco, CA 94105<br>
USA<br>
<a itemprop="url" href="http://www.magicsemantics.com">www.magicsemantics.
com</a>
 </p>
</div>
```

This example uses a few handy techniques:

- It adds new <span> elements to wrap the bits of content you need for the microdata.

- It adds the itemprop attribute to existing elements, where doing so makes sense. For example, the <b> element wraps the name information, so there's no need to add an additional <span>. (Of course, you *could* do so. For example, you might prefer to write something like <b><span itemprop="name">Mike Rowe Formatte</span></b>.

- It uses a hidden <span> to indicate the person's job title. (The text is hidden with an inline style rule that sets the display property to none, as you can see in the markup above.) This technique lets you hide redundant information, while still preserving it for search engines and other tools. That said, the content-hiding technique is a bit controversial, because some tools (like Google) ignore information that isn't made visible to the web page viewer.

It's common for microdata to have a *nested* structure that puts one microdata vocabulary inside another. For example, in the Person vocabulary you might have a set of address information nestled inside the personal details. Technically, the address information all belongs to a separate vocabulary, called PostalAddress.

To mark up the address information, you need to add a new <div> or <span> element that uses an itemprop, itemscope, or itemtype attribute. The itemprop attribute has the property name, the itemscope attribute indicates that you're starting a new vocabulary to supply the property data, and the itemtype property identifies the vocabulary by its XML namespace (in this case that's *http://schema.org/PostalAddress*). Here's how it all comes together:

```
<div itemscope itemtype="http://schema.org/Person">
 <img itemprop="image" src="face.jpg" alt="Mike's Face">
 <p>This website is the work of
  ...
```

```
<p>Or, visit Mike on the job at:<br>
<span itemprop="address" itemscope
 itemtype="http://schema.org/PostalAddress">
   ...
</span>
</div>
```

You can then fill in the address details inside the new section:

```
<div itemscope itemtype="http://schema.org/Person">
  <img itemprop="image" src="face.jpg" alt="Mike's Face">
  <p>This website is the work of

  ...

  <p>Or, visit Mike on the job at:<br>
  <span itemprop="address" itemscope
   itemtype="http://schema.org/PostalAddress">
    <span itemprop="streetAddress">42 Jordan Gordon Street,
     6th Floor</span><br>
    <span itemprop="addressLocality">San Francisco</span>,
    <span itemprop="addressRegion">CA</span>
    <span itemprop="postalCode">94105</span><br>
    <span itemprop="addressCountry">USA</span><br>
  </span>
  ...
</div>
```

This all makes perfect sense, but you might be wondering how you know *when* to define a new microdata section inside your first microdata section. Fortunately, the reference page on *http://schema.org* makes it clear (Figure 3-5).

A similar microdata-within-microdata trick takes place when you mark up the company name. Here, you need to set the person's `affiliation` property using the Organization vocabulary:

```
<p>You can contact him where he works, at
<span itemprop="affiliation" itemscope
 itemtype="http://schema.org/Organization">
  <span itemprop="name">The Magic Semantic Company</span>
</span>
```

TIP If you don't fancy filling in all the itemtypes and itemprops yourself, there are online tools that you can use to generate properly formatted microdata-enriched markup. Two examples are *http://schema-creator.org* and *www.microdatagenerator.com*. With both sites, the idea is the same—you pick your vocabulary, type your data into the supplied text boxes, and then copy the finished markup.

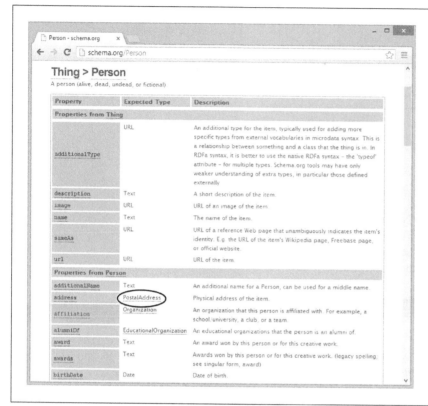

FIGURE 3-5

The Person vocabulary accepts a long list of properties (only some of which are shown here). Most properties take ordinary text, numbers, or date values. But some (like the address property, shown here) use their own vocabularies (like PostalAddress). To learn more about one of these subsections, just click the link.

Extracting Semantic Data in Your Browser

Now that you've gone to all this trouble, it's time to see what sort of benefits you can reap. Although no browser recognizes microformats on its own (at least at the time of this writing), there are a variety of plug-ins and scripts that can give browsers these capabilities. And it's not difficult to imagine useful scenarios. For example, a browser could detect the contact information on a page, list it in a side panel, and give you commands that would let you add a person to your address book as quickly as you bookmark a page. A similar trick could detect event information and let you add it to your calendar in a single click, or find locations and automatically plot them on a map.

Right now, no plug-in goes that far. However, some hardcore web developers have created a variety of JavaScript routines that can search for microformats or metadata, display it in pop-up boxes, or use it in another task. (One example is the JavaScript-powered Microdata Tool at *http://krofdrakula.github.io/microdata-tool*.) And some browsers have plug-ins that can spot different types of metadata on a web page (Figure 3-6).

FIGURE 3-6

The Semantic Inspector is a Chrome extension that extracts all the microdata on the current page. Click its toolbar button, and you'll get the semantic skinny. Here, the Semantic Inspector examines the "About Me" page.

The best bet for a microdata future may be for mainstream browsers to incorporate direct support, just like Internet Explorer and Firefox do for feeds. A *feed* is a special sort of markup document that provides up-to-date content, like a list of recently published news articles. For example, if you visit a blog with Firefox, it automatically detects the blog's RSS feed and lets you create a "live" bookmark that fetches new content automatically. This is exactly the sort of value-added feature that could make microformats really useful.

How Search Engines Use Metadata

Stuffing your page with semantic details is a great way to win yourself some serious web-nerd cred. But even hardcore web developers need some sort of payoff to make the extra work (and the messier markup) worthwhile. It's nice to think about a world of super-smart, semantically aware browsers, but right now the cold, hard reality is that web surfers have little more than a few experimental and little-known browser plug-ins.

Fortunately, there is another reason to embrace rich semantics: *search engine optimization* (SEO). SEO is the art of making your website more visible in a search engine—in other words, making it turn up more often in a results page, helping it get a better ranking for certain keywords, and making it more likely to entice a visitor to click through to your site. Good metadata can help with the last part of this equation. All you do is put the right semantic data on your page, and a search engine like Google will use it to present a fancier search listing, which can help your website stand out from the crowd.

Google Rich Snippets

Nowadays, most search engines can understand the metadata in the pages they catalog. In the rest of this chapter, you'll focus on what Google does with the metadata it finds. There are two reasons to go Google-centric. First, Google is the Earth's most popular search engine, with a commanding two-thirds share of worldwide web searches. Second, Google has been using and promoting metadata for years. The way it uses metadata today is the way other search engines will do so tomorrow.

Google uses the term *rich snippets* to lump together RDFa, microformats, and microdata. As you've already learned, these approaches share significant similarities and address the same problem. Google understands them all and attempts to treat them all equally, so it doesn't matter which approach you favor. (The following examples use microdata, with the aim of helping you get onboard with HTML5's newest semantic standard.)

To learn more about the metadata that Google supports, you can view Google's documentation at *http://tinyurl.com/GoogleRichSnippets*. Not only does it include a decent overview of RDFa, microformats, and microdata, it also shows many different snippet examples (like contact information, events, products, reviews, recipes, and so on). Best of all, Google includes an RDFa, microformat, and microdata version of each example, which can help you translate your semantic skills from one standard to another, if the need arises.

Enhanced Search Results

To see how Google's rich snippets feature works, you can use Google's Structured Data Testing Tool. This tool checks a page you supply, shows you the semantic data that Google can extract from the page, and then shows you how Google might use that information to customize the way it presents that page in someone's search results.

> **NOTE** The Structured Data Testing Tool is useful for two reasons. First, it helps validate your semantic markup. If Google isn't able to extract all the information you put in the page, or if some of it is assigned to the wrong property, then you know you've done something wrong. Second, it shows you how the semantic data can change your page's appearance in Google's search results.

To use the Structured Data Testing Tool, follow these simple steps:

1. **Go to *www.google.com/webmasters/tools/richsnippets*.**

   This simple page includes a single text box (see Figure 3-7).

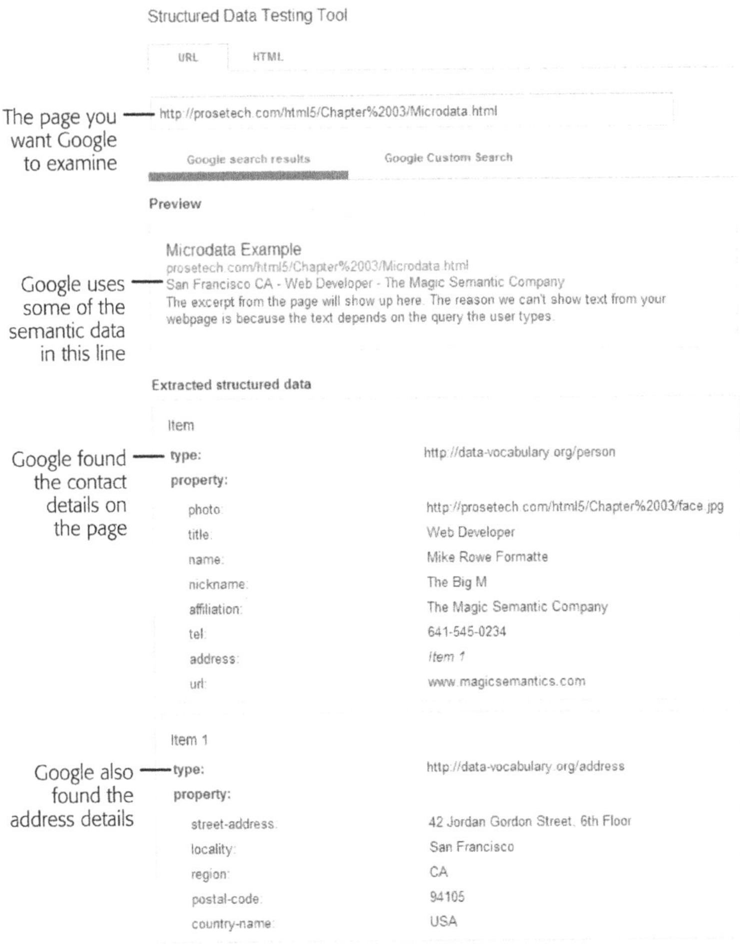

Structured Data Testing Tool

FIGURE 3-7

FIGURE 3-7

Here, Google found the person contact details and address information (from the microdata example shown on page 89). It used this information to add a gray byline under the page title with some of the personal details.

URL   HTML

The page you want Google to examine — http://prosetech.com/html5/Chapter%2003/Microdata.html

Google search results   Google Custom Search

Preview

Microdata Example
prosetech.com/html5/Chapter%2003/Microdata.html

Google uses some of the semantic data in this line — San Francisco CA - Web Developer - The Magic Semantic Company
The excerpt from the page will show up here. The reason we can't show text from your webpage is because the text depends on the query the user types.

Extracted structured data

Item

Google found the contact details on the page — **type:**		http://data-vocabulary.org/person
property:		
	photo:	http://prosetech.com/html5/Chapter%2003/face.jpg
	title:	Web Developer
	name:	Mike Rowe Formatte
	nickname:	The Big M
	affiliation:	The Magic Semantic Company
	tel:	641-545-0234
	address:	*Item 1*
	url:	www.magicsemantics.com

Item 1

Google also found the address details — **type:**		http://data-vocabulary.org/address
property:		
	street-address:	42 Jordan Gordon Street, 6th Floor
	locality:	San Francisco
	region:	CA
	postal-code:	94105
	country-name:	USA

2. **If you want to paste in your markup, click the HTML tab.**

   There are two ways to use the Structured Data Testing Tool, represented by the two tabs on the page.

   - **The URL tab** asks Google to analyze a page that's already online. You simply put in its full web address.

   - **The HTML tab** lets you paste in the chunk of markup you want to analyze (the complete page isn't necessary) into a large text box. If you haven't yet uploaded your work, this is the most convenient approach.

3. **Type in your URL or paste in your markup. Then click Preview.**

You can now review the results (see Figure 3-7). There are two important sections to review. The "Google search preview" section shows how the page may appear in a search result. The "Extracted rich snippet data from the page" shows all the raw semantic data that Google was able to pull out of your markup.

> **TIP** If you see the dreaded "Insufficient data to generate the preview" error message, there are three possible causes. First, your markup may be faulty. Review the raw data that Google extracted, and make sure it found everything you put there. If you don't find a problem here, it's possible that you're trying to use a data type that Google doesn't yet support or you haven't included the bare minimum set of properties that Google needs. To figure out what the problem is, compare your markup with one of Google's examples at *http://tinyurl.com/ GoogleRichSnippets*.

The method Google uses to emphasize contact details (Figure 3-7) is fairly restrained. However, contact details are only one of the rich data types that Google recognizes. Earlier in this chapter (page 85), you saw how to define events using microformats. Add a list of events to your page, and Google just might include them at the bottom of your search result, as shown in Figure 3-8.

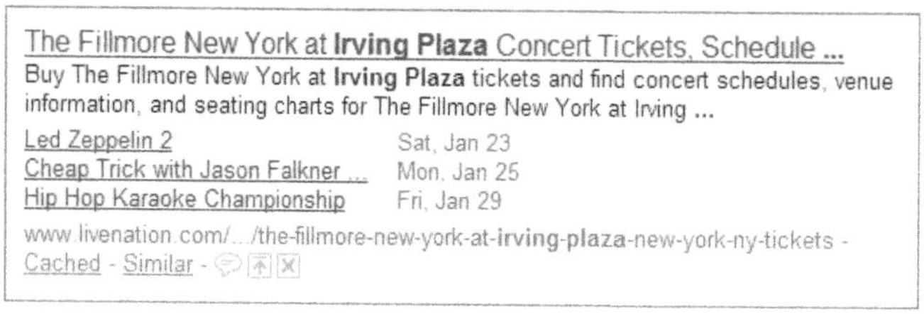

The Fillmore New York at **Irving Plaza** Concert Tickets, Schedule ...
Buy The Fillmore New York at **Irving Plaza** tickets and find concert schedules, venue information, and seating charts for The Fillmore New York at Irving ...
Led Zeppelin 2   Sat, Jan 23
Cheap Trick with Jason Falkner ...   Mon, Jan 25
Hip Hop Karaoke Championship   Fri, Jan 29
www.livenation.com/.../the-fillmore-new-york-at-**irving-plaza**-new-york-ny-tickets -
Cached - Similar - ⬚⬚⬚⬚

FIGURE 3-8

This example page has three events. If you supply a URL with your event listing (as done here), Google turns each event listing into a clickable link.

Google is also interested in business listings (which are treated in much the same way as personal contact details), recipes (which you'll take a peek at in the next section), and reviews (which you'll consider next).

The following example shows the markup you need to turn some review text into recognizable review microdata. The data standard is defined at *http://schema.org/ Review*. Key properties include itemReviewed (in this case, a restaurant), author (the person making the review) and reviewBody (the full account of the review). You can also supply a one-sentence overview (description), the date when the review was made (datePublished, which supports HTML5's <time> element), and a score that's typically made on a scale from 0 to 5 (reviewRating).

Here's an example, with all the microdata details highlighted:

```
<div itemscope itemtype="http://schema.org/Review">
  <p itemprop="description">Pretty bad, and then the Health Department showed
    up.
  </p>
```

```
<div itemprop="itemReviewed" itemscope itemtype="http://schema.org/Thing">
  <span itemprop="name">Jan's Pizza House</span>
</div>

<div>
  <span itemprop="author" itemscope itemtype="http://schema.org/Person">
    Reviewed by: <span itemprop="name">Jared Elberadi</span>
  </span>
  on <time itemprop="datePublished" datetime="2014-06-26">January 26</time>
</div>

<div itemprop="reviewBody">I had an urge to mack on some pizza, and this
  place was the only joint around. It looked like a bit of a dive, but I went
  in hoping to find an undiscovered gem. Instead, I watched a Health
  Department inspector closing the place down. Verdict? I didn't get to
  finish my pizza, and the inspector recommends a Hep-C shot.</div>

<div itemprop="reviewRating" itemscope itemtype="http://schema.org/Rating">
    Rating:<span itemprop="ratingValue">1.5</span></div>
</div>
```

If you put this microdata-formatted review in a web page, Google gives it truly
special treatment (Figure 3-9).

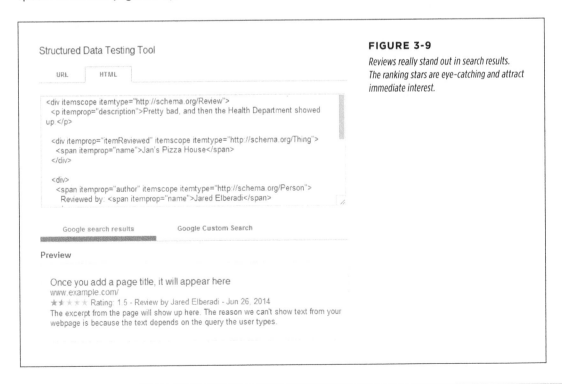

FIGURE 3-9

*Reviews really stand out in search results.
The ranking stars are eye-catching and attract
immediate interest.*

Keen eyes will notice that there are actually *four* microdata formats at work in this single review. There's one format for the review itself (*http://schema.org/Review*), one for the thing you're reviewing (*http://schema.org/Thing*), one for the person doing the reviewing (*http://schema.org/Person*), and one for the rating system (*http://schema.org/Rating*). You can use these standards to supply even more details with your review. For example, you can add the menu of the restaurant, the email address of the reviewer, or the minimum and maximum values of a custom rating system.

The *http://schema.org/Thing* data format, which is used by the itemReviewed property, is a bit different from the others. At first glance, a vocabulary for "things" sounds rather vague. This design is intentional—it gives you the flexibility to write a review about virtually anything, because Thing is a basic vocabulary upon which many more specialized categories are based. These include products, places, events, books, music recordings, and much more (see *http://schema.org/docs/full.html* for the full list of types). In this example, you could easily switch out the Thing vocabulary for the more specialized Restaurant vocabulary (defined at *http://schema.org/Restaurant*). However, as this page doesn't include any extra information about the restaurant, there's no need to take this step.

> **NOTE** You can take a similar look at how Bing (Microsoft's search engine) deals with metadata using the Bing Markup Validator at *www.bing.com/toolbox/markup-validator*. And if you speak fluent Russian, why not take a look at Yandex's microformat validator? It's available at *http://webmaster.yandex.ru/microtest.xml*.

The Recipe Search Engine

Enhanced search listings are a neat trick, and they can drive new traffic into your website. But still, it's hard not to want something even more impressive to justify your newfound semantic skills. Happily, the geniuses at Google are busy dreaming up the future of search, and it has semantics all over it.

One brilliant idea is to use the semantic information not to tweak how an item is presented in a search, but to allow smarter search filtering. For example, if people marked up their résumés using RDFa, microformats, or microdata, Google could provide a specialized résumé searching feature that looks at this data, considering résumés from every popular career website and ignoring every other type of web content. This résumé search engine could also provide enhanced filtering options—for example, allowing companies to find candidates who have specific accreditations or have worked for specific companies.

What to Do When Google Ignores Your Semantic Data

Just because Google *can* show a semantically enriched page in a certain special way doesn't mean it *will*. Google uses its own set of semi-secret rules to determine whether the semantic information is valuable to the searcher. But here are some surefire ways to make sure Google ignores your data:

- **The semantic data doesn't represent the main content.** In other words, if you slap your contact details on a page about fly-fishing, Google isn't likely to use your contact information. (After all, the odds are that when web searchers find this page, they're searching for something to do with fishing, and it doesn't make any sense to see a

byline with your address and business underneath.) On the other hand, if you put your contact details on your résumé page, they're more likely to be used.

- **The semantic data is hidden.** Google won't use any content that's hidden via CSS.

- **Your website uses just a little semantic data.** If your site has relatively few pages that use semantic data, Google might inadvertently overlook the ones that do.

Avoid these mistakes and you stand a good chance of getting an enhanced listing.

Right now, Google doesn't have a resumé search engine. However, Google has experimented with job search technology for veterans (*http://tinyurl.com/vetjobsearch*) and product searches (*www.google.ca/merchants*). But one of its more mature metadata-powered search services is a tool called Recipe View that can hunt through millions of recipes.

By now, you can probably guess what recipe data looks like when it's marked up with microdata or a microformat. The entire recipe sits inside a container that uses the Recipe data format (that's *http://data-vocabulary.org/Recipe*). There are separate properties for the recipe name, the author, and a photo. You can also add a one-sentence summary and a ranking from user reviews.

Here's a portion of recipe markup:

```
<div itemscope itemtype="http://data-vocabulary.org/Recipe">
  <h1 itemprop="name">Elegant Tomato Soup</h1>
  <img itemprop="photo" src="soup.jpg" alt="A bowl of tomato soup">
  <p>By <span itemprop="author">Michael Chiarello</span></p>
  <p itemprop="summary">Roasted tomatoes are the key to developing the rich
  flavor of this tomato soup.</p>
  ...
```

After this, you can include key details about the recipe, including its prep time, cook time, and yield. You can also add a nested section for nutritional information (with details about serving size, calories, fat, and so on):

```
  ...
  <p>Prep time: <time itemprop="prepTime" datetime="PT30M">30 min</time></p>
  <p>Cook time: <time itemprop="cookTime" datetime="PT1H">40 min</time></p>
  <p>Yield: <span itemprop="yield">4 servings</span></p>
```

```
<div itemprop="nutrition" itemscope
  itemtype="http://data-vocabulary.org/Nutrition">
  Serving size: <span itemprop="servingSize">1 large bowl</span>
  Calories per serving: <span itemprop="calories">250</span>
  Fat per serving: <span itemprop="fat">3g</span>
</div>
...
```

NOTE   The prepTime and cookTime properties are meant to represent a *duration* of time, not a single instant in time, and so they can't use the same format as the HTML5 <time> element. Instead, they use an ISO format that's detailed at *http://tinyurl.com/ISOdurations*.

After this is the recipe's ingredient list. Each ingredient is a separate nested section, which typically includes information like the ingredient name and quantity:

```
...
<ul>
  <li itemprop="ingredient" itemscope
  itemtype="http://data-vocabulary.org/RecipeIngredient">
  <span itemprop="amount">1</span>
  <span itemprop="name">yellow onion</span> (diced)
  </li>
  <li itemprop="ingredient" itemscope
  itemtype="http://data-vocabulary.org/RecipeIngredient">
  <span itemprop="amount">14-ounce can</span>
  <span itemprop="name">diced tomatoes</span>
  </li>
  ...
</ul>
...
```

Writing this part of the markup is tedious. But don't stop yet—the payoff is just ahead.

Finally, the directions are a series of paragraphs or a list of steps. They're wrapped up in a single property, like this:

```
...
<div itemprop="instructions">
  <ol>
    <li>Preheat oven to 450 degrees F.</li>
    <li>Strain the chopped canned tomatoes, reserving the juices.</li>
    ...
  </ol>
</div>
...
</div>
```

For a full recipe example, see *http://tinyurl.com/RichSnippetsRecipe*.

NOTE Recipes tend to be long and fairly detailed, so marking them up is a long and involved project. This is a clear case where a good authoring tool could make a dramatic difference. Ideally, this tool would let web authors enter the recipe details in the text boxes of a nicely arranged window. It would then generate semantically correct markup that you could place in your web page.

Once Google indexes your marked-up recipe page, it will make that recipe available through the Recipe View search feature. Here's how to try out Recipe View:

1. **Surf to *www.google.com/landing/recipes*.**

   You arrive at the Recipe View feature homepage. It includes plenty of information about how Recipe View works, including a video that shows a recipe search in action.

2. **Click the "Try Google with Recipe View" button.**

   This button takes you to the familiar Google search page. However, there's something subtly different. Under the search box, the Recipes tab is highlighted in red, which indicates that you're performing a recipe search.

3. **Type a recipe name in the search box and click the search button.**

   Google starts you out with a search for *chicken pasta*, but you can do better.

4. **Click the "Search tools" button (which appears under the right side of the search box).**

   Because Google can *understand* the structure of every recipe, it can include smarter filtering options. When you click "Search tools," Google calls up three recipe-specific filtering features, which appear in drop-down lists, just above the search results (see Figure 3-10).

   - **Ingredients** lets you choose to see only the recipes that include or omit certain ingredients. You choose by clicking a tiny Yes or No checkbox next to the corresponding ingredient. (To create the ingredient list, Google grabs the most commonly used ingredients from the search results for your search.)

   - **Any cook time** lets you pinpoint fast recipes—for example, ones that take less than an hour or less than 10 minutes (raw chicken alert).

   - **Any calories** lets you filter out recipes that come in under a specific calorie-per-portion threshold, which is handy for dieters.

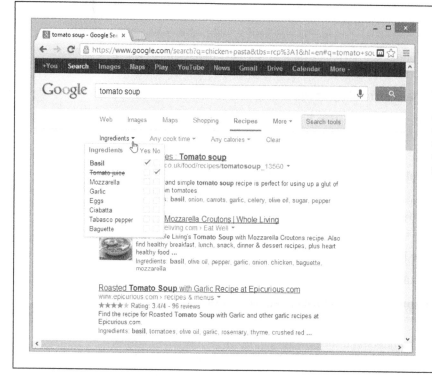

FIGURE 3-10

After you perform a recipe search, Google lets you filter the results based on some of the metadata that it found in the matching recipes. Here, a search hunts for a tomato soup recipe that's heavy on the basil but avoids tomato juice.

The semantic data you've learned about in this chapter gives web surfers a powerful information-hunting tool—and a more effective way to find your web pages.

Building Better Web Forms

HTML forms are simple HTML controls you use to collect information from website visitors. They include text boxes people can type into, list boxes they can pick from, checkboxes they can switch on or off, and so on. On the Web, forms let people do everything from getting stock quotes to buying concert tickets.

HTML forms have existed almost since the dawn of HTML, and they haven't changed a wink since last century, despite some serious efforts. Web standards-makers spent years cooking up a successor called XForms, which fell as flat as XHTML 2 (see page 4). Although XForms solved some problems easily and elegantly, it also had its own headaches—for example, XForms code was verbose and assumed that web designers were intimately familiar with XML. But the biggest hurdle was the fact that XForms wasn't compatible with HTML forms in any way, meaning that developers would need to close their eyes and jump to a new model with nothing but a whole lot of nerve and hope. But because mainstream web browsers never bothered to implement XForms—it was too complex and little used—web developers never ended up taking that leap.

HTML5 takes a different approach. It adds refinements to the existing HTML forms model, which means HTML5-enhanced forms can keep working on older browsers, just without all the bells and whistles. (This is a good thing, because Internet Explorer doesn't support any new form features in versions before IE 10.) HTML5 also adds practical form features that developers were already using but that previously required a pile of JavaScript code or a JavaScript toolkit. Now, HTML5 makes these features easily accessible.

In this chapter, you'll tour all the new features of HTML5 forms. You'll see which ones are supported, which ones aren't, and which workarounds can help you smooth over the differences. You'll also consider a feature that isn't technically part of the HTML5 forms standard but is all about interactivity—putting a rich HTML editor in an ordinary web page.

Understanding Forms

Odds are that you've worked with forms before. But if you're a bit sketchy on the details, the following recap will refresh your memory.

A *web form* is a collection of text boxes, lists, buttons, and other clickable widgets that a web surfer uses to supply some sort of information to a website. Forms are all over the Web—they allow you to sign up for email accounts, review products, and make bank transactions. The simplest possible form is the single text box that adorns search engines like Google (see Figure 4-1).

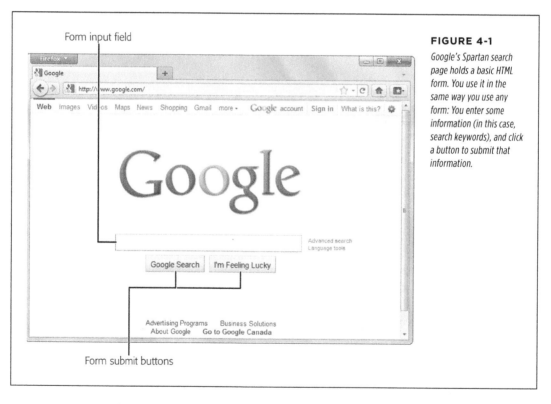

Form input field

FIGURE 4-1

Google's Spartan search page holds a basic HTML form. You use it in the same way you use any form: You enter some information (in this case, search keywords), and click a button to submit that information.

Form submit buttons

All basic web forms work in the same way. The user fills in some information and then clicks a button. At that point, the server collects all the data that the user has entered and sends it back to the web server. On the web server, some sort of application digests the information and takes the appropriate next step. The server-side program might consult a database, either to read or to store some information, before sending a new page back to the web browser.

The tricky part of this discussion is that there are hundreds of ways to build the server-side part of the equation—that's the application that processes the information that's submitted from the form. Some developers may use stripped-down scripts that let them manipulate the raw form data, while others may work with higher-level models that package the form details in neat programming objects. But either way, the task is basically the same. You examine the form data, do something with it, and then send back a new page.

NOTE This book doesn't make any assumptions about your choice of server-side programming tool. In fact, it doesn't really matter, because you still need to use the same set of form elements, and these elements are still bound by the same HTML5 rules.

UP TO SPEED

Bypassing Form Submission with JavaScript

It's worth noting that forms aren't the only way to send user-entered information to a web server (although they were, once upon a time). Today, crafty developers can use the XMLHttpRequest object (page 377) in JavaScript code to quietly communicate with a web server. For example, the Google search page uses this approach in two different ways—first, to get search suggestions, which it displays in a drop-down list; and second, to get a search results page as you type, if you've enabled the Google Instant feature (*www.google.com/instant*).

It might occur to you that JavaScript can completely bypass the form submission step, as it does in Google Instant. But while it's possible to offer this technique as a *feature*, it's not acceptable to include it as a *requirement*. That's because the JavaScript approach isn't bulletproof (for example, it may exhibit the occasional quirk on a slow connection) and there's

still a small fraction of people with no JavaScript support or with JavaScript turned off in their browsers.

Finally, it's worth noting that it's perfectly acceptable to have a page that includes a form but never *submits* that form. You've probably seen pages that perform simple calculations (for example, a mortgage interest rate calculator). These forms don't need any help from the server, because they can perform their calculations entirely in JavaScript and display the result on the current page. For that reason, these forms never need to submit their data.

From the HTML5 point of view, it really doesn't matter whether you submit your form to a server, use the data in an ordinary JavaScript routine, or pass it back to the server through XML-HttpRequest. In all cases, you'll still build your form using the standard HTML forms controls.

Revamping a Traditional HTML Form

The best way to learn about HTML5 forms is to take a typical example from today and enhance it. Figure 4-2 shows the example you'll start out with.

The markup is dishwater-dull. If you've worked with forms before, you won't see anything new here. First, the entire form is wrapped in a `<form>` element:

```
<form id="zooKeeperForm" action="processApplication.cgi">
  <p><i>Please complete the form. Mandatory fields are marked with
  a </i><em>*</em></p>

  ...
```

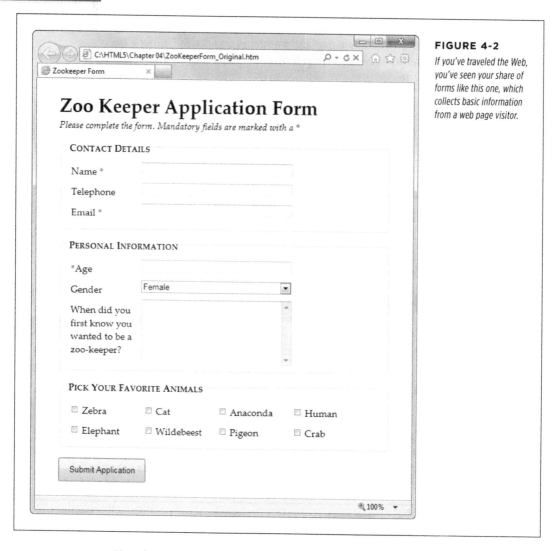

FIGURE 4-2

If you've traveled the Web, you've seen your share of forms like this one, which collects basic information from a web page visitor.

The `<form>` element bundles together all the form widgets (also known as *controls* or *fields*). It also tells the browser where to post the page when it's submitted, by providing a URL in the `action` attribute. If you plan to do all the work in client-side JavaScript code, you can simply use a number sign (#) for the `action` attribute.

NOTE HTML5 adds a mechanism for placing form controls outside of the form to which they belong. The trick is to use the new `form` attribute to refer to the form by its `id` value (as in `form="zooForm"`). However, browsers that don't support this feature will completely overlook your data when the form is submitted, which means this minor feature is still too risky to use in a real web page.

A well-designed form, like the zookeeper application, divides itself into logical chunks using the `<fieldset>` element. Each chunk gets a title, courtesy of the `<legend>` element. Here's the `<fieldset>` for the Contact Details section (which is dissected in Figure 4-3):

```
...
<fieldset>
  <legend>Contact Details</legend>
  <label for="name">Name <em>*</em></label>
  <input id="name"><br>
  <label for="telephone">Telephone</label>
  <input id="telephone"><br>
  <label for="email">Email <em>*</em></label>
  <input id="email"><br>
</fieldset>
...
```

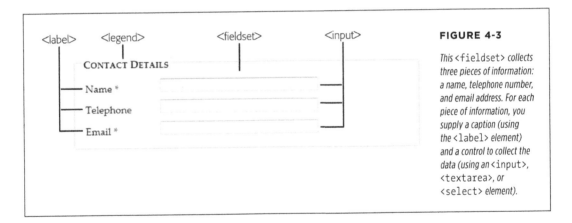

FIGURE 4-3

This `<fieldset>` collects three pieces of information: a name, telephone number, and email address. For each piece of information, you supply a caption (using the `<label>` element) and a control to collect the data (using an `<input>`, `<textarea>`, or `<select>` element).

As in all forms, the bulk of the work is handled by the all-purpose `<input>` element, which collects text and creates checkboxes, radio buttons, and list buttons. Along with `<input>`, the `<textarea>` element gives people a way to enter multiple lines of text, and the `<select>` element creates a list. If you need a refresher, Table 4-1 will fill you in.

TABLE 4-1 *Form controls*

CONTROL	HTML ELEMENT	DESCRIPTION
Single-line textbox	`<input type="text">` `<input type="password">`	Shows a text box where visitors can type in text. If you use the `password` type, the browser won't display the text. Instead, visitors see an asterisk (*) or a bullet (•) in place of each letter as they type in their password.
Multiline textbox	`<textarea>...</textarea>`	Shows a large text box that can fit multiple lines of text.
Checkbox	`<input type="checkbox">`	Shows a checkbox that can be switched on or off.
Radio button	`<input type="radio">`	Shows a radio button (a circle you can turn on or off). Usually, you have a group of radio buttons with the same value for the `name` attribute, in which case the visitor can select only one.
Button	`<input type="submit">` `<input type="image">` `<input type="reset">` `<input type="button">`	Shows the standard clickable button. A `submit` button always gathers up the form data and sends it to its destination. An `image` button does the same thing, but it lets you display a clickable picture instead of the standard text-on-a-button. A `reset` button clears the visitor's selections and text from all the input controls. A `button` button doesn't do anything unless you add some JavaScript code.
List	`<select>...</select>`	Shows a list where your visitor can select one or more items. You add an `<option>` element for each item in the list.

Here's the rest of the zookeeper form markup, with a few new details (a `<select>` list, checkboxes, and the button that submits the form):

```
...
<fieldset>
  <legend>Personal Information</legend>
    <label for="age"><em>*</em>Age</label>
    <input id="age"><br>
    <label for="gender">Gender</label>
    <select id="gender">
      <option value="female">Female</option>
      <option value="male">Male</option>
    </select><br>
```

```
        <label for="comments">When did you first know you wanted to be a
          zoo-keeper?</label>
        <textarea id="comments"></textarea>
      </fieldset>

      <fieldset>
        <legend>Pick Your Favorite Animals</legend>
        <label for="zebra"><input id="zebra" type="checkbox"> Zebra</label>
        <label for="cat"><input id="cat" type="checkbox"> Cat</label>
        <label for="anaconda"><input id="anaconda" type="checkbox"> Anaconda
        </label>
        <label for="human"><input id="human" type="checkbox"> Human</label>
        <label for="elephant"><input id="elephant" type="checkbox"> Elephant
        </label>
        <label for="wildebeest"><input id="wildebeest" type="checkbox">
          Wildebeest</label>
        <label for="pigeon"><input id="pigeon" type="checkbox"> Pigeon</label>
        <label for="crab"><input id="crab" type="checkbox"> Crab</label>
      </fieldset>
      <p><input type="submit" value="Submit Application"></p>
    </form>
```

You can find the full example, along with the relatively simple style sheet that formats it, on the try-out site (*http://prosetech.com/html5*). Look for the *Zookeeper-Form_Original.html* file to play around with a traditional, unenhanced version of the form, and *ZookeeperForm_Revised.html* to get all the HTML5 goodies.

NOTE One limit of HTML forms is that you can't change how the browser draws controls. For example, if you want to replace the standard dull gray checkbox with a big black-and-white box with a fat red checkmark image, you can't. (The alternative is to create a normal element that has checkbox-like behavior using JavaScript—in other words, it changes its appearance back and forth when someone clicks it.)

HTML5 keeps this no-customization limit in place and extends it to the new controls you'll learn about in this chapter. That means ordinary HTML5 forms aren't enough for web developers who want complete control over the look of their pages. Instead, they'll need a JavaScript toolkit like jQuery UI.

Now that you've got a form to work with, it's time to start improving it with HTML5. In the following sections, you'll start small, with placeholder text and an autofocus field.

Adding Hints with Placeholders

Forms usually start out empty. But a column of blank text boxes can be a bit intimidating, especially if it's not absolutely clear what belongs inside each text box. That's why you commonly see some sort of sample text inside otherwise-empty text boxes. This placeholder text is also called a *watermark*, because it's often given a light-gray color to distinguish it from real, typed-in content. Figure 4-4 shows a placeholder in action.

To create a placeholder, simply use the `placeholder` attribute:

```
<label for="name">Name <em>*</em></label>
<input id="name" placeholder="Jane Smith"><br>
<label for="telephone">Telephone</label>
<input id="telephone" placeholder="(xxx) xxx-xxxx"><br>
```

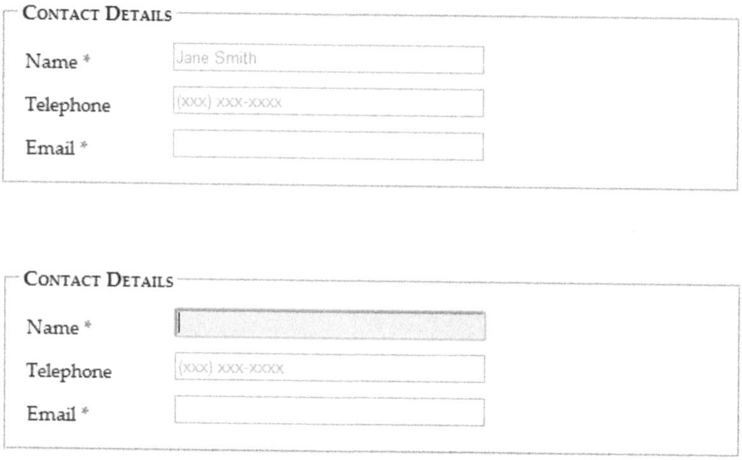

FIGURE 4-4

Top: When a field is empty, its placeholder text appears, as with the Name and Telephone fields shown here.

Bottom: When the user clicks in the field (giving it focus), the placeholder text disappears. When the form filler moves on to another field, the placeholder text reappears, as long as the text box is still empty.

Browsers that don't support placeholder text just ignore the `placeholder` attribute; Internet Explorer (before IE 10) is the main culprit. Fortunately, it's not a big deal, since placeholders are just nice form frills, not essential to your form's functioning. If it really bothers you, there are plenty of JavaScript patches that can bring IE up to speed, painlessly, at *http://tinyurl.com/polyfills*.

Right now, there's no standard, consistent way to change the appearance of placeholder text (for example, to italicize it or to change the text color). Eventually, browser makers will create the CSS styling hooks that you need—in fact, they're hashing out the details even as you read this. But to get it to work right now, you need to fiddle with browser-specific pseudo-classes (namely, `-webkit-input-placeholder` for Chrome, `-ms-input-placeholder` for Internet Explorer, and `-moz-placeholder` for Firefox). Page 443 has the full details about pseudo-classes, and page 183 explains the awkward world of browser-specific styles.

However, you can use the better-supported `focus` pseudo-class without any headaches. You use it to change the way a text box looks when it gets the focus. For example, you might want to assign a darker background color to make it stand out:

```
input:focus {
  background: #eaeaea;
}
```

UP TO SPEED

Writing Good Placeholders

You don't need placeholders for every text box. Instead, you should use them to clear up potential ambiguity. For example, no one needs an explanation about what goes in a First Name box, but the Name box in Figure 4-4 isn't quite as obvious. The placeholder text makes it clear that there's room for a first and a last name.

Sometimes placeholders include a sample value—in other words, something you might actually type into the box. For example, Microsoft's Hotmail login page (*www.hotmail.com*) uses the text *someone@example.com* for a placeholder, making it obvious that you should enter your email address in the box—not your name or any other information.

Other times, placeholders indicate the way a value should be formatted. The telephone box in Figure 4-4 is an example—it shows the value *(xxx) xxx-xxxx* to concisely indicate that telephone numbers should consist of a three-digit area code, followed by a sequence of three, then four digits. This placeholder doesn't necessarily mean that differently formatted input isn't allowed, but it does offer a suggestion that uncertain people can follow.

There are two things you shouldn't try with a placeholder. First, don't try to cram in a description of the field or instructions. For example, imagine you have a box for a credit card's security code. The text "The three digits listed on the back of your card" is *not* a good placeholder. Instead, consider adding a text note under the input box, or using the `title` attribute to make a pop-up window appear when someone hovers over the field:

```
<label for="promoCode">Promotion Code
</label>
<input id="promoCode" placeholder="QRB001"
title="Your promotion code is three
letters followed by three numbers">
```

Second, you shouldn't add special characters to your placeholder in an attempt to make it obvious that your placeholder is not real, typed-in text. For example, some websites use placeholders like *[John Smith]* instead of *John Smith*, with the square brackets there to emphasize that the placeholder is just an example. This convention can be confusing.

Focus: Starting in the Right Spot

After loading up your form, the first thing your visitors want to do is start typing. Unfortunately, they can't—at least not until they tab over to the first control, or click it with the mouse, thereby giving it *focus*.

You can make this happen with JavaScript by calling the `focus()` method of the appropriate `<input>` element. But this involves an extra line of code and can sometimes cause annoying quirks. For example, it's sometimes possible for the user to click somewhere else and start typing before the `focus()` method gets called, at which point focus is rudely transferred back to the first control. But if the browser were able to control the focus, it could be a bit smarter, and transfer focus only if the user hasn't already dived into another control.

That's the idea behind HTML5's `autofocus` attribute, which you can add to a single `<input>` or `<textarea>` element, like this:

```
<label for="name">Name <em>*</em></label>
<input id="name" placeholder="Jane Smith" autofocus><br>
```

The autofocus attribute has similar support as the placeholder attribute, which means basically every browser recognizes it except IE 9 and older. Once again, it's easy enough to plug the hole. You can check for autofocus support using Modernizr (page 31) and then run your own autofocus code if needed. Or, you can use a ready-made JavaScript polyfill that adds autofocus support (*http://tinyurl.com/polyfills*). However, it hardly seems worth it for such a minor frill, unless you're also aiming to give IE support for other form features, like the validation system discussed next.

◾ Validation: Stopping Errors

The fields in a form are there to gather information from web page visitors. But no matter how politely you ask, you might not get what you want. Impatient or confused visitors can skip over important sections, enter partial information, or just hit the wrong keys. The end result? They click Submit, and your website gets a whackload of scrambled data.

What a respectable web page needs is *validation*—a way to catch mistakes when they happen (or even better, to prevent them from happening at all). For years, developers have done that by writing their own JavaScript routines or using professional JavaScript libraries. And, truthfully, these approaches work perfectly well. But seeing as validation is so common (just about everyone needs to do error-checking), and seeing as validation generally revolves around a few key themes (for example, spotting invalid email addresses or dates), and seeing as validation is boring (no one really wants to write the same code for every form, not to mention *test* it), there's clearly room for a better way.

The creators of HTML5 spotted this low-hanging fruit and invented a way for browsers to help out, by getting them to do the validation work instead of web developers. They devised a *client-side* validation system (see the box on page 113) that lets you embed common error-checking rules into any <input> field. Best of all, this system is easy—all you need to do is insert the right attribute.

How HTML5 Validation Works

The basic idea behind HTML5 form validation is that you indicate where validation should happen, but you don't actually *implement* the tedious details. It's a bit like being promoted into a management job, just without the pay raise.

For example, imagine you decide a certain field cannot be left blank—the form filler needs to supply some sort of information. In HTML5, you can make this demand by adding the required attribute:

```
<label for="name">Name <em>*</em></label>
<input id="name" placeholder="Jane Smith" autofocus required><br>
```

Validating in Two Places

Throughout the years, crafty developers have approached the validation problem in different ways. Today, the consensus is clear. To make a bulletproof form, you need two types of error-checking:

- **Client-side validation.** These are the checks that happen in the browser, *before* a form is submitted. The goal here is to make life easier for the people filling out the form. Instead of waiting for them to complete three dozen text boxes and click a submit button, you want to catch problems in the making. That way you can pop up a helpful error message right away and in the right spot, allowing the form filler to correct the mistake before submitting the form to the server.

- **Server-side validation.** These are the checks that happen *after* a form is sent back to the web server. At this point,

it's up to your server-side code to review the details and make sure everything is kosher before continuing. No matter what the browser does, server-side validation is essential. It's the only way to defend yourself from malicious people who are deliberately trying to tamper with form data. If your server-side validation detects a problem, you send back a page with an error message.

So client-side validation (of which HTML5 validation is an example) is there to make life easier for your web page visitors, while server-side validation ensures correctness. The key thing to understand is that you need both types of validation—unless you have an exceedingly simple form where mistakes aren't likely or aren't a big deal.

Initially, there's no visual detail to indicate that a field is required. For that reason, you might want to use some other visual clue, such as giving the text box a different border color or placing an asterisk next to the field (as in the zookeeper form).

Validation kicks in only when the form filler clicks a button to submit the form. If the browser implements HTML5 forms, then it will notice that a required field is blank, intercept the form submission attempt, and show a pop-up message that flags the invalid field (Figure 4-5).

As you'll see in the following sections, different attributes let you apply different error-checking rules. You can apply more than one rule to the same input box, and you can apply the same rule to as many `<input>` elements as you want (and to the `<textarea>` element). All the validation conditions must be met before the form can be submitted.

This raises a good question: What happens if form data breaks more than one rule—for example, it has multiple required fields that aren't filled in?

Once again, nothing happens until the person filling out the form clicks the submit button. Then, the browser begins examining the fields from top to bottom. When it finds the first invalid value, it stops checking any further. It cancels the form submission and pops up an error message next to this value. (Additionally, if the offending text box isn't currently visible, the browser scrolls up just enough that it appears at the top of the page.) If the visitor corrects the problem and clicks the submit button again, the browser will stop and highlight the next invalid value.

CONTACT DETAILS

Name *

Telephone

This is a required field

Email *

CONTACT DETAILS

Name *   Jane Smith

Telephone   (xxx) xxx-xxxx   Please fill in this field.

Email *

CONTACT DETAILS

Name *   Jane Smith

Telephone   Please fill out this field.

Email *

FIGURE 4-5

Here's the same required field in Chrome (top), Internet Explorer (middle), and Firefox (bottom). Browsers are free to choose the exact way they notify people about validation problems, but they all use a pop-up box that looks like a stylized tooltip. Unfortunately, you can't customize the formatting of this box or change the wording of the validation message—at least not yet.

> **NOTE** Web browsers hold off on validation until a submit button is clicked. This ensures that the validation system is efficient and restrained, so it works for everyone.

Some web developers prefer to alert people as soon as they leave an invalid field (when they tab away or click somewhere else with the mouse). This sort of validation is handy in long forms, especially if there's a chance that someone may make a similar mistake in several different fields. Unfortunately, HTML5 doesn't have a way for you to dictate when the web browser does its validation, although it's possible that it might add one in the future. For now, if you want immediate validation messages, it's best to write the JavaScript yourself or to use a good JavaScript library.

Turning Validation Off

In some cases, you may need to disable the validation feature. For example, you might need to turn it off for testing to verify that your server-side code deals appropriately with invalid data. To turn validation off for an entire form, you add the novalidate attribute to the containing <form> element:

```
<form id="zooKeeperForm" action="processApplication.cgi" novalidate>
```

The other option is to provide a submit button that bypasses validation. This technique is sometimes useful in a web page. For example, you may want to enforce strict validation for the official submit button but provide another button that does something else (like storing half-completed data for later use). To allow this, add the `formnovalidate` attribute to the `<input>` element that represents your button:

```
<input type="submit" value="Save for Later" formnovalidate>
```

You've now seen how to use validation to catch missing information. Next, you'll learn to search for errors in different types of data.

> **NOTE** Planning to validate numbers? There's no validation rule that forces text to contain digits, but there is a new number data type, which you'll examine on page 126. Unfortunately, its support is still sketchy.

Validation Styling Hooks

Although you can't style validation messages, you can change the appearance of the input fields based on whether or not they're validated. For example, you can give invalid values a different background color, which will appear in the text box as soon as the browser detects the problem.

To use this technique, you simply need to add a few new pseudo-classes (page 443). Your options include the following:

- **required** and **optional**, which apply styles to fields based on whether they use the `required` attribute.

- **valid** and **invalid**, which apply styles to controls based on whether they contain mistakes. But remember that most browsers won't actually discover invalid values until the visitor tries to submit the form, so you won't see the invalid formatting right away.

- **in-range** and **out-of-range**, which apply formatting to controls that use the `min` and `max` attributes to limit numbers to a range (page 127).

For example, if you want to give required `<input>` fields a light-yellow background, you could use a style rule with the `required` pseudo-class:

```
input:required {
  background-color: lightyellow;
}
```

Or, you might want to highlight only those fields that are required and currently hold invalid values by combining the `required` and `invalid` pseudo-classes like this:

```
input:required:invalid {
  background-color: lightyellow;
}
```

With this setting, blank fields are automatically highlighted, because they break the required-field rule.

You can use all sorts of other tricks, like combining the validation pseudo-classes with the focus pseudo-class, or using an offset background that includes an error icon to flag invalid values. Of course, a hefty disclaimer applies: You can use these pseudo-classes to improve your pages, but make sure your form still looks good without them, because support lags in older browsers.

Validating with Regular Expressions

The most powerful (and complex) type of validation that HTML5 supports is based on regular expressions. Seeing as JavaScript already supports regular expression, adding this feature to HTML forms makes perfect sense.

A *regular expression* is a pattern written using the regular expression language. Regular expressions are designed to match patterned text—for example, a regular expression can make sure that a postal code has the right sequence of letters and digits, or that an email address has an @ symbol and a domain extension that's at least two characters long. For example, consider this expression:

```
[A-Z]{3}-[0-9]{3}
```

The square brackets at the beginning define a range of allowed characters. In other words, [A-Z] allows any uppercase letter from A to Z. The curly brackets that follow multiply this effect, so {3} means you need three uppercase letters. The dash that follows doesn't have a special meaning, so it indicates that a dash must follow the three-letter sequence. Finally, [0-9] allows a digit from 0 to 9, and {3} requires three of them.

Regular expression matching is useful for searching (finding pattern matches in a long document) and validation (verifying that a value matches a pattern). HTML5 forms use regular expressions for validation.

> **NOTE** Regular expression geeks take note: You don't need the magic ^ and $ characters to match the beginning or end of a value in a field. HTML5 assumes both details automatically, which means a regular expression must match the *entire* value in a field in order to be deemed valid.

These values are valid, because they match the pattern shown above:

```
QRB-001

TTT-952

LAA-000
```

But these values are not:

```
qrb-001

TTT-0952

LA5-000
```

Regular expressions quickly get much more complex than this example. Writing a regular expression can be quite a chore, which is why most developers simply search for a ready-made regular expression that validates the type of data they want to check. Or they get help.

TIP To learn just enough about the regular expression language to make your own super-simple expressions, check out the concise tutorials at *http://tinyurl.com/regexp-object* or *http://tinyurl.com/jsregex*. To find ready-made regular expressions that you can use with your forms, visit *http://regexlib.com*. And to become a regular expression guru, read *Mastering Regular Expressions* by Jeffrey Friedl (O'Reilly).

Once you have a regular expression, you can enforce it in any <input> or <textarea> element by adding the pattern attribute:

```
<label for="promoCode">Promotion Code</label>
<input id="promoCode" placeholder="QRB-001" title=
 "Your promotion code is three uppercase letters, a dash, then three numbers"
 pattern="[A-Z]{3}-[0-9]{3}">
```

Figure 4-6 shows what happens if you break the regular expression rule.

TIP Browsers don't validate blank values. In this example, a blank promotion code passes muster. If this isn't what you want, then combine the pattern attribute with the required attribute.

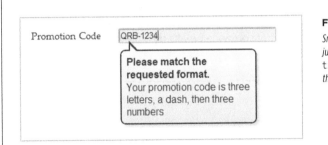

FIGURE 4-6

Smart browsers (like Google Chrome, shown here) don't just catch the mistake, they also grab the text from the title *attribute and display that as well, to help guide the person who's filling out the form.*

NOTE Regular expressions seem like a perfect match for email addresses (and they are). However, hold off on using them this way, because HTML5 already has a dedicated input type for email addresses that has the correct regular expression baked in (page 125).

Custom Validation

The HTML5 specification also outlines a set of JavaScript properties that let you find out if fields are valid (or force the browser to validate them). The most useful of these is the setCustomValidity() method, which lets you write custom validation logic for specific fields and have it work with the HTML5 validation system.

Here's how it works. First, you need to check the appropriate field for errors. You do this by handling the onInput event, which is nothing new:

```
<label for="comments">When did you first know you wanted to be a
zookeeper?</label>
<textarea id="comments" oninput="validateComments(this)"></textarea>
```

In this example, the onInput event triggers a function named validateComments(). It's up to you to write this function, check the current value of the <input> element, and then call setCustomValidity().

If the current value has problems, you need to supply an error message when you call setCustomValidity(). Or, if the current value checks out, you need to call setCustomValidity() with an empty string. This clears any error custom messages that you may have set earlier.

Here's an example that forces the text in the comment box to be at least 20 characters long:

```
function validateComments(input) {
  if (input.value.length < 20) {
    input.setCustomValidity("You need to comment in more detail.");
  }
  else {
    // There's no error. Clear any error message.
    input.setCustomValidity("");
  }
}
```

Figure 4-7 shows what happens if someone breaks this rule and then tries to submit the form.

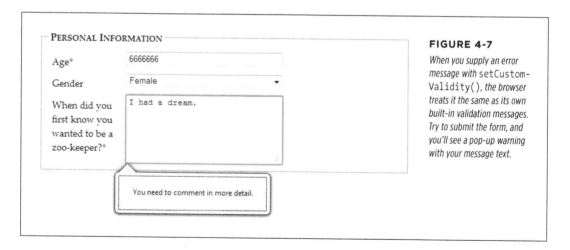

FIGURE 4-7

When you supply an error message with setCustom-Validity(), the browser treats it the same as its own built-in validation messages. Try to submit the form, and you'll see a pop-up warning with your message text.

Of course, you could solve this problem more neatly with a regular expression that requires long strings. But while regular expressions are great for validating some data types, custom validation logic can do *anything*, from complex algebra to contacting the web server.

NOTE Remember, your web page visitors can see anything you put in JavaScript, so it's no place for secret algorithms. For example, you might know that in a valid promotional code, the digits always add up to 12. But you probably don't want to reveal that detail in a custom validation routine, because it will help shifty people cook up fake codes. Instead, keep this sort of validation in the web server.

Browser Support for Web Forms and Validation

Browser makers added support for HTML5 forms in pieces. That means some browser builds support some validation features while ignoring others. Table 4-2 indicates the minimum browser versions you need to use to get solid support for all the validation tricks you've learned so far. As this table indicates, there are two potential support headaches: old versions of IE, and mobile browsers that run on smartphones and tablets.

TABLE 4-2 *Browser support for validation*

	IE	FIREFOX	CHROME	SAFARI	OPERA	SAFARI IOS	CHROME FOR ANDROID
Minimum version	10	4	10	5*	10	-	28

* Safari doesn't support the `required` attribute.

Because HTML5 validation doesn't replace the validation you do on your web server, you may see it as a frill, in which case you can accept this uneven support. Browsers that don't implement validation, like IE 9, let people submit forms with invalid dates, but you can then catch these problems on the web server and return the same page with error details.

On the other hand, your website might include complex forms with lots of potential for confusion, and you might not be ready to accept a world of frustrated IE users. In this case, you have two basic choices: Fall back on your own validation system or use a JavaScript library that adds the missing smarts. Your choice depends on the extent and complexity of your validation.

Testing for Support with Modernizr

If all your form needs is a smattering of simple validation, it's probably worth adding your own checks. Using Modernizr (page 31), you can check for a variety of HTML5 web forms features. For example, use the `Modernizr.input.pattern` property to check whether the current browser recognizes the `pattern` attribute:

```
if (!Modernizr.input.pattern) {
  // The current browser doesn't perform regular expression validation.
  // You can use the regular expression features in JavaScript instead.
  ...
}
```

> **NOTE** The `pattern` property is just one of the properties exposed by `Modernizr.input` object. Other properties that are useful for testing web form support include `placeholder`, `autofocus`, `required`, `max`, `min`, and `step`.

Of course, this example doesn't tell you *when* to perform this check or *how* to react. If you want your validation to mimic the HTML5 validation system, it makes sense to perform your validation when the person viewing the form attempts to submit it. You do this by handling the form's `onSubmit` event and then returning either `true` (which means the form is valid and the browser can submit it) or `false` (which means the form has a problem and the browser should cancel the operation):

```
<form id="zooKeeperForm" action="processApplication.cgi"
  onsubmit="return validateForm()">
```

Here's an example of a very simple custom validation routine that enforces required fields:

```
function validateForm() {
  if (!Modernizr.input.required) {
    // The required attribute is not supported, so you need to check the
    // required fields yourself.

    // First, get an array that holds all the elements.
    var inputElements = document.getElementById("zooKeeperForm").elements;

    // Next, move through that array, checking each element.
    for(var i = 0; i < inputElements.length; i++) {

      // Check if this element is required.
      if (inputElements[i].hasAttribute("required")) {
        // If this element is required, check if it has a value.
        // If not, the form fails validation, and this function returns false.
        if (inputElements[i].value == "") return false;
      }
    }
```

```
    // If you reach this point, everything worked out and the browser
    // can submit the form.
    return true;
  }
}
```

TIP This block of code relies on a number of basic JavaScript techniques, including element lookup, a loop, and conditional logic. To learn more about all these details, check out Appendix B, "JavaScript: The Brains of Your Page."

Polyfilling with HTML5Forms

If you have a complex form and you want to save some effort (while at the same time preparing for the future), you may prefer to use a JavaScript patch to solve all your problems. Technically, the approach is the same—your page will check for validation support and then perform validation manually if necessary. The difference is that the JavaScript library already has all the tedious code you need.

At *http://tinyurl.com/polyfills*, you can find a long, intimidating list of JavaScript libraries that all attempt to do more or less the same thing. One oldie but goody is the HTML5Forms library, which is available from *http://tinyurl.com/html5forms*. To get a copy, click the Download ZIP button. You'll be rewarded with a Zip folder stuffed full of files. Unzip it, and you'll find a pile of useful scripts (in the *shared/js* folder) and a long list of example pages (in the *tests/html5forms* folder).

To get started with HTML5Forms, copy the *shared* folder (with all its subfolders) to your website folder. You can rename it to something else (for example, *html5forms* instead of *shared*), as long as you tweak the name in your script references. Once you've copied the files, you need to add two references to your web page, like this:

```
<head>
  <title>...</title>
  <script src="shared/js/modernizr.com/Modernizr-2.5.3.forms.js"></script>
  <script src="shared/js/html5Forms.js" data-webforms2-support="all"
   data-webforms2-force-js-validation="true">
  </script>
  ...
<head>
```

The first reference points to a small build of Modernizr (here, it's named *Modernizr-2.5.3.forms.js*) that's included with HTML5Forms, and provides feature detection, ensuring that the validation workarounds are loaded only if the browser needs them. If you're already using Modernizr, you should omit this reference. Just make sure that your Modernizr build includes the form detection options. These are the options that begin with `forms-` (for example, `forms-validation`) on the "Non-core detects" section of the Modernizr download page.

The second reference is to the HTML5Forms library. After the familiar `src` attribute, you'll see one or more attributes that specify the features you need. In the example above, the script loads all the `webforms` features. HTML5Forms is a modular library, which means you can opt to use only some of its features. This strategy ensures that your pages don't perform any extra work to load up features you don't need. Here's an example that turns on basic support for validation, required fields, and placeholders:

```
<script src="shared/js/html5Forms.js"
  data-webforms2-support="validation,placeholder"
  data-webforms2-force-js-validation="true">
```

> **TIP** If you want to pick a different combination of features, look for a corresponding example page file in the *tests/html5forms* folder that's included with the HTML5Forms download.

HTML5Forms library also adds surprisingly good support for the form features you'll learn about next, like the slider, date picker, and color chooser. Still, there are inevitable gaps and minor bugs buried in the code. If you plan to use these newer controls, you should test your site with old browser versions (like IE 9) before you go live.

GEM IN THE ROUGH

A Few Rogue Input Attributes

HTML5 recognizes a few more attributes that can control browser behavior when editing forms, but aren't used for validation. Not all of these attributes apply to all browsers. Still, they make for good experimenting:

- **spellcheck**. Some browsers try to help you avoid embarrassment by spell-checking the words you type in an input box. The obvious problem is that not all text is meant to be real words, and there are only so many red squiggles a web surfer can take before getting just a bit annoyed. Set `spellcheck` to `false` to recommend that the browser not spellcheck a field, or `true` to recommend that it does. (Browsers differ on their default spell-checking behavior, which is what you get if you don't set the `spellcheck` attribute at all.)

- **autocomplete**. Some browsers try to save you time by offering you recently typed-in values when you enter information in a field. This behavior isn't always appropriate—as the HTML5 specification points out, some types of information may be sensitive (like nuclear attack

codes) or may be relevant for only a short amount of time (like a one-time bank login code). In these cases, set `autocomplete` to `off` to recommend that the browser not offer autocomplete suggestions. You can also set `autocomplete` to `on` to recommend it for a particular field.

- **autocorrect** and **autocapitalize**. Use these attributes to control automatic correction and capitalization features on some mobile devices—namely, the version of Safari that runs on iPads and iPhones.

- **multiple**. Web designers have been adding the `multiple` attribute to the `<select>` element to create multiple-selection lists since time immemorial. But now you can add it to certain types of `<input>` elements, including ones that use the `file` type (for uploading files) and ones that use the `email` type (page 125). On a supporting browser, the user can then pick several files to upload at once, or stick multiple email addresses in one box.

▇ New Types of Input

One of the quirks of HTML forms is that one ingredient—the vaguely named `<input>` element—is used to create a variety of controls, from checkboxes to text boxes to buttons. The `type` attribute is the master switch that determines what each `<input>` element really is.

If a browser runs into an `<input>` element with a type that it doesn't recognize, the browser treats it like an ordinary text box. That means these three elements get exactly the same treatment in every browser:

```
<input type="text">
<input type="super-strange-wonky-input-type">
<input>
```

HTML5 uses this default to its benefit. It adds a few new data types to the `<input>` element, secure in the knowledge that browsers will treat them as ordinary text boxes if they don't recognize them. For example, if you need to create a text box that holds an email address, you can use the new input type `email`:

```
<label for="email">Email <em>*</em></label>
<input id="email" type="email"><br>
```

If you view this page in a browser that doesn't directly support the `email` input type (like Internet Explorer 9), you'll get an ordinary text box, which is perfectly acceptable. But browsers that support HTML5 forms are a bit smarter. Here's what they can do:

- **Offer editing conveniences.** For example, an intelligent browser or a handy JavaScript widget might give you a way to get an email from your address book and pop it into an email field.

- **Restrict potential errors.** For example, browsers can ignore letters when you type in a number text box. Or, they can reject invalid dates (or just force you to pick one from a mini calendar, which is easier *and* safer).

- **Perform validation.** Browsers can perform more sophisticated checks when you click a submit button. For example, an intelligent browser will spot an obviously incorrect email address in an email box and refuse to continue.

The HTML5 specification doesn't give browser makers any guidance on the first point. Browsers are free to manage the display and editing of different data types in any way that makes sense, and different browsers can add different little luxuries. For example, mobile browsers take advantage of this information to customize their virtual keyboards, hiding keys that don't apply (see Figure 4-8).

FIGURE 4-8

When people use a mobile device to fill out a form, they don't have the luxury of entering information on a full keyboard. The iPod makes life easier by customizing the virtual keyboard depending on the data type, so telephone numbers get a telephone-style numeric keypad (left), while email addresses get a dedicated @ button and a smaller space bar (right).

The error-prevention and error-checking features are more important. At a bare minimum, a browser that supports HTML5 web forms must prevent a form from being submitted if it contains data that breaks the data type rules. So if the browser doesn't prevent errors (according to the second point in the previous list), it must validate them when the user submits the data (that's the third point).

Unfortunately, not all current browsers live up to this requirement. Some recognize the new data types and provide some sort of editing niceties but no validation. Many understand one data type but not another. Mobile browsers are particularly problematic—they provide some editing conveniences but currently have none of the validation.

Table 4-3 lists the new data types and the browsers that support them completely—meaning that they prevent forms from being submitted when the data type rules are broken.

TABLE 4-3 *Browser compatibility for new input types*

DATA TYPE	IE	FIREFOX	CHROME	SAFARI	OPERA
email	10	4	10	5	10.6
url	10	4	10	5	10.6
search*	n/a	n/a	n/a	n/a	n/a
tel*	n/a	n/a	n/a	n/a	n/a

DATA TYPE	IE	FIREFOX	CHROME	SAFARI	OPERA
number	10	-	10	5	9
range	10	23	6	5	11
date, month, week, time	-	-	10	-	11
color	-	-	20	-	-**

* The HTML5 standard does not require validation for this data type.
** Opera supported the color input type in versions 11 and 12, but removed this support in more recent versions.

TIP Incidentally, you can test for data type support in Modernizr using the properties of the `Modernizr.inputtypes` object. For example, `Modernizr.inputtypes.range` returns `true` if the browser supports the `range` data type.

Email Addresses

Email addresses use the `email` type. Generally, a valid email address is a string of characters (with certain symbols not allowed). An email address must contain the @ symbol and a period, and there needs to be at least one character between them and two characters after the period. These are, more or less, the rules that govern email addresses. However, writing the right validation logic or regular expression for email addresses is a surprisingly subtle task that has tripped up many a well-intentioned developer. Which is why it's great to find web browsers that support the `email` data type and perform validation automatically (see Figure 4-9).

FIGURE 4-9

Firefox refuses to accept the space in this spurious email address.

Email boxes support the `multiple` attribute, which allows the field to hold multiple email addresses. However, these multiple email addresses still look like a single piece of text—you just separate each one with a comma.

NOTE Remember, blank values bypass validation. If you want to force someone to enter a valid email address, you need the `email` data type combined with the `required` attribute (page 112).

URLs

URLs use the url type. What constitutes a valid URL is still a matter of hot debate. But most browsers use a relatively lax validation algorithm. It requires a URL prefix (which could be legitimate, like *http://*, or made up, like *bonk://*), and accepts spaces and most special characters other than the colon (:).

Some browsers also show a drop-down list of URL suggestions, which is typically taken from the browser's history of recently visited pages.

Search Boxes

Search boxes use the search type. A search box is generally meant to contain keywords that are then used to perform some sort of search. It could be a search of the entire Web (as with Google, in Figure 4-1), a search of a single page, or a custom-built search routine that examines your own catalog of information. Either way, a search box looks and behaves almost exactly like a normal text box.

On some browsers, like Safari, search boxes are styled slightly differently, with rounded corners. Also, as soon as you start typing in a search box in Safari or Chrome, a small X icon appears on the right side that you can click to clear the box. Other than these very minor differences, search boxes *are* text boxes. The value is in the semantics. In other words, you use the search data type to make the purpose of the box clear to browsers and assistive software. They can then guide visitors to the right spot or offer other smart features—maybe, someday.

Telephone Numbers

Telephone numbers use the tel type. Telephone numbers come in a variety of patterns. Some use only numbers, while others incorporate spaces, dashes, plus signs, and parentheses. Perhaps it's because of these complications that the HTML5 standard doesn't ask browsers to perform any telephone number validation at all. However, it's hard to ignore the feeling that a tel field should at least reject letters (which it doesn't).

Right now, the only value in using the tel type is to get a customized virtual keyboard on mobile browsers, which focuses on numbers and leaves out letters.

Numbers

HTML5 defines two numeric data types. The number type is the one to use for ordinary numbers.

The number data type has obvious potential. Ordinary text boxes accept anything: numbers, letters, spaces, punctuation, and the symbols usually reserved for cartoon character swearing. For this reason, one of the most common validation tasks is to check that a given value is numeric and falls in the right range. But use the number data type, and the browser automatically ignores all non-numeric keystrokes. Here's an example:

```
<label for="age">Age<em>*</em></label>
<input id="age" type="number"><br>
```

Of course, there are plenty of numbers, and they aren't all appropriate for every kind of data. The markup shown above allows ages like 43,000 and -6. To fix this, you need to use the min and max attributes. Here's an example that limits ages to the reasonable range of 0 to 120:

```
<input id="age" type="number" min="0" max="120"><br>
```

Ordinarily, the number data type accepts only whole numbers, so a fractional age like 30.5 isn't accepted. (In fact, some browsers won't even let you type the decimal point.) However, you can change this too by setting the step attribute, which indicates the acceptable intervals for the number. For example, a minimum value of 0 and a step of 0.1 means you can use values like 0, 0.1, 0.2, and 0.3. Try to submit a form with 0.15, however, and you'll get the familiar pop-up error message. The default step is 1.

```
<label for="weight">Weight (in pounds)</label>
<input id="weight" type="number" min="50" max="1000"
step="0.1"value="160"><br>
```

The step attribute also affects how the spin buttons work in the number box, as shown in Figure 4-10.

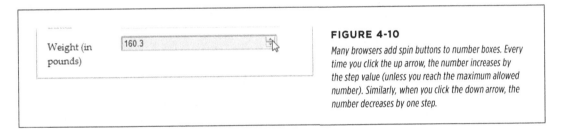

FIGURE 4-10

Many browsers add spin buttons to number boxes. Every time you click the up arrow, the number increases by the step value (unless you reach the maximum allowed number). Similarly, when you click the down arrow, the number decreases by one step.

Sliders

The range type is HTML5's other numeric data type. Like the number type, it can represent whole numbers or fractional values. It also supports the same attributes for setting the range of allowed values (min and max). Here's an example:

```
<label for="weight">Weight (in pounds)</label>
<input id="weight" type="range" min="50" max="1000" value="160"><br>
```

The difference is the way the range type presents its information. Instead of asking you to type the value you want in a text box, intelligent browsers show a slider control (Figure 4-11).

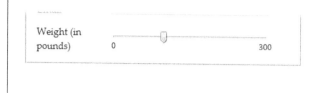

FIGURE 4-11

You've probably used range-like controls to set things like sound volume. They work well for information where there's a narrow range of values between a known minimum and a known maximum, and the specific numeric value isn't important (but the placement of that value relative to the minimum and maximum is).

To set a range type, you simply pull the tab to the position you want, somewhere between the minimum and maximum values at either end of the slider. Browsers that support the range type don't give any feedback about the specific value that's set. If you want that piece of information, you need to add a scrap of JavaScript that reacts when the slider changes (perhaps by handling the onChange event) and then displays the value nearby. Of course, you'd also want to check if the current browser supports the range type (using a tool like Modernizr). If the browser doesn't support the range type, there's no need to take any extra steps, because the value will show up in an ordinary text box.

Dates and Times

HTML5 defines several date-related types. Browsers that understand the date types can provide handy drop-down calendars for people to pick from. Not only does this clear away confusion about the right way to format the date, but it also prevents people from accidentally (or deliberately) picking a date that doesn't exist. And smart browsers can go even further—for example, adding integration with a personal calendar.

Right now, the date types are poorly supported, despite their obvious usefulness. Chrome and Opera are the only browsers that provide drop-down calendars (see Figure 4-12). Other browsers ignore date data types and show ordinary, unvalidated text boxes instead.

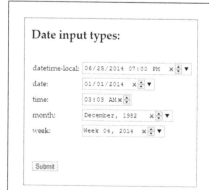
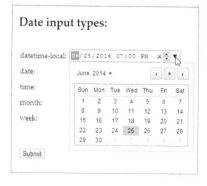

FIGURE 4-12

The <input> boxes look slightly different when storing date and time information (left). But the real convenience that supporting browsers provide is the drop-down calendar that lets you set these values with a proper date, and no formatting headaches (right).

TIP If you decide to use one of the date types, consider using a polyfill like HTML5Forms library (page 121) for older browsers. That's because it's easy for people on non-supporting browsers to enter dates in the wrong format, and it's tedious for you to validate date data and provide the appropriate guidance. (That's also why custom JavaScript date controls already exist—and why they're all over the Web.)

Table 4-4 explains the six date formats.

TABLE 4-4 *Date data types*

DATE TYPE	DESCRIPTION	EXAMPLE
date	A date in the format *YYYY-MM-DD*.	January 25, 2014: *2014-01-25*
time	A 24-hour time with an optional seconds portion, in the format *HH:mm:ss.ss*.	2:35 p.m. (and 50.2 seconds): *14:35* or *14:35:50.2*
datetime-local	A date and a time, separated by a capital T (so the format is *YYYY-MM-DDTHH:mm:ss*).	January 25, 2014, 2:35 p.m: *2014-01-15T14:35*
datetime	A date and a time, like the datetime-local data type, but with a time-zone offset. This uses the same format (*YYYY-MM-DD HH:mm:ss-HH:mm*) as the `<time>` element you considered on page 78. However, the datetime format is not supported reliably in any browser and may be removed in the future, so use datetime-local instead.	January 25, 2014, 2:35 p.m., in New York: *2014-01-15 14:35-05:00*
month	A year and month number, in the format *YYYY-MM*.	First month in 2014: *2014-01*
week	A year and week number, in the format *YYYY-Www*. Note that there can be 52 or 53 weeks, depending on the year.	Second week in 2014: *2014-W02*

TIP Browsers that support the date types also support the min and max attributes with them. That means you can set maximum and minimum dates, as long as you use the right date format. So, to restrict a date field to dates in the year 2014, you would write `<input type="date" min="2014-01-01" max="2014-12-31">`.

Colors

Colors use the color data type. The color type is an interesting, albeit little-used, frill that lets a web page visitor pick a color from a drop-down color picker, which looks like what you might see in a desktop paint program. Currently, Chrome is the only browser to add one. Opera had one briefly, in versions 10 and 11, but removed it after deciding it was too experimental.

In browsers that don't support the color type, form-fillers will need to type a hexadecimal color code on their own (or you can use the Html5Forms library described on page 121).

New Elements

So far, you've learned how HTML5 extends forms with new validation features and how it gets smarter about data by adding more input types. These are the most practical and the most widely supported new features, but they aren't the end of the HTML5 forms story.

HTML5 also introduces a few entirely new elements to fill gaps and add features. Using these nifty new elements, you can add a drop-down list of suggestions, a progress bar, a toolbar, and more. The problem with new elements is that old browsers are guaranteed not to support them, and even new browsers are slow to wade in when the specification is still changing. As a result, these details include some of the *least* supported features covered in this chapter. You may want to see how they work, but you'll probably wait to use them, unless you're comfortable inching your way out even further into the world of browser quirks and incompatibilities.

Input Suggestions with <datalist>

The <datalist> element gives you a way to fuse a drop-down list of suggestions to an ordinary text box. It gives people filling out a form the convenience to pick an option from the list, or the freedom to type exactly what they want (see Figure 4-13).

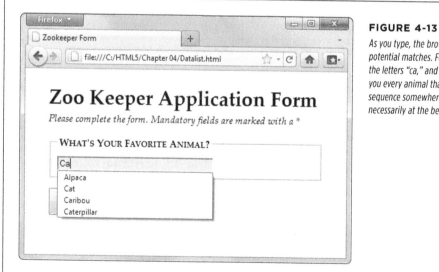

FIGURE 4-13

As you type, the browser shows you potential matches. For example, type in the letters "ca," and the browser shows you every animal that has that letter sequence somewhere in its name (and not necessarily at the beginning).

To use a datalist, you must first start with a standard text box. For example, imagine you have an ordinary <input> element like this:

```
<legend>What's Your Favorite Animal?</legend>
<input id="favoriteAnimal">
```

To add a drop-down list of suggestions, you need to create a datalist. Technically, you can place that <datalist> element anywhere you want. That's because the datalist can't display itself—instead, it simply provides data that an input box will use. However, it makes logical sense to place the <datalist> element just after or just before the <input> element that uses it. Here's an example:

```
<datalist id="animalChoices">
  <option label="Alpaca" value="alpaca">
  <option label="Zebra" value="zebra">
  <option label="Cat" value="cat">
  <option label="Caribou" value="caribou">
  <option label="Caterpillar" value="caterpillar">
  <option label="Anaconda" value="anaconda">
  <option label="Human" value="human">
  <option label="Elephant" value="elephant">
  <option label="Wildebeest" value="wildebeest">
  <option label="Pigeon" value="pigeon">
  <option label="Crab" value="crab">
</datalist>
```

The datalist uses <option> elements, just like the traditional <select> element. Each <option> element represents a separate suggestion that may be offered to the form filler. The label shows the text that appears in the text box, while the value tracks the text that will be sent back to the web server, if the user chooses that option. On its own, a datalist is invisible. To hook it up to a text box so it can start providing suggestions, you need to set the list attribute to match the ID of the corresponding datalist:

```
<input id="favoriteAnimal" list="animalChoices">
```

Current versions of Chrome, Internet Explorer, Firefox, and Opera support the datalist. They'll show the list of possible matches shown in Figure 4-13. But Safari, older versions of Internet Explorer (IE 9 and before), and mobile browsers will ignore the list attribute and the datalist markup, rendering your suggestions useless.

However, there's a clever fallback trick that makes other browsers behave properly. The trick is to put other content inside the datalist. This works because browsers that support the datalist pay attention to <option> elements only, and ignore all other content. Here's a revised example that exploits this behavior. (The bold parts are the markup that datalist-supporting browsers will ignore.)

```
<legend>What's Your Favorite Animal?</legend>
<datalist id="animalChoices">
  <span class="Label">Pick an option:</span>
```

```
<select id="favoriteAnimalPreset">
 <option label="Alpaca" value="alpaca">
  <option label="Zebra" value="zebra">
  <option label="Cat" value="cat">
  <option label="Caribou" value="caribou">
  <option label="Caterpillar" value="caterpillar">
  <option label="Anaconda" value="anaconda">
  <option label="Human" value="human">
  <option label="Elephant" value="elephant">
  <option label="Wildebeest" value="wildebeest">
  <option label="Pigeon" value="pigeon">
  <option label="Crab" value="crab">
</select>
<br>
<span class="Label">Or type it in:</span>
</datalist>
<input list="animalChoices" name="list">
```

If you remove the bold markup, you end up with the same markup you had before. That means browsers that recognize the datalist still show the single input box and the drop-down suggestion list, as shown in Figure 4-13. But on other browsers, the additional details wrap the datalist suggestion in a traditional select list, giving users the option of typing in what they want or picking it from a list (Figure 4-14).

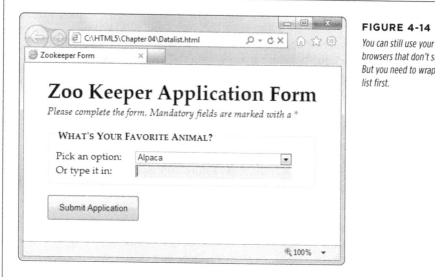

FIGURE 4-14

You can still use your suggestions on browsers that don't support the datalist. But you need to wrap them in a `<select>` list first.

This effect isn't completely seamless. When you receive the form data on the web server, you need to check for data from the list (in this example, that's favoriteAnimalPreset) and from the text box (that's favoriteAnimal). But other than this minor wrinkle, you've got a solid way to add new conveniences without leaving anyone behind.

NOTE When the datalist was first created, it had a feature that let it fetch suggestions from somewhere else—for example, it could call a web server, which could then pull a list of suggestions out of a database. This feature might still be added in a future version of the HTML standard, but for now it's possible only if you write JavaScript code to handle the fetching, with the help of the XMLHttpRequest object (page 377).

Progress Bars and Meters

The <progress> and <meter> element are two new graphical widgets that look similar but serve different purposes (Figure 4-15).

FIGURE 4-15

The <progress> and <meter> elements are nice visual conveniences, on the browsers that support them (left). Other browsers simply substitute the fallback content you've set (right).

The <progress> element indicates how far a task has progressed. It uses a gray background that's partially filled in with a pulsating green bar. The <progress> element resembles the progress bars you've probably seen before (for example, when the Windows operating system is copying files), although its exact appearance depends on the browser being used to view the page.

The <meter> element indicates a value within a known range. It looks similar to the <progress> element, but the green bar is a slightly different shade, and it doesn't pulse. Depending on the browser, the meter bar may change color when a value is classified as "too low" or "too high"—for example, in the latter case Chrome changes the bar from green to yellow. But the most important difference between <progress> and <meter> is the semantic meaning that the markup conveys.

NOTE Technically, the new <meter> and <progress> elements don't need to be in a form. In fact, they aren't even real controls (because they don't collect input from the web page visitor). However, the official HTML5 standard lumps them all together, because in some respects the <progress> and <meter> elements *feel* like form widgets, probably because they display bits of data in a graphical way.

The latest versions of all major browsers support the <progress> and <meter> elements. However, you'll run into trouble on older versions of Internet Explorer (IE 9 and before) and some mobile browsers. To guarantee support for everyone, you'll need to polyfill this feature with something like HTML5Forms (page 121).

Using the <progress> and <meter> elements is easy. First, consider the <progress> element. It takes a value attribute, which sets the percentage of progress (and thus the width of the green fill) as a fractional value from 0 to 1. For example, you could set the value to 0.25 to represent a task that's 25 percent complete:

```
<progress value="0.25"></progress>
```

Alternatively, you can use the max attribute to set an upper maximum and change the scale of the progress bar. For example, if max is 200, your value needs to fall between 0 and 200. If you set it to 50, you'd get the same 25 percent fill as in the previous example:

```
<progress value="50" max="200"></progress>
```

The scale is simply a matter of convenience. The web page viewer doesn't see the actual value in the progress bar.

NOTE The <progress> element is simply a way to display a nicely shaded progress bar. It doesn't actually *do* anything. For example, if you're using the progress bar to show the progress of a background task (say, using web workers, as demonstrated on page 414), it's up to you to write the JavaScript code that grabs hold of the <progress> element and changes its value.

Browsers that don't recognize the <progress> element simply ignore it. To deal with this problem, you can put some fallback content inside the <progress> element, like this:

```
<progress value="0.25">25%</progress>
```

Just remember that the fallback content won't appear in browsers that *do* support the <progress> element.

There's one other progress bar option. You can show an *indeterminate* progress bar, which indicates that a task is under way, but you aren't sure how close it is to completion. (Think of an indeterminate progress bar as a fancy "in progress" message.) An indeterminate progress bar looks like an empty gray bar but has a periodic green flash travel across it, from left to right. To create one, just leave out the value attribute, like this:

```
<progress>Task in progress ...</progress>
```

The `<meter>` element has a similar model, but it indicates any sort of measurement. The `<meter>` element is sometimes described as a *gauge*. Often, the specific meter value you use will correspond to something in the real world (for example, an amount of money, a number of days, an amount of weight, and so on). To control how the `<meter>` element displays this information, you're able to set both a minimum and maximum value (using the `min` and `max` attributes):

```
Your suitcase weighs: <meter min="5" max="70" value="28">28 pounds</meter>
```

Once again, the content inside the `<meter>` element is shown only if the browser doesn't know how to display a meter bar. Of course, sometimes it's important to show the specific number that the `<meter>` element uses. In this case, you'll need to add it to the page yourself, and you don't need the fallback content. The following example uses this approach. It provides all the information up front and adds an optional `<meter>` element on browsers that support it:

```
<p>Our goal is to raise $50,000 for SLF (Save the Lemmings Foundation).</p>
<p>So far we've raised $14,000. <meter max="50000" value="14000"></meter>
```

The `<meter>` element also has the smarts to indicate that certain values are too high or too low, while still displaying them properly. To do this, you use the `low` and `high` attributes. For example, a value that's above high (but still below max) is higher than it should be, but still allowed. Similarly, a value that's below low (but still above min) is lower than it should be:

```
Your suitcase weighs:
<meter min="5" max="100" high="70" value="79">79 pounds</meter>*
<p><small>* A surcharge applies to suitcases heavier than 70 pounds.
</small></p>
```

Browsers may or may not use this information. For example, Chrome shows a yellow bar for overly high values (like the one in the previous example). It doesn't do anything to indicate low values. Finally, you can flag a certain value as being an optimal value using the `optimum` attribute, but it won't change the way it shows up in today's browsers.

All in all, `<progress>` and `<scale>` are minor conveniences that will be useful once their browser support improves just a bit.

Toolbars and Menus with `<command>` and `<menu>`

Count this as the greatest feature that's not yet implemented. The idea is to have an element that represents actions the user can trigger (that's `<command>`) and another one to hold a group of them (that's `<menu>`). Depending on how you put it together and what styling tricks you use, the `<menu>` element could become anything from a toolbar docked to the side of the browser window to a pop-up menu that appears when you click somewhere on the page. But right now, no browser supports these elements, and so you'll have to wait to find out if they're really as cool as web developers hope.

■ An HTML Editor in a Web Page

As you learned in Chapter 1, HTML5 believes in paving cowpaths—in other words, taking the unstandardized features that developers use today and making them part of the official HTML5 standard. One of the single best examples is its inclusion of two odd attributes, named `contenteditable` and `designMode`, which let you turn an ordinary browser into a basic HTML editor.

These two attributes are nothing new. In fact, they were originally added to Internet Explorer 5 in the dark ages of the Internet. At the time, most developers dismissed them as more Windows-only extensions to the Web. But as the years wore on, more browsers began to copy IE's practical but quirky approach to rich HTML editing. Today, every desktop browser supports these attributes, even though they have never been part of an official standard.

When to Use HTML Editing

Before you try out rich HTML editing, it's worth asking what the feature is actually for. Despite its immediate cool factor, HTML editing is a specialized feature that won't appeal to everyone. It makes most sense if you need a quick-and-easy way for users to edit HTML content—for example, if you need to let them add blog posts, enter reviews, post classified ads, or compose messages to other users.

Even if you decide you need this sort of feature, the `contenteditable` and `designMode` attributes might not be your first choice. That's because they don't give you all the niceties of a real web design tool, like markup-changing commands, the ability to view and edit the HTML source, spell-checking, and so on. Using HTML's rich editing feature, you *can* build a much fancier editor, with a bit of work. But if you really need rich editing functionality, you may be happier using someone else's ready-made editor, which you can then plug into your own pages. Popular examples include TinyMCE (*www.tinymce.com*) and CKEditor (*http://ckeditor.com*).

Using contenteditable to Edit an Element

The first tool you have for HTML editing is the `contenteditable` attribute. Add it to any element and set its value to `true` to make the content of that element editable:

```
<div id="editableElement" contenteditable="true">You can edit this text, if
you'd like.</div>
```

You probably won't notice the difference at first. But if you load your page in a browser and click inside that `<div>`, a text-editing cursor (called a *caret*) will appear (Figure 4-16).

In this example, the editable `<div>` contains nothing but text. However, you could just as easily put other elements inside. In fact, this `<div>` element could wrap your entire page, making the whole thing editable. Similarly, you could use `contenteditable` on multiple elements to make several sections of a page editable.

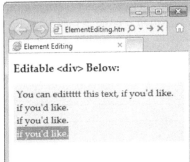

FIGURE 4-16

When you click in an edit-able region, you can move around using the arrow keys, delete text, and insert new content (left). You can also select text with the Shift key and then copy, cut, and paste it (right). It's a bit like typing in a word processor, only you won't be able to escape the confines of the <div> to get to the rest of the page.

TIP Some browsers support a few built-in commands. For example, you can get bold, italic, and underline formatting in IE using the shortcut keys Ctrl+B, Ctrl+I, and Ctrl+U. Similarly, you can reverse your last action in Firefox by pressing Ctrl+Z, and you can use all of these shortcuts in Chrome. To learn more about these editing commands and how you can create a custom toolbar that triggers them, see Opera's two-part article series at *http://tinyurl.com/htmlEdit1* and *http://tinyurl.com/htmlEdit2*.)

Usually, you won't set contenteditable in your markup. Instead, you'll turn it on using a bit of JavaScript, and you'll turn it off when you want to finish editing. Here are two functions that do exactly that:

```
function startEdit() {
  // Make the element editable.
  var element = document.getElementById("editableElement");
  element.contentEditable = true;
}

function stopEdit() {
  // Return the element to normal.
  var element = document.getElementById("editableElement");
  element.contentEditable = false;

  // Show the markup in a message box.
  alert("Your edited content: " + element.innerHTML);
}
```

And here are two buttons that use them:

```
<button onclick="startEdit()">Start Editing</button>
<button onclick="stopEdit()">Stop Editing</button>
```

Just make sure you don't place the buttons in the editable region of your page, because when a page is being edited, its elements stop firing events and won't trigger your code.

Figure 4-17 shows the result after the element has been edited and some formatting has been applied (courtesy of the Ctrl+B shortcut command).

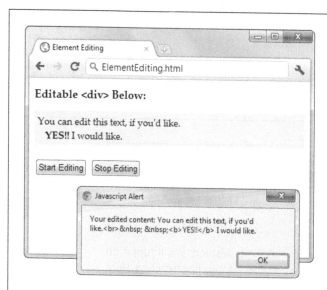

FIGURE 4-17

This proves it—editing an element really does change the in-memory content of the page. In this example, the new content is simply shown in a message box. However, a more typical page would send this data to a web server, probably using the XMLHttpRequest object described on page 377.

NOTE There are subtle differences in the way rich HTML editing works in different browsers. For example, pressing Ctrl+B in Chrome adds a <b> element, while pressing it in IE adds the <strong> element. Similar variations occur when you hit the Enter key to add a new line or Backspace to delete a tag. One of the reasons that it makes sense for HTML5 to standardize the rich HTML editing feature is the ability to enforce better consistency.

Using designMode to Edit a Page

The designMode property is similar to contenteditable, except it allows you to edit an entire web page. This may seem like a bit of a problem—after all, if the whole page is editable, how will the user click buttons and control the editing process? The solution is to put the editable document inside an <iframe> element, which then acts as a super-powered editing box (Figure 4-18).

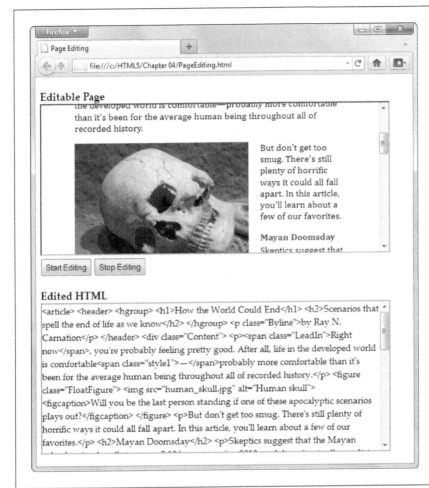

FIGURE 4-18

This page contains two boxes. The first is an `<iframe>` that shows the apocalypse page example from Chapter 2. The second is an ordinary `<div>` that shows the HTML markup of the page after it's been edited. The two buttons at the top of the page control the show, switching the `<iframe>` into design mode when the user is ready to work.

The markup in this page is refreshingly simple. Here are the complete contents of the `<body>` element in the page:

```
<h1>Editable Page</h1>
<iframe id="pageEditor" src="ApocalypsePage_Revised.html"></iframe>
<div>
  <button onclick="startEdit()">Start Editing</button>
  <button onclick="stopEdit()">Stop Editing</button>
</div>

<h1>Edited HTML</h1>
<div id="editedHTML"></div>
```

As you can see, this example relies on the startEdit() and stopEdit() methods, much like the previous example. However, the code is tweaked so that it sets the designMode attribute rather than the contenteditable attribute:

```
function startEdit() {
  // Turn on design mode in the <iframe>.
  var editor = document.getElementById("pageEditor");
  editor.contentWindow.document.designMode = "on";
}

function stopEdit() {
  // Turn off design mode in the <iframe>.
  var editor = document.getElementById("pageEditor");
  editor.contentWindow.document.designMode = "off";

  // Display the edited HTML (just to prove it's there).
  var htmlDisplay = document.getElementById("editedHTML");
  htmlDisplay.textContent =   editor.contentWindow.document.body.innerHTML;
}
```

This example gives you a better idea of the scope of the rich editing feature. For example, click on a picture and you'll see how the browser lets you manipulate it. You can resize it, drag it to a new place, or delete it completely with a single click of the Delete button. You'll have similar power over form controls, if they're in the page you're editing.

Of course, there's still a significant gap you'll need to cross if you want to turn this example into something practical. First, you'll probably want to add better editing controls. Once again, the helpful folks at Opera have your back if you're ready to make a deeper exploration into the command model, which is beyond the scope of this chapter (see *http://tinyurl.com/htmlEdit1* and *http://tinyurl.com/htmlEdit2*). Second, you'll need to do something useful with your edited markup, like sending it to your web server via XMLHttpRequest (page 377).

There's one more caveat to note. If you run this example locally from your hard drive, it won't work in all browsers. (Internet Explorer and Chrome run into security restrictions, while Firefox sails ahead without a problem.) To avoid the problem, you can run it from the try-out site at *http://prosetech.com/html5*.

Video, Graphics, and Glitz

CHAPTER 5:
Audio and Video

CHAPTER 6:
Fancy Fonts and Effects with CSS3

CHAPTER 7:
Responsive Web Design with CSS3

CHAPTER 8:
Basic Drawing with the Canvas

CHAPTER 9:
Advanced Canvas: Interactivity and Animation

Audio and Video

There was a time when the Internet was primarily a way to share academic research. Then things changed and the Web grew into a news and commerce powerhouse. Today the Internet's state-of-the-art networking technology is used less for physics calculations and more for spreading viral videos of piano-playing kittens across the planet. And network colossus Cisco reports that the trend isn't slowing down, estimating that a staggering *80 percent* of all Internet traffic will be video by 2017.

Amazingly, this monumental change happened despite the fact that—up until now— the HTML language had no built-in support for video or audio. Instead, Web surfers of the recent past relied on the Flash plug-in, which worked for most people, most of the time. But Flash has a few key gaps, including the fact that Apple devices (like iPhones and iPads) refuse to support it.

HTML5 solves these problems by adding the `<audio>` and `<video>` elements that HTML has been missing all these years. However, the transition to HTML5 audio and video has been far from seamless. Browser makers spent a few years locked in a heated name-calling, finger-pointing format war. The good news today is that much of the dust has settled, and HTML5 audio and video have become good choices for even the most cautious web developer.

The Evolution of Web Video

Without HTML5, you have a couple of ways to add video to a web page. One old-fashioned approach is to shoehorn it into a page with the <embed> element. The browser then creates a video window that uses Windows Media Player, Apple QuickTime, or some other video player, and places it on the page.

The key problem with this technique is that it puts you in a desolate no-man's-land of browser support. You have no way to control playback, you may not be able to buffer the video to prevent long playback delays, and you have no way of knowing whether your video file will be playable at all on different browsers or operating systems.

The second approach is to use a browser plug-in—like Microsoft's relative newcomer, Silverlight, or the overwhelming favorite, Adobe Flash. Up until recently, Flash had the problem of browser support solved cold. After all, Flash video works everywhere the Flash plug-in is installed, and currently that's on more than 99 percent of Internet-connected computers. Flash also gives you nearly unlimited control over the way playback works. For example, you can use someone else's prebuilt Flash video player for convenience, or you can design your own and customize every last glowy button.

But the Flash approach isn't perfect. To get Flash video into a web page, you need to throw down some seriously ugly markup that uses the <object> and <embed> elements. You need to encode your video files appropriately, and you may also need to buy the high-priced Flash developer software and learn to use it, and the learning curve can be steep. But the worst problem is Apple's mobile devices—the iPhone and iPad. They refuse to tolerate Flash at all, slapping blank boxes over the web page regions that use it.

NOTE Plug-ins also have a reputation for occasional unreliability. That's because of the way they work. For example, when you visit a page that uses Flash, the browser lets the Flash plug-in take control of a rectangular box somewhere on the web page. Most of the time, this hands-off approach works well, but minor bugs or unusual system configurations can lead to unexpected interactions and glitches, like suddenly garbled video or pages that suck up huge amounts of computer memory and slow your web surfing down to a crawl.

Still, if you watch video on the Web today, and you aren't using an iPhone or iPad, odds are that it's wrapped in a Flash mini-application. If you're not sure, try right-clicking the video player. If the menu that pops up includes a command like "About Flash Player 11," then you know you're dealing with the ubiquitous Flash plug-in. And even when you move to HTML5, you'll probably still need a Flash-powered fallback for browsers that aren't quite there yet, like Internet Explorer 8.

NOTE YouTube provides a trial HTML5 video player at *www.youtube.com/html5*. Everywhere else, YouTube sticks exclusively with Flash. The exception is if you visit YouTube using an iPhone or iPad, in which case YouTube is smart enough to switch to properly supported HTML5 video automatically.

■ Introducing HTML5 Audio and Video

A simple idea underpins HTML5's audio and video support. Just as you can add images to a web page with the `<img>` element, you should be able to insert sound with an `<audio>` element and video with a `<video>` element. Logically enough, HTML5 adds both.

Turn Back Now If...

Unfortunately, some things are beyond HTML5's new audio and video capabilities. If you want to perform any of these tricks, you'll need to scramble back to Flash (at least for now):

- **Licensed content.** HTML5 video files don't use any sort of copy protection system. In fact, folks can download HTML5 videos as easily as downloading pictures—with a simple right-click of the mouse. That said, digital rights management features are currently under development and slated for inclusion in HTML 5.1.

- **Video or audio recording.** HTML5 has no way to stream audio or video from your computer to another computer. So if you want to build a web chat program that uses the microphones and webcams of your visitors, stick with Flash. The creators of HTML5 are experimenting with a `<device>` element that might serve the same purpose, but for now there's no HTML-only solution, in any browser.

- **Adaptive video streaming.** Advanced, video-heavy websites like YouTube need fine-grained control over video streaming and buffering. They need to provide videos in different resolutions, stream live events, and adjust the video quality to fit the bandwidth of the visitor's Internet connection. Until HTML5 can provide these features, video-sharing sites may add HTML5 support, but they won't completely switch from Flash.

- **Low-latency, high-performance audio.** Some applications need audio to start with no delay or they need to play multiple audio clips in perfect unison. Examples include a virtual synthesizer, music visualizer, or a real-time game with plenty of overlapping sound effects. And while browser makers are hard at work improving HTML5's audio performance, it still can't live up to these demands.

- **Dynamically created or edited audio.** What if you could not just play recorded audio, but also analyze audio information, modify it, or generate it in real time? New specifications, like the experimental Web Audio API (*http://tinyurl.com/web-audio-API*), are competing to add on these sorts of features to HTML5 audio, but they aren't here yet.

Making Some Noise with <audio>

Here's an example of the `<audio>` element at its absolute simplest:

```
<p>Hear us rock out with our new song,
<cite>Death to Rubber Duckies</cite>:</p>
<audio src="rubberduckies.mp3" controls></audio>
```

The src attribute provides the file name of the audio file you want to play. The controls attribute tells the browser to include a basic set of playback controls. Each browser has a slightly different version of these controls, but they always serve the same purpose—to let the user start and stop playback, jump to a new position, and change the volume (Figure 5-1).

NOTE The `<audio>` and `<video>` elements must have both a start and an end tag. You can't use empty element syntax, like `<audio />`.

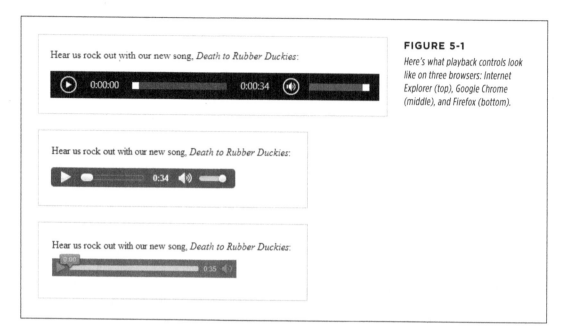

FIGURE 5-1

Here's what playback controls look like on three browsers: Internet Explorer (top), Google Chrome (middle), and Firefox (bottom).

Along with the basic `src` and `controls` attributes, the `<audio>` element supports several other attributes, which are detailed in the following sections.

Preloading Media Files

One useful attribute is `preload`, which tells the browser how it should download a media file. Set `preload` to `auto` to tell the browser to start downloading the whole file, so it's available when the user clicks the play button. Of course, this download process unfolds in the background, so your web page visitor can scroll around and read the page without waiting for the download to finish.

The `preload` attribute also supports two other values. You can use `metadata` to tell the browser to grab the first small chunk of data from the file, which is enough to determine some basic details (like the total length of the audio). Or, you can use `none`, which tells the browser to hold off completely. You might use one of these options to save bandwidth, for example, if you have a page stuffed full of `<audio>` elements and you don't expect the visitor to play more than a few of them.

```
<audio src="rubberduckies.mp3" controls preload="metadata"></audio>
```

When you use the `none` or `metadata` values, the browser downloads the audio file as soon as someone clicks the play button. Happily, browsers can play one chunk of audio while downloading the next without a hiccup unless you're working over a slow network connection.

If you don't set the `preload` attribute, browsers can do what they want, and different browsers make different assumptions. Most browsers assume `auto` as the default value, but Firefox uses `metadata`. Furthermore, it's important to note that the `preload` attribute isn't a rigid rule, but a recommendation you're giving to the browser—one that may be ignored depending on other factors. (And some slightly older browser builds don't pay attention to the `preload` attribute at all.)

> **NOTE** If you have a page stuffed with `<audio>` elements, the browser creates a separate strip of playback controls for each one. The web page visitor can listen to one audio file at a time or start them all playing at once.

Automatic Playback

Next up is the `autoplay` attribute, which tells the browser to start playback immediately once the page has finished loading. It looks like this:

```
<audio src="rubberduckies.mp3" controls autoplay></audio>
```

Without `autoplay`, it's up to the person viewing the page to click the play button.

You can use the `<audio>` element to play background music unobtrusively, or even to provide the sound effects for a browser-based game. To get background music, remove the `controls` attribute and add the `autoplay` attribute (or use JavaScript-powered playback, as described on page 160). But use this approach with caution, and remember that your page still needs some sort of audio shutoff switch.

> **NOTE** No one wants to face a page that blares music or sound effects but lacks a way to shut the sound off. If you decide to use the `<audio>` element without the `controls` attribute, you *must*, at a bare minimum, add a mute button that uses JavaScript to silence the audio.

Looping Playback

Finally, the `loop` attribute tells the browser to start over at the beginning when playback ends:

```
<audio src="rubberduckies.mp3" controls loop></audio>
```

In most browsers, playback is fluid enough that you can use this technique to create a seamless, looping soundtrack. The trick is to choose a loopable piece of audio that ends where it begins. You can find hundreds of free examples at *www.flashkit.com/loops*. (These loops were originally designed for Flash but can also be downloaded in MP3 and WAV versions.)

Getting the Big Picture with <video>

The `<video>` element pairs nicely with the `<audio>` element. Here's a straightforward example that puts it to use:

```
<p>A butterfly from my vacation in Switzerland!</p>
<video src="butterfly.mp4" controls></video>
```

Once again, the controls attribute gets the browser to generate a set of handy playback controls (Figure 5-2). In most browsers, these controls disappear when you click somewhere else on the page and return when you hover over the movie.

FIGURE 5-2

The <video> element could easily be mistaken for a Flash video window. But if you right-click the <video> element, you'll get a simpler menu that includes the option to save the video file to your computer. Depending on the browser, it may also include commands for changing the playback speed, looping the video, taking it full screen, and muting the sound.

The <video> element has the same src, controls, preload, autoplay, and loop attributes as the <audio> element. However, if you choose to enable automatic playback, you can make it less obnoxious by throwing in the muted attribute, which shuts off the sound on most browsers. The viewer can switch the audio back on by clicking the speaker icon, as usual.

The <video> element also adds three more attributes: height, width, and poster.

The height and width attributes set the size of the video window (in pixels). Here's an example that creates a video box that measures 400 x 300 pixels:

```
<video src="butterfly.mp4" controls width="400" height="300"></video>
```

This should match the natural size of the video itself, but you might choose to indicate these details explicitly so your layout doesn't get messed up before the video loads (or if the video fails to load altogether).

NOTE No matter which dimensions you use to size the video box, the video *frame* always keeps its proper proportions. For example, if you take a 400 x 300 pixel video and put it in a 800 x 450 pixel video box, you'll get the biggest video frame that fits in the box without stretching, which is 600 x 450 pixels. This leaves 100 pixels on each side of the video frame, which appear as blank space.

Finally, the poster attribute lets you supply an image that should be used in place of the video. Browsers use this picture in three situations: if the first frame of the video hasn't been downloaded yet, if you've set the preload attribute to none, or if the selected video file wasn't found.

```
<video src="butterfly.mp4" controls poster="swiss_alps.jpg"></video>
```

Although you've now learned everything there is to know about audio and video markup, there's a lot more you can do with some well-placed JavaScript. But before you can get any fancier with the <audio> and <video> elements, you need to face the headaches of audio and video codec support.

GEM IN THE ROUGH

Media Groups

The HTML5 standard specifies an unusual attribute named mediagroup that applies to both the <audio> element and the <video> element. You can use the mediagroup attribute to link multiple media files together, so their playback is synchronized. All you need to do is assign the same mediagroup name (which can be whatever you want) to each <audio> or <video> element:

```
<video src="shot12_cam1.mp4" controls
mediagroup="shot12"></video>
<video src="shot12_cam2.mp4" controls
mediagroup="shot12"></video>
```

Now if the viewer presses play in the first video window (for *shot12_cam1.mp4*), playback begins in both windows at once.

The mediagroup attribute might be a useful tool if you need to synchronize concurrent video files—for example,

recordings of a sporting event taken from different angles. You can also use it to synchronize audio and video, which is useful if you need to choose different audio tracks based on the visitor's language or accessibility needs. For example, an audio track for visually impaired users might add a voiceover that describes the action that's taking place. To accomplish this wizardry, you'd create a page with several hidden <audio> elements, give each one a different mediagroup name, and then add a bit of simple JavaScript that sets the mediagroup of your <video> element to match the mediagroup of the right <audio> element, based on the visitor's requirements.

Unfortunately, mediagroup isn't much use right now, because its browser support is still limited. Chrome and Opera understand it, but the latest versions of Internet Explorer and Firefox ignore it completely.

■ Understanding the HTML5 Media Formats

If the <video> and <audio> elements seem too good to be true, well, sometimes they are. The problem is that a media file format that works flawlessly in one browser can flummox another.

The examples you've just considered use two popular standards: MP3 audio and H.264 video. They're enough to keep most browsers happy. But use them on the Opera browser, and they won't work (Figure 5-3).

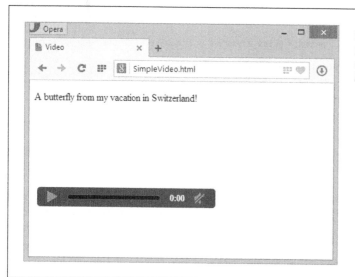

FIGURE 5-3

If you load a page that uses an H.264 video in Opera, the playback controls are disabled, and a blank space appears where the video should be.

Fortunately, you can solve this problem with a format fallback, as you'll see on page 155. But before you learn how to do that, you need to take a closer look at the range of audio and video formats on the Web today, and the current state of browser support.

Meet the Media Formats

The official HTML5 standard doesn't require support for any specific video or audio format. (Early versions did, but the recommendation was dropped after intense lobbying.) As a result, browser makers are free to choose the formats *they* want to support, despite the fact that they're congenitally unable to agree with one another.

Table 5-1 shows the standards that they're using right now.

TABLE 5-1 *Some of the audio and video standards that HTML5 browsers may support*

FORMAT	DESCRIPTION	COMMON FILE EXTENSION	MIME TYPE
MP3	The world's most popular audio format.	.mp3	audio/mp3
Ogg Vorbis	A free, open standard that offers high-quality, compressed audio comparable to MP3.	.ogg	audio/ogg
WAV	The original format for raw digital audio. Doesn't use compression, so files are staggeringly big and unsuitable for most web uses.	.wav	audio/wav

FORMAT	DESCRIPTION	COMMON FILE EXTENSION	MIME TYPE
H.264	The industry standard for video encoding, particularly when dealing with high-definition video. Used by consumer devices (like Blu-ray players and camcorders), web sharing websites (like YouTube and Vimeo), and web plug-ins (like Flash and Silverlight).	.mp4	video/mp4
Ogg Theora	A free, open standard for video by the creators of the Vorbis audio standard. Byte for byte, the quality and performance doesn't match H.264, although it's still good enough to satisfy most people.	.ogv	video/ogg
WebM	The newest video format, created when Google purchased VP8 and transformed it into a free standard. Critics argue that the quality isn't up to the level of H.264 video—yet—and that it may have unexpected links to other people's patents, which could lead to a storm of lawsuits in the future.	.webm	video/webm

Table 5-1 also lists the recommended file extensions your media files should use. To realize why this is important, you need to understand that there are actually three standards at play in a video file. First, and most obviously, is the *video codec*, which compresses the video into a stream of data (examples include H.264, Theora, and WebM). Second is the *audio codec*, which compresses one or more tracks of audio using a related standard. (For example, H.264 generally uses MP3, while Theora uses Vorbis.) Third is the *container format*, which packages everything together with some descriptive information and, optionally, other frills like still images and subtitles. Often, the file extension refers to the container format, so .mp4 signifies an MPEG-4 container, .ogv signifies an Ogg container, and so on.

Here's the tricky part: Most container formats support a range of different video and audio standards. For example, the popular Matroska container (.mkv) can hold video that's encoded with H.264 or Theora. To keep your head from exploding, Table 5-1 puts each video format with the container format that's most common and has the most reliable web support.

Table 5-1 also indicates the proper MIME type, which must be configured on your web server. If you use the wrong MIME type, browsers may stubbornly refuse to play a perfectly good media file. (If you're a little fuzzy on exactly what MIME types do and how to configure them, see the box on page 152.)

MIME Types and Why to Use Them

A *MIME type* (sometimes called a *content type*) is a piece of information that identifies the type of content in a web resource. For example, the MIME type of a web page is *text/html*.

Before a web server sends a resource to a browser, it sends the MIME type. For example, if a browser asks for the page SuperVideoPlayerPage.html, the web server sends the *text/html* MIME type, a few other pieces of information, and the actual file content. When the browser receives the MIME type, it knows what to do with the content that comes next. It doesn't need to try to make a guess based on a file name extension or some other sort of hackery.

For common file types—for example, HTML pages and images—you don't need to worry about MIME types, because every web server already handles them properly. But some web servers might not be configured with the MIME types for audio and video. That's a problem, because browsers will be thrown off course if the web server sends a media file with the wrong MIME type. Usually, they won't play the file at all.

To avoid this problem, make sure your web server is set up with the MIME types listed in Table 5-1, and use the corresponding file extensions for your audio and video files. (It's no use configuring the MIME type and then using the wrong file extension, because the web server needs to be able to pair the two together. For example, if you configure .mp4 files to use the MIME type *video/mp4*, but then you give your video file the extension *.mpFour*, the web server won't have a clue what you're trying to do.)

Configuring MIME types is an easy job, but the exact steps depend on your web hosting company (or your web server software, if you're hosting your site yourself). If your web hosting company uses the popular cPanel interface, then look for an icon named MIME Types and click it. You'll then see a page like the one shown in Figure 5-4. And if you're in any doubt, contact your web hosting company for help.

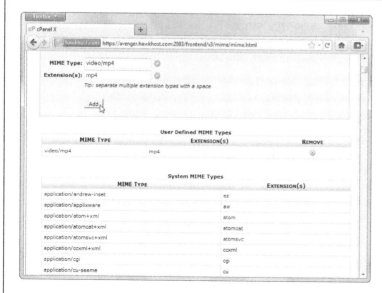

FIGURE 5-4

Here a new MIME type is being added to support H.264 video files. In many cases, you won't need to take this step, because your website will already be configured correctly.

Browser Support for Media Formats

The format headaches in HTML5 have a long history. The conflict is fueled by the different needs of browser makers. Small companies, like Mozilla (the creators of Firefox) and Opera (the creators of the Opera browser) don't want to pay stiff licensing costs for popular standards like MP3 audio and H.264 video. And it's hard to blame them—after all, they are giving away their work for free.

But bigger companies, like Microsoft and Apple, have their own reasonable-sounding excuses for shunning unlicensed standards. They complain that these standards won't perform as well (they currently lack hardware acceleration) and aren't as widespread (unlike H.264, which is used in camcorders, Blu-ray players, and a host of other devices). But the biggest problem is that these unlicensed standards may have obscure ties to someone else's intellectual property. If they do, and if big companies like Microsoft and Apple start using them, they open themselves up to pricey patent lawsuits that could drag on for years.

Fortunately, the situation is improving. In 2013, Firefox gave in and agreed to support MP3 and H.264. Google, despite threatening to remove support for H.264 in Chrome, has never taken that step and now seems unlikely to do so. Opera remains the last holdout on the desktop—for now. For the full details of browser media support, see Table 5-2 (for audio formats) and Table 5-3 (for video formats).

TABLE 5-2 *Browser support for HTML5 audio formats*

	IE	FIREFOX	CHROME	SAFARI	OPERA	SAFARI IOS	ANDROID
MP3	9	21	5	3.1	-	3	2.3
Ogg Vorbis	-	3.6	5	-	10.5	-	-
WAV	-	3.6	8	3.1	10.5	-	-

TABLE 5-3 *Browser support for HTML5 video formats*

	IE	FIREFOX	CHROME	SAFARI	OPERA	SAFARI IOS	ANDROID
H.264 Video	9	21	5	3.1	-	4*	2.3
Ogg Theora	-	3.5	5	-	10.5	-	-
WebM	-	4	6	-	10.6	-	2.3

* iOS 3.x supports video, but there are subtle video bugs hiding in older versions of the Safari browser. For example, if you set the poster attribute (page 149), you may find that the video becomes unplayable.

Mobile browsers have their own quirks. Some don't support features like autoplay and looping, because these features can drain batteries and use up valuable bandwidth. But even if you don't plan to use these features, mobile devices need special consideration to ensure good video playback performance and to minimize data usage. To make mobile-friendly videos, you should encode them with lower quality settings and, possibly, with a lower resolution.

> **TIP** As a general rule of thumb, if you want a video to be playable on a mobile device, you should encode it using the H.264 Baseline Profile (rather than High Profile). For iPhone and Android phones, use a size of 640 x 480 or smaller (and stick to 480 x 360 if you want to play it on a BlackBerry). Many encoding programs (see the box on page 156) have presets that let you prepare mobile-optimized video.

FREQUENTLY ASKED QUESTION

H.264 Licensing

I'm using H.264 for my videos. Do I have to pay licensing costs?

If you're using an H.264 decoder in your product (for example, you're creating a browser that can play H.264-encoded video), you definitely need to pay. But if you're a video provider, it's less clear cut.

First, the good news. If you're using H.264 to make free videos, you won't be asked to pay anything, ever. If you're creating videos that have a commercial purpose but aren't actually being sold (say, you're shooting a commercial or promoting yourself in an interview), you're also in the clear.

If you're *selling* H.264-encoded video content on your website, you may be on the hook to pay license fees to MPEG-LA, either

now or in the future. Right now, the key detail is the number of subscribers. If you have fewer than 100,000, there's no licensing cost, but if you have 100,000 to 250,000, you're expected to cough up $25,000 a year. This probably won't seem like much bank for a video-selling company of that size, and it may pale in comparison to other considerations, like the cost of professional encoding tools. However, these numbers could change when the licensing terms are revised in 2016. Big companies looking to make lots of money in web video might prefer to use an open, unlicensed video standard like Theora or WebM.

For the full licensing legalese on H.264, visit *http://tinyurl.com/h264-lic.*

Fallbacks: How to Please Every Browser

At this writing, an H.264 video file presented by the HTML5 <video> element works for over 80 percent of the people surfing the Web. This percentage is impressive, but it isn't good enough on its own. To create a video that *everyone* can see, you need the help of a fallback.

There are two types of fallbacks that web developers use with HTML5 video. The first is a *format fallback.* This mechanism, which is built into HTML5, lets you swap out one type of media file—say, an MP3 file—and replace it with a file in another format (for example, Ogg Vorbis). This type of fallback solves the Opera problem shown on page 150. However, it won't help when your page meets an old browser that doesn't support HTML5's media features, like Internet Explorer 8.

The second type of fallback is a *technology fallback.* If the browser that's processing your page doesn't support the <video> and <audio> element, your page can substitute a time-tested Flash player that does the job.

Conscientious web developers use *both* types of fallback. More time-constrained (or lazier) web developers sometimes omit the format fallback, in order to eliminate the work of re-encoding their video files. After all, the Opera browser (the lone desktop browser that doesn't support H.264) accounts for a mere 1 percent of worldwide browser use, and developers speculate that Opera may eventually be forced to add H.264 support. On the other hand, the Flash fallback is easier to implement, because it uses the same media file, and it fills in the support gap for a larger portion of browsers, like that dinosaur IE 8. So ignore the Flash fallback at your own peril.

The following sections explain both types of fallbacks.

Supporting Multiple Formats

The <audio> and <video> elements have a built-in format fallback system. To use it, you must remove the src attribute from the <video> or <audio> element, and replace it with a list of nested <source> elements inside. Here's an example with the <audio> element:

```
<audio controls>
  <source src="rubberduckies.mp3" type="audio/mp3">
  <source src="rubberduckies.ogg" type="audio/ogg">
</audio>
```

Here, the same <audio> element holds two <source> elements, each of which points to a separate audio file. The browser then chooses the first file it finds that has a format it supports. Firefox and Opera will grab *rubberduckies.ogg*. Internet Explorer, Safari, and Chrome will stick with *rubberduckies.mp3*. Unfortunately, it's up to you to encode your content in every alternate format you want to support—a process that wastes time, CPU power, and disk space.

In theory, a browser can determine whether or not it supports a file by downloading a chunk of it. But a better approach is to use the type attribute to supply the correct MIME type (see page 152). That way, the browser will attempt to download only a file it believes it can play. (To figure out the correct MIME type, consult Table 5-1.)

The same technique works for the <video> element. Here's an example that supplies the same video file twice, once encoded with H.264 and once with WebM, guaranteeing support for all HTML5-aware browsers:

```
<video controls width="700" height="400">
  <source src="beach.mp4" type="video/mp4">
  <source src="beach.webm" type="video/webm">
</video>
```

In this example, there's one new detail to note. When using multiple video formats, the H.264-encoded file should always come first. Otherwise, it won't work for old iPads running iOS 3.x. (The problem has since been fixed in iOS 4, but there's no disadvantage to keeping H.264 in the top spot.)

If you're really ambitious, you may opt to create a single video page that's meant for both desktop browsers and mobile devices. In this case, you not only need to worry about the H.264 and WebM video formats, but you also need to think about creating low-bandwidth versions of your video files that are suitable for devices that have less hardware power and use slower Internet connections. To make sure mobile devices get the lighter-weight video files while desktop browsers get the higher-quality ones, you need to write some crafty JavaScript or use *media queries*, as explained on page 231.

UP TO SPEED

Encoding Your Media

Now you know what combination of formats to use, but you don't necessarily know how to transform your media files into those formats. Don't despair, as there are plenty of tools. Some work on entire batches of files at once, some have a reputation for professional-grade quality (and a price tag to match), and some do their work on powerful web servers so you don't have to wait. The trick is picking through all the choices to get the encoder that works for you.

Here are some of your options:

- **Audio editors.** If you're looking to edit WAV files and save them in the MP3 or Vorbis formats, a basic audio editor can help out. Audacity (*http://audacity.sourceforge.net*) is a free editor for Mac and Windows that fits the bill, although you'll need to install the LAME MP3 encoder to get MP3 support (*http://lame1.buanzo.com.ar*). Goldwave (*www.goldwave.com*) is a similarly capable audio editor that's free to try, but sold for a nominal fee.

- **Miro Video Converter.** This free, open-source program runs on Windows and Mac OS X. It can take virtually any video file and convert it to WebM, Theora, or H.264. It also has presets that match the screen sizes and supported formats

for mobile devices, like iPads, iPhones, or Android phones. The only downside is that you can't tweak more advanced options to control how the encoding is done. To try it out, go to *www.mirovideoconverter.com*.

- **Firefogg.** This Firefox plug-in (available at *http://firefogg. org*) can create Theora or WebM video files, while giving you a few more options than Miro. It also runs right inside your web browser (although it does all its work locally, without involving a web server).

- **HandBrake.** This open-source, multi-platform program (available at *http://handbrake.fr*) converts a wide range of video formats into H.264 (and a couple of other modern formats).

- **Zencoder.** Here's an example of a professional media encoding service that you can integrate with your website. Zencoder (*http://zencoder.com*) pulls video files off your web server, encodes them in all the formats and bitrates you need, gives them the names you want, and places them in the spot they belong. A big player (say, a video sharing site) would pay Zencoder a sizable monthly fee.

Adding a Flash Fallback

The format fallback system has a key limitation: It works only on browsers that understand the <audio> and <video> elements (which is almost every browser in circulation today, except IE 8). To get your pages to work on non-HTML5 browsers, you need to add a Flash fallback.

To understand how the Flash fallback works, you first need to know that every web browser since the dawn of time deals with the tags it doesn't recognize in the same way—it ignores them. For example, if Internet Explorer 8 comes across the opening tag for the <video> element, it barrels merrily on, without bothering to check the src attribute. However, browsers don't ignore the *content* inside an unrecognized element, which is a crucial difference. It means if you have markup like this:

```
<video controls width="400" height="300">
  <source src="discoParty.mp4" type="video/mp4">
  <source src="discoParty.webm" type="video/webm">
  <p>We like disco dancing.</p>
</video>
```

Browsers that don't understand HTML5 will act as though they saw this:

```
<p>We like disco dancing.</p>
```

This fallback content provides a seamless way to deal with older browsers.

> **NOTE** Browsers that support HTML5 audio ignore the fallback section, even if they can't play the media file. For example, consider what happens if Opera finds a <video> element that uses an H.264 video file but doesn't support Theora. In this situation, the video player won't show anything at all.

So now that you know how to add fallback content, you need to decide what your fallback content should include. One example of bad fallback content is a text message (as in, "Your browser does not support HTML5 video, so please upgrade."). Website visitors consider this sort of comment tremendously impolite, and they're likely never to return when they see it.

The proper thing to include for fallback content is another working video window—in other words, whatever you'd use in an ordinary, non-HTML5 page. One possibility is a YouTube video window. If you use this approach, you need to meet YouTube's rules (make sure your video is less than 15 minutes and doesn't contain offensive or copyrighted content). You can then upload your video to YouTube in the best format you have on hand, and YouTube will re-encode the video into the formats it supports. To get started, head to *www.youtube.com/my_videos_upload*.

Another possibility is to use a Flash video player. (Or, if you're playing audio, a Flash audio player.) Happily, the world has plenty of Flash players. Many of them are free, at least for noncommercial uses. And best of all, most support H.264, a format you're probably already using for HTML5 video.

Here's an example that inserts the popular Flowplayer Flash (*http://flash.flowplayer.org*) into an HTML5 <video> element:

```
<video controls width="700" height="400">
  <source src="beach.mp4" type="video/mp4">
  <source src="beach.webm" type="video/webm">

  <object id="flowplayer" width="700" height="400"
   data="flowplayer-3.2.16.swf"
   type="application/x-shockwave-flash">
    <param name="movie" value="flowplayer-3.2.16.swf">
    <param name="flashvars" value='config={"clip":"beach.mp4"}'>
  </object>
</video>
```

Here, the bold part is a parameter that the browser passes to the Flowplayer Flash, with the file name of the video file. As you can see, even though this example has three possible outcomes (HTML5 video with H.264, HTML5 video with WebM, or Flash video with H.264), it needs only *two* video files, which saves on the encoding work. Figure 5-5 shows the result in action.

Of course, some people won't have Flash or a browser that supports HTML5. You can offer them another fallback, such as a link to download the video file and open it in an external program. You place that fallback after the Flash content, but still inside the <object> element, like this:

```
<video controls width="700" height="400">
  <source src="beach.mp4" type="video/mp4">
  <source src="beach.webm" type="video/webm">

  <object id="flowplayer" width="700" height="400"
   data="http://releases.flowplayer.org/swf/flowplayer-3.2.16.swf"
   type="application/x-shockwave-flash">
    <param name="movie" value="beach.mp4">
    <img src="beach_thumbnail.jpg" alt="A lazy day at the beach">
    <p>Your browser does not support HTML5 video or Flash.</p>
    <p>You can download the video in <a href="beach.mp4">MP4 H.264</a>
    or <a href="beach.webm">WebM</a> format.</p>
  </object>
</video>
```

FIGURE 5-5

One video, served three ways: in IE 9 (top), in Firefox (middle), and in IE 7, with Flash (bottom).

Interestingly, there's another way to implement a Flash fallback. The examples you've seen so far use HTML5 with a Flash fallback, which gives everybody HTML5 video (or audio) except for people with older browsers, who get Flash. However, you can invert this approach and use Flash first, with an HTML5 fallback. This gives everybody Flash, except for those who don't have it installed. This strategy makes sense if you're already showing video content on your website with a mature Flash video player, but you want to reach out to iPad and iPhone users. You might also choose this approach if your media requirements go beyond what HTML5 currently supports (as detailed in the box on page 145).

If you want a Flash player with an HTML fallback, you simply need to invert the previous example. Start with the <object> element, and nestle the <video> element inside, just before the closing </object> tag. Place the fallback content just after the last <source> element, like this:

```
<object id="flowplayer" width="700" height="400"
 data="http://releases.flowplayer.org/swf/flowplayer-3.2.16.swf"
 type="application/x-shockwave-flash">
  <param name="movie" value="butterfly.mp4">

  <video controls width="700" height="400">
    <source src="beach.mp4" type="video/mp4">
    <source src="beach.webm" type="video/webm">

    <img src="beach_thumbnail.jpg" alt="A lazy day at the beach">
    <p>Your browser does not support HTML5 video or Flash.</p>
    <p>You can download the video in <a href="beach.mp4">MP4 H.264</a>
    or <a href="beach.webm">WebM</a> format.</p>
  </video>
</object>
```

Incidentally, there are a number of JavaScript players that support HTML5 directly and have a built-in Flash fallback. For example, Flowplayer provides another version called Flowplayer HTML5 (get it at *http://flowplayer.org*), which uses the HTML5 <video> element if the browser supports it and performs a Flash fallback automatically if needed. The advantage is that this approach simplifies your markup, because one ingredient (the JavaScript-powered media player) handles everything. The disadvantage is that it takes you further away from a pure HTML5 solution, which is what you'll want to use one day soon when HTML5-loving browsers are ubiquitous.

■ Controlling Your Player with JavaScript

So far, you've covered some heavy ground. You've learned how to take the new <audio> and <video> elements and turn them into a reasonably supported solution that works on *more* web pages than today's Flash-based players. Not bad for a bleeding-edge technology.

That's about the most you can do with the <audio> and <video> elements if you stick to markup only. But both elements have an extensive JavaScript object model, which lets you control playback with code. In fact, you can even adjust some details—like playback speed—that aren't available in the browser's standard audio and video players.

In the following sections, you'll explore the JavaScript support by considering two practical examples. First, you'll add sound effects to a game. Next, you'll create a custom video player. And finally, you'll consider the solutions that other people have developed using this potent mix of HTML5 and JavaScript, including supercharged, skinnable players and accessible captioning.

Adding Sound Effects

The <audio> element doesn't just let web visitors play songs and voice recordings. It's also a useful tool for playing sound effects, whenever you need them. This makes it particularly useful if you need to add music and sound effects to a game.

Figure 5-6 shows a very simple example, with an interactive ball-dropping animation. You'll see the code that makes this example work when you consider the <canvas> element in Chapter 8. But for now, the only important detail is how you can add a suitable sonic backdrop.

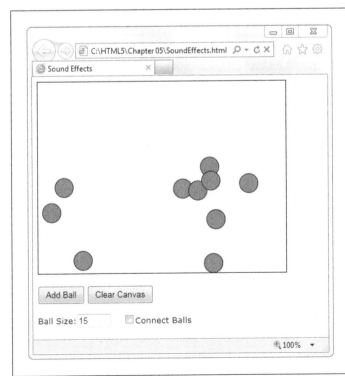

FIGURE 5-6

This web page runs a simple animation on a canvas. The visitor can click a button to add a new ball (which then falls down and bounces around the drawing surface). Or, the visitor can click a ball to send it bouncing in a new direction.

This example combines a background music track with sound effects. The background music track is the easiest part. To create it, you start by adding an invisible <audio> element to your page, like this:

```
<audio id="backgroundMusic" loop>
  <source src="TheOwlNamedOrion.mp3" type="audio/mp3">
  <source src="TheOwlNamedOrion.ogg" type="audio/ogg">
</audio>
```

This audio player doesn't include the autoplay or controls attributes, so initially it's silent and invisible. It does use the loop attribute, so once it starts playing it will repeat the music track endlessly. To control playback, you need to use two methods of the audio (or video) object: play() and pause(). Confusingly, there's no stop method—for that, you need to pause the video and then reset the currentTime property to 0, which represents the beginning of the file.

With this in mind, it's quite easy to start playback on the background audio when the first ball is created:

```
var audioElement = document.getElementById("backgroundMusic");
audioElement.play();
```

And just as easy to stop playback when the canvas is cleared:

```
var audioElement = document.getElementById("backgroundMusic");
audioElement.pause();
audioElement.currentTime = 0;
```

As you learned earlier, there's no limit on the amount of audio you can play at once. So while the background audio is playing its tune, you can concentrate on the more interesting challenge of adding sound effects.

In this example, a "boing" sound effect is played every time a ball ricochets against the ground or a wall. To keep things interesting, several slightly different boing sounds are used. This is a stand-in for a more realistic game, which would probably incorporate a dozen or more sounds.

There are several ways to implement this design, but not all of them are practical. The first option is to add a single new <audio> element to play sound effects. Then, every time a collision happens, you can load a different audio file into that element (by setting the src property) and play it. This approach hits two obstacles. First, a single <audio> element can play only a single sound at once, so if more than one ball hits the ground in quick succession, you need to either ignore the second, overlapping sound, or interrupt the first sound to start the second one. The other problem is that setting the src property forces the browser to request the audio file. And while some browsers will do this quickly (if the audio file is already in the cache), Internet Explorer doesn't. The result is laggy audio—in other words, a boing that happens half a second after the actual collision.

A better approach is to use a group of <audio> elements, one for each sound. Here's an example:

```
<audio id="audio1">
  <source src="boing1.mp3" type="audio/mp3">
  <source src="boing1.wav" type="audio/wav">
</audio>
<audio id="audio2">
  <source src="boing2.mp3" type="audio/mp3">
  <source src="boing2.wav" type="audio/wav">
</audio>
<audio id="audio3">
  <source src="boing3.mp3" type="audio/mp3">
  <source src="boing3.wav" type="audio/wav">
</audio>
```

NOTE Even though these three <audio> elements use different audio files, that isn't a requirement. For example, if you wanted to have the same boing sound effect but allow overlapping audio, you'd still use three audio players.

Whenever a collision happens, the JavaScript code calls a custom function named boing(). That method grabs the next <audio> element in the sequence and plays it.

Here's the code that makes it happen:

```
// Keep track of the number of <audio> elements.
var audioElementCount = 3;

// Keep track of the <audio> element that's next in line for playback.
var audioElementIndex = 1;

function boing() {
  // Get the <audio> element that's next in the rotation.
  var audioElementName = "audio" + audioElementIndex;
  var audio = document.getElementById(audioElementName);

  // Play the sound effect.
  audio.currentTime = 0;
  audio.play();

  // Move the counter to the next <audio> element.
  if (audioElementIndex == audioElementCount) {
    audioElementIndex = 1;
  }
  else {
    audioElementIndex += 1;
  }
}
```

TIP To get an idea of the noise this page causes with its background music and sound effects, visit the try-out
site at *http://prosetech.com/html5*.

This example works well, but what if you want to have a much larger range of audio
effects? The easiest choice is to create a hidden <audio> element for each one. If
that's impractical, you can dynamically set the src property of an existing <audio>
element. Or, you can create a new <audio> element on the fly, like this:

```
var audio = document.createElement("audio");
audio.src = "newsound.mp3";
```

Or use this shortcut:

```
var audio = new Audio("newsound.mp3");
```

However, there are two potential problems with both approaches. First, you need
to set the source well before you play the audio. Otherwise, playback will be no-
ticeably delayed, particularly on Internet Explorer. Second, you need to know what
the supported audio formats are, so you can set the right file type. This requires
using the clunky canPlayType() method. You pass in an audio or video MIME type,
and canPlayType() tells you if the browser can play that format—sort of. It actually
returns a blank string if it can't, the word "probably" if it thinks it can, and the word
"maybe" if it hopes it might but just can't make any promises. This rather embar-
rassing situation exists because supported container formats can use unsupported
codecs, and supported codecs can still use unsupported encoding settings.

Most developers settle on code like this, which attempts playback if canPlayType()
gives any answer other than a blank string:

```
if (audio.canPlayType("audio/ogg")) {
  audio.src = "newsound.ogg";
}
else if (audio.canPlayType("audio/mp3")) {
  audio.src = "newsound.mp3";
}
```

Creating a Custom Video Player

One of the most common reasons to delve into JavaScript programming with the
<audio> and <video> elements is to build your own player. The basic idea is pure
simplicity—remove the controls attribute, so that all you have is a video window,
and add your own widgets underneath. Finally, add the JavaScript code that makes
these new controls work. Figure 5-7 shows an example.

Every video player needs a basic complement of playback buttons. Figure 5-7 uses
plain-Jane buttons:

```
<button onclick="play()">Play</button>
<button onclick="pause()">Pause</button>
<button onclick="stop()">Stop</button>
```

FIGURE 5-7

Making a custom HTML5 video player is easy (making it pretty is not). This example includes the standard playback buttons, a playback progress bar, and a few extra buttons that show off what JavaScript can do with the <video> element.

These buttons trigger the following super-simple functions:

```
function play() {
  video.play();
}

function pause() {
  video.pause();
}
function stop() {
  video.pause();
  video.currentTime = 0;
}
```

The other three playback buttons are more exotic. They adjust the playbackRate property to change the speed. For example, a playbackRate of 2 plays video at twice the normal speed, but with pitch correction so the audio sounds normal, just accelerated. This is a great feature for getting through a slow training video in a hurry. Similarly, a playbackRate of 0.5 plays video at half normal speed, and a playbackRate of -1 should play video at normal speed, backward, but browsers have trouble smoothly implementing this behavior.

```
function speedUp() {
  video.play();
  video.playbackRate = 2;
}

function slowDown() {
  video.play();
  video.playbackRate = 0.5;
}

function normalSpeed() {
  video.play();
  video.playbackRate = 1;
}
```

Creating the playback progress bar is a bit more interesting. From a markup point of view, it's built out of two <div> elements, one inside the other:

```
<div id="durationBar">
  <div id="positionBar"><span id="displayStatus">Idle.</span></div>
</div>
```

> **TIP** The playback progress bar is an example where the <progress> element (page 133) would make perfect sense. However, the <progress> element still has limited support—far less than the HTML5 video feature—so this example builds something that looks similar using two <div> elements.

The outer <div> element (named durationBar) draws the solid black border, which stretches over the entire bar and represents the full duration of the video. The inner <div> element (named positionBar) indicates the current playback position, by filling in a portion of the black bar in blue. Finally, a <span> element inside the inner <div> holds the status text, which shows the current position (in seconds) during playback.

Here are the style sheet rules that size and paint the two bars:

```
#durationBar {
  border: solid 1px black;
  width: 100%;
  margin-bottom: 5px;
}

#positionBar {
  height: 30px;
  color: white;
  font-weight: bold;
```

```
    background: steelblue;
    text-align: center;
}
```

When video playback is under way, the `<video>` element triggers the `onTimeUpdate` event continuously. You can react to this event to update the playback bar:

```
<video id="videoPlayer" ontimeupdate="progressUpdate()">
  <source src="butterfly.mp4" type="video/mp4">
  <source src="butterfly.webm" type="video/webm">
</video>
```

Here, the code gets the current positioning in the video (from the `currentTime` property), divides that into the total time (from the `duration` property), and turns that into a percentage that sizes the `<div>` element named `positionBar`:

```
function progressUpdate() {
  // Resizing the blue positionBar, from 0 to 100%.
  var positionBar = document.getElementById("positionBar");
  positionBar.style.width = (video.currentTime / video.duration * 100) + "%";

  // Display the number of seconds, using two decimal places.
  displayStatus.innerHTML = (Math.round(video.currentTime*100)/100) + " sec";
}
```

TIP To get fancier, you could superimpose a download progress bar that shows how much current content has been downloaded and buffered so far. Browsers already add this feature to their built-in players. To add it to your own player, you need to handle the `onProgress` event and work with the `seekable` property. For more information about the many properties, methods, and events provided by the `<video>` element, check out Microsoft's reference at *http://tinyurl.com/video-obj-js*.

JavaScript Media Players

If you're truly independent-minded, you can create your own audio or video player from scratch. But it's not a small project, especially if you want nifty features, like an interactive playlist. And if you don't have a small art department to back you up, there's a distinct possibility that your final product will look just a little bit ugly.

Happily, there's a better option for web authors in search of the perfect HTML5 player. Instead of building one yourself, you can pick up a free, JavaScript-customized media player from the Web. Two solid choices are VideoJS (*http://videojs.com*) and, for jQuery fans, jPlayer (*www.jplayer.org*). Both of these players are lightweight, easy to use, and *skinnable*, which means you can change the look of the playback controls by plugging in a different style sheet.

Most JavaScript media players (including VideoJS and jPlayer) have built-in Flash fallbacks, which saves you from needing to find a separate Flash player. And jPlayer includes its own handy playlist feature, which lets you queue up a whole list of audio and video files (Figure 5-8).

FIGURE 5-8

Using jPlayer's playlist feature, you can offer a series of audio or video files. The user can then play them all in sequence or click to play a specific one. The example playlist here has three videos.

To use VideoJS, you start by downloading the JavaScript files from the VideoJS website. Then you add the JavaScript reference and style sheet reference shown here:

```
<!DOCTYPE html>
<html>
<head>
  <meta charset="utf-8">
  <title>...</title>
  <script src="video.js"></script>
  <link rel="stylesheet" href="video-js.css">
</head>
  ...
```

Then you use the exact same <video> element you'd normally use, with the multiple source elements and Flash fallback. (The VideoJS player sample code has the Flowplayer already slotted in for the Flash fallback, but you can remove it and use a different Flash player instead.) In fact, the only difference between a normal HTML5 video page and one that uses VideoJS is the fact that you must use a special <div> element to wrap the video player, as shown here:

```
<div class="video-js-box">
  <video class="video-js" width="640" height="264" controls ...>
    ...
  </video>
</div>
```

It's nice to see that even when extending HTML5, life can stay pretty simple.

■ Video Captions

As you've seen in previous chapters, the creators of HTML5 were often thinking about web accessibility—in other words, how people with disabilities can use rich web pages easily and efficiently.

Adding accessibility information to images is easy enough. You simply need to bolt on some suitably descriptive text with the alt attribute. But what's the equivalent to alt text for a video stream? The consensus is to use *subtitles*, text captions that pop up at the right point during playback. Subtitles can be similar to television closed-captioning, by simply transcribing dialogue, or they can add descriptive and supplementary information of their own. The point is that they give people an avenue to follow the video even if they have hearing difficulties (or if they just don't want to switch on their computer speakers to play the *Iron Man 4* movie trailer for the entire office).

Figure 5-9 shows an example of a captioned video.

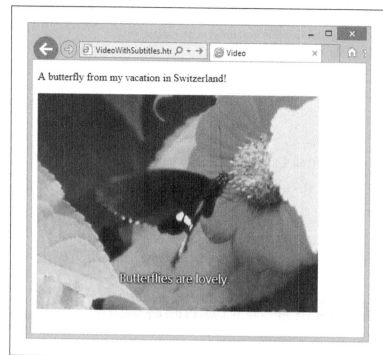

FIGURE 5-9

The subtitles in this video appear in their usual place: centered, and near the bottom of the video window.

Timed Text Tracks and WebVTT

In technical video speak, a *subtitle* is a caption that appears superimposed on a video, and a sequence of subtitles is a *timed text track*. There are a number of different formats for timed text tracks, but they all have fundamental similarities. All of them are recorded as ordinary text with time markings and are placed in chronological order in an ordinary text file. Here's an example of a timed tracks file written in WebVTT (Web Video Text Tracks Format), which is the format favored by HTML5. It holds four captions:

```
00:00:05.000 --> 00:00:10.000
This caption appears 5 seconds in and lingers until the 10 second mark.

00:01:00.000 --> 00:01:10.000
Now 1 minute has passed. Think about that for 10 seconds.

00:01:10.000 --> 00:01:15.000
This caption appears immediately after the second caption disappears.

00:01:30.000 --> 00:01:35.000
Captions can use <i>line breaks</i> and <b>simple</b> HTML markup.
```

As you can see, every entry in a WebVTT file specifies three details: the time the caption should appear (in *hour:minute:seconds* format), the time it should disappear, and the associated text. Save this content in a text file with the extension *.vtt* (as in *subtitles.vtt*), and you have a ready-to-go timed track file.

Although captioning seems simple, there are a number of fiddly details. For example, you may want to control line breaks, format your text, move the text captions to another position in the video window, or show karaoke-style captions that fill in one word at a time. That's why there are close to 50 different timed track formats. In fact, the struggle between timed text standards has been as ugly as the format war over audio and video codecs.

Currently, the official HTML5 specification doesn't specify what timed text format you should use. However, browser makers have united around WebVTT, a still-evolving specification inspired by the simple SRT format used for subtitles in desktop media players. Browser makers have chosen to ignore the more mature TTML (Timed Text Markup Language) standard, which the W3C has honed over a decade, because it's too complex. (Currently, IE 10 [and later] are the only browsers that give TTML any measure of support.)

TIP You can learn more about the WebVTT standard—including the techniques you need to format and style captions—from the specification at *http://dev.w3.org/html5/webvtt*. If you'd like some help writing your captions, you can try out Microsoft's nifty Caption Maker page (Figure 5-10), which you can find at *http://tinyurl.com/capmaker*.

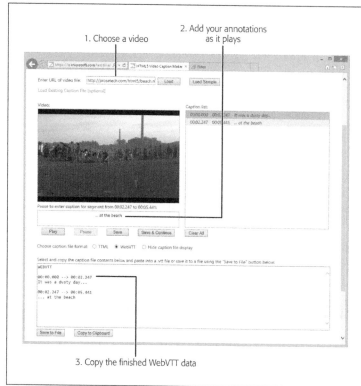

1. Choose a video
2. Add your annotations as it plays

3. Copy the finished WebVTT data

FIGURE 5-10

To use the Caption Maker, you must first point it to a video file that's already on the Web (type in the URL and click Load). While you're playing the video, it's easy to make a quick caption (type it in the box under the video window and then click Save). Then, when you're all done, you can copy the complete WebVTT listing from the text box below.

Adding Captions with <track>

Once you have a WebVTT file that contains your captions, you need a way to pair them up with your video file. The element that works this magic is named <track>. You add it inside your <video> element, after any <source> elements:

```
<video controls width="700" height="400">
  <source src="butterfly.mp4" type="video/mp4">
  <source src="butterfly.webm" type="video/webm">
  <track src="butterfly.vtt" srclang="en" kind="subtitles" label="English"
    default>
</video>
```

The <track> element takes several attributes. First is the src attribute, which identifies the timed track file. The srclang attribute identifies the language code of your subtitle file, for accessibility tools. Use en for English (or get the code for a more exotic language at *http://tinyurl.com/l-codes*).

The `kind` attribute describes the type of content in your captions. The HTML5 specification gives you five choices, but only two result in the pop-up captions you expect. Specify `subtitles` if your text consists of transcriptions or translations of dialogue), or `captions` if your text includes dialogue *and* descriptions for sound effects and musical cues.

> **TIP** Subtitles make sense when you can hear the audio but not understand it—for example, when watching a movie in another language. Captions make sense when no audio is available at all—for example, you've muted your player so you won't wake up your officemate in the cubicle beside you.

More specialized values for the `kind` attribute are `descriptions` (text that can replace the video when it's not available and may be spoken by speech synthesis), `chapters` (chapter titles, which viewers can use as a navigation aid), and `metadata` (bits of information that you can retrieve in your JavaScript code). If you choose one of these values, the video player won't show the text. It's up to another tool—or your JavaScript code—to retrieve this information and act on it.

The `label` attribute sets the text that's shown in the video player's Caption menu, which you can call up by clicking a small button under the video window. The label text is particularly important if you want to let viewers choose from multiple tracks. For example, here's a video that has two tracks:

```
<video controls width="700" height="400">
  <source src="butterfly.mp4" type="video/mp4">
  <source src="butterfly.webm" type="video/webm">
  <track src="butterfly.vtt" srclang="en" kind="subtitles" label="English"
    default>
  <track src="butterfly_fr.vtt" srclang="fr" kind="subtitles" label="French">
</video>
```

The first track has the `default` attribute, so it's the one that's initially picked. But the viewer can click the caption button and pick the other track (Figure 5-11).

Even if your video has just a single track, the caption list still includes two choices: your track and an Off option that turns off the captions. If you want to give viewers the option of captions, but you want your captions to be off initially, just make sure none of your tracks have the `default` attribute. That way, the video player starts with the Off option.

> **NOTE** Track files aren't just for accessibility and soundless playback. Search engines can also mine the information in a track file and use it to improve search results. If fact, a super-smart search engine of the future might use WebVTT information to lead a searcher directly to a specific playback location *within* a video file, by matching the search text with a timed caption.

Browser Support for Video Captions

Browsers have been slow to support the <track> element. At this writing, Firefox doesn't support it at all, but the developers at Mozilla plan to include it in the future. Table 5-4 details the current state of affairs.

FIGURE 5-11

Browsers that support the <track> element add a caption-picking button like this one. Using it, the viewer can switch tracks or turn captions off altogether.

TABLE 5-4 *Browser support for the <track> element*

	IE	FIREFOX	CHROME	SAFARI	OPERA	SAFARI IOS	ANDROID
Minimum Version	10	-	26	6*	15	-	2

* Safari doesn't provide a caption button for switching tracks or turning captions on and off.

NOTE If you're testing videos that use captions in Chrome, you'll need to upload your files first. If you simply launch the file from your computer, Chrome can play the video file, but it can't fetch the matching WebVTT file.

Fortunately, you can use the `<track>` element without worry. Browsers that don't support it simply ignore it, without a hiccup.

If you need a way to provide captions that work on every HTML5 browser, there's an easy workaround. You can use the `<track>` element as you would normally, in conjunction with a JavaScript polyfill, such as Captionator.js (*http://captionatorjs. com*). Captionator works by placing a floating element over the video window. Then, when playback reaches the appropriate points, Captionator.js retrieves the caption text from the WebVTT file and inserts it into the floating element.

Fancy Fonts and Effects with CSS3

I t would be ludicrous to build a modern website without CSS. The standard is fused into the fabric of the Web almost as tightly as HTML. Whether you're laying out pages, building interactive buttons and menus, or just making things look pretty, CSS is a fundamental tool. In fact, as HTML has increasingly shifted its focus to content and semantics (page 38), CSS has become the heart and soul of web *design*.

Along the way, CSS has become far more detailed and far more complex. When CSS evolved from its first version to CSS 2.1, it quintupled in size, reaching the size of a modest novel. Fortunately, the creators of the CSS standard had a better plan for future features. They carved the next generation of enhancements into a set of separate standards, called *modules*. That way, browser makers were free to implement the most exciting and popular parts of the standard first—which is what they were already doing, modules or not. Together, the new CSS modules fall under the catchall name *CSS3* (note the curious lack of a space, as with *HTML5*).

CSS3 has roughly 50 modules in various stages of maturity. They range from features that provide fancy eye candy (like rich fonts and animation) to ones that serve a more specialized, practical purpose (for example, speaking text aloud or varying styles based on the capabilities of the computer or mobile device). They include features that are reliably supported in the most recent versions of all modern browsers and features so experimental that no browser yet supports them.

In this chapter, you'll tour some of the most important (and best supported) parts of CSS3. First, you'll see how to use shadows, rounded corners, and other refinements to make your boxes look better. Next, you'll learn how you can use transitions to create subtle effects when the visitor hovers over an element, clicks on it, or tabs over to a control. (And you'll make these effects even better with two more CSS3 features: transforms and transparency.) Finally, you'll learn how to jazz up ordinary text with a rich variety of web fonts.

But first, before you get to any of these hot new features, it's time to consider how you can plug in the latest and most stylin' features without leaving a big chunk of your audience behind.

Using CSS3 Today

CSS3 is the unchallenged future of web styling, and it's not finished yet. Many modules are still being refined and revised, and no browser supports them all. You can see the current state of this giant family of specifications at *http://tinyurl.com/CSS3-stages*.

Because CSS3 is still being fine-tuned, it has the same complications as HTML5. Website authors like yourself need to decide what to use, what to ignore, and how to bridge the support gaps.

There are essentially three strategies you can use when you start incorporating CSS3 into a website. The following sections describe them.

> **NOTE** CSS3 is not part of HTML5. The standards were developed separately, by different people working at different times in different buildings. However, even the W3C encourages web developers to lump HTML5 and CSS3 together as part of the same new wave of modern web development. For example, if you check out the W3C's HTML5 logo-building page at *www.w3.org/html/logo*, you'll see that it encourages you to advertise CSS3 in its HTML5 logo strips. Furthermore, many hallmarks of modern web design with HTML5—such as the mobile-friendly layout techniques you'll learn about in the next chapter—require CSS3.

Strategy 1: Use What You Can

It makes sense to use features that already have solid browser support across all browser brands. One example is the web font feature (page 206). With the right font formats, you can get it working with browsers all the way back to IE 6. Unfortunately, very few CSS3 features fall into this category. The word-wrap property works virtually everywhere, and older browsers can do transparency with a bit of fiddling, but just about every other feature leaves the still-popular IE 8 browser in the dust.

> **NOTE** Unless otherwise noted, the features in this chapter work on the latest version of every modern browser, including Internet Explorer, provided you use IE 9 or later. However, they don't work on older versions of IE.

Strategy 2: Treat CSS3 Features as Enhancements

CSS3 fans have a rallying cry: "Websites don't need to look exactly the same on every browser." Which is certainly true. (They have a one-page website, too—see *http://DoWebsitesNeedToBeExperiencedExactlyTheSameInEveryBrowser.com*, which picks up a few frills on modern browsers but remains functional on laggards like IE 7.)

The idea behind this strategy is to use CSS3 to add fine touches that won't be missed by people using less-capable browsers. One example is the `border-radius` property that you can use to gently round the corners of a floating box. Here's an example:

```
header {
  background-color: #7695FE;
  border: thin #336699 solid;
  padding: 10px;
  margin: 10px;
  text-align: center;
  border-radius: 25px;
}
```

Browsers that recognize the border-radius property will know what to do. Older browsers will just ignore it, keeping the plain square corners (Figure 6-1).

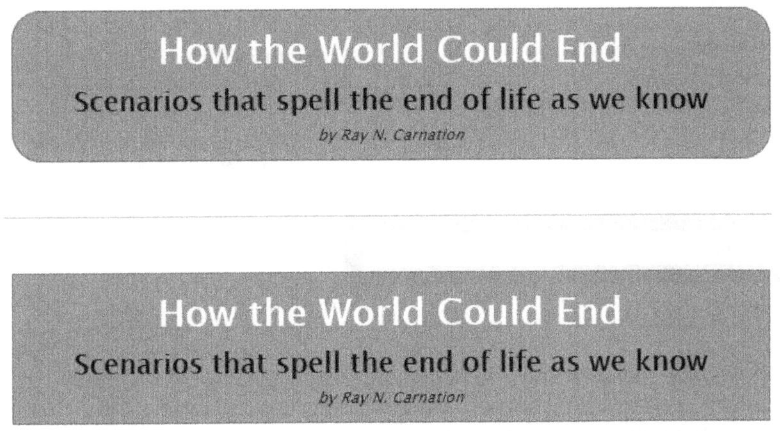

FIGURE 6-1

On Internet Explorer 9, this header box has rounded corners (top). IE 8 ignores the border-radius property but applies the rest of the style sheet properties (bottom).

This backward compatibility allows web designers to play with the latest frills in the newest version of CSS without breaking their sites on older browsers. However, there's a definite downside if you go too far. No matter how good a website looks in the latest version of your favorite browser, it can be deeply deflating if you fire up an older browser that's used by a significant slice of your clientele and find that it looks distinctly less awesome. After all, you want your website to impress everyone, not just web nerds with the best browsers.

For this reason, you may want to approach some CSS3 enhancements with caution. Limit yourself to features that are already in most browsers, even if they require the latest browser versions. And don't use CSS3 features in ways that change the experience of your website so dramatically that some people will get second-rate status.

TIP When it comes to CSS3, Internet Explorer is the straggler. There's a militant minority of web designers who believe that web designers should ignore backward browsers like IE 8 and start using CSS3 features as soon as other browsers support them. Otherwise, who will keep pressure on Microsoft and encourage the Web to get better? That philosophy makes sense, *if* the primary purpose of your website is the political one of promoting advanced web standards. But otherwise, keep in mind that dismissing a large segment of the web world will reflect poorly on you—because no matter how much you dislike someone's browser, that person is still using it to look at *your* work.

Strategy 3: Add Fallbacks with Modernizr

Using a partially supported CSS3 feature is a great idea if the website still looks great without it. But sometimes, a vital part of your website design can go missing, or the downgraded version of your website just looks ugly. For example, consider what happens if you use the Firefox-only multicolored border settings, as shown in Figure 6-2.

FIGURE 6-2

This multicolored border looks snazzy in Firefox (top). But try the same thing out in Chrome, and you'll get a thick, plain black border (bottom)—and that never looks good.

Sometimes, you can solve the problem by stacking properties in the right order. The basic technique is to start with more general properties, followed by new properties that override these settings. When this works, it satisfies every browser—the old browsers get the standard settings, while the new browsers override these settings with newer ones. For example, you can use this technique to replace an ordinary background fill with a gradient:

```
.stylishBox {
  ...
  background: yellow;
  background: radial-gradient(ellipse, red, yellow);
}
```

Figure 6-3 shows the result.

In some cases, overriding style properties doesn't work, because you need to set properties in combination. The multicolored border in Figure 6-2 is an example. The multicolored effect is set with the border-colors property, but it appears only if the border is made thick with the border-thickness property. On browsers that don't support multicolored borders, the thick border is an eyesore, no matter what single color you use.

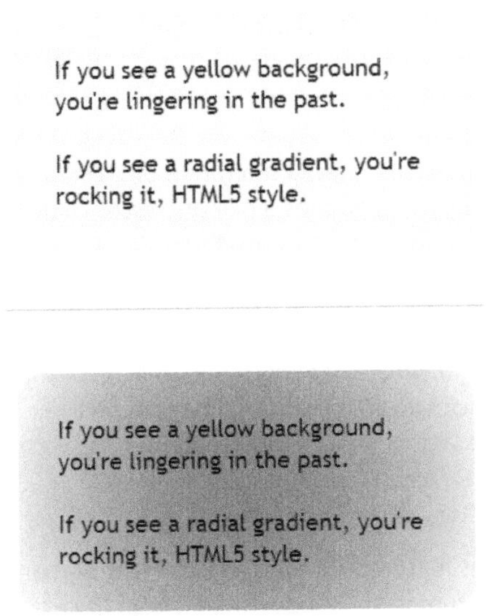

If you see a yellow background, you're lingering in the past.

If you see a radial gradient, you're rocking it, HTML5 style.

FIGURE 6-3

Top: In browsers that don't understand CSS3, the stylishBox *rule paints a yellow background.*

Bottom: In browsers that do understand CSS3, the yellow background is replaced with a radial gradient that blends from a red center point to yellow at the edges.

If you see a yellow background, you're lingering in the past.

If you see a radial gradient, you're rocking it, HTML5 style.

One way to address problems like these is with Modernizr, the JavaScript library that tests HTML5 feature support (page 31). It lets you define alternate style settings for browsers that don't support the style properties you really want. For example, imagine you want to create two versions of the header box shown in Figure 6-1. You want to use rounded corners if they're supported, but substitute a double-line border if they aren't. If you've added the Modernizr script reference to your page, then you can use a combination of style rules, like this:

```
/* Settings for all headers, no matter what level of CSS3 support. */
header {
  background-color: #7695FE;
  padding: 10px;
  margin: 10px;
  text-align: center;
}

/* Settings for browsers that support border-radius. */
.borderradius header {
  border: thin #336699 solid;
  border-radius: 25px;
}
```

```
/* Settings for browsers that don't support border-radius. */
.no-borderradius header {
  border: 5px #336699 double;
}
```

So how does this nifty trick work? When you use Modernizr in a page, you begin by adding the class="no-js" attribute to the root <html> element:

```
<html class="no-js">
```

When you load Modernizr on a page, it quickly checks if a range of HTML5, Java-Script, and CSS3 features are supported. It then applies a pile of classes to the root <html> element, separated by spaces, changing it into something like this:

```
<html class="js flexbox canvas canvastext webgl no-touch geolocation
postmessage no-websqldatabase indexeddb hashchange history draganddrop
no-websockets rgba hsla multiplebgs backgroundsize borderimage borderradius
boxshadow textshadow opacity no-cssanimations csscolumns cssgradients
no-cssreflections csstransforms no-csstransforms3d csstransitions fontface
generatedcontent video audio localstorage sessionstorage webworkers
applicationcache svg inlinesvg smil svgclippaths">
```

If a feature appears in the class list, that feature is supported. If a feature name is prefixed with the text "no-" then that feature is not supported. Thus, in the example shown here, JavaScript is supported (js) but web sockets are not (no-websockets). On the CSS3 side of things, the border-radius property works (borderradius) but CSS3 reflections do not (no-cssreflections).

You can incorporate these classes into your selectors to filter out style settings based on support. For example, a selector like .borderradius header gets all the <header> elements inside the root <html> element—if the browser supports the border-radius property. Otherwise, there will be no .borderradius class, the selector won't match anything, and the rule won't be applied.

The catch is that Modernizr provides classes for only a subset of CSS3 features. This subset includes some of CSS3's most popular and mature features, but the border-color feature in Figure 6-2 doesn't qualify because it's still Firefox-only. For that reason, it's a good idea to hold off on using multicolored borders in your pages, at least for now.

NOTE You can also use Modernizr to create JavaScript fallbacks. In this case, you simply need to check the appropriate property of the Modernizr object, as you do when checking for HTML5 support. You can use this technique to compensate if you're missing more advanced CSS3 features, like transitions or animations. However, there's so much work involved and the models are so different that it's usually best to stick with a JavaScript-only solution for essential website features.

Browser-Specific Styles with Vendor Prefixes

When the creators of CSS develop new features, they often run into a chicken-and-egg dilemma. In order to perfect the feature, they need feedback from browser makers and web designers. But in order to get this feedback, browser makers and web designers need to implement these new-and-imperfect features. The result is a cycle of trial and feedback that takes many revisions to settle down. As this process unfolds, the syntax and implementation of features change. This raises a very real danger—unknowing web developers might learn about a dazzling new feature and implement it in their real-life websites, not realizing that future versions of the standard could change the rules and break the websites.

To avoid this threat, browser makers use a system of *vendor prefixes* to change CSS property and function names while they're still under development. For example, consider the `radial-gradient()` function described on page 193. In older versions of Firefox, the `radial-gradient()` function wasn't available. However, you could use an "in progress" version of this function called `-moz-radial-gradient`:

```
.stylishBox {
  background: yellow;
  background: -moz-radial-gradient(ellipse, red, yellow);
}
```

Firefox uses the vendor prefix `-moz-` (which is short for Mozilla, the organization that's behind the Firefox project). Every browser engine has its own vendor prefix (Table 6-1), which complicates life horrendously, but for a good reason. Different browser makers add support at different times, often using different draft versions of the same specification. Although all browsers will support the same syntax for final specification, the syntax of the vendor-specific properties and functions often varies.

TABLE 6-1 *Vendor prefixes*

PREFIX	FOR BROWSERS
-moz-	Firefox
-webkit-	Chrome, Safari, and the latest versions of Opera (the same rendering engine powers all three browsers)
-ms-	Internet Explorer
-o-	Old versions of Opera (before version 15)

Here's an example that applies a radial gradient using all four of the browser-specific prefixes:

```
.stylishBox {
  background: yellow;
  background-image: -moz-radial-gradient(circle, green, yellow);
  background-image: -webkit-radial-gradient(circle, green, yellow);
  background-image: -o-radial-gradient(circle, green, yellow);
  background-image: -ms-radial-gradient(circle, green, yellow);
}
```

Clearly, when dealing with the less mature parts of CSS3, you need some bloated style sheet rules.

The obvious question for every web designer is "When do I need to use vendor prefixes, and when is it safe to use the ordinary, unprefixed property or function name?" You might think you could just fire up your browser for a quick test, but you won't have a conclusive answer unless you run your page through *every* browser out there. For example, the borderadius property works on all browsers, with no vendor prefixes required. But the radial-gradient() function is a bit trickier: At this writing, it works on most browsers but still requires the -webkit- prefix on some mobile browsers. And the transform property that you'll consider later in this chapter works with no prefix on IE and Firefox, but still requires the -webkit- prefix in Chrome, Safari, and Opera.

Further complicating life, the syntax you use to specify a property value or function argument can change. For example, IE 10 introduced a prefixed version of the radial-gradient() function during testing. The final, released version of IE 10 lets developers use either the most recent syntax with the unprefixed radial-gradient() function or the slightly older form with the prefixed -ms-radial-gradient() function. This setup is good for endless hours of debugging fun.

> **NOTE** In this chapter, you'll learn about the current state of support for all CSS3 parts covered here, including which ones need vendor prefixes. If a style sheet example in this chapter *doesn't* use vendor prefixes, you can assume that it's safe to omit them when you use the feature in your own pages.

If your head is starting to spin, don't worry—help is at hand. To get the latest information about which CSS3 features require vendor prefixes, you can turn to the virtually indispensable site *http://caniuse.com* (which you first saw on page 27). When you look up a CSS3 feature, the "Can I use..." site clearly spells out which browser versions require a vendor prefix (Figure 6-4).

> **NOTE** Using vendor prefixes is a messy business. Web developers are split on whether they're a necessary evil of getting the latest and greatest frills, or a big fat warning sign that should scare clear-thinking designers away. But one thing is certain: If you don't use the vendor prefixes, significant parts of CSS3 will be off limits for now.

◼ Building Better Boxes

From the earliest days of CSS, web designers were using it to format boxes of content. As CSS became more powerful, the boxes became more impressive, creating everything from nicely shaded headers to floating, captioned figures. And when CSS cracked the hovering problem, floating boxes were even turned into rich, glowy buttons, taking over from the awkward JavaScript-based approaches of yore. With this in mind, it's no surprise that some of the most popular and best-supported CSS3 features can make your boxes look even prettier, no matter what they hold.

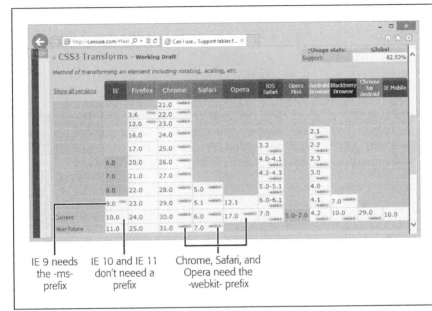

FIGURE 6-4

If you need to use a prefix, the "Can I use..." website lets you know in a tiny yellow text bubble. For example, the CSS3 transforms feature doesn't need a vendor prefix in the latest versions of Firefox or IE, but it does in all other browsers.

IE 9 needs the -ms- prefix

IE 10 and IE 11 don't need a prefix

Chrome, Safari, and Opera need the -webkit- prefix

GEM IN THE ROUGH

Adding Vendor Prefixes Automagically

If you make heavy use of the parts of CSS3 that still require vendor prefixes, you can quickly get worn down updating massive style sheets and adding multiple versions of the same style sheet property over and over again. Before you lose your sanity, consider a miraculously clever JavaScript tool called -prefix-free.

To use -prefix-free, you create an ordinary style sheet, using CSS3 properties as you need them, without worrying about vendor prefixes. Then, in your web pages, you add a reference to the -prefix-free script.

When someone views one of your pages, the -prefix-free script springs into action. It examines the current browser and automatically tweaks your style sheet to suit by adding all the vendor prefixes that that browser needs. (Yes, this automatic tweaking takes a bit of extra time, but you'll probably find it's so fast as to be undetectable.) Of course, -prefix-free can't make a browser support a feature that it otherwise wouldn't, but it can transform ordinary, sensibly named properties into the messy, vendor-specific names that some browsers need to support new and evolving features. For many developers, adding an extra JavaScript file is a small price to pay for managing the chaos of CSS3 prefixes.

To download the -prefix-free library, or play with an interactive page that lets you type some CSS and test the script's prefix-adding ability, visit *http://leaverou.github.io/prefixfree*.

Transparency

The ability to make partially transparent pictures and colors is one of the most basic building blocks in CSS3. There are two ways to do it.

Your first option is to use the rgba() color function, which accepts four numbers. The first three values are the red, green, and blue components of the color, from 0 to 255. The final value is the *alpha*, a fractional value number from 0 (fully transparent) to 1 (fully opaque).

Here's an example that creates a 50 percent transparent lime green color:

```
.semitransparentBox {
  background: rgba(170,240,0,0.5);
}
```

Browsers that don't support rgba() will just ignore this rule, and the element will keep its default, completely transparent background. So the second, and better, approach is to start by declaring a solid fallback color, and then replace that color with a semitransparent one:

```
.semitransparentBox {
  background: rgb(170,240,0);
  background: rgba(170,240,0,0.5);
}
```

This way, browsers that don't support the rgba() function will still color the element's background, just without the transparency.

> **TIP** To make this fallback better, strive to use a color that more accurately reflects the semitransparent effect. For example, if you're putting a semitransparent lime green color over a mostly white background, the color will look lighter because the white shows through. Your fallback color should reflect this fact, if possible.

CSS3 also adds a style property named opacity, which works just like the alpha value. You can set opacity to a value from 0 to 1 to make any element partially transparent:

```
.semitransparentBox {
  background: rgb(170,240,0);
  opacity: 0.5;
}
```

Figure 6-5 shows two examples of semitransparency, one that uses the rgba() function and one that uses the opacity property.

The opacity property is a better tool than the rgba() function if you want to do any of the following:

- Make more than one color semitransparent. With opacity, the background color, text color, and border color of an element can become transparent.

- Make something semitransparent, even if you don't know its color (for example, because it might be set by another style sheet or in JavaScript code).

- Make an image semitransparent.

- Use a transition, an animated effect that can make an element fade away or reappear (page 199).

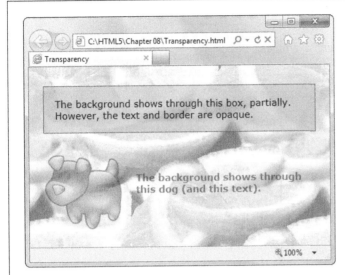

FIGURE 6-5

This page serves up semitransparency two different ways: to fade out a picture (using the opacity property) and to let the background show through a box (using a background color created with the rgba() function).

Rounded Corners

You've already learned about the border-radius property, which lets you shave the hard corners off boxes. But what you haven't yet seen is how you can tweak this setting to get the curve you want.

First, you can choose a different, single value for the border-radius property, since the property specifies the radius of the circle that's used to draw the rounded edge. (You don't see the entire circle—just enough to connect the vertical and horizontal sides of the box.) Set a bigger border-radius value, and you'll get a bigger curve and a more gently rounded corner. As with most measurements in CSS, you can use a variety of units, including pixels and percentages. You can also adjust each corner separately by supplying four values:

```
.roundedBox {
  background: yellow;
  border-radius: 25px 50px 25px 85px;
}
```

But that's not all—you can also stretch the circle into an ellipse, creating a curve that stretches longer in one direction. To do this, you need to target each corner separately (using properties like border-top-left-radius) and then supply two numbers: one for the horizontal radius and one for the vertical radius:

```
.roundedBox {
  background: yellow;
  border-top-left-radius: 150px 30px;
  border-top-right-radius: 150px 30px;
}
```

Figure 6-6 shows some examples.

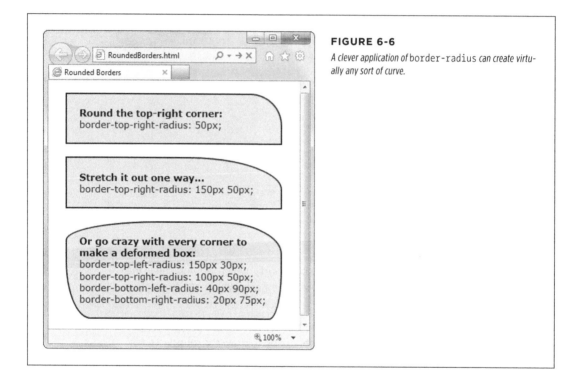

FIGURE 6-6
A clever application of border-radius can create virtually any sort of curve.

Backgrounds

One shortcut to attractive backgrounds and borders is to use images. CSS3 introduces two new features to help out here. First is multiple background support, which
lets you combine two or more images in a single element's background. Here's an
example that uses two backgrounds to embellish the top-left and bottom-right
corner of a box:

```
.decoratedBox {
  margin: 50px;
  padding: 20px;
  background-image: url('top-left.png'), url('bottom-right.png');
  background-position: left top, right bottom;
  background-repeat: no-repeat, no-repeat;
}
```

This first step is to supply a list with any number of images, which you use to set the background-image property. You can then position each image and control whether it repeats, using the background-position and background-repeat properties. The trick is to make sure that the order matches, so the first image is positioned with the first background-position value, the second image with the second background-position value, and so on. Figure 6-7 shows the result.

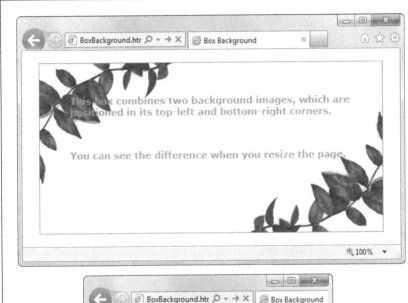

FIGURE 6-7

It doesn't matter how big this box grows—the two background images stay fixed at either corner.

NOTE If browsers don't support multiple backgrounds, they'll completely ignore your attempt to set the background. To avoid this problem, start by setting the background or background-image property with a fallback color or picture. Then, attempt to set multiple backgrounds by setting background-image with a list of pictures.

And here's a revised example that uses the *sliding doors* technique—a time-honored web design pattern that creates a resizable graphic out of three pieces: an image for the left, an image for the right, and an extremely thin sliver that's tiled through the middle:

```
.decoratedBox {
  margin: 50px;
  padding: 20px;
  background-image: url('left.png'), url('middle.png'), url('right.png');
  background-position: left top, left top, right bottom;
  background-repeat: no-repeat, repeat-x, no-repeat;
}
```

You could use markup like this to draw a background for a button. Of course, with all of CSS3's fancy new features, you'll probably prefer to create those using shadows, gradients, and other image-free effects.

Shadows

CSS3 introduces two types of shadows: box shadows and text shadows. Of the two, box shadows are generally more useful. You can use a box shadow to throw a rectangular shadow behind any <div> (but don't forget your border, so it still looks like a box). Shadows even follow the contours of boxes with rounded corners (see Figure 6-8).

FIGURE 6-8

Shadows can make text float (top), boxes pop out (middle), or buttons look glowy (bottom).

The two properties that make shadows work are box-shadow and text-shadow. Here's a basic box shadow example:

```
.shadowedBox {
  border: thin #336699 solid;
  border-radius: 25px;
  box-shadow: 5px 5px 10px gray;
}
```

The first two values set the horizontal and vertical offset of the shadow. Using positive values (like 5 pixels for both, in the above example) displaces the shadow down and to the right. The next value sets the *blur* distance—in this example, 10 pixels—which increases the fuzziness of the shadow. At the end is the shadow color. If there's any content underneath the box, consider using the rgba() function (page 186) to supply a semitransparent shadow.

If you want to tweak your shadow, you can tack on two details. You can add another number between the blur and the color to set the shadow *spread*, which expands the shadow by thickening the solid part before the blurred edge starts:

```
box-shadow: 5px 5px 10px 5px gray;
```

And you can add the word inset on the end to create a shadow that reflects inside an element, instead of outside. This works best if you use a shadow that's directly on top of the element, with no horizontal or vertical offset:

```
box-shadow: 0px 0px 20px lime inset;
```

This creates the bottom example in Figure 6-8. You can use inset shadows to add hover effects to a button (page 196).

> **NOTE** You can even supply multiple shadows by separating each one with a comma. But getting shadow-crazy is usually a waste of effort and computing power.

The text-shadow property requires a similar set of values, but in a different order. The color comes first, followed by the horizontal and vertical offsets, followed by the blur:

```
.textShadow {
  font-size: 30px;
  font-weight: bold;
  text-shadow: gray 10px 10px 7px;
}
```

Box shadows and text shadows don't show up in old versions of Internet Explorer. Box shadows require IE 9 or later, while text shadows require IE 10 or later.

Gradients

Gradients are blends of color that can create a range of effects, from the subtle shading behind a menu bar to a psychedelic button that's colored like a 1960s revival party. Figure 6-9 shows some examples.

NOTE Many web gradients are faked with background images. But CSS3 lets you define the gradient you want and gets the browser to do the work. The advantage is fewer image files to schlep around and the ability to create gradients that seamlessly resize themselves to fill any amount of space.

CSS supports two types of gradients: linear gradients that blend from one band of color to another, and radial gradients that blend from a central point to the outer edges of your region.

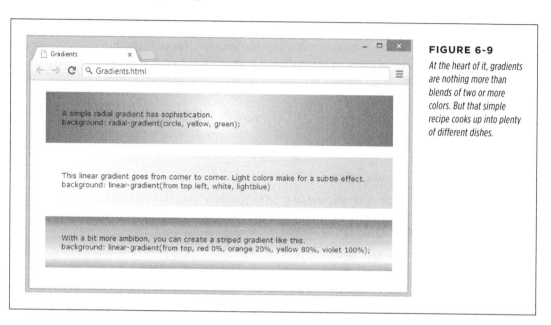

FIGURE 6-9

At the heart of it, gradients are nothing more than blends of two or more colors. But that simple recipe cooks up into plenty of different dishes.

There are no special CSS properties for creating gradients. Instead, you can use a gradient function to set the background property. Just remember to set the property to a solid color first to create a fallback for browsers that don't support gradients (like versions of Internet Explorer before IE 10).

■ LINEAR GRADIENTS

There are four gradient functions. The first function is linear-gradient(). Here it is in one of its simpler forms, shading a region from white at the top to blue at the bottom:

```
.colorBlendBox {
  background: linear-gradient(from top, white, blue);
}
```

The word from indicates that the top is the starting point for the first color (white). You can replace this with to, which reverses the gradient so it blends from blue at the bottom to white at the top:

```
background: linear-gradient(to top, white, blue);
```

Similarly, you can replace top with left to go from one side to another. Or use both to blend diagonally from the top-left corner:

```
background: linear-gradient(from top left, white, lightblue)
```

If you want multiple-color bands, you simply supply a list of colors. Here's how you create a series of three horizontal color stripes, starting with red at the top:

```
background: linear-gradient(from top, red, orange, yellow);
```

Finally, you can control where each color starts (bumping some together or off to one side), using *gradient stops*. Each gradient stop is a percentage, with 0 percent being at the very start of the gradient and 100 percent being at the very end. Here's an example that extends the orangey-yellow section in the middle:

```
background: linear-gradient(from top, red 0%, orange 20%, yellow 80%,
    violet 100%);
```

The syntax of the linear-gradient() function is easy to follow. But here's the bad news: To guarantee support on Android browsers and slightly older versions of Safari (before Safari 7), you need to also add the -webkit- vendor prefix. And what's worse, the -webkit-linear-gradient() function is subtly different from the true linear-gradient() function. Unlike linear-gradient(), -webkit-linear-gradient() doesn't use the to or from values to specify direction. Instead, from is assumed automatically.

Here's a fully outfitted style sheet rule that satisfies slightly older browsers by adding a vendor-prefixed gradient:

```
.colorBlendBox {
  background: lightblue;
  background: -webkit-linear-gradient(top left, white, lightblue);
  background: linear-gradient(from top left, white, lightblue);
}
```

Fortunately, there's no need to add other vendor prefixes (like -moz- and -o-), unless you want to support *much* older versions of Firefox and Opera.

TIP In all these examples, gradients were used with the background property. However, you can also use gradient functions to set the background-image property in exactly the same way. The advantage here is that background-image lets you use an image fallback. First, set background-image to a suitable fallback image for less-equipped browsers, and then set it again using a gradient function. Most browsers are smart enough that they won't download the gradient image unless they need it, which saves bandwidth.

■ RADIAL GRADIENTS

To set a radial gradient, you use the radial-gradient() function. You need to supply a color for the center of the circle and a color for the outer edge of the circle, where it meets the boundaries of the element. Here's a radial gradient that places a white point in the center and fades out to blue on the edges:

```
background: radial-gradient(circle, white, lightblue);
```

Once again, you need to add a -webkit- version of the function to be safe:

```
background: -webkit-radial-gradient(circle, yellow, green);
```

Replace the word circle with ellipse if you want to stretch your gradient out into an oblong shape to better fit its container.

As with a linear gradient, you can supply a whole list of colors. Optionally, you can add percentages to tweak how quickly the gradient blends from one color to the next. Here's an example that starts yellow, blends slowly into green, and then quickly blends through blue, white, and black near the outside edge of the element:

```
background: radial-gradient(circle, yellow 10%, green 70%, blue, white,
black);
```

You can also place the center of your gradient using percentages. For example, if you want the center point of your circle to be near the top-right corner of your element, you might use this sort of radial gradient:

```
background: radial-gradient(circle at 90% 5%, white, lightblue);
```

These percentages tell the browser to start the gradient 90% from the left edge (which is almost all the way to the right side) and 5% from the top edge.

> **NOTE** The syntax of the radial-gradient() function has changed since it was first created. The at keyword, which positions the gradient's center point, is a relatively new detail. Although it's safe to use at with the radial-gradient() function, don't attempt to use it with the vendor-specific -webkit-radial-gradient() function.

▓ REPEATING GRADIENTS

CSS3 also includes two functions that let you create more dizzying gradients: repeating-linear-gradient() and repeating-radial-gradient(). Whereas linear-gradient() and radial-gradient() blend through your list of colors once, the repeating-linear-gradient() and repeating-radial-gradient() functions cycle through the same set of colors endlessly, until they fill up all the available space in your element with blended stripes of color. The result is a psychedelic tie-dye effect that just might fool you into thinking you've stepped back in time to the '70s.

The syntax of repeating-linear-gradient() and repeating-radial-gradient() is essentially the same as the syntax of linear-gradient() and radial-gradient(). The only difference is that you need to make sure you limit the size of your gradient so it can repeat.

For example, this repeating gradient won't look any different from a normal gradient, because its size isn't limited. Instead, it starts with yellow in the center and blends to green at the outer edge:

```
background: repeating-radial-gradient(circle, yellow, green);
```

The following gradient is different. It keeps the yellow in the center, but sets the green to kick in at the 10% mark. After that, the gradient repeats, starting with the yellow color again. The result is a striped effect of blurry yellow and green lines.

```
background: repeating-radial-gradient(circle, yellow, green 10%);
```

You can have as many colors as you like in a repeating gradient. The key detail is to make sure that the final color includes a percentage or pixel value, which sets that color's position. That way, the color won't be placed at the edge of your element.

Instead of using a percentage value, you can use a pixel width, like this:

```
background: repeating-linear-gradient(to top, red, orange, white, yellow,
red 30px);
```

This gradient creates a slightly different effect. Now each stripe always has the same thickness (30 pixels), and the number of stripes depends on the available space. By comparison, the previous example always had the 10 proportionately sized stripes, each one filling 10% of the available space.

TIP Repeating gradients come with two caveats. First, you may include only the to keyword but never from, because a repeating gradient can be filled in only one direction. Second, if you want your gradient to blend seamlessly without a sharp break between colors each time the gradient repeats itself, make sure the final color in your list is the same as the first color in your list.

GEM IN THE ROUGH

Fancy Gradients with Less Fuss

Creating complex gradients is a fiddly business. To speed up the process, you may want to try an online gradient-generating tool. The idea is simple: You play with the controls in your browser until the gradient looks fabulous, and the tool spits out the markup you need (complete with different vendor-prefixed versions, just in case you need them). Two good gradient-generating tools are the Ultimate CSS Gradient Generator (*www.colorzilla.com/gradient-editor*) and Microsoft's CSS Gradient Background Maker (*http://tinyurl.com/ms-gradient*).

■ Creating Effects with Transitions

Back in the day when CSS 2.1 was hot stuff, web developers were excited about a new feature called *pseudo-classes* (page 443). Suddenly, with the help of :hover and :focus, developers could create interactive effects without writing any JavaScript code. For example, to create a hover button, you simply supply a set of new style properties for the :hover pseudo-class. These styles kick in automatically when the visitor moves the mouse pointer over your button.

TIP If you're the last web developer on earth who hasn't rolled your own hover button, you can find a detailed tutorial in *Creating a Website: The Missing Manual,* or in an online article at *www.elated.com/articles/ css-rollover-buttons.*

Great as they are, pseudo-classes aren't cutting edge any longer. The problem is their all-or-nothing nature. For example, if you use the :hover pseudo-class, then your style settings spring into action immediately when someone hovers over an element. But in Flash applications or in desktop programs, the effect is usually more refined. The hovered-over button may shift its color, move, or begin to glow using a subtle animation that takes a fraction of a second to complete.

Some web developers have begun to add effects like these to their pages, but it usually requires the help of someone else's JavaScript animation framework. But CSS3 has a simpler solution—a *transitions* feature that lets you smoothly switch from one group of settings to another.

A Basic Color Transition

To understand how transitions work, you need to see a real example. Figure 6-10 shows a color-changing button that's bolstered with some CSS3 transition magic.

FIGURE 6-10

If this were an ordinary rollover button, its background would jump from green to yellow in one step. But with transitions, the green blends into yellow, taking half a second to make the change. Move the mouse off, and the same transition plays out in reverse, returning the button to its normal state. The result is a button that just feels more polished. (To try if for yourself, head to the try-out page at http:// prosetech.com/html5.)

First, consider how you'd style this button the ordinary way, without using transitions. This task is basic CSS, requiring one style rule to set the button's initial appearance and a second style rule to change it when it's hovered on:

```
.slickButton {
  color: white;
  font-weight: bold;
  padding: 10px;
  border: solid 1px black;
  background: lightgreen;
  cursor: pointer;
}

.slickButton:hover {
  color: black;
  background: yellow;
}
```

Here's a button that uses these style rules:

```
<button class="slickButton">Hover Here!</a>
```

This approach is all well and good, but it lacks a certain finesse. To smooth out the green-to-yellow color change, you can create a CSS3 transition using the `transition` property. You do this in the normal `slickButton` style (not the `:hover` pseudo-class).

At a minimum, every transition needs two pieces of information: the CSS property that you want to animate and the time the browser should take to make the change. In this example, the transition acts on the `background` property, and the duration is 0.5 seconds:

```
.slickButton {
  color: white;
  font-weight: bold;
  padding: 10px;
  border: solid 1px black;
  background: lightgreen;
  cursor: pointer;
  -webkit-transition: background 0.5s;
  transition: background 0.5s;
}

.slickButton:hover {
  color: black;
  background: yellow;
}
```

As you'll no doubt notice, this example adds two transition properties instead of the promised one. That's because the CSS3 transitions standard is not quite final and some browsers still require the `-webkit-` vendor prefix.

There's one quirk in this example. The hovered-over button changes two details: its background color and its text color. But the transition applies to the background color only. As a result, the text blinks from white to black in an instant, while the new background color fades in slowly.

There are two ways to patch this up. Your first option is to set the transition property with a comma-separated list of transitions, like this:

```
.slickButton {
  ...
  -webkit-transition: background 0.5s, color 0.5s;
  transition: background 0.5s, color 0.5s;
  ...
}
```

But there's a shortcut if you want to set transitions for all the properties that change and you want to use the same duration for each one. In this case, you can simply add a single transition and use `all` for the property name:

```
-webkit-transition: all 0.5s;
transition: all 0.5s;
```

Right now, transitions work in the latest version of every browser. Old versions of Internet Explorer (IE 9 and before) don't have any transition support, and vendor prefixes won't help. However, this lack of support isn't the problem it seems. Even if a browser ignores the transition property, it still applies the effect. It just makes the change immediately, rather than smoothly fading it in. That's good news—it means a website can use transitions and keep the essentials of its visual style intact on old browsers.

More Transition Ideas

It's gratifying to see that CSS transitions can make a simple color change look good. But if you're planning to build a slick rollover effect for your buttons or menus, there are plenty of other properties you can use with a transition. Here are some first-rate ideas:

- **Transparency.** By modifying the opacity property, you can make an image fade away into the background. Just remember not to make the picture completely transparent, or the visitor won't know where to hover.

- **Shadow.** Earlier, you learned how the box-shadow property can add a shadow behind any box (page 190). But the right shadow can also make a good hover effect. In particular, consider shadows with no offset and lots of blur, which create more of a traditional glow effect. You can also use an inset shadow to put the effect inside the box.

- **Gradients.** Change up a linear gradient or add a radial one—either way, it's hard not to notice this effect.

- **Transforms.** As you'll learn on page 201, transforms can move, resize, and warp any element. That makes them a perfect tool for transitions.

On the flip side, it's usually not a good idea to use transitions with padding, margins, and font size. These operations take more processing power (because the browser needs to recalculate layout or text hinting), which can make them slow and jerky. If you're trying to make something move, grow, or shrink, you're better off using a transform (page 201).

Triggering Transitions with JavaScript

As you've seen, transitions kick in when an element switches from one style to another. If you want a nice, code-free way to make this happen, you can use pseudo-classes like :hover and :focus. But this approach has obvious limits. For example, it won't work if you want your transition to take place at another time or in response to a different event. It also won't work if you want your transition to be triggered by one element but then *affect* a different element. In situations like these, you need to chip in with a bit of JavaScript code.

Fortunately, it's easy to create a JavaScript-powered transition. As with an ordinary transition, you begin by creating two style rules, one for your element's initial state, and one for its transitioned state. Then you add the JavaScript code that finds your element and changes its style when the time is right.

Don't Leave Old Browsers Behind

As you know, browsers that don't support transitions switch between states immediately, which is usually a good thing. However, if you use CSS3 glitter to make your states look different (for example, you're adding a shadow or a gradient to a hovered-over button), old browsers ignore that, too. That's not so good. It means that visitors with less capable browsers get *no* hover effect at all.

To solve this problem, use a fallback that older browsers understand. For example, you might create a hover state that sets a different background color and *then* sets a gradient. This way, older browsers will see the background change to a new solid color when the button is hovered over. More capable browsers will see the background change to a gradient fill. For even more customizing power, you can use Modernizr, which lets you define completely different styles for older browsers (page 31).

Figure 6-11 shows an example that uses a code-powered transition. In this page, two images are layered over each other—an image of a city skyline in the day and an image of the same skyline at night. The buttons use a few simple lines of JavaScript to trigger a transition that hides or shows the night-time image.

The first step to creating this example is adding an image-formatting style sheet rule. It does two things: switches the images to absolute positioning (so they can be placed on top of one another in their containing <div>), and defines the type of transition you plan to carry out. In this case, it's a 10-second transition that alters the opacity of the nighttime image.

```
img {
  position: absolute;
  -webkit-transition: opacity 10s;
  transition: opacity 10s;
}
```

You also need two style rules to represent the different possible states for the nighttime image, which begins fully transparent but can become solid at the click of a button:

```
.solid {
  opacity: 1;
}

.transparent {
  opacity: 0;
}
```

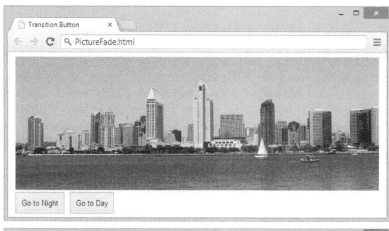

FIGURE 6-11

Initially, the image with the night skyline is completely transparent (top). But click the To Night button and the night image fades in, gradually blotting out the day skyline (bottom).

The page markup places both images into a `<div>`, taking care to apply the transparent class to the second image, and defines two buttons that are hard-wired into the JavaScript functions you need.

```
<div>
  <img src="day.png" alt="Daytime view">
  <img id="nightImage" src="night.png" alt="Night-time view"
class="transparent">
</div>

<button onclick="toNight()">Go to Night</button>
<button onclick="toDay()">Go to Day</button>
```

The final step is to add the code that reacts to the button clicks, finds the nighttime image, and switches its style:

```
function toNight() {
  var nightImage = document.getElementById("nightImage");
  nightImage.className = "solid";
}

function toDay() {
  var nightImage = document.getElementById("nightImage");
  nightImage.className = "transparent";
}
```

Although this seems like a single abrupt act, the change will phase in steadily over 10 seconds, thanks to the transition that's defined for all <img> elements.

Remember, transitions take place only if your visitor has a modern browser. If someone visits your site with IE 9 and clicks the To Night or To Day button, the page will shift abruptly from one style to the other, with no 10-second blending effect. Unfortunately, there's no easy polyfill to patch this gap, and it's all too easy to ignore what your pages will look like on less capable browsers when you start weaving transitions into your code

NOTE If animated effects are an essential part of your pages, you're probably not quite ready to embrace CSS3. Instead, the most practical solution for transitions today is a JavaScript library like jQuery UI or MooTools. But CSS3 is the clear future of web effects, once the standards settle down and modern browsers have colonized the computers of the world.

Transforms

A *transform* is a powerful tool that lets you move, scale, skew, or rotate an element, warping its appearance. With CSS3 transforms, you use them to change the appearance of an element. Like transitions, transforms are a new and experimental feature. To use them, you need to use the transform property. Here's an example that rotates an element and all its contents:

```
.rotatedElement {
  transform: rotate(45deg);
}
```

To get your transforms to work on Chrome, Safari, and Opera, you need to add the -webkit- vendor prefix. On Internet Explorer 9, you need the -ms- prefix (although IE 10 and later don't need any prefix). Firefox doesn't need a prefix. So unless you're using the -prefix-free tool (page 185), the proper way to use a transform looks like this:

```
.rotatedElement {
  -ms-transform: rotate(45deg);
  -webkit-transform: rotate(45deg);
  transform: rotate(45deg);
}
```

POWER USERS' CLINIC

Making More Natural Transitions

The `transition` property is an all-in-one property that combines several details. So far, you've seen how to give a transition a duration and specify the property it acts on. However, there are two more details you can use to fine-tune your transition.

First, you can choose a *timing function* that controls how the transition effect flows—for example, whether it starts slow and then speeds up or starts fast and then decelerates. In a short transition, the timing function you choose doesn't make much of a difference. But in a longer, more complex animation, it can change the overall feel of the effect. Here's an example that uses the `ease-in-out` timing function so that a transition starts slow, then accelerates, and then slows back down at the end:

```
transition: opacity 10s ease-in-out;
```

Other timing functions include `linear` (the transition has a constant rate from start to finish), `ease-in` (the transition starts slow and then goes at a constant rate), `ease-out` (the transition starts at a constant rate but slows at the end), and `cubic-bezier` (the transition goes according to a Bézier curve that you define, you math lover, you).

No matter what timing function you choose, the whole transition takes the same amount of time—the duration you've specified. The difference is in how the transition speeds up or slows down as it takes place. To review the different timing functions and get a feel for how each one alters the pace of a transition, you can see them in action with a helpful series of rolling square animations at *http://css3.bradshawenterprises.com/transitions/*.

The other transition detail that you can add is an optional delay that holds off the start of the transition for some period of time. Here's an example that waits 0.1 seconds:

```
transition: opacity 10s ease-in-out 0.1s;
```

In this example, the `rotate()` function does the work, twisting an element 45 degrees around its center. However, there are many more transform functions that you can use, separately or at the same time. For example, the following style chains three transforms together. It enlarges an element by half (using the `scale` transform), moves it 10 pixels to the left (using the `scaleX` transform), and skews it for effect (using the `skew` transform):

```
.rotatedElement {
  -ms-transform: scale(1.5) scaleX(10px) skew(10deg);
  -webkit-transform: scale(1.5) scaleX(10px) skew(10deg);
  transform: scale(1.5) scaleX(10px) skew(10deg);
}
```

A skew twists an element out of shape. For example, imagine pushing the top edge of a box out to the side, while the bottom edge stays fixed (so it looks like a parallelogram).

Table 6-2 lists all the two-dimensional transform functions you can use. To remove all your transforms, set the transform property to none.

NOTE Transforms don't affect other elements or the layout of your web page. For example, if you enlarge an element with a transform, it simply overlaps the adjacent content.

TABLE 6-2 *Transform functions*

FUNCTION	DESCRIPTION
translateX(x)	Moves an element horizontally. Use a positive value to shift it to the right, and a negative value to shift it to the left.
translateY(y)	Moves an element vertically. Use a positive value to shift it down, and a negative value to shift it up.
translate(x, y)	Moves an element vertically and horizontally.
scaleX(x)	Scales an element horizontally. Use a value greater than 1.0 to enlarge it (2.0 is twice as big) and a value between 0 and 1.0 to shrink it (0.5 is half as big). Use a negative value to flip the element around the y-axis, creating a right-to-left mirror image.
scaleY(y)	Scales an element vertically. Use a value greater than 1.0 to enlarge it and a value between 0 and 1.0 to shrink it. Use a negative value to flip the element around the x-axis, creating a bottom-to-top mirror image.
scale(x, y)	Scales an element horizontally and vertically.
rotate(angle)	Rotates an element clockwise around its center. Use a negative value to rotate the element counter-clockwise. If you want to rotate an element around another point, use the CSS transform-origin property.
skewX(angle)	Tilts an element horizontally. The top and bottom edges remain level, but the sides are pulled out of alignment.
skewY(angle)	Tilts an element vertically. The left and right edges remain in place, but the top and bottom are slanted.
skew(x-angle, y-angle)	Tilts an element horizontally and vertically.
matrix(n1, n2, n3, n4, n5, n6)	Uses matrix multiplication to move each of the corners of the element. The matrix, which is represented by six numbers, can duplicate any other transform (or any combination of transforms). However, you're unlikely to build the matrix you need yourself, even if you're a math nerd. Instead, you'll probably use a tool that provides you with the ready-made matrix you want.

NOTE When you get tired of moving an element around in two dimensions, you can use 3-D transforms to move, rotate, and warp it in three-dimensional space. You'll find several good, interactive examples of 3-D transforms at *http://tinyurl.com/3d-transitions*.

POWER USERS' CLINIC

How to Shift the Starting Point

Ordinarily, transforms are made using the center point of your element as a reference point. You can shift this reference point by using the transform-origin property before you apply your transform. For example, here's how you can rotate a shape around its top-left corner:

```
.rotatedElement {
  -ms-transform-origin: 0% 0%;
  -webkit-transform-origin: 0% 0%;
  transform-origin: 0% 0%;

  -ms-transform: rotate(45deg);
```

```
  -webkit-transform: rotate(45deg);
  transform: rotate(45deg);
}
```

To rotate around the top-right corner, you'd use a value of 100% 0%. You can even specify a far-off origin that doesn't appear in your element (like 50% 200%, which puts the reference point halfway across the element, and a distance down that's equal to twice the element's height).

By default, the transform-origin property is set to 50% 50%, which puts the center point exactly in the middle of your element.

Transitions That Use Transforms

Transforms and transitions make a natural pair. For example, imagine you want to create an image gallery, like the one shown in Figure 6-12.

FIGURE 6-12

Here, a transform makes the hovered-over image stand out.

This example starts out simple enough, with a bunch of images wrapped in a `<div>` container:

```
<div class="gallery">
  <img src="bunny.jpg">
  <img src="cat.jpg">
  <img src="dog.jpg">
  <img src="platypus.jpg">
  <img src="goose.jpg">
</div>
```

Here's the style for the `<div>` that holds all the images:

```
.gallery {
  margin: 0px 30px 0px 30px;
  background: #D8EEFE;
  padding: 10px;
}
```

And here's how each `<img>` element starts off:

```
.gallery img {
  margin: 5px;
  padding: 5px;
  width: 75px;
  border: solid 1px black;
  background: white;
}
```

Notice that all the images are given explicit sizes with the `width` property. That's because this example uses slightly bigger pictures that are downsized when they're shown on the page. This technique is deliberate: It makes sure the browser has all the picture data it needs to enlarge the image with a transform. If you didn't take this step, and used thumbnail-sized picture files, the enlarged versions would be blurry.

Now for the hover effect. When the user moves the mouse over an image, the page uses a transform to rotate and expand the image slightly:

```
.gallery img:hover {
  -ms-transform: scale(2.2) rotate(10deg);
  -webkit-transform: scale(2.2) rotate(10deg);
  transform: scale(2.2) rotate(10deg);
}
```

Right now, this transform snaps the picture to its new size and position in one step. But to make this effect look more fluid and natural, you can define an all-encompassing transition in the normal state:

```
.gallery img {
  margin: 5px;
  padding: 5px;
  width: 75px;
  border: solid 1px black;
```

```
    -ms-transition: all 1s;
    -webkit-transition: all 1s;
    transition: all 1s;
    background: white;
}
```

Now the picture rotates and grows over a time span of 1 second. Move the mouse away, and it takes another second to shrink back to its original position.

Web Fonts

With all its pizzazzy new features, it's hard to pick the best of CSS3. But if you had to single out just one feature that opens an avalanche of new possibilities and is ready to use *right now*, that feature may just be web fonts.

In the past, web designers had to work with a limited set of web-safe fonts. These are the few fonts that are known to work on different browsers and operating systems. But as every decent designer knows, type plays a huge role in setting the overall atmosphere of a document. With the right font, the same content can switch from coolly professional to whimsical, or from old-fashioned to futuristic.

> **NOTE** There were good reasons why web browsers didn't rush to implement custom web fonts. First, there are optimization issues, because computer screens offer far less resolution than printed documents. If a web font isn't properly tweaked for onscreen viewing, it'll look like a blurry mess at small sizes. Second, most fonts aren't free. Big companies like Microsoft were understandably reluctant to add a feature that could encourage web developers to take the fonts installed on their computers and upload them to a website without proper permission. As you'll see in the next section, font companies now have good solutions for both problems.

CSS3 adds support for fancy fonts with the @font-face feature. Here's how it works:

1. You upload the font to your website (or, more likely, multiple versions of that font to support different browsers).

2. You register each font-face you want to use in your style sheet, using the @font-face command.

3. You use the registered font in your styles, by name, just as you use the web-safe fonts.

4. When a browser encounters a style sheet that uses a web font, it downloads the font to its temporary cache of pages and pictures. It then uses that font for just your page or website (Figure 6-13). If other web pages want to use the same font, they'll need to register it themselves and provide their own font files.

> **NOTE** Technically, @font-face isn't new. It was a part of CSS 2, but dropped in CSS 2.1 when browser makers couldn't cooperate. Now, in CSS3, there's a new drive to make @font-face a universal standard.

The following sections walk you through these essential steps.

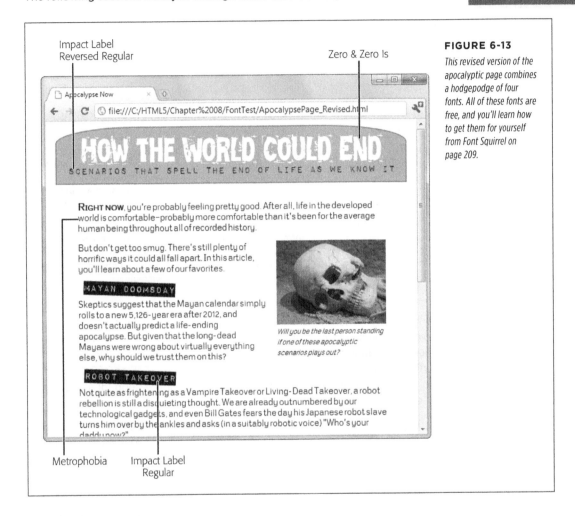

Impact Label
Reversed Regular

Zero & Zero Is

Metrophobia

Impact Label
Regular

FIGURE 6-13

This revised version of the apocalyptic page combines a hodgepodge of four fonts. All of these fonts are free, and you'll learn how to get them for yourself from Font Squirrel on page 209.

Web Font Formats

Although all current browsers support @font-face, they don't all support the same *types* of font files. Internet Explorer, which has supported @font-face for years, supports only EOT (Embedded OpenType) font files. This format has a number of advantages—for example, it uses compression to reduce the size of the font file, and it allows strict website licensing so a font can't be stolen from one website and used on another. However, the EOT format never caught on, and no other browser uses it. Instead, other browsers have (until recently) stuck with the more familiar font standards used in desktop computer applications—that's TTF (TrueType) and OTF (OpenType PostScript). But the story's still not complete without two more acronyms—SVG and WOFF. Table 6-3 puts all the font formats in perspective.

TABLE 6-3 *Embedded font formats*

FORMAT	DESCRIPTION	USE WITH
WOFF (Web Open Font Format)	The single font format of the future. Newer browsers support it.	Any browser that supports it, starting with Internet Explorer 9, Firefox 3.6, and Chrome 6.
EOT (Embedded Open Type)	A Microsoft-specific format that never caught on with browsers except Internet Explorer.	Internet Explorer (before IE 9)
TTF (TrueType) OTF (OpenType PostScript)	Your font will probably begin in one of these common desktop formats.	Mobile devices using the Android operating system and (optionally) non-IE browsers, such as Firefox, Chrome, Safari, and Opera
SVG (Scalable Vector Graphics)	An all-purpose graphics format you can use for fonts, with good but not great results (it's slower to display and produces lower-quality text).	Old mobile versions of Safari (before iOS 4.2), and (optionally) mobile devices using the Android operating system.

Bottom line: If you want to use the @font-face feature and support a wide range of browsers, you need to distribute your font in several different formats. The best practice is to include a WOFF file (for optimum performance on modern browsers), an EOT file (to fill in the gaps on old versions of IE), and a TTF or OTF file (to fill in support for Android and older non-IE browsers). It's also a good idea to supply a lower-quality SVG file to satisfy old iPads and iPhones.

If you think that's too many font files to manage, you can strip this down to an absolute minimum and cover most browsers with just two files: a font in the TTF or OTF format (either one is fine), and a font in the EOT format. This won't satisfy everyone, but it will give fancy fonts to the vast majority of people who visit your site.

NOTE Fortunately, font vendors and online font services will usually supply you with all four font formats you need, so you can guarantee the best possible level of browser support.

Finding a Font for Your Website

Now that you know where you can get the font files you need for your website, in which formats, you need to get your hands on them. You have two possibilities:

- **Download a free web font.** This way, you don't need to worry about licensing details. You can keep your wallet closed.

- **Convert a desktop font you already have into a web font.** This approach lets you use a font that you've already fallen in love with. It's also great for consistency—for example, if you work in a company that already has a standard set of fonts that it uses in logos, memos, and publications, it makes sense to stick with the same typefaces online. However, you'll need to do a bit of research to figure out the licensing situation, and you may need to cough up some more cash.

In the following sections, you'll try both approaches.

TROUBLESHOOTING MOMENT

Ironing Out the Quirks

Even if you follow the rules and supply all the required font formats, expect a few quirks. Here are some problems that occasionally crop up with web fonts:

- Many fonts look bad on the ancient but still-popular Windows XP operating system, because Windows XP computers often have the anti-aliasing display setting turned off. (And fonts without anti-aliasing look as attractive as mascara on a mule.)

- Some people have reported that some browsers (or some operating systems) have trouble printing certain embedded fonts.

- Some browsers suffer from a problem known as FOUT (which stands for Flash of Unstyled Text). This phenomenon occurs when an embedded font takes a few seconds to download, and the page is rendered first using a fallback font, and then re-rendered using the embedded font. This problem is most noticeable on old builds of Firefox. If it really bothers you, Google provides a JavaScript library that lets you define fallback styles that kick in for unloaded fonts, giving you complete control over the rendering of your text at all times (see *http://tinyurl.com/font-loader*).

Although these quirks are occasionally annoying, most are being steadily ironed out in new browser builds. For example, Firefox now minimizes FOUT by waiting for up to 3 seconds to download an embedded font before using the fallback font.

Getting a Free Font from Font Squirrel

One of the best places to find free web fonts is the Font Squirrel website at *www.fontsquirrel.com*. It provides a catalog of roughly 1,000 free-to-use fonts (see Figure 6-14).

When you find a font you like in Font Squirrel's list, start by checking the tiny icons underneath (Figure 6-15). These icons indicate how the font is licensed. Solid icons indicate that the font can be used in a particular context; white outlines indicate that it cannot.

If a font's licensing details check out (and on Font Squirrel, they almost always do), the next step is to take a closer look at your font. Click on the font text to switch to a font preview page, which shows every letter of the font and lets you test drive it on some text you type in.

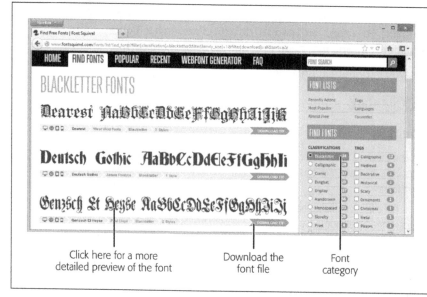

FIGURE 6-14

Font Squirrel gives you several options for font hunting, but the most effective way to find what you want is to browse by type ("Calligraphic," "Novelty," and "Retro," for example). Best of all, most fonts are free to use wherever you want—on your personal computer to create documents, or on the Web to build web pages.

Click here for a more detailed preview of the font

Download the font file

Font category

FIGURE 6-15

The first two icons are the most important—they indicate that the font is allowed both on the desktop and on the Web. Virtually all Font Squirrel fonts include these two icons. The next two icons indicate whether you can use the font in ebooks and custom-built applications. (If you're not sure what an icon means, just click it to find out.)

This font cannot be included in a custom application

This font cannot be embedded in an eBook

This font allows online use

This font allows desktop use

If you like what you see, the final step is to download the font. Depending on the font, you may be able to download a complete web-ready font kit, or—more likely—you'll need to download just the TTF or OTF file and then create your own kit. This quirk is largely due to the messy world of font licensing. Many fonts use the SIL Open Font License, which makes the font free for everyone to use but doesn't allow a service like Font Squirrel to repackage it. Fortunately, creating your own kit is easy—and perfectly legit. You'll learn how to do that in the next section.

Using a Font on Your Computer

Can I use the same font for web work and printed documents?

If you find a hot new font to use in your website, you can probably put it to good use on your computer, too. For example, you might want to use it in an illustration program to create a logo. Or, your business might want to use it for other print work, like ads, fliers, product manuals, and financial reports.

Modern Windows and Mac computers support TrueType (.ttf) and OpenType (.otf) fonts. Every font package includes a font in one of these formats—usually TrueType. To install it in Windows, make sure you've pulled it out of the ZIP download file. Right-click the font file and then choose Install. (You can do this with multiple font files at once.) On a Mac, double-click the font file to open the Font Book utility. Then, click the Install Font button.

Preparing a Font for the Web

Using Font Squirrel, you can convert a standard desktop TTF or OTF format font file into a web-ready font that you can use in any web page. You can do this with any of the free fonts you download from Font Squirrel. You *may* also be able to do this with the fonts on your own computer, but it's important to understand the licensing issues that you'll face first (see the box below). Using an ordinary desktop font in an online website without permission is likely to be a breach of copyright—and, if the font maker has asked Font Squirrel to blacklist the font, you won't be allowed to perform the desktop-to-web conversion anyway.

Understanding the Rules of Font Licensing

Ordinary fonts used in desktop software aren't free. It's not kosher to take a font you have on your computer and use it on your website, unless you have explicit permission from the font's creator.

For example, Microsoft and Apple pay to include certain fonts with their operating systems and applications so you can use them to, say, create a newsletter in a word processor. However, this license doesn't give you permission to put these fonts on a web server and use them in your pages.

If you have a favorite font, the only way to know whether you need to pay for it is to contact the company or individual that made it. Some font makers charge licensing fees based on the amount of traffic your website receives. Other font creators may let you use their fonts for a nominal amount or for free, provided you meet certain criteria (for example, you include some small-print note about the font you're using, or you have a noncommercial website that isn't out to make boatloads of money). There's also a side benefit to reaching out: Skilled font makers often provide versions of their creations that are optimized for web viewing.

Once you know that you're allowed to use a specific font, you can convert it using Font Squirrel's handy web font generator. To get there, click on the Webfont Generator tab near the top of the Font Squirrel site, or just surf directly to *www.fontsquirrel.com/fontface/generator*. Figure 6-16 shows you the three-step process you need to follow.

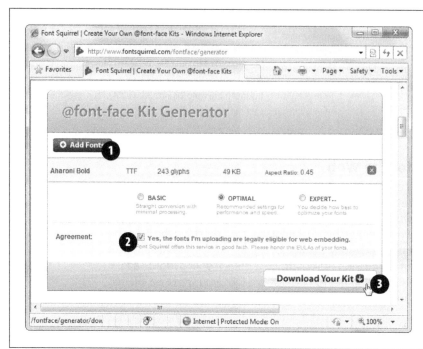

FIGURE 6-16

First, click Add Fonts to upload a font file from your computer (#1). Then, add a checkmark to the setting "Yes, the fonts I'm uploading are legally eligible for web embedding," assuming you've reviewed their license requirements, as described on page 211 (#2). Finally, click Download Your Kit (#3).

When you download a font kit, you get a compressed Zip file that contains a number of files. For example, if you download the Chantelli Antiqua font, then you get these files:

```
Bernd Montag License.txt
Chantelli_Antiqua-webfont.eot
Chantelli_Antiqua-webfont.svg
Chantelli_Antiqua-webfont.ttf
Chantelli_Antiqua-webfont.woff
demo.html
stylesheet.css
```

The text file (*Bernd Montag License.txt*) provides licensing information that basically says you can use the font freely but never sell it. The Chantelli_Antiqua-webfont files provide the font in four different file formats. (Depending on the font you pick, you may get additional files for different variations of that font—for example, in bold, italic, and extra-dark styles.) Finally, the *stylesheet.css* file contains the style sheet rule you need to apply the font to your web page, and *demo.html* displays the font in a sample web page.

To use the Chantelli Antiqua font, you need to copy all the Chantelli_Antiqua-webfont files to the same folder as your web page. Then you need to register the font so that it's available for use in your style sheet. To do that, you use a complex @font-face rule at the beginning of your style sheet, which looks like this (with the lines numbered for easy reference):

```
1  @font-face {
2    font-family: 'ChantelliAntiquaRegular';
3    src: url('Chantelli_Antiqua-webfont.eot');
4    src: local('Chantelli Antiqua'),
5      url('Chantelli_Antiqua-webfont.woff') format('woff'),
6      url('Chantelli_Antiqua-webfont.ttf') format('truetype'),
7      url('Chantelli_Antiqua-webfont.svg') format('svg');
8  }
```

To understand what's going on in this rule, it helps to break it down line by line:

- **Line 1.** @font-face is the tool you use to officially register a font so you can use it elsewhere in your style sheet.

- **Line 2.** You can give the font any name you want. You'll use this name later, when you apply the font.

- **Line 3.** The first format you specify must be the file name of the EOT file. That's because Internet Explorer gets confused by the rest of the rule and ignores the other formats. The url() function is a style sheet technique that tells a browser to download another file at the location you specify. If you put the font in the same folder as your web page, then you can simply provide the file name here.

- **Line 4.** The next step is running the local() function. This function tells the browser the font name, and if that font just happens to be installed on the visitor's computer, the browser uses it. However, in rare cases this can cause a problem (for example, it could cause Mac OS X to show a security dialog box, depending on where your visitor has installed the font, or it could load a different font that has the same name). For these reasons, web designers sometimes use an obviously fake name to ensure that the browser finds no local font. One common choice is to use a meaningless symbol like local('☺').

- **Lines 5 to 7.** The final step is to tell the browser about the other font files it can use. If you have a WOFF font file, suggest that first, as it offers the best quality. Next, tell the browser about the TTF or OTF file, and finally about the SVG file.

TIP Of course, you don't need to type the @font-face rule by hand (and you definitely don't need to understand all the technical underpinnings described above). You can simply copy the rule from the *stylesheet. css* file that's included in the web font kit.

Once you register an embedded font using the @font-face feature, you can use it in any style sheet. Simply use the familiar font-family property, and refer to the font family name you specified with @font-face (in line 2). Here's an example that leaves out the full @font-face details:

```
@font-face {
  font-family: 'ChantelliAntiquaRegular';
  ...
}

body {
  font-family: 'ChantelliAntiquaRegular';
}
```

This rule applies the font to the entire web page, although you could certainly restrict it to certain elements or use classes. However, you must register the font with @font-face *before* you use it in a style rule. Reverse the order of these two steps, and the font won't work properly.

Even Easier Web Fonts with Google

If you want a simpler way to use a fancy font on your website, Google has got you covered. It provides a service called Google Fonts (formerly Google Web Fonts), which hosts free fonts that anyone can use. The beauty of Google Fonts is that you don't need to worry about font formats, because Google detects the user's browser and automatically sends the right font file. All you need to do is add a link to a Google-generated style sheet.

To use a Google font in your pages, follow these steps:

1. **Go to *www.google.com/fonts*.**

   Google shows you a long list of available fonts (Figure 6-17).

2. **At the top of the page, click a tab title (Word, Sentence, or Paragraph) to choose how you preview fonts.**

   For example, if you're hunting for a font to use in a heading, you'll probably choose Word or Sentence to take a close look at a single word or line of text. But if you're looking for a font to use in your body text, you'll probably choose Paragraph to study a whole paragraph of text at once. No matter what option you choose, you can type in your own preview text and set an exact font size for your previews.

3. **Set your search options.**

   If you have a specific font in mind, type it into the search box. Otherwise, you'll need to scroll down, and that could take ages. To help you get what you want more quickly, start by setting a sort order and some filtering options, if they apply (for example, you might want to find the most popular bold sans-serif fonts). Figure 6-17 shows you where to find these options.

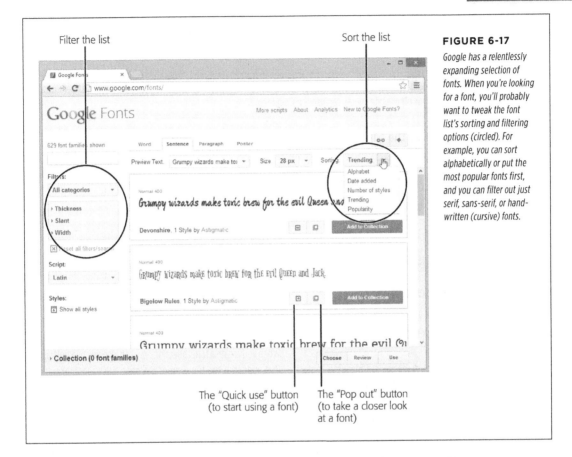

FIGURE 6-17

Google has a relentlessly expanding selection of fonts. When you're looking for a font, you'll probably want to tweak the font list's sorting and filtering options (circled). For example, you can sort alphabetically or put the most popular fonts first, and you can filter out just serif, sans-serif, or hand-written (cursive) fonts.

4. **When you see a font that's a candidate for your site, click the "Pop out" button.**

   Google pops open an informative window that describes the font and shows each of its characters.

5. **If you like the font, click the "Quick-use" button to get the information you need to use it.**

   Google shows you the code you need to use this font. It consists of a style sheet link (which you must add to your web page) and an example of a style sheet rule that uses the font.

6. **Add a style sheet link to your web page.**

   For example, if you picked the Metrophobic font, Google wants you to place the following link in the <head> section of your page:

```
<link href="http://fonts.googleapis.com/css?family=Metrophobic"
rel="stylesheet">
```

This style sheet registers the font, using @font-face, so you don't have to. Best of all, Google provides the font files, so you don't need to upload anything extra to your website.

> **NOTE** Remember to put the link for the Google font style sheet before your other style sheet links. That way, your other style sheets can use the Google font.

7. **Use the font, by name, wherever you want.**

For example, here's how you could use the newly registered Metrophobic font in a heading, with fallbacks in case the browser fails to download the font file:

```
h1 {
    font-family: 'Metrophobic', arial, serif;
}
```

POWER USERS' CLINIC

Creating a Font Collection

These steps show the fastest way to get the markup you need for a font. However, you can get more options by creating a *font collection*.

A font collection is a way to package up multiple fonts. To start creating one, you simply click the "Add to Collection" button next to a font you like. As you add fonts to your collection, each one appears in the fat blue footer at the bottom of the page.

When you're finished picking the fonts you want, click the Use button in the footer. Google then shows a page that's similar to the "Quick-use" page, except that it allows you to create a

single style sheet reference that supports *all* the fonts from your custom-picked collection.

When you create a font collection, you can also use two buttons that appear at the top right of the page. Click the Bookmark button (which looks like a link in a chain) to create a browser bookmark that lets you load up the same collection at some point in the future, so you can tweak it. Click the Download button (which looks like a down-pointing arrow) to download copies of the fonts to your computer, so you can install the fonts and use them for print work.

> **TIP** Still looking for the perfect font? Popular font subscription sites like *http://fonts.com* and *http://typekit.com* give you access to thousands of ultra-high-quality typefaces from legendary font foundries like Linotype and Monotype. Font-addicted web developers will need to pay from $10 to $100 a year, with more money needed to outfit super-popular sites that get avalanches of web traffic.

Putting Text in Multiple Columns

Fancy fonts aren't the only innovation CSS3 has for displaying text. It also adds a module for multicolumn text, which gives you a flexible, readable way to deal with lengthy content.

Using multiple columns is almost effortless, and you have two ways to create them. Your first option is to set the number of columns you want using the `column-count` property, like this:

```
.Content {
  text-align: justify;
  column-count: 3;
}
```

As of this writing, the `column-count` property works only in Internet Explorer 10 and 11. Although multiple columns are supported by Chrome, Firefox, Safari, and Opera, you need to use the vendor-prefixed versions of the `column-count` property, like this:

```
.Content {
  text-align: justify;
  -moz-column-count: 3;
  -webkit-column-count: 3;
  column-count: 3;
}
```

This approach—creating a set number of columns—works well for fixed-size layouts. But if you have a space that grows and shrinks with the browser window, your columns may grow too wide and become unreadable. In this situation, it's better *not* to set the exact number of columns. Instead, tell the browser how big each column should be using the `column-width` property:

```
.Content {
  text-align: justify;
  -moz-column-width: 10em;
  -webkit-column-width: 10em;
  column-width: 10em;
}
```

The browser can then create as many columns as it needs to fill up the available space (see Figure 6-18).

> **NOTE** You can use pixel units to size a column, but em units make more sense. That's because em units adapt to the current font size. So if a web page visitor ratchets up the text size settings in her browser, the column width grows proportionately to match. To get a sense of size, 1 em is equal to two times the current font size. So if you have a 12 pixel font, 1 em works out to 24 pixels.

our favorites.

MAYAN DOOMSDAY

Skeptics suggest that the Mayan calendar simply rolls to a new 5,126-year era after 2012, and doesn't actually predict a life-ending apocalypse. But given that the long-dead Mayans were wrong about virtually everything else, why should we trust them on this?

ROBOT TAKEOVER

Not quite as frightening as a Vampire Takeover or Living-Dead Takeover, a robot rebellion is still a disquieting thought. We are already outnumbered by our technological gadgets, and even Bill Gates fears the day his Japanese robot slave turns him over by the ankles and asks (in a suitably robotic voice) "Who's your daddy now?"

66 We don't know how the universe started, so we can't

Will you be the last person standing if one of these apocalyptic scenarios plays out?

But don't get too smug. There's still plenty of horrific ways it could all fall apart. In this article, you'll learn about a few of our favorites.

MAYAN DOOMSDAY

Skeptics suggest that the Mayan calendar simply rolls to a new 5,126-year era after 2012, and doesn't actually predict a life-ending apocalypse. But given that the long-dead

are already outnumbered by our technological gadgets, and even Bill Gates fears the day his Japanese robot slave turns him over by the ankles and asks (in a suitably robotic voice) "Who's your daddy now?"

66 We don't know how the universe started, so we can't be sure it won't just end, maybe today. 99

UNEXPLAINED SINGULARITY

We don't know how the universe started, so we can't be sure it won't just

contend with vicious storms, widespread food shortages, and surly air conditioning repairmen.

GLOBAL EPIDEMIC

Some time in the future, a lethal virus could strike. Predictions differ about the source of the disease, but candidates include monkeys in the African jungle, bioterrorists, birds and pigs with the flu, warriors from the future, an alien race, hospitals that use too many antibiotics, vampires, the CIA, and unwashed brussel sprouts. Whatever the source, it's clearly bad news.

These apocalyptic predictions do not reflect the views of the author.
About Us Disclaimer Contact Us
Copyright © 2014

FIGURE 6-18

In a narrow window (top), Firefox can accommodate just one column. But widen the window, and you'll get as many more as can fit (bottom).

CSS3 provides a few more properties for tailoring the look of your columns. You can adjust the size of the spacing between columns with column-gap. You can also add a vertical line to separate them with column-rule, which accepts a thickness, border style, and color (just like the border property). Here's an example that makes a red, 1-pixel-wide column rule:

```
-webkit-column-rule: 1px solid red;
-moz-column-rule: 1px solid red;
column-rule: 1px solid red;
```

You can also use the column-span property to let figures and other elements span columns. The default value of column-span is 1, which means the element is locked in the single column where it appears. The only other acceptable value is all, which lets an element stretch across the entire width of all the columns. There's currently no way to let an element span some but not all columns.

Here's an example (shown in Figure 6-19) that uses column spanning with a figure:

```
.SpanFigure {
  -moz-column-span: all;
  -webkit-column-span: all;
  column-span: all;
}
```

This technique doesn't work for figures that set the float property to something other than none. That's because floating figures already have the ability to float free of your layout and any columns it contains.

> **NOTE** Columns work well if you need to break up text to make it more readable on wide layouts. However, columns aren't the best choice for truly large amounts of content, since there's currently no way to tie the height of a column to the height of the browser window. So if you split a lengthy essay into three columns, the reader will need to scroll from top to bottom to read the first column, then back to the top, then down to the bottom to read the second column, and again for the third. If the content is more than a screenful or two, all this scrolling gets old fast.

FIGURE 6-19

This tweaked-up multicolumn page adds a rule between columns and lets figures span multiple columns.

RIGHT NOW, you're probably feeling pretty good. After all, life in the developed world is comfortable–probably more comfortable than it's been for the average human being throughout all of recorded history.

Will you be the last person standing if one of these apocalyptic scenarios plays out?

But don't get too smug. There's still plenty of horrific ways it could all fall apart. In this article, you'll learn about a few of our favorites.

MAYAN DOOMSDAY

Skeptics suggest that the Mayan calendar simply rolls

UNEXPLAINED SINGULARITY

We don't know how the universe started, so we can't be sure it won't just end, maybe today, and maybe with nothing more exciting than a puff of anti-matter and a slight fizzing

Responsive Web Design with CSS3

When web designers first started putting their content into HTML pages, they faced a challenge. Whereas print designers could rely on certain assumptions about how their documents would be arranged on paper and how they would be read by their audiences, the online world was loose and lawless. Depending on the user's browser (and personal preferences), the same HTML page might appear wedged in a tiny window or floating in a giant one. This made complex layouts risky. A layout that looked perfect in one window could easily turn into an awkward and ungainly mess when viewed in a window with different proportions.

Today, this variability has only increased. Not only do web designers need to think about different sizes of browser windows on desktop computers, but they also need to accommodate different sizes of *devices*, like tablets and smartphones. And at the same time, website layouts have become more intricate, with most sites now composed of menus, navigation aids, sidebars, and so on. If your goal is to create a single website that can shift gracefully between different viewing contexts, these details present a significant challenge.

Because web designers have long since outsourced the layout and formatting work of their web pages to CSS, it makes sense for CSS to provide the solution for this problem. Fortunately, CSS3 has the perfect tool: a feature called *media queries*, which lets your website seamlessly switch from one set of styles to another depending on the window size or the viewing device.

Media queries are an essential technique for mobile web development. But even if you don't expect any visitors to surf your site on a smartphone, media queries will still help you ensure that your layout adapts itself to the viewer—for example, dropping an extra column when there's no space to show it comfortably, or moving the navigation links from the top of a page to its side. This sort of adaptation is part of a wildly popular web design philosophy called *responsive design*, which you'll explore in this chapter.

Responsive Design: The Basics

The problem of varying window sizes has been around since the dawn of the Web. Over the years, web designers have cooked up a variety of complementary techniques—some elegant, some messy—to cope with the challenges of responsive design.

Before you learn how to use media queries, it's important to consider the following traditional tactics. All of them are still important today—but, as you'll see, they don't form a complete solution on their own. Once you recognize their limits, you'll understand how CSS3 patches the gaps.

Fluid Layout

The simplest solution to the problem of resizing windows is to make a *proportional* layout—one that simply sucks up the available space, no matter how large or small it is.

Creating a proportional layout is easy enough in theory. The basic principle is to carve up your page into columns using percentage sizes instead of pixel sizes. Say, for example, you have a two-column layout like this:

```
<body>
  <div class="leftColumn">
    ...
  </div>

  <div class="rightColumn">
    ...
  </div>
</body>
```

The style rules for a fixed layout might look like this:

```
.leftColumn {
  width: 275px;
  float: left;
}

.rightColumn {
  width: 685px;
  float: left;
}
```

```
body {
   margin: 0px;
}
```

But the style rules for a proportionately sized layout would look like this:

```
.leftColumn {
   width: 28.6%;
   float: left;
}

.rightColumn {
   width: 71.4%;
   float: left;
}

body {
   margin: 0px;
}
```

Here, the left column has a width of 28.6%, so it takes 28.6% of the width of its container, which is the <body> element. In this example, the <body> element has no margins, so it takes up the full width of the browser window, and the left column gets 28.6% of that.

As you would expect, the percentages of the two columns combined add up to exactly 100%, filling the page. No matter what the size of the browser window, the columns expand or shrink to match. Proportional layouts are also called *fluid layouts*, because the content flows seamlessly into whatever space is available.

NOTE   In this example, the left column width of 28.6% is calculated by dividing the fixed width of the column (275 pixels) into the fixed width of the entire layout (which, previously, was set at the relatively common default width of 960 pixels). Because most layouts are initially planned using fixed widths, web developers are accustomed to using this sort of calculation when they create fluid layouts.

Of course, it's not enough to adjust column sizes alone. You also need to think about margins, padding, and borders. When novice web developers create their first fluid layouts, they often leave in fixed margins and padding (using pixel values), while sizing their columns proportionately. As a result, the columns can occupy only the space that's left over after the margins are subtracted. However, the column width percentages are calculated according to the full page width, without taking the margins into account. This discrepancy can lead to problems in narrow windows, when the fixed-width margins crowd out the proportional columns.

For example, imagine you create styles like this:

```
.leftColumn {
   width: 27%;
```

```
    margin: 5px;
    float: left;
}


.rightColumn {
    width: 68%;
    margin: 5px;
    float: left;
}
```

These two columns occupy a combined 95%, leaving an extra 5% for the margin space. This is enough for mid- to large-sized windows, but if you size the window small enough, the leftover 5% can't accommodate the fixed margin space. To see this problem in action, simply give each column a different background color using the background property and then try resizing the window, as shown in Figure 7-1.

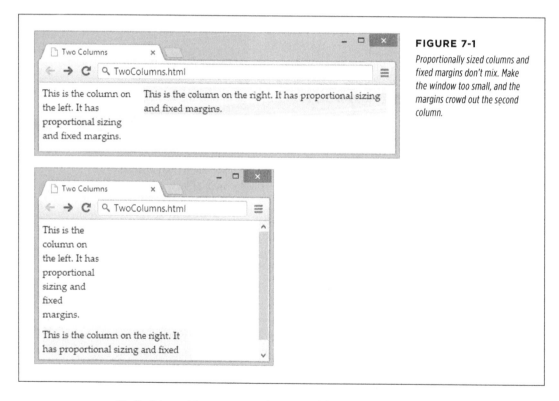

FIGURE 7-1

Proportionally sized columns and fixed margins don't mix. Make the window too small, and the margins crowd out the second column.

To fix this problem, any margins you add between proportional columns must also use proportional sizing. So if the columns leave 5% of the page width unclaimed, you can use that for your margins. Split it into three 1.66% sections—one for the left edge of the window, one for the right edge of the window, and one for the space between the columns, like this:

```
.leftColumn {
  width: 27%;
  margin-left: 1.66%;
  margin-right: 1.66%;
  background: #FFFFCC;
  float: left;
}

.rightColumn {
  width: 68%;
  margin-right: 1.66%;
  background: #CCFFCC;
  float: left;
}
```

Figure 7-2 shows the solution, with both margins and columns sized proportionally using percentages.

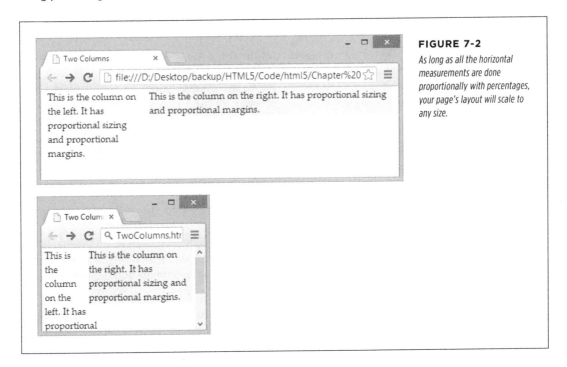

FIGURE 7-2

As long as all the horizontal measurements are done proportionally with percentages, your page's layout will scale to any size.

Depending on the effect you want, you may find that proportional margins don't look quite right. If you don't want your margins to change based on the size of the web browser window, you can use a workaround. For example, you can place another element inside one of your proportional columns and give that element its own fixed margins or padding. Because this element is placed *inside* the top-level layout that you've already established, and because your layout is fully proportional, it will fit snugly into any window size.

Borders present a similar problem. If you add borders to your columns, the extra space they require will break your layout in the same way as the fixed margins shown in Figure 7-1. In this situation, you can't solve the problem with proportional measurements, because borders don't accept percentage widths. Instead, the easiest solution is to use the workaround suggested above: Add a <div> element inside your proportional column, and apply the border to the <div>. This time-honored technique makes your markup a bit messier (because you need an extra layer of layout), but it ensures that your layout works at any size.

CSS3 Box-Sizing and calc()

The layout problems you've touched on in this section are common—so common that CSS3 is brimming with potential solutions. Here are two of the most promising (although not perfect, as you'll see).

- **Box-sizing.** Ordinarily, borders are added to the outside of elements, which means you need to subtract the border space from your layout calculations. But CSS3 adds a new box-sizing property that, if set to border-box, puts the border on the *inside* of your box. The border looks the same, but the size calculation is different. For example, it means that a 67%-wide column stays 67% wide, no matter how thick its border.

- **The calc() function.** If you need to combine proportional and fixed measurements, you can ask CSS3 to do the calculations for you—and use the results in your layout—thanks to the nifty calc() function. For example, imagine you need to create a column that's 67% wide, less 5px of margin space. Careless web developers might fudge the issue by sizing the column down to 65% (causing the inconsistent spacing issue shown in Figure 7-1). But with CSS3 you can set the width property to calc(67%-5px), which makes sure your column mops up exactly all of the available space—and not a pixel more.

Unfortunately, in both cases the cure may not be much better than the disease. The box-sizing setting fails on IE 7, and requires the vendor-specific -moz- prefix (page 183) on Firefox. The calc() function fails on IE 7, IE 8, and the pre-Chrome Android browser, and older versions of Safari require the -webkit- prefix. There are polyfills that can smooth out these issues, but for now it's easier to avoid these features altogether until more people inch forward to newer, more modern browsers.

Fluid Images

Achieving a multicolumn, proportional layout is the first step in responsive design. However, there's plenty more to occupy yourself with when you begin to consider the content in those columns.

One issue is images. Ordinarily, image boxes are sized to fit their content—in other words, the exact pixel dimensions of your picture file. However, this arrangement can lead to a problem in small-sized windows. If there's not enough room to accommodate the picture, it will spill out of its column and sprawl over other elements, obscuring them and generally looking sloppy.

The solution to this annoyance is simple. Cap each image at the maximum width of its container, with a style rule that looks like this:

```
img {
  max-width: 100%;
}
```

As always, the 100% is relative to the element's container. In this case, that's the column that contains the image, not the whole page. Now your image can grow until it reaches its full size *or* until it meets the boundaries of its container, whichever comes first (Figure 7-3).

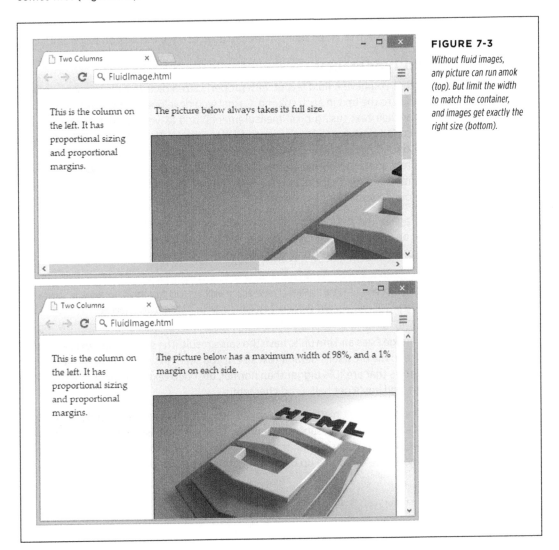

FIGURE 7-3

Without fluid images, any picture can run amok (top). But limit the width to match the container, and images get exactly the right size (bottom).

TIP If you decide to add a margin around your image, make sure the percentages you use for the margin-left, margin-right, and max-width total 100% (and not more).

One limitation of fluid images is that the browser needs to download the full-sized image file no matter what size the image is displayed at. This wastes a small amount of time and bandwidth, which is inconvenient for mobile devices. Sadly, CSS can't correct this problem on its own. But there are other potential solutions that attempt to deal with this issue using some combination of server-side code, web services, and JavaScript libraries. If you're serving up an image-heavy site to large numbers of mobile users, you may want to consider these techniques, which are discussed in a Smashing Magazine article at *http://tinyurl.com/responsive-img* (but most web developers won't bother). Happily, there is a way to solve the analogous but more serious problem of video sizes on mobile devices—see the box on page 244.

Fluid Typography

Now that you have a fluid layout with properly sized pictures, it's time to turn your attention to the text in each column. Casual web developers pick an attractive fixed size for their text (using pixel measurements) and leave it at that. However, such hard-coded sizes break the responsive layout model, because text that's properly sized on a desktop display will be vanishingly tiny on mobile devices. And while website readers can always zoom in to see small text, the goal of responsive design is to make a page that fits any window without requiring excessive zooming and side-to-side scrolling.

Once again, the solution involves avoiding using fixed units of measurement like pixels and points. Instead, you want to set your text sizes relatively, using percentages or em units. The *em* unit, named after the letter M, is the most popular choice.

> **NOTE** The em has a long tradition of representing widths in print typography. For example, the term *em dash* originally referred to a dash that was the width of a capital M in the current typeface.

Percentage sizes and em units have the same result: The size of your text is adjusted relative to the browser's default text size. If you set a text size of 110% or 1.1em, you'll get letters that are 10% bigger than normal, unstyled text. Set a text size of 50% or 0.5em, and you'll get half-sized characters.

Although it doesn't matter whether you use percentages or ems, most responsive web designs follow the same convention. They set the base text size of the page to 100% (just to emphasize that this is the baseline from which all other text is sized), and then tweak that size up or down in other elements with ems:

```
body {
  font-size: 100%
}


p {
  font-size: 0.9em
}
```

```
h1 {
  font-size: 2em
}
```

Experienced web developers don't stop there. Instead, they use ems for all other fixed measurements in their layouts. For example, if you have a border or a bit of margin or padding space deep inside your layout, you're better off to set it with ems than pixels. That way, these sizes are tweaked to match the size of the text. It's a subtle adjustment, but one that creates a more polished appearance.

For example, imagine you've created a two-level layout that places a <div> inside your left column. You use this <div> to get the extra spacing you want around your content, without breaking the proportionally sized column layout:

```
<body>
  <div class="leftColumn">
    <div class="leftColumnContent">
      ...
    </div>
  </div>

  <div class="rightColumn">
    ...
  </div>
</body>
```

You could set the border, margins, and padding of your left column content <div> using pixels. Your layout would still work and it would still be fluid. But it's even better if you use ems, as shown here:

```
.leftColumn {
  width: 28.6%;
  background: #FFFFCC;
  float: left;
}

.rightColumn {
  width: 71.4%;
  background: #CCFFCC;
  float: left;
}

.leftColumnContent {
  border: 0.07em solid gray;
  margin: 0.3em;
  padding: 0.2em 0.3em 0.4em 0.4em;
}
```

NOTE In most layouts, the chief benefit of using ems for borders, margins, and padding is that it prevents these elements from being too large in tiny windows and dominating your layout on mobile devices.

FEATURE FROM THE FUTURE

CSS3: When an Em Becomes a Rem

There's one quirk that faces web designers when using text in complex responsive layouts. Proportionately sized text units, like ems and percentages, size their text with respect to the containing element. That's no problem in a simple example like the one considered on page 229, because the containing element is the <body> element that holds the page, or another element that inherits the font settings of the <body> element. The headaches happen when you apply proportional sizing to *multiple* levels of your layout.

For example, suppose you create a <div> and give it a text size of 1.1em. Then, inside that <div> you add an <h1> heading with a size of 2em. You might expect that the heading is twice the default text size, but it's actually twice the size of its *container*, which is 1.1em. That works out to a heading that's 2.2 times the default text size.

To avoid this compounding effect, you need to be disciplined about where you apply your text sizing. Ideally, you should do it at only one layout level. However, CSS3 has a new unit that neatly solves the problem, called *rems* (which stands for "root em"). Essentially, a rem is a relative measurement just like an em, but with a twist: No matter where you put it, a rem is always calculated relative to the text size of the <html> element, not the text size of the containing element. Thus, 2rem is always two times the size of normal text, no matter where you apply it.

Rems have surprisingly good support—they work in every modern browser. The problem is the familiar stragglers, IE 8 and IE 7, which don't understand rems at all. And while it's technically possible to polyfill the gap with JavaScript (see *http://tinyurl.com/rem-polyfill*), most sensible web developers avoid adding yet another script simply to switch their unit system and stick to the slightly inconvenient em units for now.

Of course there's much more to typography than the size of your typeface. To create text that remains readable on a range of displays, you need to think about line-lengths, margins, line height, and even multicolumn text (as demonstrated on page 217). You can't deal with any of these issues using ordinary fluid layouts and proportional sizing. However, you *can* create more flexible style sheets that tweak these other details using media queries, as you'll see shortly. But first, there's one more consideration that you need to unravel: the automatic scaling behavior of mobile phones.

Understanding Viewports: Making Your Layout Work on a Smartphone

In theory, the two-column example you've seen so far can fit into any window size. But in practice there's another complication that comes into play for small mobile devices: the size of the *viewport*.

Apple introduced the viewport concept so its iPhones could do a respectable job displaying the ordinary websites of the time, which didn't use the techniques of responsive web design. Instead of showing just a tiny fragment of a large web page, mobile browsers like Safari show a zoomed-out view that fits in more content. This zoomed-out display area is called the viewport.

The viewport technique is a bit of a tradeoff. It ensures that the page looks more like it would on a desktop browser, but it also makes most ordinary text illegible. It reduces the need to scroll back and forth, but it increases the need to zoom in and out. It makes it easier for viewers to orient themselves in the page, but it prevents them from comfortably reading the content.

> **NOTE** Although Apple introduced the viewport feature, all other mobile developers now follow the same practice. The only difference is how big the viewport is and how much of the web page gets crammed into view at once.

If you're creating a traditional desktop website, you don't have to worry about the devices' viewport settings. They'll ensure that your site looks reasonably good on super-small mobile screens (even though mobile visitors won't find the scaled-down site completely convenient). On the other hand, if you're planning to go all the way with responsive design and create a true, mobile-friendly website, you need to make viewport changes. You need to tell mobile browsers *not* to perform their automatic viewport scaling, which you can easily do by adding the following <meta> element to the page's <head> section:

```
<meta content="initial-scale=1.0" name="viewport">
```

This line tells mobile devices to use the true scale of your page, with no zooming out. For example, it means a modern iPhone will fit your page into a 320-pixel wide window and display that at full size. Without this scale adjustment, the iPhone will give your page a desktop-sized 980 pixels of width and then shrink that down to fit. Figure 7-4 shows the difference.

> **NOTE** You're probably aware that there are plenty of online simulators that let you see what your website looks like on different mobile devices. For example, on *http://mobiletest.me* you can compare your site's appearance on the latest iPhones, iPads, and Android devices. However, most simulators don't replicate the automatic scaling behavior. In other words, when you preview your site in a simulator, it may look as though you set the initial scale to 1.0 with the <meta> element shown above. If you haven't, you won't get an accurate reflection of what you'll see on the device itself, so tread with caution.

■ Adapting Your Layout with Media Queries

You've now seen how to create a fluid layout that can grow or shrink to fit any browser window. This approach guarantees that your page will fit into any window. However, it doesn't ensure that your page will always look good.

Simple fluid layouts tend to break down at the extremes. In a very tiny window, multiple columns are compacted down to embarrassingly thin dimensions, crowding text and pictures into an unreadable jumble. In a very large window, columns become dauntingly large, and it's hard to follow a line across the vast expanse of the page without losing your place.

FIGURE 7-4

Left: The iPhone's automatic rescaling treats this fluid layout like a desktop-optimized web page. As a result, its text is unreadable without zooming.

Right: Turn off the scaling, and you see your page as it truly is. The next step is to simplify the layout at small sizes using media queries.

One way to deal with these issues is to set limits on how far your layout can expand or contract. You can do that with the max-width and min-width properties. Expand a page beyond its maximum width, and you'll end up with an extra margin of space on the right. Shrink a page past its minimum width, and the columns will lock into their dimensions, while the browser adds scroll bars to let you move around. Maximum and minimum width settings give you a bit of basic protection against extreme layouts. However, they also reduce the value of your responsive design. For example, if your page can't shrink down to the dimensions of an iPhone window, it's not much use to mobile visitors.

A better solution is to gracefully tweak the *structure* of the layout when your page size changes. For example, a really small window needs a streamlined layout with no sidebars or ad panels. And a really big window presents the opportunity for scaled up text or multiple columns of text (page 217).

Enter *media queries*. This CSS3 feature gives you a simple way to vary styles for different viewing settings. Used carefully, they can help you serve everything from an ultra-widescreen desktop computer to an iPhone—without altering a single line of HTML.

The Anatomy of a Media Query

Media queries work by latching onto a key detail about the device that's viewing your page (like its size, resolution, color capabilities, and so on). Based on that information, you can apply different styles, or even swap in a completely different style sheet.

At its simplest, a media query is a separate section in your style sheet. That section starts with the word @media, followed by a condition in parentheses, and then a series of related styles in curly brackets. Here's the basic structure:

```
@media (media-feature-name: value) {
  /* New styles go here. */
}
```

A media query is similar to a block of conditional JavaScript code. If the current browser meets the condition that you've set out in parentheses, the styles inside come into effect. But if the browser doesn't satisfy the condition, the styles are ignored.

> **NOTE** The styles that lie outside of your @media section are always applied, no matter what. The conditional media query styles are applied in *addition* to the other styles. For that reason, the conditional media query styles often have the job of overriding the other style settings—for example, hiding something that was previously visible, moving a section to a new location, applying new text sizes, and so on.

To use a media query, you need to know what sorts of conditions you can construct. The media query standard lets you examine various details, which it calls *media features*. For example, you can find out the width of the display area and then change your styles when it shrinks beyond a certain limit. Table 7-1 lists the most commonly used media features. (There are also several vendor-specific, experimental media features that aren't supported consistently. These aren't included in this table.)

TABLE 7-1 *Most useful media features for building media queries*

FEATURE NAME	VALUE	COMMONLY USED TO...
width min-width max-width	The width of the display area (or rendering surface, on a printer).	Change the layout to accommodate very narrow displays (like a smartphone) or very wide displays.
height min-height max-height	The height of the display area.	Change the layout to accommodate very tall or very short displays.
device-width min-device-width max-device-width	The full width of the screen on the current computer or device (or the full width of a page in a printout).	Adjust the layout to specifically target different devices, like smartphones.

FEATURE NAME	VALUE	COMMONLY USED TO...
device-height min-device-height max-device-height	The full height of the screen or page.	Adjust the layout to specifically target different devices, like smartphones.
orientation	One of two values: landscape or portrait.	Change the layout for different orientations on a table computer.
device-aspect-ratio min-device-aspect-ratio max-device-aspect-ratio	The proportions of the display area, as a ratio. For example, an aspect ratio of 1/1 is completely square.	Adjust styles to fit different window shapes (although this approach quickly gets complicated).
color min-color max-color	The number of color bits. For example, 1-bit color is monochrome, while modern displays typically use 24-bit color, which accommodates millions of colors.	Check for the presence of color (for example, for a printable version of a page), or assess the level of color support.

NOSTALGIA CORNER

CSS Media Types

Interestingly, the creators of CSS took a crack at the multiple-device problem in CSS 2.1, using a feature called *media types*. You may already be using this standard to supply a separate style sheet for printouts:

```
<head>
...
<!-- Use this stylesheet to display the
     page onscreen. -->
<link rel="stylesheet" media="screen"
  href="styles.css">

<!-- Use this stylesheet to print the
```

```
     page. -->
<link rel="stylesheet" media="print"
  href="print_styles.css">
</head>
```

The media attribute also accepts the value handheld, which is meant for low-bandwidth, small-screen mobile devices. As a result, many modern mobile browsers ignore handheld style sheets anyway, making the media attribute a woefully inadequate tool for dealing with the wide range of web-connected devices that exists today. However, it's still a good way to clean up printouts.

Creating a Simple Media Query

You'll notice that most media query features have several versions, which let you set maximum or minimum limits. These limits are important, because most media queries apply to a range of values.

To use media queries, you must first choose the property you want to examine. For example, if you wanted to create a new set of styles that comes into effect for narrow windows, you'd choose the max-width setting. It's then up to you to choose a suitable limit. For example, the following media query creates a block of conditional styles that spring into action when the width of the browser window is 480 pixels or less:

```
@media (max-width: 480px) {
    ...
}
```

> **TIP** Right now, the most popular media features are `max-device-width` (for creating mobile versions of your pages), `max-width` (for varying styles based on the current size of the browser window), and `orientation` (for changing your layout based on whether a tablet computer like an iPad is turned horizontally or vertically).

For a simple test, use a media query to make an obvious change. For example, this media query alters the background color of a column:

```
@media (max-width: 480px) {
    .leftColumn {
        background: lime;
    }
}
```

Now you can check whether your media query is working. In your browser, slowly resize the browser window. As soon as the display area of the window shrinks to less than 480 pixels, the new style kicks in and the column changes to a fetching shade of lime green. All the other style properties that you've applied to the `leftColumn` class (for example, its size and positioning) stay in place, because the media query doesn't override them.

> **NOTE** Browsers that don't understand media queries, like Internet Explorer 8, will simply ignore these new styles and keep applying the original styles, no matter how big or small the browser window becomes.

If you want, you can add another media query section that overrides these rules at a still-smaller size. For example, this section will apply new rules when the browser width creeps under 250 pixels:

```
@media (max-width: 250px) {
    ...
}
```

Just remember that these rules are overriding everything that's been applied so far—in other words, the cumulative set of properties that have been set by the normal styles and the media query section for under 450 pixels. If this seems too confusing, don't worry—you'll learn to work around it with more tightly defined media queries on page 239. But first, it's time to consider a more practical example.

Building a Mobile-Friendly Layout

With media queries, you have the essential building blocks you need to create a website that looks just as respectable in a smartphone browser as a desktop browser. All you need to do is apply them.

Figure 7-5 shows a revamped example of the *ApocalypseSite.html* page you first saw in Chapter 2 (page 54). The original page used a fixed layout with hard-coded column widths. The revised version uses all of the techniques explored in this chapter. It has a fluid layout with proportional sizing (page 222) that fits any window width. It uses em units for margins, padding, border widths, and text sizes, ensuring that these details are adjusted in harmony on different devices (page 228). The site header image grows or shrinks to fit the available space, and the ad image in the sidebar uses the fluid image technique to make sure it never oversteps its bounds (page 226). It also uses the <meta> element fix to prevent mobile browsers from zooming out (page 231).

FIGURE 7-5

Behind the scenes, this page uses the best practices of responsive web design. You can peruse the complete CSS on the try-out site at http://prosetech.com/html5.

In short, the new *ApocalypseSite.html* page is mobile-ready. However, its layout still isn't mobile-*friendly*. That's because no matter how small the two side-by-side columns compress themselves, they won't fit cleanly in a tiny window. To correct this oversight, you need to use a media query.

Before you crack open your style sheet, you need to consider what the mobile version of your site should look like. Usually, mobile sites slim themselves down to a single column. Sidebars are either hidden completely or inserted above or below the main content. Figure 7-6 shows a cleaned-up version of the *ApocalypseSite. html* on an iPhone.

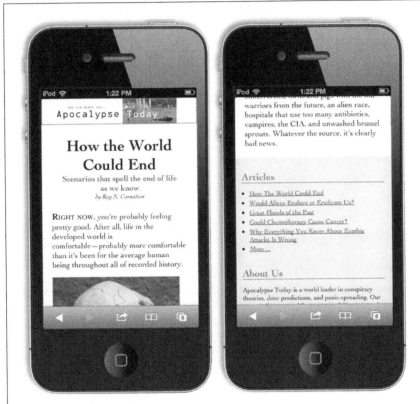

FIGURE 7-6

Here are two snapshots of the mobile version of the ApocalypseSite.html *page. The page starts with a small site header, followed by the article content (left). The article links and ad block from the sidebar are placed after the article footer (right).*

It's surprisingly easy to create the mobile version of the *ApocalypseSite.html* page. The shrunken site header and nicely sized text happen automatically, thanks to the page's use of fluid images and em units. The only task left for your media query is to rearrange the columns.

Initially, the two columns are defined with these two style rules:

```
.NavSidebar {
  float: left;
  width: 22%;
  font-size: small;
}
```

```
.Content {
  float: left;
  width: 78%;
}
```

The sidebar is floated on the left with a width of 22%. The content is floated next to it and given a width of 78%.

Because the layout stops working at small widths, it makes sense to use the popular max-width media feature. As you learned in the previous section, max-width gets the current size of the page in the browser window. If this value is small, two columns aren't appropriate.

Here's the media query that removes the floats and resizes the section so the columns take the full available width:

```
@media (max-width: 568px) {
  .NavSidebar {
    float: none;
    width: auto;
  }

  .Content {
    float: none;
    width: auto;
  }
}
```

These styles are applied in addition to the normal styles you've already defined. Thus, you may need to reset properties you've already changed to their default values. In this example, the media query styles reset the float property to none, and the width property to auto (although it would work equally well if you set the width to 100%). These are the default values, but the original sidebar style changed them. You'll also notice that the original NavSidebar style set the font size. The media query doesn't override this detail, so it stays in place.

Technically, this media query creates styles that apply to any narrow window, regardless of whether it's in a mobile browser or in a micro-sized window on a desktop browser. This makes perfect sense, but you can get more particular and create one set of styles for tiny desktop windows and another for mobile devices. To target tiny desktop windows, you'd use max-width, and to spot mobile devices, you'd use max-device-width, as detailed in Table 7-1.

TIP It's up to you when you want to switch to your simplified layout, but the 568-pixel mark is a good choice. That's because 568 pixels is the width of your page in an iPhone when it's turned sideways, in landscape orientation. (It works for Android devices too, as explained on page 243.)

This example needs one more adjustment. In the original version of the page, the NavSidebar section is defined before the Content section in the HTML markup. This lets you float them both on the left side, and makes sure the NavSidebar is on the left. Unfortunately, when you remove the floating behavior, the mobile version of the site is forced to show the sections in the order they appear, which means the NavSidebar appears at the top of the page, followed by the Content section underneath. This layout is a bit off-putting to mobile viewers, since they'd rather not scroll through a set of links and advertisements before they get to the meat of the page.

When faced with a challenge like this, the solution is to start by arranging your markup to suit the mobile version of the site, and *then* layer on extra CSS rules to create the more sophisticated multicolumn layout. This gold-standard technique is called *mobile-first* development.

In this example, that means putting the Content section before the NavSidebar section. This solves the problem in the mobile version of the page, but it also forces the sidebar to the right column on the full-sized version of the page. To correct this quirk, simply tweak the Content section so it floats to the right:

```
.Content {
  float: right;
  width: 78%;
}
```

Now the Content section returns to its place on the right, while the NavSidebar clings to the left, restoring the full-size layout shown in Figure 7-5.

At this point, you may want to consider adding another media query to also change your styles for very wide windows. For example, you could break your text into multiple columns (using the CSS properties described on page 217) to make sure your text remains readable.

TIP Looking for some examples to inspire you? Try out a ready-made responsive template. There are plenty of examples on the Web. To get started, start browsing *http://html5up.net*, *www.typeandgrids.com*, or *http://responsify.it*.

More Advanced Media Query Conditions

Sometimes you might want to make your styles even more specific, so they depend on multiple conditions. Here's an example:

```
@media (min-width: 400px) and (max-width: 700px) {
  /* These styles apply to windows from 400 to 700 pixels wide. */
}
```

Hiding and Replacing Sections

If you're ambitious, there are many more changes you can make to differentiate the mobile version of your site from its full-size incarnation. For example, you can use the CSS `display` property to hide and show entire *sections* of your page.

Before you use this approach, consider its drawbacks. If you switch large sections of your page, you'll be left with messy markup, which you'll need to maintain, keep consistent, and test on different devices. Also, if your hidden sections contain images, browsers will still download them, even if they're never shown. On a mobile device, this can become a performance drag and a waste of bandwidth.

However, there *is* an appropriate time to use the section-switching technique: when you need to replace a complex navigation aid or menu with a slimmer, simpler mobile version. For example, it's common practice to give mobile users a drop-down list for navigation instead of an unwieldy tree. (There's even a clever style technique that can convert a row of links into a drop-down list, as detailed at *http://css-tricks.com/convert-menu-to-dropdown*).

Sometimes, simple tricks and small alterations aren't enough. You may want to revamp the mobile version of your site more radically. Here, you have a range of options, ranging in complexity and sophistication. At one extreme, you could create a completely separate mobile site and host it on a different web domain (as the New York Times does with its mobile site at *http://mobile.nytimes.com*). This option is a lot more work, and without some sort of content management system running on your web server, you'll never keep your mobile site in sync with your standard site. Another way is to write web server code that checks every request, figures out what web browser is on the other end, and sends the appropriate type of content. This sort of solution is great, if you have the time and skills.

A more modest approach is to use a JavaScript tool that lets you alter your pages dynamically based on the viewer. One example is Modernizr, which provides a method named `Modernizr.mq()` for testing media queries in your code (read about it at *http://modernizr.com/docs*). This approach is more powerful than media queries, but it also introduces more complexity into your page design.

This type of media query comes in handy if you want to apply several sets of mutually exclusive styles, but you don't want the headaches of several layers of overlapping rules. Here's an example:

```
/* Normal styles here */

@media (min-width: 600px) and (max-width: 700px) {
  /* Override the styles for 600-700 pixel windows. */
}

@media (min-width: 400px) and (max-width: 599.99px) {
  /* Override the styles for 400-600 pixel windows. */
}

@media (max-width: 399.99px) {
  /* Override the styles for sub-400 pixel windows. */
}
```

In this case, if the browser window is 380 pixels, exactly two sets of styles will apply: the standard styles and the styles in the final @media block. Whether this approach simplifies your life or complicates it depends on what you're trying to accomplish. If you're using complex styles and changing them a lot, the no-overlap approach shown here is often the simplest way to go.

Notice that you have to take care that your rules don't unexpectedly overlap. For example, if you set the maximum width of one rule to 400 pixels and the minimum width of another rule to 400 pixels, you'll have one spot where both style settings suddenly combine. The slightly awkward solution is to use fractional values, like the 399.99 pixel measurement used in this example.

Another option is to use the not keyword. There's no functional difference, but if the following style sheet makes more sense to you, feel free to use this approach:

```css
/* Normal styles here */

@media (not max-width: 600px) and (max-width: 700px) {
  /* Override the styles for 600-700 pixel windows. */
}

@media (not max-width: 400px) and (max-width: 600px) {
  /* Override the styles for 400-600 pixel windows. */
}

@media (max-width: 400px) {
  /* Override the styles for sub-400 pixel windows. */
}
```

In these examples, there's still one level of style overriding to think about. That's because every @media section starts off with the standard, no-media-query style rules. Depending on the situation, you may prefer to separate your style logic completely (for example, so a mobile device gets its own, completely independent set of styles). To do so, you need to use media queries with external style sheets, as described next.

Replacing an Entire Style Sheet

If you have simple tweaks to make, the @media block is handy, because it lets you keep all your styles together in one file. But if the changes are more significant, you may decide that it's easier to create a whole separate style sheet. You can then use a media query to create a link to that style sheet:

```html
<head>
  <link rel="stylesheet" href="standard.css">
  <link rel="stylesheet" media="(max-width: 568px)" href="small_styles.css">
  ...
</head>
```

The browser will download the second style sheet (*small_styles.css*) with the page but won't apply it unless the browser width falls under the maximum.

As in the previous example, the new styles will override the styles you already have in place. In some cases, you want completely separate, independent style sheets. If so, you first need to add a media query to your standard style sheet to make sure it kicks in only for large sizes:

```
<link rel="stylesheet" media="(min-width: 568.01px)" href="standard.css">
<link rel="stylesheet" media="(max-width: 568px)" href="small_styles.css">
```

The problem with this approach is that browsers that don't understand media queries will ignore *both* style sheets. You can fix this up for old versions of Internet Explorer by adding your main style sheet again, but with conditional comments:

```
<link rel="stylesheet" media="(min-width: 568.01px)" href="standard.css">
<link rel="stylesheet" media="(max-width: 568px)" href="small_styles.css">
<!--[if lt IE 9]>
  <link rel="stylesheet" href="standard.css">
<![endif]-->
```

This example still has one small blind spot. Old versions of Firefox (earlier than 3.5) don't understand media queries and don't use the conditionally commented IE section. You could solve the problem by detecting the browser in your code and then using JavaScript to swap in a new page, but it's messy. Fortunately, old versions of Firefox are becoming increasingly rare.

Incidentally, you can combine media queries with the media types described in the box on page 234. When you do so, always start with the media type, and don't put it in parentheses. For example, here's how you could create a print-only style sheet for a specific page width:

```
<link rel="stylesheet" media="print and (min-width: 25cm)"
 href="NormalPrintStyles.css" >
<link rel="stylesheet" media="print and (not min-width: 25cm)"
 href="NarrowPrintStyles.css" >
```

Recognizing Specific Mobile Devices

As you've already learned, you can distinguish between normal computers and mobile devices by writing a media query that uses max-device-width. But what widths should you use?

If you're looking for mobile phones, check for a max-device-width of 568 pixels. This is a good rule of thumb, since it catches current iPhone and Android phone models, whether they're in portrait or landscape orientation:

```
<link rel="stylesheet" media="(max-device-width: 568px)"
  href="mobile_styles.css">
```

If you're a hardware geek, this rule may have raised a red flag. After all, modern mobile devices use tiny, super-high-resolution screens. For example, the iPhone 5 crams a grid of 640 x 1136 pixels into view at once. You might think you'd need larger device widths to recognize these devices. Surprisingly, though, that isn't the case.

For example, consider the iPhone 5. It claims that it has a pixel width of 320 pixels (in portrait orientation), even though it actually has twice as many physical pixels. It uses this quirk to prevent websites from concluding that 640-pixel wide iPhone displays should receive the full desktop version of a website. Although the iPhone can certainly display such a site, its tiny pixels would make it all but impossible to read.

Most modern, high-resolution devices behave this way. They add in a fudge factor called the *pixel ratio*. In the iPhone (version 4 and later), every CSS pixel is two physical pixels wide, so the pixel ratio is 2. In fact, you can create a media query that matches the iPhone 4 but ignores older iPhones, using the following media query:

```
<link rel="stylesheet"
 media="(max-device-width: 480px) and (-webkit-min-device-pixel-ratio: 2)"
 href="iphone4.css">
```

Table 7-2 lists the device widths of some popular devices. Keep in mind that there's often a bit of pixel ratio fudgery at work. For example, all versions of the iPad report a device width of 768, even though the number of physical pixels doubled in the iPad 3.

TABLE 7-2 *Common device widths*

DEVICE	DEVICE WIDTH (IN PORTRAIT MODE)	DEVICE WIDTH (IN LANDSCAPE MODE)
Apple iPhone 4	320	480
Apple iPhone 5	320	568
Apple iPad	768	1024
Samsung Galaxy S4	360	640
Google Nexus 4	384	640
Kindle Fire	600	1024

TIP New devices are released all the time. For current information, consult a site like *www.mobitest.me/ devices.*

Tablets like the iPad pose a special challenge: Users can turn them to show content vertically or horizontally. And although this changes the max-width, it doesn't alter the max-device-width. In both portrait and landscape orientation, the iPad reports a device width of 768 pixels. Fortunately, you can combine the max-device-width property with the orientation property if you want to vary styles based on the iPad's orientation:

```
<link rel="stylesheet"
 media="(max-device-width: 768px) and (orientation: portrait)"
 href="iPad_portrait.css">

<link rel="stylesheet"
 media="(max-device-width: 768px) and (orientation: landscape)"
 href="iPad_landscape.css">
```

Of course, this rule isn't limited to iPads. Other devices that have similar screen sizes (in this case, 768 pixels or less) will get the same style rules.

NOTE On their own, media queries probably aren't enough to turn a normal website into a mobile-friendly one. You'll also need to think about the user experience. You may need to break content down into smaller pieces (so less scrolling is required) and avoid effects and interactions that are difficult to navigate with a touch interface (like pop-up menus).

GEM IN THE ROUGH

Media Queries for Video

One obvious difference between desktop websites and mobile websites is the way they use video. A mobile website may still include video, but it will typically use a smaller video window and a smaller media file. The reasons are obvious—not only do mobile browsers have slower, more expensive network connections to download video, but they also have less powerful hardware to play it back.

Using the media query techniques you've just learned, you can easily change the size of a <video> element to suit a mobile user. However, it's not as easy to take care of the crucial second step and link to a slimmed-down video file.

HTML5 has a solution: It adds a media attribute directly to the <source> element. As you learned in Chapter 5, the <source> element specifies the media file a <video> element should play. By adding the media attribute, you can limit certain media files to certain device types.

Here's an example that hands the *butterfly_mobile.mp4* file out to small-screened devices. Other devices get *butterfly.*

mp4 or *butterfly.ogv*, depending on which video format they support.

```
<video controls width="400" height="300">
  <source src="butterfly_mobile.mp4"
   type="video/mp4"
   media="(max-device-width: 480px)">
  <source src="butterfly.mp4"
  type="video/mp4">
  <source src="butterfly.ogv"
  type="video/ogg">
</video>
```

It's still up to you to encode a separate copy of your video for mobile users. Encoding tools usually have device-specific profiles that can help you out. For example, they might have an option for encoding "iPad video." It's also still up to you to make sure that you use the right media format for your device (usually, that will be H.264) and supply video formats for every other browser.

Basic Drawing with the Canvas

As you learned in Chapter 1, one of HTML5's goals is to make it easier to put *rich applications* inside otherwise ordinary web pages. In this case, the word "rich" doesn't have anything to do with your bank account. Instead, a rich application is one that's decked out with slick graphics, interactive features, and showy frills like animation.

One of the most important HTML5 tools for rich applications is the *canvas*, a drawing surface where you can let your inner Picasso loose. Compared with every other HTML element, the canvas is unique because it *requires* JavaScript. There's no way to draw shapes or paint pictures without it. That means the canvas is essentially a programming tool—one that takes you far beyond the original document-based idea of the Web.

At first, using the canvas can feel like stuffing your page with a crude version of Windows Paint. But dig deeper, and you'll discover that the canvas is the key to a range of graphically advanced applications, including some you've probably already thought about (like games, mapping tools, and dynamic charts) and others that you might not have imagined (like musical lightshows and physics simulators). In the not-so-distant past, these applications were extremely difficult without the help of a browser plug-in like Flash. Today, with the canvas, they're all possible, provided you're willing to put in a fair bit of work.

In this chapter, you'll learn how to create a canvas and fill it up with lines, curves, and simple shapes. Then you'll put your skills to use by building a simple painting program. And, perhaps most importantly, you'll learn how you can get canvas-equipped pages to work on old browsers that don't support HTML5.

NOTE For some developers, the canvas will be indispensable. For others, it will just be an interesting diversion. (And for some, it may be interesting but still way too much work compared with a mature programming platform like Flash.) But one thing is certain: This straightforward drawing surface is destined to be much more than a toy for bored programmers.

Getting Started with the Canvas

The <canvas> element is the place where all your drawing takes place. From a markup point of view, it's as simple as can be. You supply three attributes: id, width, and height:

```
<canvas id="drawingCanvas" width="500" height="300"></canvas>
```

The id attribute gives the canvas a unique name, which you'll need when your script code goes searching for it. The width and height attributes set the size of your canvas, in pixels.

NOTE You should always set the size of your canvas through the width and height attributes, not the width and height style sheet properties. To learn about the possible problem that can occur if you use style sheet sizing, see the box on page 277.

Ordinarily, the canvas shows up as a blank, borderless rectangle (which is to say it doesn't show up at all). To make it stand out on the page, you can apply a background color or a border with a style sheet rule like this:

```
canvas {
  border: 1px dashed black;
}
```

Figure 8-1 shows this starting point.

To work with a canvas, you need to fire off a bit of JavaScript that takes two steps. First, your script must use the indispensable document.getElementById() method to grab hold of the canvas object. In this example, you'll name the canvas drawing-Canvas, so the code looks like this:

```
var canvas = document.getElementById("drawingCanvas");
```

This code is nothing new, as you use the getElementById() method whenever you need to find an HTML element on your page.

NOTE If you aren't familiar with JavaScript, you won't get far with the canvas. To brush up with the absolute bare-minimum essentials, read Appendix B, "JavaScript: The Brains of Your Page."

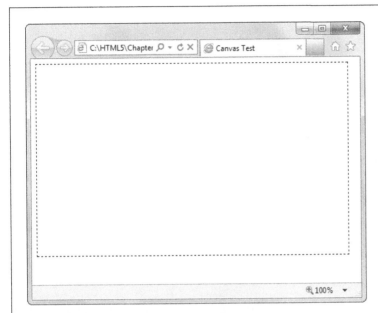

FIGURE 8-1

Every canvas begins as an empty rectangle somewhere on a web page. To put even a single line inside, you need to write some JavaScript code.

Once you have the canvas object, you can take the second essential step. You use the canvas object's getContext() method to retrieve a two-dimensional *drawing context*, like this:

```
var context = canvas.getContext("2d");
```

You can think of the context as a supercharged drawing tool that handles all your canvas tasks, like painting rectangles, writing text, pasting an image, and so on. It's a sort of one-stop shop for canvas drawing operations.

> **NOTE** The fact that the context is explicitly called *two-dimensional* (and referred to as 2d in the code) raises an obvious question—namely, is there a three-dimensional drawing context? Not yet, but the creators of HTML5 have clearly left space for one in the future.

You can grab the context object and start drawing at any point: for example, when the page first loads, when the visitor clicks a button, or at some other point. When you're just starting out with the canvas, you probably want to create a practice page that gets to work straightaway. Here's a template for a page that does just that:

```
<!DOCTYPE html>
<html lang="en">
<head>
  <meta charset="utf-8">
  <title>Canvas Test</title>
```

```
  <style>
canvas {
  border: 1px dashed black;
}
  </style>

  <script>
window.onload = function() {
  var canvas = document.getElementById("drawingCanvas");
  var context = canvas.getContext("2d");

  // (Put your fabulous drawing code here.)
};
  </script>
</head>

<body>
  <canvas id="drawingCanvas" width="500" height="300"></canvas>
</body>
</html>
```

The <body> of this page includes the <canvas> element and no other markup. The <style> section of this page makes the canvas stand out with a border. The <script> section handles the window.onload event, which occurs once the browser has completely loaded the page. The code then gets the canvas, creates a drawing context, and gets ready to draw. You can use this example as the starting point for your own canvas experiments.

NOTE Of course, when you're using the canvas in a real page on your website, you'll want to declutter a bit by snipping out the JavaScript code and putting it in an external script file (page 455). But for now, this template gives you single-page convenience. If you want to type the examples in on your own, you can get this markup from the CanvasTemplate.html file on the try-out site (*http://prosetech.com/html5*).

Straight Lines

Now you're just about ready to start drawing. But before you add anything on a canvas, you need to understand its coordinate system. Figure 8-2 shows you how it works.

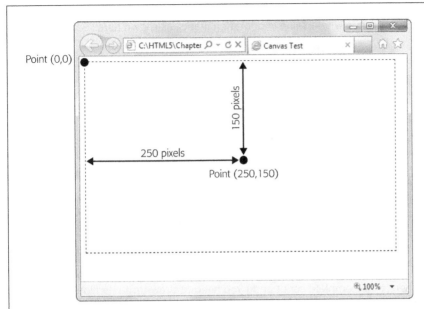

FIGURE 8-2

As with every other HTML element, the canvas designates its top-left corner as the point (0,0). As you move right, the x-value increases, and as you move down, the y-value increases. If a canvas is 500 x 300 pixels, then the bottom-right corner is point (500, 300).

The simplest thing you can draw on a canvas is a solid line. Doing that takes three actions with the drawing context. First, you use the moveTo() method to move to the point where you want the line to start. Second, you use the lineTo() method to travel from the current point to the end of the line. Third, you call the stroke() method to make the line actually appear:

```
context.moveTo(10,10);
context.lineTo(400,40);
context.stroke();
```

Or think of it this way: First you lift up your pen and put it where you want (using moveTo), then you drag the pen across the canvas (using lineTo), then you make the line appear (using stroke). This result is a thin (1-pixel) black line from point (10,10) to point (400,40).

Happily, you can get a little fancier with your lines. At any point before you call the stroke() method that winks your line into existence, you can set three drawing context properties: lineWidth, strokeStyle, and lineCap. These properties affect everything you draw from that point on, until you change them.

You use lineWidth to set the width of your lines, in pixels. Here's a thick, 10-pixel line:

```
context.lineWidth = 10;
```

You use strokeStyle to set the color of your lines. You can use an HTML color name, an HTML color code, or the CSS rgb() function which lets you assemble a color from red, green, and blue components. (This approach is useful because most drawing and painting programs use the RGB system.) No matter which one you use, you need to wrap the whole value in quotation marks, as shown here:

```
// Set the color (brick red) using an HTML color code:
context.strokeStyle = "#cd2828";

// Set the color (brick red) using the rgb() function:
context.strokeStyle = "rgb(205,40,40)";
```

> **NOTE** This property is named strokeStyle rather than strokeColor because you aren't limited to plain colors. As you'll see later on, you can use color blends called gradients (page 284) and image-based patterns (page 283).

Finally, use lineCap to decide how you want to cap off the ends of your lines. The default is to make a squared-off edge with butt, but you can also use round (to round off the edge) or square (which looks the same as butt, but extends the line an amount equal to half its thickness on each end).

And here's the complete script code you need to draw three horizontal lines, with different line caps (Figure 8-3). To try this code out, pop it into any JavaScript function you want. To make it run right away, put it in the function that handles the window.onload event, as shown on page 248:

```
var canvas = document.getElementById("drawingCanvas");
var context = canvas.getContext("2d");

// Set the line width and color (for all the lines).
context.lineWidth = 20;
context.strokeStyle = "rgb(205,40,40)";

// Draw the first line, with the standard butt ending.
context.moveTo(10,50);
context.lineTo(400,50);
context.lineCap = "butt";
context.stroke();

// Draw the second line, with a round cap.
context.beginPath();
context.moveTo(10,120);
context.lineTo(400,120);
context.lineCap = "round";
context.stroke();
```

```
// Draw the third line, with a square cap.
context.beginPath();
context.moveTo(10,190);
context.lineTo(400,190);
context.lineCap = "square";
context.stroke();
```

This example introduces one new feature: the `beginPath()` method of the drawing context. When you call `beginPath()`, you start a new, separate segment of your drawing. Without this step, every time you call `stroke()`, the canvas will attempt to draw everything over again. This is a particular problem if you're changing other context properties. In this case, you'd end up drawing over your existing content with the same shapes but a new color, thickness, or line cap.

NOTE While you do need to begin new segments by calling `beginPath()`, you don't need to do anything special to end a segment. Instead, the current segment is automatically considered "finished" the moment you create a new segment.

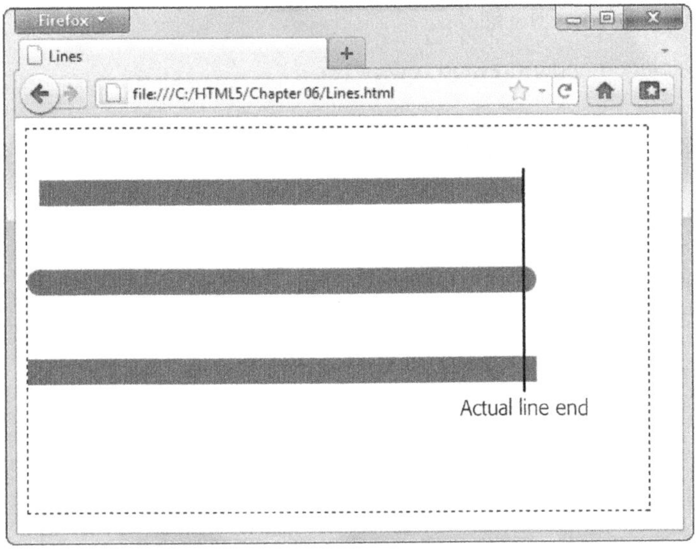

FIGURE 8-3

The top line uses the standard `butt` *ending, while the lines below have added caps (*`round` *or* `square`*), which extend the line by an amount equal to half the line's thickness.*

Paths and Shapes

In the previous example, you separated different lines by starting a new path for each one. This method lets you give each line a different color (and a different width and cap style). Paths are also important because they allow you to fill custom shapes. For example, imagine you create a red-outlined triangle using this code:

```
context.moveTo(250,50);
context.lineTo(50,250);
context.lineTo(450,250);
context.lineTo(250,50);

context.lineWidth = 10;
context.strokeStyle = "red";
context.stroke();
```

But if you want to *fill* that triangle, the stroke() method won't help you. Instead, you need to close the path by calling closePath(), pick a fill color by setting the fillStyle property, and then call the fill() method to make it happen:

```
context.closePath();
context.fillStyle = "blue";
context.fill();
```

It's worth tweaking a couple of things in this example. First, when closing a path, you don't need to draw the final line segment, because calling closePath() automatically draws a line between the last drawn point and the starting point. Second, it's best to fill your shape first, and *then* draw its outline. Otherwise, your outline may be partially overwritten by the fill.

Here's the complete triangle-drawing code:

```
var canvas = document.getElementById("drawingCanvas");
var context = canvas.getContext("2d");

context.moveTo(250,50);
context.lineTo(50,250);
context.lineTo(450,250);
context.closePath();

// Paint the inside.
context.fillStyle = "blue";
context.fill();

// Draw the outline.
context.lineWidth = 10;
context.strokeStyle = "red";
context.stroke();
```

Notice that you don't need to use beginPath() in this example, because the canvas starts you off with a new path automatically. You need to call beginPath() only when you need a *new* path—for example, when changing line settings or drawing a new shape. Figure 8-4 shows the result of running this JavaScript.

> **NOTE** When drawing connecting line segments (like the three sides of this triangle), you can set the drawing context's lineJoin property to round or bevel the edges (by using the values round or bevel—the default is mitre).

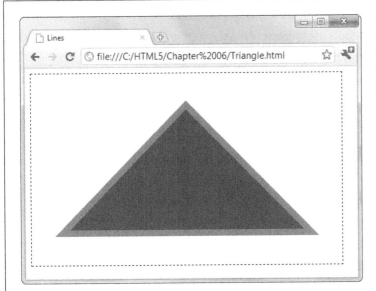

FIGURE 8-4

To create a closed shape like this triangle, use moveTo() *to get to the starting point,* lineTo() *to draw each line segment, and* closePath() *to complete the shape. You can then fill it with* fill() *and outline it with* stroke().

Most of the time, when you want a complex shape, you'll need to assemble a path for it, one line at a time. But there's one shape that's important enough to get special treatment: the rectangle. You can fill a rectangular region in one step using the fillRect() method. You supply the coordinate for the top-left corner, the width, and the height.

For example, to place a 100 x 200 pixel rectangle starting at point (0,10), use this code:

```
fillRect(0,10,100,200);
```

The fillRect() method gets the color to use from the fillStyle property, just like the fill() method.

Similarly, you can use strokeRect() to draw the outline of a rectangle in one step:

```
strokeRect(0,10,100,200);
```

The strokeRect() method uses the current lineWidth and strokeStyle properties to determine the thickness and color of the outline, just as the stroke() method does.

Curved Lines

If you want something more impressive than lines and rectangles (and who doesn't?), you'll need to understand four methods that can really throw you for a curve: arc(), arcTo(), bezierCurveTo(), and quadraticCurveTo(). All of these methods draw curved lines in different ways, and they all require at least a smattering of math (and some need a whole lot more).

The arc() method is the simplest of the bunch. It draws a portion of a circle's outline. To draw an arc, you first need to visualize an imaginary circle, and then decide which part of the edge you need, as explained in Figure 8-5. You'll then have all the data you need to pass to the arc() method.

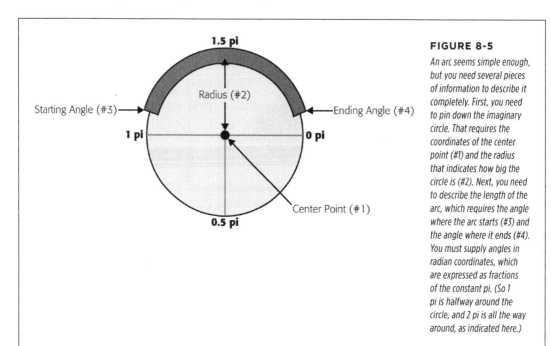

FIGURE 8-5

An arc seems simple enough, but you need several pieces of information to describe it completely. First, you need to pin down the imaginary circle. That requires the coordinates of the center point (#1) and the radius that indicates how big the circle is (#2). Next, you need to describe the length of the arc, which requires the angle where the arc starts (#3) and the angle where it ends (#4). You must supply angles in radian coordinates, which are expressed as fractions of the constant pi. (So 1 pi is halfway around the circle, and 2 pi is all the way around, as indicated here.)

Once you've sorted out all the details you need, you can call the arc() method:

```
var canvas = document.getElementById("drawingCanvas");
var context = canvas.getContext("2d");

// Create variables to store each detail about the arc.
var centerX = 150;
var centerY = 300;
var radius = 100;
var startingAngle = 1.25 * Math.PI;
var endingAngle = 1.75 * Math.PI;
```

```
// Use this information to draw the arc.
context.arc(centerX, centerY, radius, startingAngle, endingAngle);
context.stroke();
```

Or, call closePath() before you call stroke() to add a straight line between the two ends of the arc. This creates a closed semi-circle.

Incidentally, a circle is simply an arc that stretches all the way around. You can draw it like this:

```
var canvas = document.getElementById("drawingCanvas");
var context = canvas.getContext("2d");

var centerX = 150;
var centerY = 300;
var radius = 100;
var startingAngle = 0;
var endingAngle = 2 * Math.PI;

context.arc(centerX, centerY, radius, startingAngle, endingAngle);
context.stroke();
```

> **NOTE** The arc() method doesn't let you draw an ellipse (a flattened circle). To get that, you need to do more work—either use some of the more sophisticated curve methods described next, or use a transform (page 256) to stretch out an ordinary circle as you draw it.

The three other curve methods—arcTo(), bezierCurveTo(), and quadraticCurveTo()— are a bit more intimidating to the geometrically challenged. They involve a concept called *control points*—points that aren't included in the curve, but influence the way it's drawn. The most famous example is the Bézier curve, which is used in virtually every computer illustration program ever created. It's popular because it creates a curve that looks smooth no matter how small or big you draw it. Figure 8-6 shows how control points shape a Bézier curve.

And here's the code that creates the curve from Figure 8-6:

```
var canvas = document.getElementById("drawingCanvas");
var context = canvas.getContext("2d");

// Put the pen where the curve starts.
context.moveTo(62, 242);

// Create variables for the two control points and the end point of the curve.
var control1_x = 187;
var control1_y = 32;
var control2_x = 429;
var control2_y = 480;
```

```
var endPointX = 365;
var endPointY = 133;

// Draw the curve.
context.bezierCurveTo(control1_x, control1_y, control2_x, control2_y,
 endPointX, endPointY);
context.stroke();
```

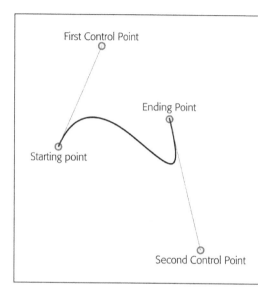

FIGURE 8-6

A Bézier curve has two control points. The start of the curve runs parallel to the first control point. The end of the curve runs parallel to the second control point. In between, the line curves. The amount of curvature is influenced by the distance to the control point—the farther away the point is, the stronger its "pull." It's sort of like gravity, but in reverse.

The outline of a complex, organic shape often involves a series of arcs and curves glued together. Once you're finished, you can call closePath() to fill or outline the entire shape. The best way to learn about curves is to play with one on your own. You can find a perfect test page at *http://tinyurl.com/html5bezier* (Figure 8-7).

Transforms

A transform is a drawing technique that lets you shift the canvas's coordinate system. For example, imagine you want to draw the same square in three places. You could call fillRect() three times, with three different points:

```
var canvas = document.getElementById("drawingCanvas");
var context = canvas.getContext("2d");

// Draw a 30x30 square, at three places.
context.rect(0, 0, 30, 30);
context.rect(50, 50, 30, 30);
context.rect(100, 100, 30, 30);

context.stroke();
```

Or you could call `fillRect()` three times, with the *same* point, but shift the coordinate system each time so the square actually ends up in three different spots, like so:

```
var canvas = document.getElementById("drawingCanvas");
var context = canvas.getContext("2d");

// Draw a square at (0,0).
context.rect(0, 0, 30, 30);

// Shift the coordinate system down 50 pixels and right 50 pixels.
context.translate(50, 50);
context.rect(0, 0, 30, 30);

// Shift the coordinate system down a bit more. Transforms are cumulative,
// so now the (0,0) point will actually be at (100,100).
context.translate(50, 50);
context.rect(0, 0, 30, 30);

context.stroke();
```

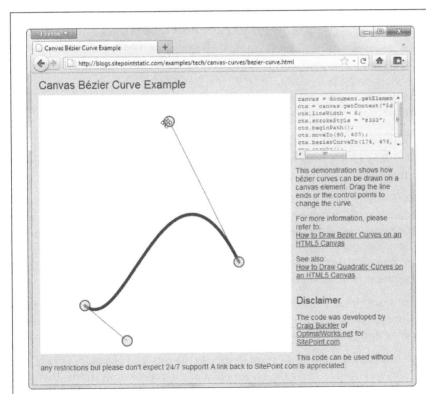

FIGURE 8-7

This page (found at http://tinyurl.com/html5bezier) lets you tweak all the details of a Bézier curve by clicking and pulling with the mouse. Best of all, as you drag the starting point, control points, and end point, the page generates the corresponding snippet of HTML5 canvas code that you can use to create the same curve on your own canvas. You can find a similarly great test page for quadratic curves at http://tinyurl.com/html5quadratic.

Canvas Drawing for Math-Phobes

How do I get all the shapes with none of the headaches?

If you're hoping to use the canvas to create eye-catching graphics, but you don't want to pick up a degree in geometry, you might be a bit frustrated. Fortunately, there are several approaches that can help you draw what you want without worrying about the mathematical underpinnings:

- **Use a drawing library.** Why draw everything the hard way when you can use someone else's drawing library to draw circles, triangles, ellipses, and polygons in a single step? The idea is simple—you call a higher-level method (say, fillEllipse(), with the appropriate coordinates), and the JavaScript library translates that to the correct canvas operations. Two good examples are Fabric.js (*http://fabricjs.com*) and KineticJS (*http://kineticjs.com*). However, these libraries (and more) are still evolving—and rapidly. It's too soon to say which ones will have real staying power, but you could read a lively debate and some developer suggestion on the popular question-and-answer Stack Overflow site (*http://tinyurl.com/canvas-libraries*).

- **Draw bitmap images.** Instead of painstakingly drawing each shape you need, you can copy ready-made graphics to your canvas. For example, if you have an image of a circle with a file name *circle.png*, you can insert that into your canvas using the approach shown on page 276. However, this technique won't give you the same flexibility to manipulate your image (for example, to stretch it, rearrange it, remove part of it, and so on).

- **Use an export tool.** If you have a complex graphic and you need to manipulate it on the canvas or make it interactive, drawing a fixed bitmap isn't good enough. But a conversion tool that can examine your graphic and generate the right canvas-creation code just might solve your problem. One intriguing example is the Ai→Canvas plug-in for Adobe Illustrator (*http://visitmix.com/labs/ai2canvas*), which converts Adobe Illustrator artwork to an HTML page with JavaScript code that painstakingly recreates the picture on a canvas.

Both versions of this code have the same effect: They draw three squares, in the same three spots.

At first glance, transforms may seem like nothing more than a way to make a somewhat complicated drawing task even more complicated. But transforms can work magic in some tricky situations. For example, suppose you have a function that draws a series of complex shapes that, put together, create a picture of a bird. Now, say you want to animate that bird, so it appears to fly around the canvas. (You'll see a basic example of animation on the canvas on page 301.)

Without transforms, you'd need to adjust every coordinate in your drawing code each time you drew the bird. But with transforms, you can leave your drawing code untouched and simply tweak the coordinate system over and over again.

Transforms come in several different flavors. In the previous example, a translate transform was used to move the center point of the coordinate system—that's the (0,0) point that's usually placed in the top-left corner of the canvas. Along with the translate transform, there's also a scale transform (which lets you draw things bigger or smaller), a rotate transform (which lets you turn the coordinate system around), and a matrix transform (which lets you stretch and warp the coordinate system in virtually any way—provided you understand the complex matrix math that underpins the visual effect you want).

Transforms are cumulative. The following example moves the (0,0) point to (100,100) with a translate transform and then rotates the coordinate system around that point several times. Each time, it draws a new square, creating the pattern shown in Figure 8-8:

```
var canvas = document.getElementById("drawingCanvas");
var context = canvas.getContext("2d");

// Move the (0,0) point. This is important, because
// the rotate transform turns around this point.
context.translate(100, 100);

// Draw 10 squares.
var copies = 10;
for (var i=1; i<copies; i++) {
  // Before drawing the square, rotate the coordinate system.
  // A complete rotation is 2*Math.PI. This code does a fraction of this
  // for each square, so that it has rotated around completely by the time
  // it's drawn the last one.
  context.rotate(2 * Math.PI * 1/(copies-1));

  // Draw the square.
  context.rect(0, 0, 60, 60);
}
context.stroke();
```

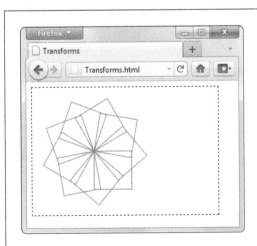

FIGURE 8-8

By drawing a series of rotated squares, you can create Spirograph-like patterns.

Transforms are somewhat beyond the scope of this chapter. If you want to explore them in more detail, Mozilla (the company that created Firefox) has some helpful documentation and examples at *http://tinyurl.com/canvas-transforms*.

Transparency

So far, you've been dealing with solid colors. However, the canvas also lets you use partial transparency to layer one shape over another. There are two ways to use transparency with the canvas. The first approach is to set a color (through the fillStyle or strokeStyle properties) with the rgba() function, instead of the more common rgb() function. The rgba() function takes four arguments—the numbers for the red, green, and blue color components (from 0 to 255), and an additional number for the alpha value (from 0 to 1), which sets the color's opacity. An alpha value of 1 is completely solid, while an alpha value of 0 is completely invisible. Set a value in between—for example, 0.5—and you get a partially transparent color that any content underneath shows through.

Here's an example that draws a circle and a triangle. They both use the same fill color, except that the triangle sets the alpha value to 0.5, making it 50 percent opaque:

```
var canvas = document.getElementById("drawingCanvas");
var context = canvas.getContext("2d");

// Set the fill and outline colors.
context.fillStyle = "rgb(100,150,185)";
context.lineWidth = 10;
context.strokeStyle = "red";

// Draw a circle.
context.arc(110, 120, 100, 0, 2*Math.PI);
context.fill();
context.stroke();
```

```
// Remember to call beginPath() before adding a new shape.
// Otherwise, the outlines of both shapes will
// be merged together in an unpredictable way.
context.beginPath();

// Give the triangle a transparent fill.
context.fillStyle = "rgba(100,150,185,0.5)";

// Now draw the triangle.
context.moveTo(215,50);
context.lineTo(15,250);
context.lineTo(315,250);
context.closePath();
context.fill();
context.stroke();
```

Figure 8-9 shows the result.

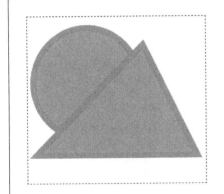
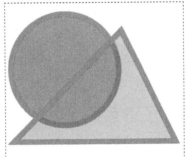

FIGURE 8-9

Left: Two solid shapes, one on top of the other.

Right: One solid shape, with a semitransparent shape on top. Semitransparent shapes look lighter (because they let the white background through), and they allow you to see whatever content you've drawn underneath. Notice that in this example, the semitransparent shape uses a fully opaque color for its border.

The other way to use transparency is to set the drawing context's globalAlpha property, like this:

```
context.globalAlpha = 0.5;

// Now this color automatically gets an alpha value of 0.5:
context.fillStyle = "rgb(100,150,185)";
```

Do that, and everything you draw from that point on (until you change globalAlpha again) will use the same alpha value and get the same degree of transparency. This includes both stroke colors and fill colors.

So which approach is better? If you need just a single transparent color, use rgba(). If you need to paint a variety of shapes with different colors, and they all need the same level of transparency, use globalAlpha. The globalAlpha property is also useful if you want to paint semitransparent images on your canvas, as you'll learn to do on page 301.

Composite Operations

So far, this chapter has assumed that when you put one shape on top of another, the second shape paints over the first, obscuring it. The canvas works this way most of the time. However, the canvas also has the ability to use more complex *composite operations*.

A composite operation is a rule that tells the canvas how to display two images that overlap. The default composite operation is source-over, which tells the canvas that the new shape should be painted *over* the first shape (that is, on top of the first shape). If the new shape overlaps with the first shape, the new shape obscures it.

> **NOTE** In the lingo of composite operations, the *source* is the new object you're drawing, and the *destination* is the existing content on the canvas that you've already drawn.

But other composition options are possible. For example, you can use xor, which tells the canvas to show nothing at all in the area where the shapes overlap. Figure 8-10 shows an overview of the different composite operations.

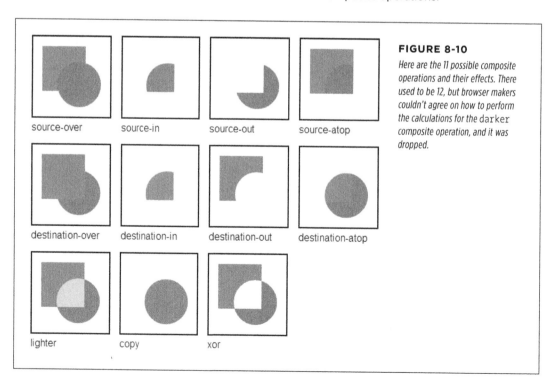

FIGURE 8-10

Here are the 11 possible composite operations and their effects. There used to be 12, but browser makers couldn't agree on how to perform the calculations for the darker *composite operation, and it was dropped.*

source-over   source-in   source-out   source-atop

destination-over   destination-in   destination-out   destination-atop

lighter   copy   xor

To change the current composite operation that the canvas uses, simply set the drawing context's globalCompositeOperation property before you draw the second shape, like this:

```
context.globalCompositeOperation = "xor";
```

For example, to create the source-atop combination shown in the top-right corner of Figure 8-10, you'd use this code:

```
var canvas = document.getElementById("drawingCanvas");
var context = canvas.getContext("2d");

// Draw a rectangle.
context.fillStyle = "blue";
context.fillRect(15,15,70,70);

// Choose the global composite operation.
context.globalCompositeOperation = "source-atop";

// Draw a circle overtop.
context.fillStyle = "red";
context.beginPath();
context.arc(75, 75, 35, 0, Math.PI*2, true);
context.fill();
```

Used cleverly, a composite operation can provide shortcuts for certain drawing tasks, like drawing complex shapes. Hard-core canvas coders can even use these shortcuts to improve performance by reducing the number of drawing operations they perform.

In the recent past, browsers didn't quite agree on how to deal with certain composite operations. Fortunately, these quirks have now been ironed out. The only issue is with any polyfills that you use to get canvas support on old browsers. Right now, the only polyfill that supports composite operations is FlashCanvas Pro (page 273).

■ Building a Basic Paint Program

The canvas still has a fair bit more in store for you. But you've covered enough ground to build your first practical canvas-powered program. It's the simple painting program shown in Figure 8-11.

The JavaScript that makes this example work is longer than the examples you've seen so far, but still surprisingly straightforward. You'll consider it piece by piece in the following sections.

TIP If you're curious about the style sheet rules that create the blue toolbars above and below the canvas, you want to see the whole example in one piece, or you just want to paint something in your browser, then you can use the *Paint.html* file on the try-out site (*http://prosetech.com/html5*).

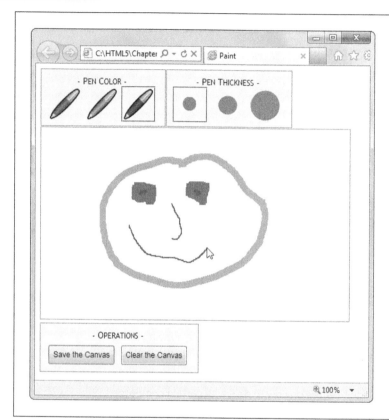

FIGURE 8-11

To express yourself with this paint program, just pick a pen color, pick a pen thickness, and scribble away with the mouse.

Preparing to Draw

First, when the page loads, the code grabs the canvas object and attaches functions that will handle several JavaScript events for different mouse actions: onMouseDown, onMouseUp, onMouseOut, and onMouseMove. (As you'll see, these events control the drawing process.) At the same time, the page also stores the canvas in a handy global variable (named canvas), and the drawing context in another global variable (named context). This way, these objects will be easily available to the rest of the code:

```
var canvas;
var context;

window.onload = function() {
  // Get the canvas and the drawing context.
  canvas = document.getElementById("drawingCanvas");
  context = canvas.getContext("2d");
```

```
  // Attach the events that you need for drawing.
  canvas.onmousedown = startDrawing;
  canvas.onmouseup = stopDrawing;
  canvas.onmouseout = stopDrawing;
  canvas.onmousemove = draw;
};
```

To get started with the paint program, the person using the page chooses the pen color and pen thickness from the two toolbars at the top of the window. These toolbars are simple <div> elements styled to look like nice steel-blue boxes, with a handful of clickable <img> elements in them. For example, here's the toolbar with the three color choices:

```
<div class="Toolbar">
  - Pen Color -<br>
  <img id="redPen" src="pen_red.gif" alt="Red Pen"
   onclick="changeColor('rgb(212,21,29)', this)">
  <img id="greenPen" src="pen_green.gif" alt="Green Pen"
   onclick="changeColor('rgb(131,190,61)', this)">
  <img id="bluePen" src="pen_blue.gif" alt="Blue Pen"
   onclick="changeColor('rgb(0,86,166)', this)">
</div>
```

The important part of this markup is the <img> element's onclick attribute. Whenever the web page visitor clicks a picture, the <img> element calls the changeColor() function. The changeColor() function accepts two pieces of information—the new color, which is set to match the icon, and a reference to the <img> element that was clicked. Here's the code:

```
// Keep track of the previous clicked <img> element for color.
var previousColorElement;

function changeColor(color, imgElement) {
  // Change the current drawing color.
  context.strokeStyle = color;

  // Give the newly clicked <img> element a new style.
  imgElement.className = "Selected";

  // Return the previously clicked <img> element to its normal state.
  if (previousColorElement != null) previousColorElement.className = "";
  previousColorElement = imgElement;
}
```

The changeColor() code takes care of two basic tasks. First, it sets the drawing context's strokeStyle property to match the new color; this takes a single line of code. Second, it changes the style of the clicked <img> element, giving it a solid border, so it's clear which color is currently active. This part requires a bit more work, because the code needs to keep track of the previously selected color so it can remove the solid border around that <img> element.

The changeThickness() function performs an almost identical task, only it alters the lineWidth property to have the appropriate thickness:

```
// Keep track of the previously clicked <img> element for thickness.
var previousThicknessElement;


function changeThickness(thickness, imgElement) {
  // Change the current drawing thickness.
  context.lineWidth = thickness;

  // Give the newly clicked <img> element a new style.
  imgElement.className = "Selected";

  // Return the previously clicked <img> element to its normal state.
  if (previousThicknessElement != null) {
    previousThicknessElement.className = "";
  }
  previousThicknessElement = imgElement;
}
```

This code gets all the drawing setup out of the way, but this example still isn't ready to run. The next (and final) step is to add the code that performs the actual drawing.

Drawing on the Canvas

Drawing begins when the user clicks down on the canvas with the mouse button. The paint program uses a global variable named isDrawing to keep track of when drawing is taking place, so the rest of the code knows whether it should be writing on the drawing context.

As you saw earlier, the onMouseDown event is linked to the startDrawing() function. It sets the isDrawing variable, creates a new path, and then moves to the starting position to get ready to draw something:

```
var isDrawing = false;

function startDrawing(e) {
  // Start drawing.
  isDrawing = true;

  // Create a new path (with the current stroke color and stroke thickness).
  context.beginPath();

  // Put the pen down where the mouse is positioned.
  context.moveTo(e.pageX - canvas.offsetLeft, e.pageY - canvas.offsetTop);
}
```

In order for the paint program to work properly, it needs to start drawing at the current position—that's where the mouse is hovering when the user clicks down. However, getting the right coordinates for this point is a bit tricky.

The onMouseDown event provides coordinates (through the pageX and the pageY properties shown in this example), but these coordinates are relative to the whole page. To calculate the corresponding coordinate on the canvas, you need to subtract the distance between the top-left corner of the browser window and the top-left corner of the canvas.

The actual drawing happens while the user is moving the mouse. Every time the user moves the mouse, even just a single pixel, the onMouseMove event fires and the code in the draw() function runs. If isDrawing is set to true, then the code calculates the current canvas coordinate—where the mouse is *right now*—and then calls lineTo() to add a tiny line segment to the new position and stroke() to draw it:

```
function draw(e) {
  if (isDrawing == true) {
    // Find the new position of the mouse.
    var x = e.pageX - canvas.offsetLeft;
    var y = e.pageY - canvas.offsetTop;

    // Draw a line to the new position.
    context.lineTo(x, y);
    context.stroke();
  }
}
```

If the user keeps moving the mouse, the draw() function keeps getting called, and another short piece of line keeps getting added. This line is so short—probably just a pixel or two—that it doesn't even look like a straight line when the user starts scribbling.

Finally, when the user releases the mouse button or moves the cursor off to the side, away from the canvas, the onMouseUp or onMouseOut events fire. Both of these trigger the stopDrawing() function, which tells the application to stop drawing:

```
function stopDrawing() {
  isDrawing = false;
}
```

So far, this code covers almost all there is to the simple paint program. The only missing details are the two buttons under the canvas, which offer to clear or save the current work. Click clear, and the clearCanvas() function blanks out the entire surface, using the drawing context's clearRect() method:

```
function clearCanvas() {
  context.clearRect(0, 0, canvas.width, canvas.height);
}
```

The save option is slightly more interesting, and you'll consider it next.

Saving the Picture in the Canvas

When it comes to saving the picture in a canvas, there are countless options. First, you need to decide how you're going to get the data. The canvas gives you three basic options:

- **Use a data URL.** Converts the canvas to an image file and then converts that image data to a sequence of characters, formatted as a URL. This gives you a nice, portable way to pass the image data around (for example, you can hand it to an <img> element or send it off to the web server). The paint program uses this approach.

- **Use the getImageData() method.** Grabs the raw pixel data, which you can then manipulate as you please. You'll learn to use getImageData() on page 313.

- **Store a list of "steps."** Lets you store, for example, an array that lists every line you drew on the canvas. Then you can save that data and use it to recreate the image later. This approach takes less storage space, and it gives you more flexibility to work with or edit the image later on. Unfortunately, it works only if you keep track of all the steps you're taking, using a technique like the one you'll see in the circle-drawing example (page 294).

If that seems a bit intimidating, well, you're not done quite yet. Once you decide what you want to save, you still need to decide *where* to save it. Here are some options for that:

- **In an image file.** For example, you can let the web surfer save a PNG or JPEG on the computer. That's the approach you'll see next.

- **In the local storage system.** You'll learn how that works in Chapter 10.

- **On the web server.** Once you transfer the data, the web server could store it in a file or a database and make it available the next time the web page user visits.

To make the save feature work in the paint program, the code uses a feature called *data URLs*. To get a URL for the current data, you simply use the canvas's toDataURL() method:

```
var url = canvas.toDataURL();
```

When you call toDataURL() without supplying any arguments, you get a PNG-formatted picture. Alternatively, you can supply an image type to request that format instead:

```
var url = canvas.toDataURL("image/jpeg");
```

But if the browser is unable to honor your format request, it will still send you a PNG file, converted to a long string of letters.

At this point, you're probably wondering what a data URL looks like. Technically, it's a long string of base-64 encoded characters that starts with the text *data:image/png;base64*. It looks like gobbledygook, but that's OK, because it's supposed to be readable by computer programs (like browsers). Here's a data URL for the current canvas picture:

```
data:image/png;base64,iVBORw0KGgoAAAANSUhEUgAAAfQAAAEsCAYAAAA1uOHIAAAAAXNSR
0IArs4c6QAAAARnQU1BAACxjwv8YQUAACqRSURBVHhe7Z1bkB1Hecdn5uxFFzzA2FWOnsEEGiiew
nZgKsrWLrZXMRU9JgZQKhoSHVK...gAAEIQAACEIBAiAT+HxAYpeqDfKieAAAAAElFTkSuQmCC
```

This example leaves out a huge amount of the content in the middle (where the ellipsis is) to save space. If it was all left in, this data URL would fill five pages in this book.

NOTE   Base-64 encoding is a system that converts image data to a long string of characters, numbers, and a small set of special characters. It avoids punctuation and all the bizarre extended characters, so the resulting text is safe to stick in a web page (for example, to set the value of a hidden input field or the `src` attribute in an `<img>` element).

So, it's easy to convert a canvas to image data in the form of a data URL. But once you have that data URL, what can you do with it? One option is to send it to the web server for long-term storage. You can see an example of a web page that does that, using a sprinkling of PHP script on the server, at *http://tinyurl.com/5uud9ob*.

If you want to keep your data on the client, your options are a bit more limited. Some browsers will let you navigate directly to a data URL. That means you can use code like the following to navigate to the image:

```
window.location = canvas.toDataURL();
```

A more reliable technique is to hand the data URL over to an `<img>` element. Here's what the paint program does (Figure 8-12):

```
function saveCanvas() {
  // Find the <img> element.
  var imageCopy = document.getElementById("savedImageCopy");

  // Show the canvas data in the image.
  imageCopy.src = canvas.toDataURL();

  // Unhide the <div> that holds the <img>, so the picture is now visible.
  var imageContainer = document.getElementById("savedCopyContainer");
  imageContainer.style.display = "block";
}
```

This code doesn't exactly "save" the image data, because the image hasn't yet been stored permanently, in a file. However, it takes just one more step to save the data once it's in an image. The web page visitor simply needs to right-click the image and choose the Save command. This isn't quite as convenient as a file download or the Save dialog box, but it's the only client-side option that works reliably in all browsers.

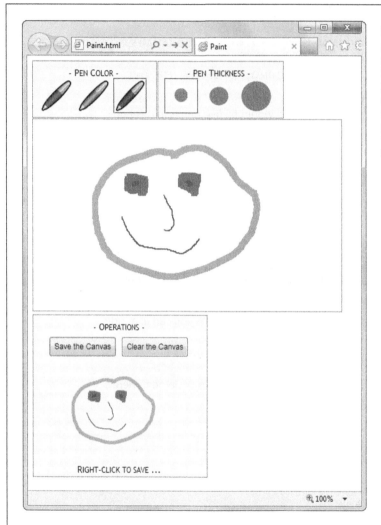

FIGURE 8-12

Here, the data URL is used to transmit information to an <img> element. The <img> element has been given a smaller size, to distinguish it from the main canvas. If you want to save this image as a respectable .png file, simply right-click the image and choose "Save picture as," just as you would with any other picture in a web page.

Canvas-Based Paint Programs

A paint program is one of the first examples that comes to mind when people start exercising their canvas-programming muscles. It's thus no surprise that you can Google up many more paint program examples on the Web, including some ridiculously advanced versions. Here are two favorites:

- **iPaint** (*http://tinyurl.com/js-ipaint*). This straightforward program looks like Microsoft Paint in a web browser. However, it adds at least one feature traditional Paint

doesn't—the ability to select and manipulate the objects in your picture after you've drawn them.

- **Sketchpad** (*http://mugtug.com/sketchpad*). This amazingly tricked-out painting program has support for advanced illustration features like shape manipulation, marquee selection, textures, and even Spirograph drawing.

Browser Compatibility for the Canvas

You've come a long way with the canvas already. Now it's time to step back and answer the question that hangs over every new HTML5 feature: When is it safe to use it?

Fortunately, the canvas is one of the better-supported parts of HTML5. The latest version of every mainstream browser supports it. Of course, the more up-to-date the browser, the better—later builds of these browsers improve the drawing speed of the canvas and remove occasional glitches.

You're not likely to run into an old browser that doesn't support the canvas, except for versions of Internet Explorer before IE 9. And that's the clear issue that today's canvas users will be thinking about: How can you put the canvas in your pages without locking out IE 8 and IE 7?

As with many HTML5 features, you have two compatibility choices. Your first option is to detect when canvas support is missing and try to fall back on a different approach. Your second option is to fill the gap with another tool that can simulate the HTML5 canvas, so your pages will work—as written—on old browsers. In the case of the canvas, the second approach is the surprise winner, as you'll learn in the next section.

Polyfilling the Canvas with ExplorerCanvas

There are several solid workarounds that grant canvas-like abilities to aging copies of IE. The first is the ExplorerCanvas library (also called excanvas), by Google engineer and JavaScript genius Erik Arvidsson. It simulates the HTML5 canvas in Internet Explorer 7 or 8, using nothing but JavaScript and a now out-of-date technology called VML (Vector Markup Language).

NOTE VML is a specification for creating line art and other illustrations using markup in an HTML document. It's now been replaced by a similar, but better supported, standard called SVG (Scalable Vector Graphics), which browsers are just beginning to support. Today, VML still lingers in a few Microsoft products, like Microsoft Office and Internet Explorer. This makes it a reasonable substitute for the canvas, albeit with some limitations.

You can download ExplorerCanvas from *http://code.google.com/p/explorercanvas*. To use it, copy the *excanvas.js* file to the same folder as your web page, and add a script reference like this to your web page:

```
<head>
  <title>...</title>
  <!--[if lt IE 9]>
    <script src="excanvas.js"></script>
  <![endif]-->
  ...
<head>
```

Notice that this reference is conditional. Versions of Internet Explorer that are *earlier* than IE 9 will use it, but IE 9 and non-IE browsers will ignore the script altogether.

From this point, you can use the <canvas> without any serious headaches. For example, this change is all you need to get the basic paint program (shown on page 263) working in old versions of IE.

NOTE If you plan to draw text on your canvas (a feature discussed on page 279), you'll also need the help of a second JavaScript library, called Canvas-text, which works in conjunction with ExplorerCanvas. You can download it from *http://code.google.com/p/canvas-text*.

Polyfilling the Canvas with FlashCanvas

Of course, the ExplorerCanvas isn't perfect. If you use advanced features, you'll probably run into something that doesn't look right. The main features that aren't supported in ExplorerCanvas include radial gradients, shadows, clipping regions, raw pixel processing, and data URLs. And although someone may update Explorer-Canvas in the future to add these features, it doesn't seem likely—the current build of ExplorerCanvas is a few years old and the code hasn't been touched in a while.

If you have really ambitious plans—for example, you're planning to create complex animations or a side-scrolling game—you might find that ExplorerCanvas isn't fast enough to keep up. In this situation, you can consider switching to a different poly-fill that uses a high-performance browser plug-in like Silverlight or Flash. You can review all your options on GitHub's polyfill page at *http://tinyurl.com/polyfills*. Or, go straight to one of the best: the free FlashCanvas library at *http://code.google.com/p/flashcanvas*. Like ExplorerCanvas, you can plug it into your page using a single line of JavaScript. But unlike ExplorerCanvas, it uses the Flash plug-in, without a trace of VML.

FlashCanvas also has a grown-up professional version called FlashCanvas Pro. It adds support for a few additional features, like global composite operations (page 262) and shadows (page 281).

FlashCanvas Pro is free for noncommercial use (get it at *http://flashcanvas.net/ download*). Or, if you're a business or an individual planning to make some money, you can buy FlashCanvas Pro for a small fee (currently $31) at *http://flashcanvas.net/ purchase*. You can compare the canvas support of ExplorerCanvas, FlashCanvas, and FlashCanvas Pro at *http://flashcanvas.net/docs/canvas-api*.

Like ExplorerCanvas, the FlashCanvas project isn't seeing much action these days. However, in its current state it remains a reliable choice for canvas support in old browsers. If you're planning to create a truly ambitious canvas-powered site—for example, a real-time game—you'll need to test out FlashCanvas to see if it supports everything you need to do.

NOTE When you combine a canvas-powered page with a library like FlashCanvas, you get truly impressive support on virtually every browser known to humankind. Not only do you get support for slightly older versions of IE through Flash, but you also get support for Flash-free mobile devices like the iPad and iPhone through HTML5.

The Canvas Fallback and Feature Detection

The most popular way to extend the reach of pages that use the canvas is with ExplorerCanvas and FlashCanvas. However, they aren't the only options.

The <canvas> element supports fallback content, just like the <audio> and <video> elements you explored in the last chapter. For example, you could apply this sort of markup to use the canvas (if it's supported) or to display an image (if it isn't):

```
<canvas id="logoCreator" width="500" height="300">
  <p>The canvas isn't supported on your computer, so you can't use our
  dynamic logo creator.</p>
  <img src="logo.png" alt="Standard Company Logo">
</canvas>
```

This technique is rarely much help. Most of the time, you'll use the canvas to draw dynamic graphics or to create some sort of interactive graphical application, and a fixed graphic just can't compensate. One alternative is to place a Flash application inside the <canvas> element. This approach is especially good if you already have a Flash version of your work but you're moving to the canvas for future development. It lets you offer a working Flash-based solution to old versions of IE, while letting everyone else use the plug-in-free canvas.

If you're using Modernizr (page 31), you can test for canvas support in your JavaScript code. Just test the Modernizr.canvas property, and check the Modernizr.canvastext property to look for the canvas's text-drawing feature (which was a later addition to the canvas drawing model). If you don't detect canvas support in the current browser, then you can use any workaround you'd like.

Canvas Accessibility

Is it possible to make the canvas more accessible?

One of the key themes of HTML5, the semantic elements, and the past few chapters is *accessibility*—designing a page that provides information to assistive software, so it can help people with disabilities use your website. After all this emphasis, it may come as a shock that one of HTML5's premier new features has no semantics or accessibility model *at all*.

The creators of HTML5 are working to patch the hole. However, no one is quite certain of the best solution. One proposal is to create a separate document model for assistive devices, which would then mirror the canvas content. The problem here is that it's up to the author to keep this "shadow" model in sync with the visuals, and lazy or overworked developers are likely to pass on this responsibility if it's at all complicated.

A second proposal is to extend image maps (an existing HTML feature that divides pictures into clickable regions) so they act as a layer over the top of the canvas. Because an image map is essentially a group of links, it could hold important information for assistive software to read and report to the user.

Currently, there's no point in thinking too much about either of these ideas, because they're both still being debated. In the meantime, it makes sense to use the canvas for a variety of graphical tasks, like arcade games (most of which can't practically be made accessible) and data visualization (as long as you have the data available in text form elsewhere on the page). However, the canvas isn't a good choice for an all-purpose page design element. So if you're planning to use the canvas to create a fancy heading or a menu for your website, hold off for now.

Advanced Canvas: Interactivity and Animation

The canvas is a huge, sprawling feature. In the previous chapter, you learned how to draw line art and even create a respectable drawing program in a few dozen lines of JavaScript. But the canvas has more up its sleeve than that. Not only can it show dynamic pictures and host paint programs, but it can also play animations, process images with pixel-perfect control, and run interactive games. In this chapter, you'll learn the practical beginnings for all these tasks.

First, you'll start by looking at drawing context methods that let you paint different types of content on a canvas, including images and text. Next, you'll learn how to add some graphical pizzazz with shadows, patterned fills, and gradients. Finally, you'll learn practical techniques to make your canvas interactive and to host live animations. Best of all, you can build all of these examples with nothing more than ordinary JavaScript and raw ambition.

> **NOTE** For the first half of this chapter, you'll focus on small snippets of drawing code. You can incorporate this code into your own pages, but you'll need to first add a <canvas> element to your page and create a drawing context, as you learned on page 246. In the second half of this chapter, you'll look at much more ambitious examples. Although you'll see most (or all) of the canvas-drawing code that these examples use, you won't get every page detail. To try out the examples for yourself, visit the try-out site at *http://prosetech.com/html5*.

Other Things You Can Draw on the Canvas

Using the canvas, you can painstakingly recreate any drawing you want, from a bunch of lines and triangles to a carefully shaded portrait. But as the complexity of your drawing increases, so does the code. It's extremely unlikely that you'd write by hand all the code you need to create a finely detailed picture.

Fortunately, you have other options. The drawing context isn't limited to lines and curves—it also has methods that let you slap down pre-existing images, text, patterns, and even video frames. In the following sections, you'll learn how to use these methods to get more content on your canvas.

Drawing Images

You've probably seen web pages that build maps out of satellite images, downloaded and stitched together. That's an example of how you can take images you already have and combine them to get the final image that you want.

The canvas supports ordinary image data through the drawing context's logically named drawImage() method. To put an image in your canvas, you call drawImage() and pass in an image object and your coordinates, like this:

```
context.drawImage(img, 10, 10);
```

But before you can call drawImage(), you need the image object. HTML5 gives you three ways to get it. First, you can build it yourself out of raw pixels, one pixel at a time, using createImageData(). This approach is tedious and slow (although you'll learn more about per-pixel manipulation on page 313).

Your second option is to use an <img> element that's already on your page. For example, if you have this markup:

```
<img id="arrow_left" src="arrow_left.png">
```

You can copy that picture onto the canvas with this code:

```
var img = document.getElementById("arrow_left");
context.drawImage(img, 10, 10);
```

The third way that you can get an image for use with drawImage() is by creating an image object and loading an image picture from a separate file. The disadvantage to this approach is that you can't use your image with drawImage() until that picture has been completely downloaded. To prevent problems, you need to wait until the image's onLoad event occurs before you do anything with the image.

To understand this pattern, it helps to look at an example. Imagine you have an image named *maze.png* that you want to display on a canvas. Conceptually, you want to take this series of steps:

```
// Create the image object.
var img = new Image();

// Load the image file.
img.src = "maze.png";
```

```
// Draw the image. (This could fail, because the picture
// might not be downloaded yet.)
context.drawImage(img, 0, 0);
```

The problem here is that setting the `src` attribute starts an image download, but your code carries on without waiting for it to finish. The proper way to arrange this code is like this:

```
// Create the image object.
var img = new Image();

// Attach a function to the onload event.
// This tells the browser what to do after the image is loaded.
img.onload = function() {
  context.drawImage(img, 0, 0);
};

// Load the image file.
img.src = "maze.png";
```

This may seem counterintuitive, since the order in which the code is listed doesn't match the order in which it will be *executed*. In this example, the `context.draw Image()` call happens last, shortly after the `img.src` property is set.

Images have a wide range of uses. You can use them to add embellishments to your line drawings, or as a shortcut to avoid drawing by hand. In a game, you can use images for different objects and characters, positioned appropriately on the canvas. And fancy paint programs use them instead of basic line segments so the user can draw "textured" lines. You'll see some practical examples that use image drawing in this chapter.

TROUBLESHOOTING MOMENT

My Pictures Are Squashed!

If you attempt to draw a picture and find that it's inexplicably stretched, squashed, or otherwise distorted, the most likely culprit is a style sheet rule.

The proper way to size the canvas is to use its height and width attributes in your HTML markup. You might think you could remove these in your markup, leaving a tag like this:

```
<canvas></canvas>
```

And replace them with a style sheet rule that targets your canvas, like this one:

```
canvas {
  height: 300px;
  width: 500px;
}
```

But this doesn't work. The problem is that the CSS height and width properties aren't the same as the canvas height and width properties. If you make this mistake, what actually happens is that the canvas gets its default size (300 x 150 pixels). Then, the CSS size properties stretch or squash the canvas to fit, causing it to resize its contents accordingly. As a result, when you put an image on the canvas, it's squashed too, which is decidedly unappealing.

To avoid this problem, always specify the canvas size using its height and width attributes. And if you need a way to change the size of the canvas based on something else, use a bit of JavaScript code to change the `<canvas>` element's height and width when needed.

Slicing, Dicing, and Resizing an Image

The drawImage() function accepts a few optional arguments that let you alter the way your image is painted on the canvas. First, if you want to resize the image, you can tack on the width and height you want, like this:

```
context.drawImage(img, 10, 10, 30, 30);
```

This function makes a 30 x 30 pixel box for the image, with the top-left corner at point (10,10). Assuming the image is naturally 60 x 60 pixels, this operation squashes it by half in both dimensions, leaving it just a quarter as big as it would ordinarily be.

If you want to crop a piece out of the picture, you can supply the four extra arguments to drawImage() at the beginning of the argument list. These four points define the position and size of the rectangle you want to cut out of the picture, as shown here:

```
context.drawImage(img, source_x, source_y, source_width, source_height, x, y,
width, height);
```

The last four arguments are the same as in the previous example—they define the position and size that the cropped picture should have on the canvas.

For example, imagine you have a 200 x 200 pixel image and you want to paint just the top half. To do that, you create a box that starts at point (0,0) and has a width of 200 and a height of 100. You can then draw it on the canvas at point (75,25), using this code:

```
context.drawImage(img, 0, 0, 200, 100, 75, 25, 200, 100);
```

Figure 9-1 shows exactly what's happening in this example.

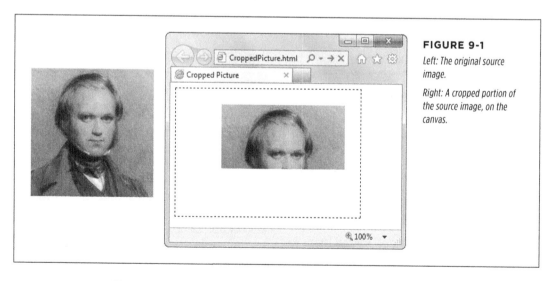

FIGURE 9-1

Left: The original source image.

Right: A cropped portion of the source image, on the canvas.

If you want to do more—for example, skew or rotate an image before you draw it, the drawImage() method can't keep up. However, you can use transforms to alter the way you draw anything and everything, as explained on page 256.

Drawing a Video Frame

The first parameter of the drawImage() method is the image you want to draw. As you've seen, this can be an Image object you've just created, or an <img> element that's elsewhere on the page.

But that's not the whole story. HTML5 actually allows two more substitutions. Instead of an image, you can throw in a complete <canvas> element (not the one you're drawing on). Or, you can use a currently playing <video> element, with no extra work:

```
var video =
  document.getElementById("videoPlayer");

context.drawImage(video, 0, 0,
  video.clientWidth, video.clientWidth);
```

When this code runs, it grabs a single frame of video—the frame that's being played at the very instant the code runs. It then paints that picture onto the canvas.

This ability opens the door to a number of interesting effects. For example, you can use a timer to grab new video frames while playback is under way and keep painting them on a canvas. If you do this fast enough, the copied sequence of images on the canvas will look like another video player.

To get more exotic, you can change something about the copied video frame before you paint it. For example, you could scale it larger or smaller, or dip into the raw pixels and apply a Photoshop-style effect. For an example, read the article at *http://html5doctor.com/video-canvas-magic*. It shows how you can play a video in grayscale simply by taking regular snapshots of the real video and converting each pixel in each frame to a color-free shade of gray.

Drawing Text

Text is another thing that you wouldn't want to assemble yourself out of lines and curves. And the HTML5 canvas doesn't expect you to. Instead, it includes two drawing context methods that can do the job.

First, before you draw any text, you need to set the drawing context's font property. You use a string that uses the same syntax as the all-in-one CSS font property. At a bare minimum, you must supply the font size, in pixels, and the font name, like this:

```
context.font = "20px Arial";
```

You can supply a list of font names, if you're not sure that your font is supported:

```
context.font = "20px Verdana,sans-serif";
```

And optionally, you can add italics or bold at the beginning of the string, like this:

```
context.font = "bold 20px Arial";
```

You can also use a fancy web font, courtesy of CSS3. All you need to do is register the font name first, using a style sheet (as described on page 206).

Once the font is in place, you can use the fillText() method to draw your text. Here's an example that puts the top-left corner of the text at the point (10,10):

```
context.textBaseline = "top";
context.fillStyle = "black";
context.fillText("I'm stuck in a canvas. Someone let me out!", 10, 10);
```

You can put the text wherever you want, but you're limited to a single line. If you want to draw multiple lines of text, you need to call fillText() multiple times.

> **TIP** If you want to divide a solid paragraph over multiple lines, you can create your own *word wrapping algorithm.* The basic idea is this: Split your sentence into words, and see how many words fit in each line using the drawing context's measureText() method. It's tedious to do, but the sample code at *http://tinyurl.com/6ec7hld* can get you started.

Instead of using fillText(), you can use the other text-drawing method, stroke-Text(). It draws an outline around your text, using the strokeStyle property for its color and the lineWidth property for its thickness. Here's an example:

```
context.font = "bold 40px Verdana,sans-serif";
context.lineWidth = "1";
context.strokeStyle = "red";
context.strokeText("I'm an OUTLINE", 20, 50);
```

When you use strokeText(), the middle of the text stays blank. Of course, you can use fillText() followed by strokeText() if you want colored, outlined text. Figure 9-2 shows both pieces of text in a canvas.

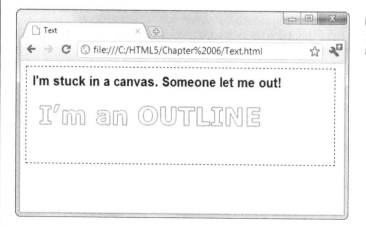

FIGURE 9-2

The canvas makes it easy to draw solid text and outlined text.

> **TIP** Drawing text is much slower than drawing lines and images. The speed isn't important if you're creating a static, unchanging image (like a chart), but it may be an issue if you're creating an interactive, animated application. If you need to optimize performance, you may find that it's better to save your text in an image file and then draw it on the canvas with drawImage().

Shadows and Fancy Fills

So far, when you've drawn lines and filled shapes on the canvas, you've used solid colors. And while there's certainly nothing wrong with that, ambitious painters will be happy to hear that the canvas has a few fancier drawing techniques. For example, the canvas can draw an artfully blurred shadow behind any shape. Or, it can fill a shape by tiling a small graphic across its surface. But the canvas's fanciest painting frill is *gradients*, which you can use to blend two or more colors into a kaleidoscope of patterns.

In the following sections, you'll learn to use all these features, simply by setting different properties in the canvas's drawing context.

Adding Shadows

One handy canvas feature is the ability to add a shadow behind anything you draw. Figure 9-3 shows some snazzy shadow examples.

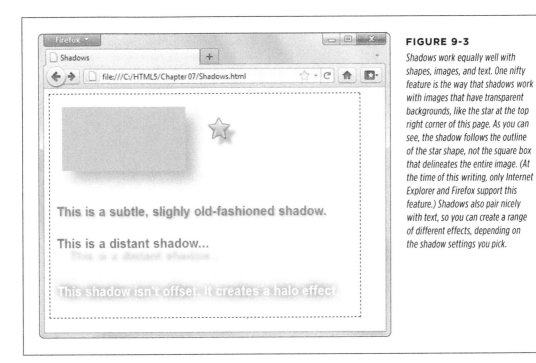

FIGURE 9-3

Shadows work equally well with shapes, images, and text. One nifty feature is the way that shadows work with images that have transparent backgrounds, like the star at the top right corner of this page. As you can see, the shadow follows the outline of the star shape, not the square box that delineates the entire image. (At the time of this writing, only Internet Explorer and Firefox support this feature.) Shadows also pair nicely with text, so you can create a range of different effects, depending on the shadow settings you pick.

Essentially, a shadow looks like a blurry version of what you would ordinarily draw (lines, shapes, images, or text). You control the appearance of shadows using several drawing context properties, as outlined in Table 9-1.

TABLE 9-1 *Properties for creating shadows*

PROPERTY	DESCRIPTION
shadowColor	Sets the shadow's color. You could go with black or a tinted color, but a nice midrange gray is generally best. Another good technique is to use a semitransparent color (page 185) so the content that's underneath still shows through. When you want to turn shadows off, set shadowColor back to transparent.
shadowBlur	Sets the shadow's "fuzziness." A shadowBlur of 0 creates a crisp shadow that looks just like a silhouette of the original shape. By comparison, a shadowBlur of 20 is a blurry haze, and you can go higher still. Most people agree that some fuzz (a blur of at least 3) looks best.
shadowOffsetX and shadowOffsetY	Positions the shadow relative to the content. For example, set both properties to 5, and the shadow will be bumped 5 pixels to the right and 5 pixels down from the original content. You can also use negative numbers to move the shadow the other way (left and up).

The following code creates the assorted shadows shown in Figure 9-3:

```
// Draw the shadowed rectangle.
context.rect(20, 20, 200, 100);
context.fillStyle = "#8ED6FF";
context.shadowColor = "#bbbbbb";
context.shadowBlur = 20;
context.shadowOffsetX = 15;
context.shadowOffsetY = 15;
context.fill();

// Draw the shadowed star.
context.shadowOffsetX = 10;
context.shadowOffsetY = 10;
context.shadowBlur = 4;
img = document.getElementById("star");
context.drawImage(img, 250, 30);

context.textBaseline = "top";
context.font = "bold 20px Arial";

// Draw three pieces of shadowed text.
context.shadowBlur = 3;
context.shadowOffsetX = 2;
context.shadowOffsetY = 2;
```

```
context.fillStyle = "steelblue";
context.fillText("This is a subtle, slightly old-fashioned shadow.", 10, 175);

context.shadowBlur = 5;
context.shadowOffsetX = 20;
context.shadowOffsetY = 20;
context.fillStyle = "green";
context.fillText("This is a distant shadow...", 10, 225);

context.shadowBlur = 15;
context.shadowOffsetX = 0;
context.shadowOffsetY = 0;
context.shadowColor = "black";
context.fillStyle = "white";
context.fillText("This shadow isn't offset. It creates a halo effect.", 10,
  300);
```

Filling Shapes with Patterns

So far, you've filled the shapes you've drawn with solid or semitransparent colors.
But the canvas also has a fancy fill feature that lets you slather the inside with a
pattern or a gradient. Using these fancy fills is a sure way to jazz up plain shapes.
Using a fancy fill is a two-step affair. First, you create the fill. Then, you attach it to
the fillStyle property (or, occasionally, the strokeStyle property).

To make a pattern fill, you start by choosing a small image that you can tile seamlessly over a large area (see Figure 9-4). You need to load the picture you want to
tile into an image object using one of the techniques you learned about earlier, such
as putting a hidden <img> on your page (page 276), or loading it from a file and
handling the onLoad event of the <img> element (page 277). This example uses
the first approach:

```
var img = document.getElementById("brickTile");
```

Once you have your image, you can create a pattern object using the drawing
context's createPattern() method. At this point, you pick whether you want the
pattern to repeat horizontally (repeat-x), vertically (repeat-y), or in both dimensions (repeat):

```
var pattern = context.createPattern(img, "repeat");
```

The final step is to use the pattern object to set the fillStyle or strokeStyle
property:

```
context.fillStyle = pattern;
context.rect(0, 0, canvas.width, canvas.height);
context.fill();
```

This creates a rectangle that fills the canvas with the tiled image pattern, as shown
in Figure 9-4.

FIGURE 9-4

Left: An image that holds a single tile.

Right: The pattern created by tiling the image over an entire canvas.

Filling Shapes with Gradients

The second type of fancy fill is a gradient, which blends two or more colors. The canvas supports linear gradients and radial gradients, and Figure 9-5 compares the two.

FIGURE 9-5

A linear gradient (top left) blends from one line of color to another. A radial gradient (top right) blends from one point of color to another. Both types support more than two colors, allowing you to create a banded effect with linear gradients (bottom left) or a ring effect with radial gradients (bottom right).

Unsurprisingly, the first step to using a gradient fill is creating the right type of gradient object. The drawing context has two methods that handle this task: cre-ateLinearGradient() and createRadialGradient(). Both work more or less the same way: They hold a list of colors that kick in at different points.

The easiest way to understand gradients is to start by looking at a simple example. Here's the code that's used to create the gradient for the top-left heart in Figure 9-5:

```
// Create a gradient from point (10,0) to (100,0).
var gradient = context.createLinearGradient(10, 0, 100, 0);

// Add two colors.
gradient.addColorStop(0, "magenta");
gradient.addColorStop(1, "yellow");

// Call another function to draw the shape.
drawHeart(60, 50);

// Paint the shape.
context.fillStyle = gradient;
context.fill();
context.stroke();
```

When you create a new linear gradient, you supply two points that represent the starting point and ending point of a *line*. This line is the path over which the color change takes place.

The gradient line is important, because it determines what the gradient looks like (see Figure 9-6). For example, consider a linear gradient that transitions from magenta to yellow. It could make this leap in a few pixels, or it could blend it out over the entire width of the canvas. Furthermore, the blend could be from left to right, top to bottom, or slanted somewhere in between. The line determines all these details.

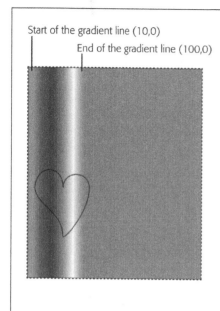

Start of the gradient line (10,0)

End of the gradient line (100,0)

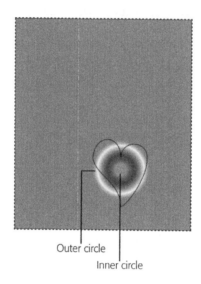

Outer circle

Inner circle

FIGURE 9-6

Left: Here's the gradient generated for the bottom-left heart from Figure 9-5. When you use that gradient to fill a shape, you see just a portion of it.

Right: The same is true for this radial gradient, which is used for the bottom-right heart in Figure 9-5.

In this example, the gradient line starts at point (10,0) and ends at point (100,0). These points tell you several important things:

- **The gradient is horizontal.** That means it blends colors from left to right. You know this because the two points have the same y-coordinate. If, on the other hand, you wanted to blend from top to bottom, you could use points like (0,10) and (0,100). If you wanted it to stretch diagonally from top left to bottom right, you could use (10,10) and (100,100).

- **The actual color blend spans just 90 pixels (starting when the x-coordinate is 10 and ending when the x-coordinate is 100).** In this example, the heart shape is just slightly smaller than the gradient dimensions, which means you see most of the gradient in the heart.

- **Beyond the limits of this gradient, the colors become solid.** So if you make the heart wider, you'll see more solid magenta (on the left) and solid yellow (on the right).

> **TIP** Often, you'll create a gradient that's just barely bigger than the shape you're painting, as in this example. However, other approaches are possible. For example, if you want to paint several shapes using different parts of the same gradient, you might decide to create a gradient that covers the entire canvas.

To actually set the colors in a gradient, you call the gradient's addColorStop() method. Each time you do, you supply an offset from 0 to 1, which sets where the color appears in the blend. A value of 0 means the color appears at the very start of the gradient, while a value of 1 puts the color at the very end. Change these numbers (for example, to 0.2 and 0.8), and you can compress the gradient, exposing more solid color on either side.

When you create a two-color gradient, 0 and 1 make most sense for your offsets. But when you create a gradient with more colors, you can choose different offsets to stretch out some bands of colors while compressing others. The bottom-left heart in Figure 9-5 splits its offsets evenly, giving each color an equal-sized band:

```
var gradient = context.createLinearGradient(10, 0, 100, 0);
gradient.addColorStop("0", "magenta");
gradient.addColorStop(".25", "blue");
gradient.addColorStop(".50", "green");
gradient.addColorStop(".75", "yellow");
gradient.addColorStop("1.0", "red");

drawHeart(60, 200);
context.fillStyle = gradient;
context.fill();
context.stroke();
```

NOTE If the room is starting to revolve around you, don't panic. After all, you don't need to understand everything that happens in a gradient. You can always just tweak the numbers until an appealing blend of colors appears in your shape.

You use the same process to create a radial gradient as you do to create a linear one. But instead of supplying two points, you must define two circles. That's because a radial gradient is a blend of color that radiates out from a small circle to a larger, containing circle. To define each of these circles, you supply the center point and radius.

In the radial gradient example shown in the top right of Figure 9-5, the colors blend from a center point inside the heart, at (180,100). The inner color is represented by a 10-pixel circle, and the outer color is a 50-pixel circle. Once again, if you go beyond these limits, you get solid colors, giving the radial gradient a solid magenta core and solid yellow surroundings. Here's the code that draws the two-color radial gradient:

```
var gradient = context.createRadialGradient(180, 100, 10, 180, 100, 50);
gradient.addColorStop(0, "magenta");
gradient.addColorStop(1, "yellow");

drawHeart(180, 80);
context.fillStyle = gradient;
context.fill();
context.stroke();
```

> **NOTE** Most often, you'll choose the same center point for both the inner and outer circles. However, you could offset one from the other, which can stretch, squash, and distort the blend of colors in interesting ways.

Using this example, you can create the final, multicolored radial gradient that's in the bottom-right corner of Figure 9-5. You simply need to move the center point of the circles to the location of the heart and add a different set of color stops—the same ones that you used for the multicolored linear gradient:

```
var gradient = context.createRadialGradient(180, 250, 10, 180, 250, 50);
gradient.addColorStop("0","magenta");
gradient.addColorStop(".25","blue");
gradient.addColorStop(".50","green");
gradient.addColorStop(".75","yellow");
gradient.addColorStop("1.0","red");

drawHeart(180, 230);
context.fillStyle = gradient;
context.fill();
context.stroke();
```

Now you have the smarts to create more psychedelic patterns than a 1960s revival party.

Putting It Together: Drawing a Graph

Now that you've slogged your way through the better part of the canvas's drawing features, it's time to pause and enjoy the fruits of your labor. In the following example, you'll take some humdrum text and numbers and use the canvas to create simple, standout charts.

Figure 9-7 shows the starting point: a two-page personality test that's light on graphics. The user answers the questions on the first page and then clicks Get Score to move to the second page. The second page reports the personality scores according to the infamous five-factor personality model (see the box on page 290).

The JavaScript code that makes this example work is pretty straightforward. When the user clicks a number button, its background is changed to indicate the user's choice. When the user completes the quiz, a simple algorithm runs the answers through a set of scoring formulas to calculate the five personality factors. If you want to examine this code or to take the test, visit the try-out site at *http://prosetech.com/html5*.

So far, there's no HTML5 magic. But consider how you could improve this two-page personality test by *graphing* the personality scores so that each factor is shown visually. Figure 9-8 shows the revamped version of the personality test results page, which uses this technique.

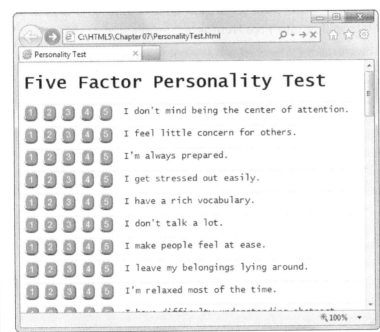

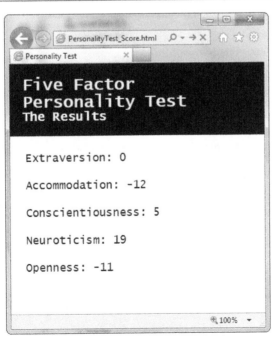

FIGURE 9-7

Click your way through the questions (top), and then review the scores (bottom). Unfortunately, without a scale or any kind of visual aid, it's difficult for ordinary people to tell what these numbers are supposed to mean.

How to Convert One Personality into Five Numbers

This five-factor personality test ranks you according to five personality "ingredients," which are usually called openness, conscientiousness, extraversion, agreeableness, and neuroticism. These factors were cooked up when researchers analyzed the thousands of personality-describing adjectives in the English language.

To pick just five factors, psychologists used a combination of hard-core statistics, personality surveys, and a computer. They identified which adjectives people tend to tick off together and used that to distill the smallest set of personality super-traits.

For example, people who describe themselves as *outgoing* usually also describe themselves as *social* and *gregarious*, so it makes sense to combine all these traits into a single personality factor (which psychologists call *extraversion*). By the time the researchers had finished chewing through their set of nearly 20,000 adjectives, they had managed to boil them down to five closely interrelated factors.

You can learn more about the five-factor personality model at *http://tinyurl.com/big-five-p*, or in the book *Your Brain: The Missing Manual* (by this author).

To show these charts, the page uses five separate canvases, one for each personality factor. Here's the markup:

```
<header>
  <h1>Five Factor Personality Test</h1>
  <p>The Results</p>
</header>

<div class="score">
  <h2 id="headingE">Extraversion: </h2>
  <canvas id="canvasE" height="75" width="550"></canvas>
</div>

<div class="score">
  <h2 id="headingA">Accommodation: </h2>
  <canvas id="canvasA" height="75" width="550"></canvas>
</div>

<div class="score">
  <h2 id="headingC">Conscientiousness: </h2>
  <canvas id="canvasC" height="75" width="550"></canvas>
</div>

<div class="score">
  <h2 id="headingN">Neuroticism: </h2>
  <canvas id="canvasN" height="75" width="550"></canvas>
</div>
```

```
<div class="score">
  <h2 id="heading0">Openness: </h2>
  <canvas id="canvas0" height="75" width="550"></canvas>
</div>
```

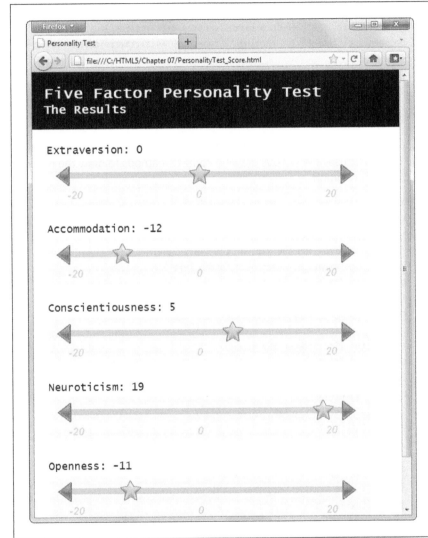

FIGURE 9-8

*This page combines
several different types of
canvas drawing, including
lines, images, and text. But
the most interesting part
of it is the way it dynamically draws these simple
graphs, based on your
answers in the personality
quiz.*

Each chart is drawn by the same custom JavaScript function, named plotScore().
The page calls this function five times, using different arguments each time. For
example, to draw the extraversion chart at the top of the page, the code passes the
topmost canvas element, the extraversion score (as a number from -20 to 20), and
the text title ("Extraversion"):

```
window.onload = function() {
  ...
  // Get the <canvas> element for the extraversion score.
  var canvasE = document.getElementById("canvasE");

  // Add the score number to the corresponding heading.
  // (The score is stored in a variable named extraversion.)
  document.getElementById("headingE").innerHTML += extraversion;

  // Plot the score in the corresponding canvas.
  plotScore(canvasE, extraversion, "Extraversion");
  ...
}
```

The plotScore() function runs through a bit of drawing code that will seem familiar
to you by now. It uses the various drawing context methods to draw the different
parts of the score graph:

```
function plotScore(canvas, score, title) {
  var context = canvas.getContext("2d");

  // Draw the arrows on the side of the chart line.
  var img = document.getElementById("arrow_left");
  context.drawImage(img, 12, 10);
  img = document.getElementById("arrow_right");
  context.drawImage(img, 498, 10);

  // Draw the line between the arrows.
  context.moveTo(39, 25);
  context.lineTo(503, 25);
  context.lineWidth = 10;
  context.strokeStyle = "rgb(174,215,244)";
  context.stroke();

  // Write the numbers on the scale.
  context.fillStyle = context.strokeStyle;
  context.font = "italic bold 18px Arial";
  context.textBaseline = "top";

  context.fillText("-20", 35, 50);
  context.fillText("0", 255, 50);
  context.fillText("20", 475, 50);

  // Add the star to show where the score ranks on the chart.
  img = document.getElementById("star");
  context.drawImage(img, (score+20)/40*440+35-17, 0);
}
```

The most important bit is the final line, which plots the star at the right position using this slightly messy equation:

```
context.drawImage(img, (score+20)/40*440+35-17, 0);
```

Here's how it works. The first step is to convert the score into a percentage from 0 to 100 percent. Ordinarily, the score falls between -20 and 20, so the first operation the code needs to carry out is to change it to a value from 0 to 40:

```
score+20
```

You can then divide that number by 40 to get the percentage:

```
(score+20)/40
```

Once you have the percentage, you need to multiply it by the length of the line. That way, 0 percent ends up at the far left side, while 100 percent ends up at the opposite end, and everything else falls somewhere in between:

```
(score+20)/40*440
```

This code would work fine if the line stretched from the *x*-coordinate 0 to the *x*-coordinate 400. But in reality the line is offset a bit from the left edge, to give it a bit of padding. You need to offset the star by the same amount:

```
(score+20)/40*440+35
```

But this lines the left edge of the start up with the proper position, when really you want to line up its midpoint. To correct this issue, you need to subtract an amount that's roughly equal to half the start's width:

```
(score+20)/40*440+35-17
```

This gives you the final *x*-coordinate for the star, based on the score.

NOTE It's a small jump to move from fixed drawings to dynamic graphics like the ones in this example, which tailor themselves according to the latest data. But once you've made this step, you can apply your skills to build all sorts of interesting data-driven graphics, from traditional pie charts to infographics that use dials and meters. And if you're looking for a way to simplify the task, check out one of the canvas graphic libraries, which include pre-written JavaScript routines for drawing common types of graphs based on your data. Two good examples are RGraph (*www.rgraph.net*) and ZingChart (*www.zingchart.com*).

■ Making Your Shapes Interactive

The canvas is a *non-retained* painting surface. That means that the canvas doesn't keep track of what drawing operations you've performed. Instead, it just keeps the final result—the grid of colored pixels that makes up your picture.

For example, if you draw a red square in the middle of your canvas, the moment you call stroke() or fill(), that square becomes nothing more than a block of red pixels. It may look like a square, but the canvas has no memory of its squareness.

This model makes drawing fast. However, it also makes life difficult if you want to add interactivity to your drawing. For example, imagine you want to create a smarter version of the painting program you saw on page 263. You want people to be able to not only draw a line, but also draw a rectangle. (That part's easy.) And you want people to be able to not only draw a rectangle, but also select it, drag it to a new place, resize it, change its color, and so on. Before you can give them all that power, you need to deal with several complications. First, how do you know if someone has clicked on the rectangle? Second, how do you know the details about the rectangle—its coordinates, size, stroke color, and fill color? And third, how do you know the details about every *other* shape on the canvas—which you'll need to know if you need to change the rectangle and repaint the canvas?

To solve these problems and make your canvas interactive, you need to keep track of every object you paint. Then, when users click somewhere, you need to check whether they're clicking one of the shapes (a process known as *hit testing*). If you can tackle these two tasks, the rest—changing one of your shapes and repainting the canvas—is easy.

Keeping Track of What You've Drawn

In order to be able to change and repaint your picture, you need to know everything about its contents. For example, consider the circle-drawing program shown in Figure 9-9. To keep things simple, it consists entirely of separately sized, differently colored circles.

To keep track of an individual circle, you need to know its position, radius, and fill color. Rather than create dozens of variables to store all this information, it makes sense to put all four details in a small package. That package is a *custom object*.

If you haven't created a custom object before, here's the standard technique. First, you create a function that's named after your type of object. For example, if you want to build a custom object for a circle creation, you might name the function Circle(), like this:

```
function Circle() {
}
```

Next, you need your object to store some data. You do that by using a keyword named this to create properties. For example, if you want to give your circle object a property named radius, so you can keep track of its size, you would assign a starting value to this.radius inside the Circle() function.

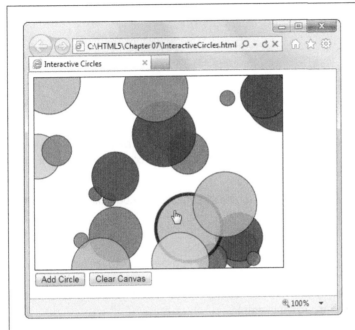

FIGURE 9-9

This circle-drawing program is interactive. You can click to select a circle (at which point it becomes highlighted with a different border color) and drag it to a new position.

Here's a function that defines a circle with three details: the *x*- and *y*-coordinates, and the radius of the circle:

```
function Circle() {
  this.x = 0;
  thix.y = 0;
  this.radius = 15;
}
```

The numbers you set in the Circle() function are just default values. When you use the function to create a new circle object, you can change each property value.

Once you've added all the properties you need, you're ready to use your function to create live objects. In this case, that means using the Circle() function to create a new circle object. The trick is that you don't want to call the function—instead, you want to create a new copy of it with the new keyword. Here's an example:

```
// Create a new circle object, and store it in a variable named myCircle.
var myCircle = new Circle();
```

Once you have a live circle object, you can access all the circle details as properties:

```
// Change the radius.
myCircle.radius = 20;
```

If you want to get a bit fancier, you can pass arguments to the Circle() function. That way, you can create a circle object and set all the circle properties in one step. Here's the version of the Circle() function that's used for the page in Figure 9-9:

```
function Circle(x, y, radius, color) {
  this.x = x;
  this.y = y;
  this.radius = radius;
  this.color = color;
  this.isSelected = false;
}
```

The isSelected property takes a true or false value. When someone clicks the circle, isSelected is set to true, and then the drawing code knows to paint a different border around it.

Using this version of the Circle() function, you can use code like this to create a circle object:

```
var myCircle = new Circle(0, 0, 20, "red");
```

Of course, the whole point of the circle-drawing program is to let people draw as many circles as they want. That means just one circle object won't do. Instead, you need to create an array that can hold all the circles. Here's the global variable that makes this work in the current example:

```
var circles = [];
```

The rest of the code is easy. When someone clicks the Add Circle button to create a new circle, it triggers the addRandomCircle() function. The addRandomCircle() function creates a new circle with a random size, color, and position:

```
function addRandomCircle() {
  // Give the circle a random size and position.
  var radius = randomFromTo(10, 60);
  var x = randomFromTo(0, canvas.width);
  var y = randomFromTo(0, canvas.height);

  // Give the circle a random color.
  var colors = ["green", "blue", "red", "yellow", "magenta",
   "orange", "brown", "purple", "pink"];
  var color = colors[randomFromTo(0, 8)];

  // Create the new circle.
  var circle = new Circle(x, y, radius, color);

  // Store it in the array.
  circles.push(circle);
```

```
    // Redraw the canvas.
    drawCircles();
  }
```

This code makes use of a custom function named `randomFromTo()`, which generates random numbers in a set range.

(To play with the full code, visit *http://prosetech.com/html5.*)

The final step in this sequence is actually painting the canvas, based on the current collection of circles. After a new circle is created, the `addRandomCircle()` function calls another function, named `drawCircles()`, to do the job. The `drawCircles()` function moves through the array of circles, using this loop:

```
for(var i=0; i<circles.length; i++) {
  var circle = circles[i];
  ...
}
```

This code uses the trusty for loop (which is described in Appendix B, "JavaScript: The Brains of Your Page"). The block of code in the braces runs once for each circle. The first line of code grabs the current circle and stores it in a variable, so it's easy to work with.

Here's the complete `drawCircles()` function, which fills the canvas with the current collection of circles:

```
function drawCircles() {
  // Clear the canvas and prepare to draw.
  context.clearRect(0, 0, canvas.width, canvas.height);
  context.globalAlpha = 0.85;
  context.strokeStyle = "black";

  // Go through all the circles.
  for(var i=0; i<circles.length; i++) {
    var circle = circles[i];

    // Draw the circle.
    context.beginPath();
    context.arc(circle.x, circle.y, circle.radius, 0, Math.PI*2);
    context.fillStyle = circle.color;

    context.fill();
    context.stroke();
  }
}
```

NOTE Each time the circle-drawing program refreshes the display, it starts by clearing everything away with the clearRect() method. Paranoid programmers might worry that this step would cause a flicker, as the canvas goes blank and the circles disappear, then reappear. However, the canvas is optimized to prevent this problem. It doesn't actually clear or paint *anything* until all your drawing logic has finished, at which point it copies the final product to the canvas in one smooth step.

Right now, the circles still aren't interactive. However, the page has the all-important plumbing that keeps track of every circle that's drawn. Although the canvas is still just a block of colored pixels, the code knows the precise combination of circles that creates the canvas—and that means it can manipulate those circles at any time.

In the next section, you'll see how you can use this system to let the user select a circle.

Hit Testing with Coordinates

If you're creating interactive shapes, you'll almost certainly need to use *hit testing*, a technique that checks whether a given point has "hit" another shape. In the circle-drawing program, you want to check whether the user's click has hit upon a circle or just empty space.

More sophisticated animation frameworks (like those provided by Flash and Silverlight) handle hit testing for you. And there are add-on JavaScript libraries for the canvas (like KineticJS) that aim to offer the same conveniences, but none is mature enough to recommend without reservations. So the best bet is for canvas fans to start by learning to write their own hit testing logic. (After you've done that, you can consider pumping up the canvas with one of the JavaScript libraries discussed in the box on page 307.)

To perform hit testing, you need to examine each shape and calculate whether the point is inside the bounds of that shape. If it is, the click has "hit" that shape. Conceptually, this process is straightforward, but the actual details—the calculations you need to figure out whether a shape has been clicked—can get messy.

The first thing you need is a loop that moves through all the shapes. This loop looks a little different from the one that the drawCircles() function uses:

```
for (var i=circles.length-1; i>=0; i--) {
  var circle = circles[i];
  ...
}
```

Notice that the code actually moves backward through the array, from finish to start. It starts at the end (where the index is equal to the total number of items in the array, minus 1), and counts back to the beginning (where the index is 0). The backward looping is deliberate, because in most applications (including this one), the objects are drawn in the same order they're listed in the array. That means later objects are superimposed over earlier ones, and when shapes overlap, it's always the shape on top that should get the click.

To determine if a click has landed in a shape, you need to use some math. In the case of a circle, you need to calculate the straight-line distance from the clicked point to the center of the circle. If the distance is less than or equal to the radius of the circle, then the point lies inside its bounds.

In the current example, the web page handles the onClick event of the canvas to check for circle clicks. When the user clicks the canvas, it triggers a function named canvasClick(). That function figures out the click coordinates and then sees if they intersect any circle:

```
function canvasClick(e) {
  // Get the canvas click coordinates.
  var clickX = e.pageX - canvas.offsetLeft;
  var clickY = e.pageY - canvas.offsetTop;

  // Look for the clicked circle.
  for (var i=circles.length; i>0; i--) {
    // Use Pythagorean theorem to find the distance from this point
    // and the center of the circle.
    var distanceFromCenter =
    Math.sqrt(Math.pow(circle.x - clickX, 2) + Math.pow(circle.y - clickY, 2))

    // Does this point lie in the circle?
    if (distanceFromCenter <= circle.radius) {
      // Clear the previous selection.
      if (previousSelectedCircle != null) {
        previousSelectedCircle.isSelected = false;
      }
      previousSelectedCircle = circle;

      // Select the new circle.
      circle.isSelected = true;

      // Update the display.
      drawCircles();

      // Stop searching.
      return;
    }
  }
}
```

NOTE You'll look at another way to do hit testing—by grabbing raw pixels and checking their color—when you create a maze game, on page 313.

To finish this example, the drawing code in the `drawCircles()` function needs a slight tweak. Now it needs to single out the selected circle for special treatment (in this case, a thick, bold border):

```
function drawCircles() {
  ...

  // Go through all the circles.
  for(var i=0; i<circles.length; i++) {
    var circle = circles[i];

    if (circle.isSelected) {
      context.lineWidth = 5;
    }
    else {
      context.lineWidth = 1;
    }
    ...
  }
}
```

There's no end of ways that you can build on this example and make it smarter. For example, you can add a toolbar of commands that modify the selected circle—for example, changing its color or deleting it from the canvas. Or, you can let the user drag the selected circle around the canvas. To do that, you simply need to listen for the onMouseMove event of the canvas, change the circle coordinates accordingly, and call the `drawCircles()` function to repaint the canvas. (This technique is essentially a variation of the mouse-handling logic in the paint program on page 263, except now you're using mouse movements to drag a shape, not draw a line.) The try-out site (*http://prosetech.com/html5*) includes a variation of this example named *InteractiveCircles_WithDrag.html* that demonstrates this technique.

The lesson is clear: If you keep track of what you draw, you have unlimited flexibility to change it and redraw it later on.

■ Animating the Canvas

Drawing one perfect picture can seem daunting enough. So it's no surprise that even seasoned web developers approach the idea of drawing several dozen each second with some trepidation. The whole challenge of animation is to draw and redraw canvas content fast enough that it looks like it's moving or changing right in front of your visitors.

Animation is an obvious and essential building block for certain types of applications, like real-time games and physics simulators. But simpler forms of animation make sense in a much broader range of canvas-powered pages. You can use animation to highlight user interactivity (for example, making a shape glow, pulse, or twinkle when someone hovers over it). You can also use animation to draw attention to changes in content (for example, fading in a new scene or creating graphs and charts that "grow" into the right positions). Used in these ways, animation is a powerful way to give your web applications some polish, make them feel more responsive, and even help them stand out from the crowd of web competitors.

A Basic Animation

It's easy enough to animate a drawing on an HTML5 canvas. First, you set a timer that calls your drawing over and over again—typically 30 or 40 times each second. Each time, your code repaints the entire canvas from scratch. If you've done your job right, the constantly shifting frames will blend into a smooth, lifelike animation.

JavaScript gives you two ways to manage this repetitive redrawing:

- **Use the setTimeout() function.** This tells the browser to wait a few milliseconds and then run a piece of code—in this case, that's your canvas-drawing logic. Once your code finishes, you call setTimeout() to ask the browser to call it again, and so on, until you want your animation to end.

- **Use the setInterval() function.** Tells your browser to run a piece of code at regular intervals (say, every 20 milliseconds). It has much the same effect as setTimeout(), but you need to call setInterval() only once. To stop the browser from calling your code, you call clearInterval().

If your drawing code is quick, both of these have the same effect. If your drawing code is less than snappy, then the setInterval() approach will do a better job of keeping your redraws precisely on time, but possibly at the expense of performance. (In the worst-case situation, when your drawing code takes a bit longer than the interval you've set, your browser will struggle to keep up, your drawing code will run continuously, and your page may briefly freeze up.) For this reason, the examples in this chapter use the setTimeout() approach.

When you call setTimeout(), you supply two pieces of information: the name of the function you want to run, and the amount of time to wait before running it. You give the amount of time as a number of milliseconds (thousandths of a second), so 20 milliseconds (a typical delay for animation) is 0.02 seconds. Here's an example:

```
var canvas;
var context;

window.onload = function() {
  canvas = document.getElementById("canvas");
  context = canvas.getContext("2d");

  // Draw the canvas in 0.02 seconds.
  setTimeout(drawFrame, 20);
};
```

This call to setTimeout() is the heart of any animation task. For example, imagine you want to make a square fall from the top of the page to the bottom. To do this, you need to keep track of the square's position using two global variables:

```
// Set the square's initial position.
var squarePosition_y = 0;
var squarePosition_x = 10;
```

Now, you simply need to change the position each time the drawFrame() function runs, and then redraw the square in its new position:

```
function drawFrame() {
  // Clear the canvas.
  context.clearRect(0, 0, canvas.width, canvas.height);

  // Call beginPath() to make sure you don't redraw
  // part of what you were drawing before.
  context.beginPath();

  // Draw a 10x10 square, at the current position.
  context.rect(squarePosition_x, squarePosition_y, 10, 10);
  context.lineStyle = "black";
  context.lineWidth = 1;
  context.stroke();

  // Move the square down 1 pixel (where it will be drawn
  // in the next frame).
  squarePosition_y += 1;

  // Draw the next frame in 20 milliseconds.
  setTimeout(drawFrame, 20);
}
```

Run this example, and you'll see a square that plummets from the top of the canvas and carries on, disappearing past the bottom edge.

In a more sophisticated animation, the calculations get more complex. For example, you may want to make the square accelerate to simulate gravity, or bounce at the bottom of the page. But the basic technique—setting a timer, calling a drawing function, and redrawing the entire canvas—stays exactly the same.

Animating Multiple Objects

Now that you've learned the basics of animation and the basics of making interactive canvas drawings, it's time to take the next step and merge them together. Figure 9-10 shows a test page with an animation of falling, bouncing balls. The page uses the familiar setTimeout() method you met in the last section, but now the drawing code has to manage an essentially unlimited number of flying balls.

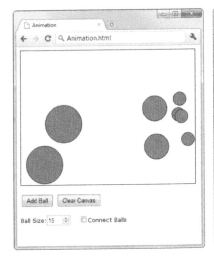 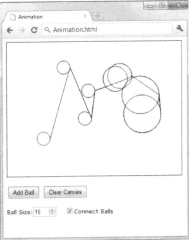

FIGURE 9-10

This test page lets you add as many balls as you want. You can choose the size of each ball (the default is a 15-pixel radius), and you can switch on connecting lines (shown on right). Once added, each ball begins its own independent journey, falling down and picking up speed until it collides with the bottom of the canvas and bounces off somewhere else.

TIP Pictures can't do justice to animations. To find out how animations like the one in Figure 9-10 look and feel, you can try out the examples for yourself at *http://prosetech.com/html5*.

Animation Performance

Because of these rapid redraws, it's clear that animation will tax the abilities of the canvas far more than ordinary drawing does. However, the canvas holds up surprisingly well. Modern browsers use performance-enhancing features like *hardware acceleration*, which farms out some of the graphical work to the computer's video card, rather than using its CPU for everything. And even though JavaScript isn't the fastest language on the block, it's quite possible to create a complex, high-speed animation—even a real-time arcade game—without using anything except script code and the canvas.

However, canvas performance *can* become a problem for people using underpowered mobile devices, like iPhones or phones running Google's Android operating system. Tests have shown that an animation that can run at 60 fps (frames per second) on a desktop browser probably tops out at a jerky 10 fps on a smartphone. So if you want to create an application for mobile visitors, make sure you test before you get too far into your design, and be prepared to sacrifice some of the animation eye candy to keep things running smoothly.

To manage all the balls in Figure 9-10, you need to reuse the custom object trick you picked up on page 295. Only now you need to track an array of ball objects, and each ball needs not only a position (represented by the properties x and y), but also a speed (represented by dx or dy):

```
// These are the details that represent an individual ball.
function Ball(x, y, dx, dy, radius) {
  this.x = x;
  this.y = y;
  this.dx = dx;
  this.dy = dy;
  this.radius = radius;
  this.color = "red";
}

// This is an array that will hold all the balls on the canvas.
var balls = [];
```

NOTE In mathematics lingo, dx is the rate that x is changing, and dy is the rate that y is changing. So as the ball is falling, each frame x increases by the dx amount and y increases by the dy amount.

When the visitor clicks the Add Ball button, a simple bit of code creates a new ball object and stores it in the balls array:

```
function addBall() {
  // Get the requested size.
  var radius = parseFloat(document.getElementById("ballSize").value);

  // Create the new ball.
  var ball = new Ball(50,50,1,1,radius);

  // Store it in the balls array.
  balls.push(ball);
}
```

The Clear Canvas button has the complementary task of emptying the balls array:

```
function clearBalls() {
  // Remove all the balls.
  balls = [];
}
```

However, neither the addBall() nor the clearBalls() function actually draws anything. Neither one even calls a drawing function. Instead, the page sets itself up to call the drawFrame() function, which paints the canvas in 20 milliseconds intervals:

```
var canvas;
var context;

window.onload = function() {
  canvas = document.getElementById("canvas");
  context = canvas.getContext("2d");
```

```
    // Redraw every 20 milliseconds.
    setTimeout(drawFrame, 20);
  };
```

The `drawFrame()` function is the heart of this example. It not only paints the balls on the canvas, but it also calculates their current position and speed. The `drawFrame()` function uses a number of calculations to simulate more realistic movement—for example, making balls accelerate as they fall and slow down when they bounce off of obstacles. Here's the complete code:

```
function drawFrame()    // Clear the canvas.
  context.clearRect(0, 0, canvas.width, canvas.height);
  context.beginPath();

  // Go through all the balls.
  for(var i=0; i<balls.length; i++) {
    // Move each ball to its new position.
    var ball = balls[i];
    ball.x += ball.dx;
    ball.y += ball.dy;

    // Add in a "gravity" effect that makes the ball fall faster.
    if ((ball.y) < canvas.height) ball.dy += 0.22;

    // Add in a "friction" effect that slows down the side-to-side motion.
    ball.dx = ball.dx * 0.998;

    // If the ball has hit the side, bounce it.
    if ((ball.x + ball.radius > canvas.width) || (ball.x - ball.radius < 0)) {
      ball.dx = -ball.dx;
    }

    // If the ball has hit the bottom, bounce it, but slow it down slightly.
    if ((ball.y + ball.radius > canvas.height) || (ball.y - ball.radius < 0))
    {
      ball.dy = -ball.dy*0.96;
    }

    // Check if the user wants lines.
    if (!document.getElementById("connectedBalls").checked) {
      context.beginPath();
      context.fillStyle = ball.fillColor;
    }
    else {
      context.fillStyle = "white";
    }
```

```
    // Draw the ball.
    context.arc(ball.x, ball.y, ball.radius, 0, Math.PI*2);
    context.lineWidth = 1;
    context.fill();
    context.stroke();
  }

  // Draw the next frame in 20 milliseconds.
  setTimeout(drawFrame, 20);
}
```

> **TIP** If you're fuzzy about how the `if` statements work in this example, and what operators like `!` and `||` really mean, check out the summary of logical operators on page 463 in Appendix B, "JavaScript: The Brains of Your Page."

The sheer amount of code can seem a bit intimidating. But the overall approach hasn't changed. The code performs the same steps:

1. Clear the canvas.

2. Loop through the array of balls.

3. Adjust the position and velocity of each ball.

4. Paint each ball.

5. Set a timeout so the `drawFrame()` method will be called again, 20 milliseconds later.

The complex bit is step 3, where the ball is tweaked. This code can be as complicated as you like, depending on the effect you're trying to achieve. Gradual, natural movement is particularly difficult to model, and it usually needs more math.

Finally, now that you've done all the work tracking each ball, it's easy to add interactivity. In fact, you can use virtually the same code you used to detect clicks in the circle-drawing program on page 298. Only now, when a ball is clicked, you want something else to happen—for example, you might choose to give the clicked ball a sudden boost in speed, sending it ricocheting off to the side. (The downloadable version of this example, available at *http://prosetech.com/html5*, does exactly that.)

To see this example carried to its most impressive extreme, check out the bouncing Google balls at *http://tinyurl.com/6byvnk5*. When left alone, the balls are pulled, magnet-like, to spell the word "Google." But when your mouse moves in, they're repulsed, flying off to the far corners of the canvas and bouncing erratically. And if you're still hungry for more animation examples, check out the poke-able blob at *http://www.blobsallad.se* and the somewhat clichéd flying star field at *http://tinyurl.com/crn3ed*.

FREQUENTLY ASKED QUESTION

Canvas Animations for Busy (or Lazy) People

Do I really need to calculate everything on my own? For real?

The most significant drawback to canvas animation is the fact that you need to do everything yourself. For example, if you want a picture to fly from one side of the canvas to the other, you need to calculate its new position in each frame, and then draw the picture in its proper location. If you have several things being animated at the same time in different ways, your logic can quickly get messy. By comparison, life is much easier for programmers who are using a browser plug-in like Flash or Silverlight. Both technologies have built-in animation systems, which allow developers to give instructions like "Move this shape from here to there, taking 45 seconds." Or, even better, "Move this shape from the top of the window to the bottom, using an accelerating effect that ends with a gentle bounce."

To fill this gap, enterprising JavaScript developers have begun creating higher-level drawing and animation systems that sit on top of the canvas. Using these JavaScript libraries, you can pick the effects you want, without having to slog through all the math. The catch? There are at least a half-dozen high quality frameworks for canvas animation, each with its own distinct model and subtle quirks. And it's impossible to pick which of the evolving toolkits of today will become the best-supported and most widely accepted leaders of tomorrow. Some of the most worthy candidates today are Fabric.js (*http://fabricjs.com*), Paper.js (*http://paperjs.org*), EaselJS (*www.createjs.com*), and KineticJS (*http://kineticjs.com*). You can read some recent developer opinions on these libraries at *http://tinyurl.com/canvas-libraries*.

■ A Practical Example: The Maze Game

So far, you've explored how to combine the canvas with some key programming techniques to make interactive drawings and to perform animations. These building blocks take the canvas beyond mere drawing and into the realm of complete, self-contained applications—like games or Flash-style mini-apps.

Figure 9-11 shows a more ambitious example that takes advantage of what you've learned so far and builds on both concepts. It's a simple game that invites the user to guide a small happy face icon through a complex maze. When the user presses an arrow key, the happy face starts moving in that direction (using animation) and stops only when it hits a wall (using hit testing).

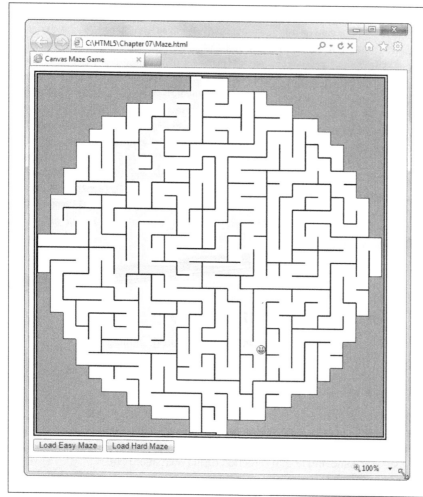

FIGURE 9-11

Guide the face through the maze. To a user, it looks like a fun game. To a developer, it's a potent mix of the HTML5 canvas and some smart JavaScript.

Of course, there's a trade-off. If you're going to rely on the canvas to build something sophisticated, you'll need to dig your way through a significant amount of code. The following sections show you the essentials, but be prepared to flex your JavaScript muscles.

NOTE You can run this example from your local computer if you're using Internet Explorer 9. But on other browsers, it works only if you first put your page (and the graphics it uses) on a test web server. To save the trouble, run this example from the try-out site at *http://prosetech.com/html5*.

Setting Up the Maze

Before anything can happen, the page needs to set up the canvas. Although you could paint the entire maze out of lines and rectangles, you'd need a lot of drawing code. Writing that drawing code by hand would be extremely tedious. You'd need to have a mental model of the entire maze, and then draw each short wall segment using a separate drawing operation. If you went this route, you'd almost certainly use a tool that automatically creates your drawing code. For example, you might draw the maze in Adobe Illustrator and then use a plug-in to convert it to canvas code (page 258).

Another option is to take a preexisting graphic of a maze and paint that on the canvas. This is particularly easy, because the web is filled with free pages that will create mazes for you. Using one of these pages, you set a few details—for example, the size, shape, colors, density, and complexity of the maze—and the page creates a downloadable graphic. (To try it out for yourself, just Google *maze generator*.)

This example uses maze pictures. When the page first loads, it takes a picture file (named *maze.png*) and draws that on the canvas. Here's the code that kicks that process off when the page first loads:

```
// Define the global variables for the canvas and drawing context.
var canvas;
var context;

window.onload = function() {
  // Set up the canvas.
  canvas = document.getElementById("canvas");
  context = canvas.getContext("2d");

  // Draw the maze background.
  drawMaze("maze.png", 268, 5);

  // When the user presses a key, run the processKey() function.
  window.onkeydown = processKey;
};
```

This code doesn't actually draw the maze background. Instead, it hands the work off to another function, named drawMaze().

Because this example uses a separate maze-drawing function, it's not limited to a single maze. Instead, it lets you load any maze graphic you want. You simply need to call drawMaze() and pass in the file name of the maze picture, along with the coordinates for where the happy face should start. Here's the drawMaze() code that does the job:

```
// Keep track of the current face position.
var x = 0;
var y = 0;
```

```
function drawMaze(mazeFile, startingX, startingY) {
  // Load the maze picture.
  imgMaze = new Image();
  imgMaze.onload = function() {
    // Resize the canvas to match the size of the maze picture.
    canvas.width = imgMaze.width;
    canvas.height = imgMaze.height;

    // Draw the maze.
    var imgFace = document.getElementById("face");
    context.drawImage(imgMaze, 0,0);

    // Draw the face.
    x = startingX;
    y = startingY;

    context.drawImage(imgFace, x, y);
    context.stroke();

    // Draw the next frame in 10 milliseconds.
    setTimeout(drawFrame, 10);
  };
  imgMaze.src = mazeFile;
}
```

This code uses the two-step image drawing method explained on page 276. First, it sets a function that will handle the image's onLoad event and draw the maze image after it loads. Second, it sets the src attribute on the image object, which loads the image and triggers the code. This two-step process is a bit more complicated than just pulling the picture out of a hidden <img> element on the page, but it's necessary if you want to create a function that's flexible enough to load any maze picture you want.

When the maze image is loaded, the code adjusts the size of the canvas to match, places the face at its proper position, and then paints the face image. Finally, it calls setTimeout() to start drawing frames.

> **NOTE** The downloadable version of this example (at *http://prosetech.com/html5*) is slightly more sophisticated. It lets the user load a new maze at any time—even while the happy face is still moving around the current maze. To make this work, it adds a bit of extra code in the drawMaze() function to stop the happy face (if it's currently moving) and halt the animating process, before loading the background and starting it again.

Animating the Face

When the user hits a key, the face begins moving. For example, if the user presses the down key, the happy face continues moving down until it hits a barrier or another key is pressed.

To make this work, the code uses two global variables that track the happy face's speed—in other words, how many pixels it will move in the *x* or *y* dimension, per frame. The variables that do this are named dx and dy, just as they were in the bouncing ball example (page 304). The difference is that you don't need an array for this page, because there's only one happy face:

```
var dx = 0;
var dy = 0;
```

When the user presses a key, the canvas calls the processKey() function. The function then checks if one of the arrow keys was pressed and adjusts the speed accordingly. To identify an arrow key, the code checks its key code against a known value. For example, a key code of 38 always represents the up arrow key. The processKey() function ignores all other keys except the arrow keys:

```
function processKey(e) {
  // If the face is moving, stop it.
  dx = 0;
  dy = 0;

  // The up arrow was pressed, so move up.
  if (e.keyCode == 38) {
    dy = -1;
  }

  // The down arrow was pressed, so move down.
  if (e.keyCode == 40) {
    dy = 1;
  }

  // The left arrow was pressed, so move left.
  if (e.keyCode == 37) {
    dx = -1;
  }

  // The right arrow was pressed, so move right.
  if (e.keyCode == 39) {
    dx = 1;
  }
}
```

The processKey() function doesn't change the current position of the happy face, or attempt to draw it. Instead, this task happens every 10 milliseconds, when the drawFrame() function is called.

The drawFrame() code is fairly straightforward, but detailed. It performs several tasks. First, it checks if the face is moving in either direction. If not, there's really no work to be done:

```
function drawFrame() {
   if (dx != 0 || dy != 0) {
```

If the face is moving, the drawFrame() code draws a yellow patch in the current face position (which creates the "trail" effect. It then moves the face to its new position:

```
context.beginPath();
context.fillStyle = "rgb(254,244,207)";
context.rect(x, y, 15, 15);
context.fill()

// Increment the face's position.
x += dx;
y += dy;
```

Next, the code calls checkForCollision() to see if this new position is valid. (You'll see the code for this hit testing function in the next section.) If the new position isn't valid, the face has hit a wall, and the code must move the face back to its old position and stop it from moving:

```
if (checkForCollision()) {
   x -= dx;
   y -= dy;
   dx = 0;
   dy = 0;
}
```

Now the code is ready to draw the face, where it belongs:

```
var imgFace = document.getElementById("face");
context.drawImage(imgFace, x, y);
```

And check if the face has reached the bottom of the maze (and has thus completed it). If so, the code shows a message box:

```
if (y > (canvas.height - 17)) {
   alert("You win!");
   return;
}
}
```

If not, the code sets a timeout so the drawFrame() method will be called again, 10 milliseconds later:

```
    // Draw a new frame in 10 milliseconds.
    setTimeout(drawFrame, 10);
  }
```

You've now seen all the code for the maze game, except the innovative bit of logic in the checkForCollision() function, which handles the hit testing. That's the topic you'll tackle next.

Hit Testing with Pixel Colors

Earlier in this chapter, you saw how you can use mathematical calculations to do your hit testing. However, there's another approach you can use. Instead of looking through a collection of objects you've drawn, you can grab a block of pixels and look at their colors. This approach is simpler in some ways, because it doesn't need all the objects and the shape tracking code. But it works only if you can make clear-cut assumptions about the colors you're looking for.

NOTE The pixel-based hit-testing approach is the perfect approach for the maze example. Using this sort of hit testing, you can determine when the happy face runs into one of the black walls. Without this technique, you'd need a way to store all the maze information in memory and then determine if the current happy-face coordinates overlap one of the maze's wall lines.

The secret to the color-testing approach is the canvas's support for manipulating individual pixels—the tiny dots that comprise every picture. The drawing context provides three methods for managing pixels: getImageData(), putImageData(), and createImageData(). You use getImageData() to grab a block of pixels from a rectangular region and examine them (as in the maze game). You can also modify the pixels and use putImageData() to write them back to the canvas. And finally, createImageData() lets you create a new, empty block of pixels that exists only in memory, the idea being that you can customize them and then write them to the canvas with putImageData().

To understand a bit more about the pixel-manipulation methods, consider the following code. First, it grabs a 100 x 50 square of pixels from the current canvas, using getImageData():

```
// Get pixels starting at point (0,0), and stretching out 100 pixels to
// the right and 50 pixels down.
var imageData = context.getImageData(0, 0, 100, 50);
```

Then, the code retrieves the array of numbers that has the image data, using the data property:

```
var pixels = imageData.data;
```

You might expect that there's one number for each pixel, but life isn't that simple. There are actually *four* numbers for each pixel, one each to represent its red, green, blue, and alpha components. So if you want to examine each pixel, you need a loop that bounds through the array four steps at a time, like this:

```
// Loop over each pixel and invert the color.
for (var i = 0, n = pixels.length; i < n; i += 4) {

  // Get the data for one pixel.
  var red = pixels[i];
  var green = pixels[i+1];
  var blue = pixels[i+2];
  var alpha = pixels[i+3];

  // Invert the colors.
  pixels[i] = 255 - red;
  pixels[i+1] = 255 - green;
  pixels[i+2] = 255 - blue;
}
```

Each number ranges from 0 to 255. The code above uses one of the simplest image manipulation methods around—it inverts the colors. Try this with an ordinary picture, and you get a result that looks like a photo negative.

To see the results, you can write the pixels back to the canvas, in their original positions (although you could just as easily paint the content somewhere else):

```
context.putImageData(imageData, 0, 0);
```

The pixel-manipulation methods certainly give you a lot of control. However, they also have drawbacks. The pixel operations are slow, and the pixel data in the average canvas is immense. If you grab off a large chunk of picture data, you'll have tens of thousands of pixels to look at. And if you were already getting tired of drawing complex pictures using basic ingredients like lines and curves, you'll find that dealing with individual pixels is even more tedious.

That said, the pixel-manipulation methods can solve certain problems that would be difficult to deal with in any other way. For example, they provide the easiest way to create fractal patterns and Photoshop-style picture filters. In the maze game, they let you create a concise routine that checks the next move of the happy face icon and determines whether it collides with a wall. Here's the checkForCollision() function that handles the job:

```
function checkForCollision() {
  // Grab the block of pixels where the happy face is, but extend
  // the edges just a bit.
  var imgData = context.getImageData(x-1, y-1, 15+2, 15+2);
  var pixels = imgData.data;

  // Check these pixels.
  for (var i = 0; n = pixels.length, i < n; i += 4) {
    var red = pixels[i];
    var green = pixels[i+1];
    var blue = pixels[i+2];
```

```
    var alpha = pixels[i+3];

    // Look for black walls (which indicates a collision).
    if (red == 0 && green == 0 && blue == 0) {
      return true;
    }

    // Look for gray edge space (which indicates a collision).
    if (red == 169 && green == 169 && blue == 169) {
      return true;
    }
  }
  // There was no collision.
  return false;
}
```

This completes the canvas maze game, which is the longest and most code-packed example you'll encounter in this book. It may take a bit more review (or a JavaScript brush-up) before you really feel comfortable with all the code it contains, but once you do you'll be able to use similar techniques in your own canvas creations.

If you're hungering for more canvas tutorials, you may want to check out a complete book on the subject, such as *HTML5 Canvas* (by Steve Fulton and Jeff Fulton) or *Core HTML5 Canvas* (by David Geary). Either book will take you deeper into the raw and gritty details of do-it-yourself canvas drawing.

POWER USERS' CLINIC

Eye-Popping Canvas Examples

There's virtually no limit to what you can do with the canvas. If you want to look at some even more ambitious examples that take HTML5 into the world of black-belt coding, the Web is your friend. Here's a list of websites that demonstrate some mind-blowing canvas mojo:

- **Canvas Demos.** This canvas example site has enough content to keep you mesmerized for days. Entries include the game Mutant Zombie Masters and the stock-charting tool TickerPlot. Visit *www.canvasdemos.com* to browse them all.

- **Wikipedia knowledge map.** This impressive canvas application shows a graphical representation of Wikipedia articles, with linked topics connected together by slender, web-like lines. Choose a new topic, and you zoom into

that part of the knowledge map, pulling new articles to the forefront with a slick animation. See it at *http://en.inforapid.org*.

- **3D Walker.** This example lets you walk through a simple 3D world of walls and passages (similar to the ancient Wolfenstein 3D game that kicked off the first-person-shooter gaming craze way back in 1992). Take it for a spin at *www.benjoffe.com/code/demos/canvascape*.

- **Chess.** This HTML5 chess simulator lets you try your hand against a computer opponent with a canvas-drawn board that's rendered from above or with a three-dimensional perspective, depending on your preference. Challenge yourself to a game at *http://htmlchess.sourceforge.net/demo/example.html*.

Building Web Apps

CHAPTER 10:
Storing Your Data

CHAPTER 11:
Running Offline

CHAPTER 12:
Communicating with the Web Server

CHAPTER 13:
Geolocation, Web Workers, and History Management

Storing Your Data

On the Web, there are two places to store information: on the web server, or on the web client (the viewer's computer). Certain types of data belong on one, while others work better on the other.

The web server is the place to store sensitive information and data you don't want people tampering with. For example, if you fill your shopping cart at an online bookstore, your potential purchases are stored on the web server, as are the catalog of books, the history of past sales, and just about everything else. The only data your computer keeps is a tiny bit of tracking information that tells the website who you are, so it knows which shopping cart is yours. Even with HTML5, there's no reason to change this setup—it's safe, secure, and efficient.

But server-side storage isn't the best bet for every website. Sometimes, it's easier to keep nonessential information on the web surfer's computer. For example, local storage makes sense for *user preferences* (for example, settings that influence how the web page tailors its display) and *application state* (a snapshot of where the web application is right now, so the web visitor can pick up at the same spot later on). And if the data takes time to calculate or retrieve from the web server, you may be able to improve performance by storing it on the visitor's computer.

Before HTML5, the only way to get local storage was to use *cookies*, a mechanism originally devised to transmit small bits of identifying information between web browsers and web servers. Cookies work perfectly well for storing small amounts of data, but the JavaScript model for using them is a bit clunky. Cookies also force you to fiddle with expiry dates and needlessly send your data back and forth over the Internet with every web request.

HTML5 introduces a better alternative that lets you store information on your visitor's computer simply and easily. This data stays on the client indefinitely, isn't sent to the web server (unless you do it yourself), has plenty of room, and works through a couple of simple, streamlined JavaScript objects. This feature—called *web storage*—is a particularly nice fit with the offline application feature explored in Chapter 11, because it lets you build self-sufficient offline applications that can store all the information they need, even when there's no web connection.

In this chapter, you'll explore every corner of the web storage feature. You'll also look at two additional, newer standards: the File API, which lets the web browser read the content from other files on the computer's hard drive; and IndexedDB, which lets web developers run a complete, miniature database engine right inside the browser.

■ Web Storage Basics

HTML5's web storage feature lets a web page store some information on the viewer's computer. That information could be short-lived (so it disappears once the browser is shut down), or it could be long-lived (so it's still available days later, on subsequent visits to the website).

> **NOTE** The name *web storage* is more than a little misleading. That's because the information a page stores is never on the Web—in fact, it never leaves the web surfer's computer.

There are two types of web storage, and they revolve around two objects:

- **Local storage** uses the `localStorage` object to store data permanently and make it accessible to any page in your website. If a web page stores local data, it will still be there when the visitor returns the next day, the next week, or the next year. Of course, most browsers also include a way to let users clear out local storage. Some web browsers provide an all-or-nothing command that lets people wipe out local data, in much the same way that you can clear out your cookies. (In fact, in some browsers the two features are linked, so that the only way to clear local data is to clear the cookies.) Other browsers may let their users review the storage usage of each website and clear the local data for specific sites.

- **Session storage** uses the `sessionStorage` object to store data temporarily, for a single window (or tab). The data remains until the visitor closes that tab, at which point the session ends and the data disappears. However, the session data stays around if the user goes to another website and then returns to your site, provided that this all happens in the same window tab.

TIP From the point of view of your web page code, both local storage and session storage work exactly the same. The difference is just how long the data lasts. Using local storage is the best bet for information you want to keep for future visits. Use session storage for data that you want to pass from one page to another. (You can also use session storage to keep temporary data that's used in just one page, but ordinary JavaScript variables work perfectly well for that purpose.)

Both local storage and session storage are linked to your website domain. So if you use local storage on a page at *www.GoatsCanFloat.org/game/zapper.html*, that data will be available on the page *www.GoatsCanFloat.org/contact.html*, because the domain is the same (*www.GoatsCanFloat.org*). However, other websites won't be able to see it or manipulate it.

Also, because web storage is stored on your computer (or mobile device), it's linked to that computer; a web page can't access information that was stored locally on someone else's computer. Similarly, you get different local storage if you log onto your computer with a different user name or fire up a different browser.

NOTE Although the HTML5 specification doesn't lay down any hard rules about maximum storage space, most browsers limit local storage to 5 MB. That's enough to pack in a lot of data, but it falls short if you want to use local storage to optimize performance by caching large pictures or videos (and truthfully, this isn't what local storage is designed to do). For space-hoggers, the still-evolving IndexedDB database storage standard (see page 340) offers much more room—typically hundreds of megabytes, if the user agrees.

Storing Data

To put a piece of information away into local storage or session storage, you first need to think of a descriptive name for it. This name is called a *key*, and you need it to retrieve your data later on.

To store a piece of data, you use the localStorage.setItem() method, as follows:

```
localStorage.setItem(keyName, data);
```

For example, imagine you want to store a piece of text with the current user's name. For this data, you might use the key name user_name, as shown here:

```
localStorage.setItem("user_name", "Marky Mark");
```

Of course, it doesn't really make sense to store a hard-coded piece of text. Instead, you'd store something that changes—for example, the current date, the result of a mathematical calculation, or some text that the user has typed into a text box. Here's an example of that last one:

```
// Get a text box.
var nameInput = document.getElementById("userName");

// Store the text from that text box.
localStorage.setItem("user_name", nameInput.value);
```

Pulling something out of local storage is as easy as putting it in, provided you use the localStorage.getItem() method. For example, here's a line of code that grabs the previously stored name and shows it in a message box:

```
alert("You stored: " + localStorage.getItem("user_name"));
```

This code works whether the name was stored five seconds ago or five months ago.

Of course, it's possible that nothing was stored at all. If you want to check whether a storage slot is empty, you can test for a null reference. Here's an example of that technique:

```
if (localStorage.getItem("user_name") == null) {
  alert ("You haven't entered a name yet.");
}
else {
  // Put the name into a text box.
  document.getElementById("userName").value = localStorage.getItem("user_
name");
}
```

Session storage is just as simple. The only difference is that you use the session-Storage object instead of the localStorage object:

```
// Get the current date.
var today = new Date();

// Store the time as a piece of text in the form HH:mm.
var time = today.getHours() + ":" + today.getMinutes();
sessionStorage.setItem("lastUpdateTime", time);
```

Figure 10-1 shows a simple test page that puts all of these concepts together.

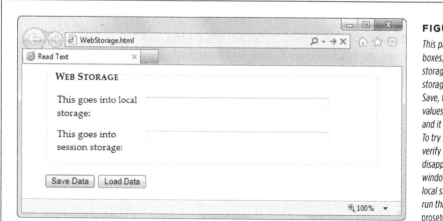

FIGURE 10-1

This page has two text boxes, one for session storage and one for local storage. When you click Save, the page stores the values. Click Load Data, and it brings them back. To try this out (and to verify that session storage disappears when the window is closed but that local storage lives forever), run this page at http://prosetech.com/html5.

NOTE Web storage also supports two alternate syntaxes for accessing data. Instead of using the getItem( ) and setItem( ) methods that you've already seen, you can use property names or an indexer. With property names, you access a storage slot called "user_name" as localStorage.user_name. With an indexer, you access the same storage slot as localStorage["user_name"]. You can choose a syntax based on your preference, but most web experts believe the getItem( ) and setItem( ) methods are best because they offer the least ambiguity.

TROUBLESHOOTING MOMENT

Web Storage Fails Without a Web Server

There's an unexpected problem that can trip up your web storage testing. In many browsers, web storage works only when you're requesting the pages from a live web server. It doesn't matter whether that web server is located on the Internet or if it's just a test server running on your own computer—the important detail is that you aren't just launching the pages from your local hard drive.

This quirk is a side effect of the way browsers dole out their local storage space. As you've already learned, they limit each website to 5 MB, and in order to do that, they need to associate every page that wants to use local storage to a website domain.

So what happens if you break this rule and open a web page that uses web storage, straight from a file? It depends. In Internet Explorer, the browser appears to lose its web storage support completely. The localStorage and sessionStorage objects disappear, and trying to use them causes a JavaScript error. In Firefox, the localStorage and sessionStorage objects remain, and support *appears* to be there (even to Modernizr), but everything you try to store quietly disappears into a void. And in Chrome, the result is different again—most of web storage works fine, but some features (like the onStorage event) don't work. You'll see the same issues when you use the File API (page 332). So do yourself a favor and put your pages on a test server, so you're not tripped up by unexpected quirks. Or, run the examples in this chapter from the try-out site at *http://prosetech.com/html5*.

A Practical Example: Storing the Last Position in a Game

At this point, you might have the impression that there isn't much to web storage, other than remembering to pick a name and put it in square brackets. And you'd be mostly right. But you can put local storage to some more practical purposes without any extra effort.

For example, consider the canvas-based maze game you saw in Chapter 9 (page 307). A maze might be too much trouble to solve in one go, in which case it makes sense to store the current position when the user closes the window or navigates to a new page. When the user returns to the maze page, your code can then restore the happy face to its previous position in the maze.

There are several possible ways to implement this example. You could simply save a new position after each move. Local storage is fast, so this wouldn't cause any problem. Or, you could react to the page's onBeforeUnload event to ask the game player whether it's worth storing the current position (Figure 10-2).

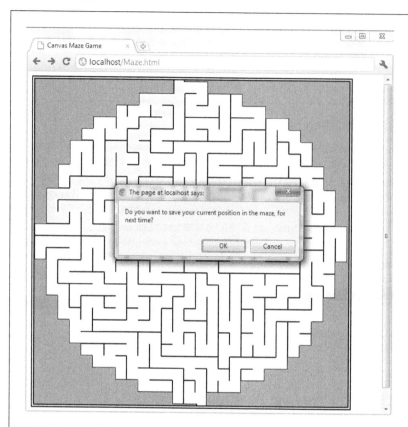

Here's the code that offers to store the position details:

```
window.onbeforeunload = function(e) {
  // Check if the localStorage object exists (as there's no reason to offer
  // to save the position if it won't work).
  if (localStorage) {

    // Ask to save the position.
    if (confirm(
"Do you want to save your current position in the maze, for next time?")) {
      // Store the two coordinates in two storage slots.
      localStorage.setItem("mazeGame_currentX", x);
      localStorage.setItem("mazeGame_currentY", y);
    }
  }
}
```

TIP Long key names, like mazeGame_currentX, are good. After all, it's up to you to ensure that key names are unique, so two web pages on your website don't inadvertently use the same name to store different pieces of data. With just a single container that holds all your data, it's all too easy to run into naming conflicts, which is the one glaring weakness in the web storage system. To prevent problems, come up with a plan for creating logical, descriptive key names. For example, if you have separate maze games on separate pages, consider incorporating the page name into the key name, as in Maze01_currentX.

This example shows how to store an *application state* (the current position). If you wanted to avoid showing the same message each time the user leaves the game, you could add an "Automatically save position" checkbox. You would then store the position if the checkbox is switched on. Of course, you'd want to save the value of the checkbox too, and that would be an example of storing *application preferences*.

When the page loads the next time, you can check to see whether there's a previously stored position:

```
// Is the local storage feature supported?
if (localStorage) {
  // Try to get the data.
  var savedX = localStorage.getItem("mazeGame_currentX");
  var savedY = localStorage.getItem("mazeGame_currentY");

  // If the variables are null, no data was saved.
  // Otherwise, use the data to set new coordinates.
  if (savedX != null) x = Number(savedX);
  if (savedY != null) y = Number(savedY);
}
```

This example also uses the JavaScript Number() function to make sure the saved data is converted to valid numbers. You'll learn why that's important on page 327.

Browser Support for Web Storage

Web storage is one of the best-supported HTML5 features in modern browsers. The only browser that you're likely to find that doesn't support web storage is the thankfully endangered IE 7.

If you need a workaround for IE 7, you can simulate web storage using cookies. The fit isn't perfect, but it works. And although there's no official piece of script that plugs that gap, you can find many decent starting points on the GitHub polyfill page at *http://tinyurl.com/polyfill* (just look under the "Web Storage" section heading).

One web storage feature that enjoys slightly less support is the onStorage event, which you'll consider on page 330. In particular, IE 8 supports web storage but not the onStorage event. (IE 9 and later versions correct the problem, with full web storage support.) This situation is fine if you're using onStorage to add a nonessential feature, but otherwise be warned.

Deeper into Web Storage

You now know the essentials of web storage—how to put information in, and how to get it out again. However, there are several finer points and a few useful techniques left to cover before you put it to use. In the following sections, you'll see how to remove items from web storage and how to examine all the currently stored items. You'll also learn to deal with different data types, to store custom objects, and to react when the collection of stored items changes.

Removing Items

It couldn't be easier. You use the removeItem() method, and the key name, to get rid of a single piece of data you don't want:

```
localStorage.removeItem("user_name");
```

Or, if you want to empty out all the local data your website has stored, use the more radical clear() method:

```
sessionStorage.clear();
```

Finding All the Stored Items

To get a single piece of data out of web storage, you need to know its key name. But here's another neat trick. Using the key() method, you can pull every single item out of local or session storage (for the current website), even if you don't know any key names. This is a nifty technique when you're debugging, or if you just want to review what other pages in your site are storing, and what key names they're using.

Figure 10-3 shows a page that puts this technique into practice.

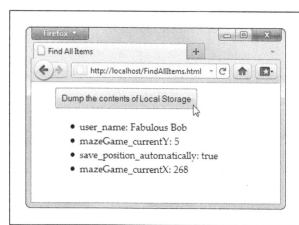

FIGURE 10-3

Click the button, and this page fills a list with the local storage contents.

When you click the button in this example, it triggers the findAllItems() function, which scans through the collection of items in local storage. Here's the code:

```
function findAllItems() {
  // Get the <ul> element for the list of items.
  var itemList = document.getElementById("itemList");

  // Clear the list.
  itemList.innerHTML = "";

  // Do a loop over all the items.
  for (var i=0; i<localStorage.length; i++) {
    // Get the key for the item at the current position.
    var key = localStorage.key(i);

    // Get the item that's stored with this key.
    var item = localStorage.getItem(key);

    // Create a new list item with this information,
    // and add it to the page.
    var newItem = document.createElement("li");
    newItem.innerHTML = key + ": " + item;
    itemList.appendChild(newItem);
  }
}
```

Storing Numbers and Dates

So far, the exploration into web storage has glossed over one important detail. Whenever you store something in the localStorage or sessionStorage object, that data is automatically converted to a string of text. For values that are already text (like the user name typed into a text box), there's no problem. But numbers aren't as forgiving. Consider the example on page 324, which stores the most recent maze position in local storage. If you forget to convert the coordinates from text to numbers, you can run into this sort of problem:

```
// Get the last x-coordinate position.
// For example, this might return the text "35"
x = localStorage.getItem("mazeGame_currentX");

// Attempt to increment the position (incorrectly).
x += 5;
```

Unfortunately, this code doesn't have the result you want. Because x is a string, JavaScript converts the number 5 to a string as well. And instead of adding 35+5, JavaScript actually performs the string combination "35"+"5", which returns a result of 355. This clearly isn't what you want. In fact, this code will cause the happy face to jump to completely the wrong position, or right out of the maze.

The issue here is that JavaScript assumes you're trying to stick two pieces of text together, rather than perform a mathematical operation. To solve the problem, you need to give JavaScript a hint that you're trying to work with numbers. Several solutions are possible, but the Number() function works well:

```
x = Number(localStorage.getItem("mazeGame_currentX"));

// Now JavaScript calculates 35+10 properly, and returns 40.
x += 10;
```

Text and numbers are easy to deal with, but if you want to place other sorts of data into web storage, you'll need to handle them with care. Some data types have handy conversion routines. For example, imagine you store a date like this:

```
var today = new Date();
```

This code doesn't store a date object, but a text string, like "Sat Jun 07 2014 13:30:46". Unfortunately, there's no easy way to convert this text back into a date object when you pull it out of storage. And if you don't have a date object, you won't be able to manipulate the date in the same way—say, calling date methods and performing date calculations.

To solve this problem, it's up to you to explicitly convert the date into the text you want, and then convert it back into a proper date object when you retrieve it. Here's an example:

```
// Create a date object.
var today = new Date();

// Turn the date into a text string in the standard form YYYY/MM/DD,
// and store that text.
var todayString = today.getFullYear() + "/" +
 today.getMonth() + "/" + today.getDate();
sessionStorage.setItem("session_started", todayString);

...

// Now retrieve the date text and use it to create a new date object.
// This works because the date text is in a recognizable format.
today = new Date(sessionStorage.getItem("session_started"));

// Use the methods of the date object, like getFullYear().
alert(today.getFullYear());
```

Run this code, and the year appears in a message box, confirming that you've successfully recreated the date object.

Storing Objects

In the previous section, you saw how to convert numbers and dates to text and back again, so you can store them with web storage. These examples work because the JavaScript language helps you out, first with the handy Number() function, and then with the text-to-date conversion smarts that are hard-wired into date objects. However, there are plenty of other objects that you can't convert this way, especially if you create a custom object of your own.

For example, consider the personality quiz you first saw in Chapter 9 (page 290). The personality quiz uses two pages. On the first, the quiz-taker answers some questions and gets a score. On the second, the results are shown. In the original version of this page, the information is passed from the first page to the second using query string arguments that are embedded in the URL. This approach is traditional HTML (although a cookie would work too). But in HTML5, local storage is the best way to shuffle data around.

But here's the challenge. The quiz data consists of five numbers, one for each per-sonality factor. You *could* store each personality factor in a separate storage slot. But wouldn't it be neater and cleaner to create a custom object that packages up all the personality information in one place? Here's an example of a PersonalityScore object that does the trick:

```
function PersonalityScore(o, c, e, a, n) {
  this.openness = o;
  this.conscientiousness = c;
  this.extraversion = e;
  this.accommodation = a;
  this.neuroticism = n;
}
```

If you create a PersonalityScore object, you need just one storage slot, instead of five. (For a refresher about how custom objects work in JavaScript, see page 468.)

To store a custom object in web storage, you need a way to convert the object to a text representation. You could write some tedious code that does the work. But fortunately, there's a simpler, standardized approach called *JSON encoding*.

JSON (JavaScript Object Notation) is a lightweight format that translates structured data—like all the values that are wrapped in an object—into text. The best thing about JSON is that browsers support it natively. That means you can call JSON. stringify() to turn any JavaScript object into text, complete with all its data, and JSON.parse() to convert that text back into an object. Here's an example that puts this to the test with the PersonalityScore object. When the test is submitted, the page calculates the score (not shown), creates the object, stores it, and then redi-rects to the new page:

```
// Create the PersonalityScore object.
var score = new PersonalityScore(o, c, e, a, n);
```

```
// Store it, in handy JSON format.
sessionStorage.setItem("personalityScore", JSON.stringify(score));

// Go to the results page.
window.location = "PersonalityTest_Score.html";
```

On the new page, you can pull the JSON text out of storage and use the JSON.parse() method to convert it back to the object you want. Here's that step:

```
// Convert the JSON text to a proper object.
var score = JSON.parse(sessionStorage.getItem("personalityScore"));

// Get some data out of the object.
lblScoreInfo.innerHTML = "Your extraversion score is " + score.extraversion;
```

To see the complete code for this example, including the calculations for each personality factor, visit *http://prosetech.com/html5*. To learn more about JSON and take a peek at what JSON-encoded data actually looks like, check out *http://en.wikipedia.org/wiki/JSON*.

Reacting to Storage Changes

Web storage also gives you a way to communicate among different browser windows. That's because whenever a change happens to local storage or session storage, the window.onStorage event is triggered in every other window that's viewing the same page or another page on the same website. So if you change local storage on *www.GoatsCanFloat.org/storeStuff.html*, the onStorage event will fire in a browser window for the page *www.GoatsCanFloat.org/checkStorage.html*. (Of course, the page has to be viewed in the same browser and on the same computer, but you already knew that.)

The onStorage event is triggered whenever you add a new object to storage, change an object, remove an object, or clear the entire collection. It doesn't happen if your code makes a storage operation that has no effect (like storing the same value that's already stored, or clearing an already-empty storage collection).

Consider the test page shown in Figure 10-4. Here, the visitor can add any value to local storage, with any key, just by filling out two text boxes. When a change is made, the second page reports the new value.

To create the example shown in Figure 10-4, you first need to create the page that stores the data. In this case, clicking the Add button triggers a short addValue() function that looks like this:

```
function addValue() {
  // Get the values from both text boxes.
  var key = document.getElementById("key").value;
  var item = document.getElementById("item").value;
```

```
    // Put the item in local storage.
    // (If the key already exists, the new item replaces the old.)
    localStorage.setItem(key, item);
  }
```

The second page is just as simple. When the page first loads, it attaches a function to the window.onStorage event, using this code:

```
window.onload = function() {
  // Connect the onStorage event to the storageChanged() function.
  window.addEventListener("storage", storageChanged, false);
};
```

This code looks a little different than the event handling code you've seen so far. Instead of setting window.onstorage, it calls window.addEventListener(). That's because this code is the simplest that works on all current browsers. If you set window.onstorage directly, your code will work in every browser except Firefox.

> **NOTE** Web graybeards may remember that the addEventListener() method doesn't work on Internet Explorer 8 (or older). In this example, that limitation is no cause for concern, because IE 8 doesn't support storage events anyway.

The storageChanged() function has a simple task. It grabs the updated information and displays it on the page, in a <div> element:

```
function storageChanged(e) {
  var message = document.getElementById("updateMessage");
  message.innerHTML = "Local storage updated.";
  message.innerHTML += "<br>Key: " + e.key;
  message.innerHTML += "<br>Old Value: " + e.oldValue;
  message.innerHTML += "<br>New Value: " + e.newValue;
  message.innerHTML += "<br>URL: " + e.url;
}
```

As you can see, the onStorage event provides several pieces of information, including the key of the value that was changed, the old value, the newly applied value, and the URL of the page that made the change. If the onStorage event is a reaction to the insertion of a new item, the e.oldValue property is either null (in most browsers) or an empty string (in Internet Explorer).

> **NOTE** If you have several pages open for the same website, the onStorage event occurs in each one, except the page that made the change (in the current example, that's *StorageEvents1.html*). However, Internet Explorer is the exception—it doesn't follow this rule, and fires the onStorage event in the original page as well.

FIGURE 10-4

To see the onStorage *event in action, open* Storage Events1.html *and* StorageEvents2.html *at the same time. When you add or change a value in the first page (top), the second page captures the event and reports it in the page (bottom).*

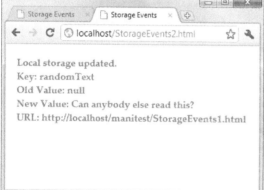

Reading Files

Web storage is a solidly supported part of HTML5. But it's not the only way to access information. Several new standards are creeping onto the field for different types of storage-related tasks. One example is a standard called the File API, which technically isn't a part of HTML5, but has good support across modern browsers, with the exception of Internet Explorer (which didn't add support until IE 10).

Based on its rather vague name, you might expect that the File API is a sweeping standard for reading and writing files on a web browser's hard drive. However, it's not that ambitious or powerful. Instead, the File API gives a way for a visitor to pick a file from his hard drive and hand it directly to the JavaScript code that's running on the web page. This code can then open the file and explore its data, whether it's simple text or something more complicated. The key thing is that the file goes directly to the JavaScript code. Unlike a normal file upload, it never needs to travel to the web server.

It's also important to note what the File API *can't* do. Most significantly, it can't change a file or create a new one. If you want to store any data, you'll need to use another mechanism—for example, you can send your data to a web server through XMLHttpRequest (page 377), or you can put it in local storage.

You might think that the File API is less useful than local storage—and for most websites, you'd be right. However, the File API is also a toehold into a world where HTML has never gone before, at least not without a plug-in to help.

NOTE   Right now, the File API is an indispensable feature for certain types of specialized applications, but in the future its capabilities may expand to make it much more important. For example, future versions may allow web pages to *write* local files, provided the user has control over the file name and location, using a Save dialog box. Browser plug-ins like Flash already have this capability.

Getting Hold of a File

Before you can do anything with the File API, you need to get hold of a file. There are three strategies you can use, but they are the same in one key fact—namely, your web page gets a file only if the visitor explicitly picks it and gives it to you.

Here are your options:

- **The <input> element.** Set the type attribute to file, and you've got the standard file upload box. But with a bit of JavaScript and the File API, you can open it locally.

- **A hidden <input> element.** The <input> element is ugly. To get right with the style police, you can hide your <input> element and make a nicer browser button. When it's clicked, use JavaScript to call the click() method on the hidden <input> element. This shows the standard file-selection dialog box.

- **Drag-and-drop.** If the browser supports it, you can drag a file from the desktop or a file browser window and drop it on a region in the web page.

In the following sections, you'll see all three approaches.

Reading a Text File with <input>

One of the easiest things you can do with the File API is read the content from a simple text file. Figure 10-5 shows a web page that uses this technique to read the markup in a web page and then display it.

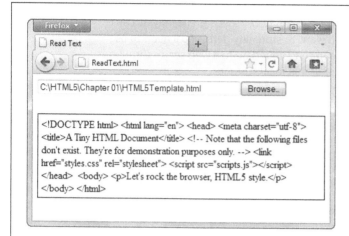

FIGURE 10-5

Click the Browse button (or Choose File, as it's named in Chrome), choose a file, and then click OK. Instead of the usual upload, the web page JavaScript takes it from there, copying the content into your page.

To build this example, you start with the `<input type="file">` element, which creates the infamous text box and Browse button combination:

```
<input id="fileInput" type="file" onchange="processFiles(this.files)">
```

However, whereas an `<input>` element usually belongs in a `<form>` container so the file can be posted to the web server, this `<input>` element goes its own way. When the web page visitor picks a file, it triggers the `<input>` element's onChange event, and that triggers the processFiles() function. It's here that the file is opened, in ordinary JavaScript.

Now you'll consider the processFiles() function, one piece at a time. The first order of business is to grab the first file from the collection of files that the `<input>` element provides. Unless you explicitly allow multiple file selection (with the multiple attribute), the files collection is guaranteed to hold just one file, which will be at position 0 in the files array:

```
function processFiles(files) {
  var file = files[0];
```

> **NOTE** Every file object has three potentially useful properties. The name property gives you its file name (not including the path), the size property tells you how many bytes big it is, and the type property tells you the MIME type of the file (page 152), if it can be determined. You could read these properties and add additional logic—for example, you could refuse to process files above a certain size, or allow files of only a certain type.

Next, you create a FileReader object that allows you to process the file:

```
var reader = new FileReader();
```

It's almost time to call one of the FileReader's methods to extract the file content. All of these methods are *asynchronous*, which means they start the file-reading task but don't wait for the data. To get the data, you first need to handle the onLoad event:

```
reader.onload = function (e) {
  // When this event fires, the data is ready.
  // Copy it to a <div> on the page.
  var output = document.getElementById("fileOutput");
  output.textContent = e.target.result;
};
```

Finally, with that event handler in place, you can call the FileReader's readAsText() method:

```
  reader.readAsText(file);
}
```

This method dumps all the file content into a single long string, which is provided in the e.target.result that's sent to the onLoad event.

The readAsText() method works properly only if the file holds text content (not binary content). That means it suits HTML files perfectly well, as shown in Figure 10-5. However, there are other useful formats that use plain text. One good example is the CSV format, which is a basic export format supported by all spreadsheet programs. Another example is the XML format, which is a standard way of exchanging bunches of data between programs. (It's also the foundation of the Office XML formats, which means you can hand .docx and .xlsx files directly to the readAsText() method as well.)

NOTE The JavaScript language even has a built-in XML parser, which means you can browse around an XML file and dig out just the content you need. Of course, the code this requires is considerable, it performs poorly for large files, and it's rarely easier than just uploading the file to a web server and running your file-processing logic there. However, you can start to see how the File API can open up new possibilities that HTML lovers didn't dare imagine even just a few years ago.

The readAsText() method isn't the only way to pull your data out of a file. The FileReader object also includes the following file-reading methods: readAsBinaryString(), readAsArrayBuffer(), and readAsDataUrl().

The readAsBinaryString() method gives your application the ability to deal with binary-encoded data, although it somewhat awkwardly sticks it into a text string, which is inefficient. And if you actually want to *interpret* that data, you need to struggle through some horribly convoluted code.

The readAsArryaBuffer() method is a better bet for web developers who need to do some serious do-it-yourself data processing. This method reads the data into an array (page 465), where each element represents a single byte of data. The advantage of this package is that you can use it to create Blob objects and slice out smaller sections of binary data, so you can process it one chunk at a time.

NOTE Blob is shorthand for *binary large object*—in other words, a fat chunk of raw data. Blobs are an advanced part of the File API; to learn more, you can take a look at Mozilla's steadily evolving documentation on the subject at *http://tinyurl.com/file-blob*.

Lastly, the readAsDataURL() method gives you an easy way to grab picture data. You'll use that on page 339. But first, it's time to make the page in this example a bit prettier.

Replacing the Standard Upload Control

Web developers agree: The standard <input> control for file submission is ugly. And although you do need to use it, you don't need to let anyone see it. Instead, you can simply hide it, with a style rule like this:

```
#fileInput {
  display: none;
}
```

Now add a new control that will trigger the file-submission process. An ordinary link button will do, which you can make look as pretty as you want:

```
<button onclick="showFileInput()">Analyze a File</button>
```

The final step is to handle the button click and use it to manually trigger the <input> element, by calling *its* click() method:

```
function showFileInput() {
  var fileInput = document.getElementById("fileInput");
  fileInput.click();
}
```

Now, when the button is clicked, the showFileInput() function runs, which clicks the hidden Browse button and shows the dialog box where the visitor can pick a file. This, in turn, triggers the hidden <input> element's onChange event, which runs the processFiles() function, just like before.

Reading Multiple Files at Once

There's no reason to limit people to submitting one file at a time. HTML5 allows multiple file submission, but you need to explicitly allow it by adding the multiple attribute to the <input> element:

```
<input id="fileInput" type="file" onchange="processFiles(this.files)"
multiple>
```

Now the user can select more than one file in the Open dialog box (for example, by pressing Ctrl on a Windows computer while clicking several files, or by dragging a box around a group of them). Once you allow multiple files, your code needs to accommodate them. That means you can't just grab the first file from the files collection, as in the previous example. Instead, you need a for loop that processes each file, one at a time:

```
for (var i=0; i<files.length; i++) {
  // Get the next file
  var file = files[i];

  // Create a FileReader for this file, and run the usual code here.
  var reader = new FileReader();
  reader.onload = function (e) {
    ...
  };
  reader.readAsText(file);
}
```

Reading an Image File with Drag-and-Drop

As you've seen, `FileReader` handles text content in a single, simple step. It deals will images just as easily, thanks to the `readAsDataURL()` method.

Figure 10-6 shows an example that introduces two new features: image support, and file drag-and-drop. The submitted image is used to paint the background of an element, although you could just as easily paint it on a canvas and process it using the canvas's raw pixel features (page 313). For example, you could use this technique to create a page where someone can drop in a picture, draw on it or modify it, and then upload the final result using an `XMLHttpRequest` call (page 377).

FIGURE 10-6

There are two ways to provide an image to this page: Use the file controls below, or drag one or more images onto the drop box.

To create this page, you first need to decide what element will capture the dropped files. In this example, it's a `<div>` element named `dropBox`:

```
<div id="dropBox">
  <div>Drop your image here...</div>
</div>
```

Some straightforward style sheet magic gives the drop box the size, borders, and colors you want:

```
#dropBox {
  margin: 15px;
  width: 300px;
  height: 300px;
  border: 5px dashed gray;
  border-radius: 8px;
  background: lightyellow;
  background-size: 100%;
  background-repeat: no-repeat;
  text-align: center;
}

#dropBox div {
  margin: 100px 70px;
  color: orange;
  font-size: 25px;
  font-family: Verdana, Arial, sans-serif;
}
```

Keen eyes will notice that the drop box sets the background-size and background-repeat properties in preparation for what comes next. When the image is dropped onto the <div>, it's set as the background. The background-size property ensures that the picture is compressed down so you can see all of it at once. The background-repeat property ensures that the picture isn't tiled to fill the leftover space.

To handle file drops, you need to handle three events: onDragEnter, onDragOver, and onDrop. When this page first loads, it attaches event handlers for all three:

```
var dropBox;

window.onload = function() {
  dropBox = document.getElementById("dropBox");
  dropBox.ondragenter = ignoreDrag;
  dropBox.ondragover = ignoreDrag;
  dropBox.ondrop = drop;
};
```

The ignoreDrag() function handles both onDragEnter (which fires when the mouse pointer enters the drop box, with a file attached) and onDragOver (which fires continuously, as the file-dragging mouse pointer moves over the drop box). That's because you don't need to react to either of these actions, other than to tell the browser to hold off from taking any actions of its own. Here's the code you need:

```
function ignoreDrag(e) {
  // Make sure nobody else gets this event, because you're handling
  // the drag and drop.
```

```
        e.stopPropagation();
        e.preventDefault();
    }
```

The onDrop event is more important. It's at this point that you get the file and process it. However, because there are actually two ways to submit files to this page, the drop() function calls the processFiles() function to do the actual work:

```
function drop(e) {
    // Cancel this event for everyone else.
    e.stopPropagation();
    e.preventDefault();

    // Get the dragged-in files.
    var data = e.dataTransfer;
    var files = data.files;

    // Pass them to the file-processing function.
    processFiles(files);
}
```

The processFiles() function is the last stop in the drag-and-drop journey. It creates a FileReader, attaches a function to the onload event, and calls readAsDataURL() to transform the image data into a data URL (page 269):

> **NOTE** As you learned when you explored the canvas, a data URL is a way of representing image data in a long text string that's fit for URL. This gives you a portable way to move the image data around. To show the image content in a web page, you can set the src property of an <img> element (as on page 276), or you can set the CSS background-image property (as in this example).

```
function processFiles(files) {
    var file = files[0];

    // Create the FileReader.
    var reader = new FileReader();

    // Tell it what to do when the data URL is ready.
    reader.onload = function (e) {
        // Use the image URL to paint the drop box background
        dropBox.style.backgroundImage = "url('" + e.target.result + "')";
    };

    // Start reading the image.
    reader.readAsDataURL(file);
}
```

The `FileReader` provides several more events, and when reading image files you might choose to use them. The `onProgress` event fires periodically during long operations, to let you know how much data has been loaded so far. (You can cancel an operation that's not yet complete by calling the `FileReader`'s `abort()` method.) The `onError` event fires if there was a problem opening or reading the file. And the `onLoadEnd` event fires when the operation is complete for any reason, including if an error forced it to end early.

Browser Support for the File API

The File API has solid browser support, but it isn't quite as reliable as web storage. Table 10-2 shows which browsers include it.

TABLE 10-1 *Browser support for the File API*

	IE	FIREFOX	CHROME	SAFARI	OPERA	SAFARI IOS	ANDROID
Minimum version	10	3.6	13	6	11.1	6	3

Because the File API requires some privileges that ordinary web pages don't have, you can't patch the missing feature with more JavaScript. Instead, you need to rely on a plug-in like Flash or Silverlight. For example, you can find a polyfill at *https://github.com/MrSwitch/dropfile* that uses Silverlight to intercept a dragged file, open it, and then pass the details to the JavaScript code on the page.

■ IndexedDB: A Database Engine in a Browser

You're probably familiar with the concept of *databases*—carefully structured catalogs of information that can swallow lists of people, products, sales, and just about any other sort of data you want to stuff them with. Many websites use databases that are stored on the web server. For example, when you look up a book on Amazon, the page extracts the details from Amazon's staggeringly big database. Much the same thing happens when you look for an article on Wikipedia or a video on YouTube, or when you perform a web search on Google.

For years, the story ended there. Databases were the province of the web server; conversation closed. But HTML5 introduces another possibility. What if the browser had the ability to create a *local* database—a database that's stored on the client's computer rather than the far-off web server? Different ideas cropped up, including a briefly popular and now abandoned specification called Web SQL Databases. More recently, the still-evolving IndexedDB specification rose to prominence as the official HTML5-sanctioned solution for local databases.

NOTE The name "IndexedDB" emphasizes the fact that the databases use *indexes* to identify and arrange data. Indexes ensure that you don't end up with the same record of data stored in two places, and they also speed up data retrieval when you have acres of information.

The Difference Between Server-Side and Client-Side Databases

There are plenty of ways for websites to use server-side databases, but none of them have anything to do with HTML5. To understand why, you need to remember that the HTML5 universe is centered on the mix of markup, styles, and JavaScript that's loaded in the client's browser. There's no direct way for a browser on your computer to access a database on the web server. Even if it were technically possible, this kind of contact would raise all kinds of security issues. Instead, to interact with a server-side database you need code that runs on the web server. For example, websites commonly use PHP or C# code (although there are many other technologies) to take care of server-side database tasks like generating a page of search results or logging a customer's purchase.

Before going ahead, it's important to understand exactly what role IndexedDB can play in a web application. For a host of reasons, IndexedDB can never replace the server-side databases described earlier. Most significantly, there's this: IndexedDB creates a separate database for every user. Websites that use server-side data need a single, centralized catalog of information that they can share with everyone.

However, IndexedDB is useful in several other special scenarios:

- **Making a self-sufficient offline application.** In Chapter 11, you'll learn how HTML5 caching lets you run a web page even without a web connection—a feat that's particularly useful for mobile devices. You can make your offline apps even more capable by using IndexedDB storage. For example, your page can retrieve the data it needs from a database on the web server when it's connected (using the XMLHttpRequest object demonstrated on page 377), and store that data in a local database so it's available even when the network isn't.

- **Enhancing performance.** Some applications use masses of data, and if you're continually retrieving the same data every time you need it, you'll slow down your pages. Similarly, if you create an application that generates data using complex calculations, you don't want to waste time performing the same work more than once. The solution is to store everything you need in an IndexedDB database. Treat it like your own super-customizable cache.

- **Improving local storage.** As you learned earlier, local storage provides a place to stash some data between browser sessions, and pass it from one page to another. If your data is relatively simple in structure and small in size, ordinary JavaScript variables and objects will hold it fine. But if you have an extraordinarily large or complex batch of data, you may find that it's easier and faster to manage it with an IndexedDB database.

> **NOTE** The IndexedDB storage system behaves like local storage in several key ways. Most importantly, an IndexedDB database belongs to a single person, using a particular browser and a particular computer, and visiting a specific site. If you change any of these details—for example, switching browsers, logging on with a different user account, or switching to your smartphone—the web page gets a new IndexedDB database.

Learning to use IndexedDB can be daunting. First, the specification is complex (some less charitable developers say ugly). You, the web developer, are responsible for creating the database, building its tables, and filling them with data. Second, IndexedDB uses an *asynchronous model*, which means that database tasks happen in the background, without stalling your code or locking up the page. The drawback is that this forces you to use a more complex model that scatters your code into different places. For example, the code you use to start a database task isn't in the same place as the code you use to handle the outcome of that task. Following the sequence and figuring out how each piece of code fits together takes some practice.

Figure 10-7 shows the database-powered web page that you'll analyze through the rest of this chapter. It puts the IndexedDB feature through a set of basic operations with a database that stores link information. Each record in the database consists of a URL and some relevant information about that URL, like its name and a description. Using the *FavoriteSiteTracker.html* page, you can add new link records, browse the ones that already exist, and change or delete individual records—all of which are fundamental tasks for code that deals with any type of database.

The Data Object

Before you get started with the link tracker example, it's time to learn about the data it stores—the LinkRecord object. Traditional databases are all about tables and fields, but IndexedDB simplifies life by storing *objects*. So before you create your database, it's a good idea to define your data structure in JavaScript.

In the link tracker example, the database has a single table, and each record in that table holds the information for a single link. You can package all the link details in JavaScript using an object-definition function, like this:

```
function LinkRecord(name, url, description, notes) {
  this.name = name;
  this.url = url;
  this.description = description;
  this.notes = notes;
}
```

Once you've added this function to your code, you can call it when needed to create a LinkRecord object, complete with a descriptive name, URL, full description, and notes. (If you're a bit fuzzy on object-creation with JavaScript, refer to page 468 for a review.)

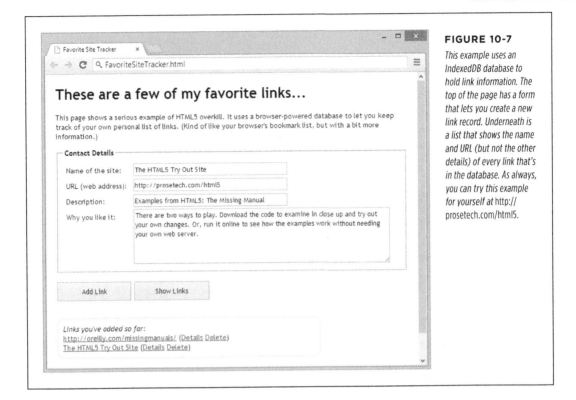

FIGURE 10-7

This example uses an IndexedDB database to hold link information. The top of the page has a form that lets you create a new link record. Underneath is a list that shows the name and URL (but not the other details) of every link that's in the database. As always, you can try this example for yourself at http:// prosetech.com/html5.

Creating and Connecting to a Database

In any web page that uses IndexedDB, the first task is to connect to your database. Since you'll usually perform this task when the page first loads, it makes sense to handle the window.onload event and put your code there. Here's the basic skeleton:

```
var database;

window.onload = function () {
  ...
}
```

The database variable goes outside your function. That way, once you set the database variable, you can access it everywhere else in your code.

So, what does your code need to do when the page loads? That depends on what you've done before:

- If this is the first time the user is visiting the page, you need to create the database and set up its tables from scratch.

- If the user has been here before, you only need to open the database and set the database variable, so it's ready for use.

Either way, your starting point is the open() function that's provided by the window. indexedDB object. It takes two arguments: the name of the database you want to use (or create), and its version number. If you're starting out with a brand new database, you need to set the version to 1:

```
var request = window.indexedDB.open("LinksDB", 1);
```

> **NOTE** It doesn't matter what name you give your database, so long as you stay consistent and aren't already using that name in another page on the same website.

As explained earlier, everything in IndexedDB land is asynchronous. Accordingly, when you call the open() method, nothing is actually opened. Instead, you're making a *request*. In this case, your request is for the browser to open the database when it gets the chance, and preferably on a background thread so it won't freeze up the page for even a moment.

You'll find this pattern of asynchronous requests—and the same request object— with just about every task you perform with IndexedDB. To react when the task is finished, you need to attach at least two event handlers: one that handles a successful result (onSuccess) and one that handles an unexpected failure (onError). In addition, when using the open() method, you need a third event handler for an event called onUpgradeNeeded.

When opening a database, the onSuccess event indicates that the right version of your database already exists. At this point you need to set the database variable so you can use it later. Optionally, you can get to work reading data. In the link tracker example, a separate function named showLinks() does that job (page 349).

```
request.onsuccess = function(event) {
  alert("Created or opened database successfully.");

  // Make the database available everywhere in the code.
  database = request.result;

  // Call the showLinks() function to read the database and display the
  // list of links that already exist.
  showLinks();
};
```

The onError event is equally straightforward. Depending on the error, you may be able to take corrective action, or you may simply choose to report it to the user with a message either in a pop-up box or right on the page.

```
request.onerror = function(event) {
  alert(request.error + " occurred.");
};
```

> **WARNING** Don't make the mistake of omitting the onError event handler. If you do, problems will slip by without any notification at all, and you'll have no clue what went wrong.

The onUpgradeNeeded event is the most interesting of the three. It fires when the database version you requested isn't available. For example, if you requested database version 2 and the computer currently has database version 1, this event fires. At this point, you can upgrade the database—for example, by adding a new table. (You can find out the version of the current database from the event.oldVersion argument.) The onUpgradeNeeded event also fires if the database doesn't exist at all, in which case the browser obligingly creates a blank database and waits for you to fill in the tables you want.

To create a table, you must first grab the database object from the request.result property. Then, you call its createObjectStore() method. Here's the code that adds a table named Links to the LinksDB database:

```
request.onupgradeneeded = function(event) {
  var db = request.result;
  var objectStore = db.createObjectStore("Links", { keyPath: "url" });
  }
};
```

In traditional database programming, you need to specify field names and data types when you create a table. But IndexedDB uses a simpler, object-focused model. When you create a table, you supply just two details: the name of the table and the *key path*, which is the property of your object that should be used for the primary key.

> **NOTE** The key path identifies a property in your data object. In this example, the word *url* is written in lowercase so it matches the name of the property of the data object. If you flip back to page 342, you'll see that the LinkRecord object defines a property named url.

Understanding Primary Keys

The *primary key* is the bit of information that uniquely identifies each record. In the case of the Links table, each link record has a unique URL, so it makes sense to use that for the key. This setup prevents you from accidentally creating two records for the same address. It also forces the browser to create an index for the Links table that will let you look up any link record by URL.

If your data doesn't include an obvious candidate for the primary key—in other words, it doesn't have an essential piece of information that's guaranteed to be unique—you can use the time-honored database technique of adding a numeric ID number. Even better, you can get the browser to generate unique numbers for you automatically and fill them in whenever you insert a new record. To do that, set the autoIncrement property to true when you create the database:

```
var objectStore =
db.createObjectStore("Links",
  { keyPath: "id", autoIncrement: true });
```

If your database needs to have multiple tables, you can call createObjectStore() multiple times, with different data objects. The request.onError event fires if the browser encounters a problem. Once the tables are added successfully, the request.onSuccess event will fire and your code can finish setting up the page.

NOTE The databases you create with IndexedDB are stored permanently, just like the objects you store in local storage. However, you can delete a database using the window.indexedDB.deleteDatabase() method, and some browsers allow users to review how much data each website is storing and remove whatever they don't want.

Storing Records in the Database

Database geeks use the term *data manipulation* to describe every database operation that works with table data, whether it involves reading, changing, inserting, or updating information. In the IndexedDB world, data manipulation operations always follow the same four basic steps. Once you understand this pattern, you'll have an easier time following the code for different database tasks.

Here are the steps:

1. **Create a transaction.**

   Whenever you want to do anything with an IndexedDB database, whether it's writing data or reading it, you must first begin by creating a transaction. In a database, a *transaction* is one or more data operations that are committed together, as a unit. If any part of a transaction fails, every operation inside the transaction is reversed, restoring the database to its pre-transaction state.

Transactions are important in the IndexedDB world because there are so many ways that a database operation can be interrupted. For example, if the user closes the browser while the page is still at work, the browser interrupts your code mid-task. The transaction system guarantees that even when these rude interruptions occur, the database is kept in a consistent state. In fact, transactions are so important that there's no way to perform IndexedDB operations without one.

NOTE To understand the problems you can run into without transactions, imagine you're transferring money from one bank account to another. In a transactional world, the first step (removing money from account A) and the second step (depositing it in account B) either succeed or fail together. But without transactions, you could end up in an unhappy situation: a successful debit from account A, but a failed deposit to account B, leading to some serious missing cash.

---

2. **Retrieve the object store for your transaction.**

   Object store is a fancy name for table. Because every record in an IndexedDB table is actually a data object, this name makes sense.

3. **Call one of the object store methods.**

   The object store is the gateway to all the table-manipulation features. For example, to add a record you call its put() method. To delete a record, you call its delete() method. The method returns a request object, which you must use for the next step.

4. **Handle the success and error events.**

   As you already know, virtually everything in IndexedDB is asynchronous. If you want to do something when an operation is finished, and if you want to catch errors before they metastasize into more serious problems, you need to handle the onSuccess and onError events, just as you did when opening the database.

With these steps in mind, you're ready to look at the code in the addLink() function, which runs when the web page visitor clicks the Add Link button.

Before you do anything with your database, you need your data on hand. In the link tracker example, the code grabs the typed-in data from the form and uses it to create a LinkRecord object. This task is basic JavaScript—you simply need to find your elements, pull out the corresponding values, and use the LinkRecord() function shown on page 342.

```
function addLink() {
  // Collect the data from the form.
  var name = document.getElementById("name").value;
  var url = document.getElementById("url").value;
  var description = document.getElementById("description").value;
  var notes = document.getElementById("notes").value;
```

```
// Create the LinkRecord object.
var linkRecord = new LinkRecord(name, url, description, notes);
```

Now you're ready to follow step 1 from the list and create your transaction. To do that, you call the database.transaction() method and provide two parameters:

```
var transaction = database.transaction(["Links"], "readwrite");
```

The first parameter is a list of all the tables involved in the transaction. This information enables IndexedDB to lock the tables, preventing other pieces of code from making overlapping and possibly inconsistent changes at the same time. Technically, this parameter is an array that holds a list of table names, which is why you wrap the whole thing in square brackets. But in this example, there's just one table involved in the task.

The second parameter is a string that identifies the type of transaction. Use the word readwrite if you want to create a transaction that changes the table in any way, whether it's inserting, updating, or deleting records. But if all you need to do is retrieve data, use the word readonly instead.

This brings you to step 2—getting the indispensable object store for your table. You can do so easily with the transaction.objectStore() property. Just supply the name of the table, like this:

```
var objectStore = transaction.objectStore("Links");
```

To add a record, use the put() method of the object store and supply the data object:

```
var request = objectStore.put(linkRecord);
```

Finally, you need to handle the onError and onSuccess events to find out whether the record was successfully added:

```
request.onerror = function(event) {
  alert(request.error + " occurred.");
};

request.onsuccess = function(event) {
  // The record has been added.
  // Refresh the display. (For better performance, you could add just the
  // one new item, rather than refresh the whole list.)
  showLinks();
};
}
```

NOTE If you call put() to add a record that has the same primary key as an existing record (for example, a link with an existing URL), the browser quietly replaces the existing record with your new data.

Querying All the Records in a Table

Querying is the essential job of retrieving your stored information. You pick out a single record, search for a group of records that match certain criteria, or travel through all the records in your table, whichever you prefer.

The link tracker performs a complete table scan and a single-record search. It uses the table scan to create the list of links that appears under the link-adding form. It uses the record search to get the full details for a specific site when you click one of the Details links in the list, as you'll see shortly.

The first task is the more complex one. That's because you need the help of a cursor to browse through an IndexedDB table. (A database *cursor* is an object that keeps track of your current position in a table and lets you step through its records.)

You begin by creating a transaction and getting the object store. This time, you don't need to make any changes, so a read-only transaction fits the bill:

```
function showLinks() {
  var transaction = database.transaction(["Links"], "readonly");
  var objectStore = transaction.objectStore("Links");
```

Next, you create the cursor using the openCursor() method of the object store:

```
  var request = objectStore.openCursor();
```

Then, you attach your code to the familiar onError and onSuccess events. The onError event handler is nothing special:

```
  request.onerror = function(event) {
    alert(request.error + " occurred.");
  };
```

The onSuccess event handler is more interesting. It has the job of stepping through the records in the Links table, one by one. As it travels, it builds up a string of HTML with the list of links.

```
  // Prepare the string of markup that will be inserted into the page.
  var markupToInsert = "";

  request.onsuccess = function(event) {
    // Create a cursor.
    var cursor = event.target.result;
```

Initially, the cursor is positioned on the first record of the table, if it exists. You check for data by testing whether the cursor is true or false. If it's true, there's a record there ready for you to read. You can get the record from the cursor.value property:

```
    if (cursor) {
      var linkRecord = cursor.value;
```

Your data is returned to you as an object. In the link tracker example, each record is a genuine LinkRecord object, complete with the name, url, description, and notes properties outlined in the object-definition function on page 342.

Once you retrieve your object, it's up to you to decide what to do with it. In the current example, the code uses the LinkRecord data to construct an <a> element. It uses the site name for the link text and the URL for the link address:

```
markupToInsert += "<a href=" + linkRecord.url + ">" + linkRecord.name +
    "</a>";
```

For now, the <a> is stored in a variable called markupToInsert. When the code is finished examining every LinkRecord in the database and adding all their information to the markupToInsert variable, it will finally be ready to copy the markup to the page.

The link tracker example gets a bit fancier by adding two clickable bits of text after every link. One is named "Details" and the other is named "Delete," and you can see them both in Figure 10-7 (near the very bottom of the screen).

These bits of text look like ordinary links, but they are actually <span> elements that are hard-wired to call two other JavaScript functions in the page (getLinkDetails and deleteLink) when clicked. Here's the code that creates them:

```
markupToInsert += "(" +
    "<span class='linkButton' data-url='" + linkRecord.url +
    "' onclick='getLinkDetails(this)'>Details</span>" + " " +
    "<span class='linkButton' data-url='" + linkRecord.url +
    "' onclick='deleteLink(this)'>Delete</span>" +
    ")<br>";
```

There's a neat trick here. The Details and Delete commands are <span> elements. To simplify life, the URL of the corresponding element is stored in each <span> element using an attribute. That way, when one of these commands is clicked, the page can quickly retrieve the URL and use it to look up the corresponding record in the Links table.

> **NOTE** The attribute that stores the URL is named data-url, according to HTML5 convention. The data-prefix indicates that you're using the attribute to hold custom data, which the browser can ignore. You can use whatever you want for the rest of the attribute name—here, url makes sense because the attribute is storing a URL.

So far, you've seen how the code processes a single record during a search. When you're ready to move to the next record, you call the cursor.continue() method. However, you *don't* attempt to process any more data. That's because stepping through your records is an asynchronous operation. When the cursor reaches the next record, the onSuccess event fires again, triggering the same code a second time, at which point you can add the markup for the next record, if it exists.

```
    cursor.continue();
}
```

When you reach the last record in the table, the cursor will evaluate to false. At this point, it's time to copy your markup into the page:

```
      else {
        // If there wasn't at least one result, substitute some placeholder text.
        if (markupToInsert == "") {
          markupToInsert = "<< No links. >>";
        }
        else {
          markupToInsert = "<i>Links you've added so far: </i><br>" +
            markupToInsert;
        }

        // Insert the markup.
        var resultsElement = document.getElementById("links");
        resultsElement.innerHTML = markupToInsert;
      }
    };
  }
```

Querying a Single Record

Querying an individual record in a table is easier than getting them all, because you don't have to mess around with cursors. Instead, you follow the well-established four-step procedure you saw on page 346, using the get() method from the object store.

If you click one of the "Details" links in the link tracker example, the following code springs into action. It grabs the corresponding LinkRecord object and extracts all of its information.

```
function getLinkDetails(element) {
  // Get the URL for this link from the handy data-url attribute we added
  // earlier.
  var url = element.getAttribute("data-url");

  var transaction = database.transaction(["Links"], "readonly");
  var objectStore = transaction.objectStore("Links");

  // Find the record that has this URL.
  var request = objectStore.get(url);

  request.onerror = function(event) {
    alert(request.error + " occurred.");
  };

  request.onsuccess = function(event) {
    var linkRecord = request.result;
```

```
      var resultsElement = document.getElementById("linkDetails");
      resultsElement.innerHTML = "<b>" + linkRecord.name + "</b><br>" +
        "<b>URL:</b> " + linkRecord.url + "<br>" +
        "<b>Description:</b> " + linkRecord.description + "<br>" +
        "<b>Notes:</b> " + linkRecord.notes;
    }
  }
```

The information from the LinkRecord object is used to create a snippet of HTML markup, which is then inserted into the page in a separate box under the link list. Figure 10-8 shows the result.

Deleting a Record

By this point, you're familiar with the four-step sequence that underpins every data operation. Deleting a record isn't any different. You simply need to use the delete() method of the object store.

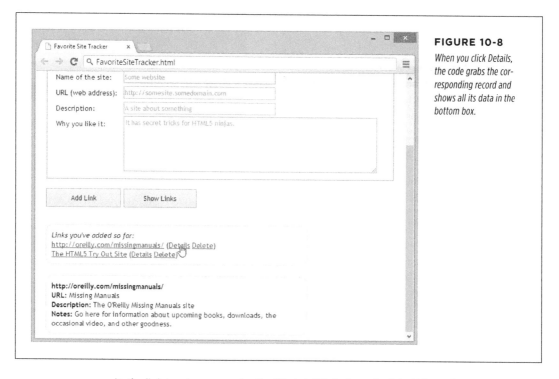

FIGURE 10-8

When you click Details, the code grabs the corresponding record and shows all its data in the bottom box.

In the link tracker example, the "Delete" link does the job. When clicked, it removes the LinkRecord with the matching URL, using this code:

```
function deleteLink(element) {
  var url = element.getAttribute("data-url");

  var transaction = database.transaction(["Links"], "readwrite");
  var objectStore = transaction.objectStore("Links");

  var request = objectStore.delete(url);

  request.onerror = function(event) {
    alert(request.error + " occurred.");
  };

  request.onsuccess = function (event) {
    // The record has been deleted.
    // Refresh the display.
    showLinks();
  }
}
```

You've now seen the key methods that you can use to manipulate data with IndexedDB. You've learned how to use the object store to add records or update them
(with the put() method) and delete them (with delete). You've also learned how to
retrieve individual records by key value (with get) or browse through them all (with
openCursor). But if you want to get deeper into databases, check out Mozilla's helpful documentation for the object store at *http://tinyurl.com/objectstore*, or explore
the nitty-gritty details of the IndexedDB standard at *www.w3.org/TR/IndexedDB*.

Browser Support for IndexedDB

IndexedDB is a relatively new specification,and requires a relatively recent browser.
Table 10-2 shows the current state of affairs.

TABLE 10-2 *Browser support for IndexedDB*

	IE	FIREFOX	CHROME	SAFARI	OPERA	SAFARI IOS	CHROME FOR ANDROID
Minimum version	10	10	23	-	15	-	29

Sadly, IndexedDB isn't yet available on desktop or mobile versions of Safari. This
support gap exists because the developers of Safari invested their effort in the
now-abandoned Web SQL Database standard. If you need Safari support, you
can use a polyfill that converts IndexedDB operations to the corresponding Web
SQL commands. (Download it at *http://tinyurl.com/DBpolyfill*.) But if you want
IndexedDB support on a browser that doesn't support IndexedDB or Web SQL,
such as Internet Explorer version 9 or 8, you're unfortunately out of luck.

Running Offline

I f you want to view a website, you need to connect to the Internet. Everybody knows that. So why a chapter about offline applications? The very notion seems so last century. After all, didn't web applications overthrow several generations of offline, desktop applications on their way to conquering the world? And there are plenty of tasks—from following the latest Kardashian sightings to ordering a new office chair—that just wouldn't be possible without a live, real-time connection. But remember, even web applications aren't meant to stay *permanently* online. Instead, they're designed to keep working during occasional periods of downtime when a computer loses its network connection. In other words, a useful offline web application can tolerate intermittent network disruptions.

This fact is particularly important for people using smartphones and tablets. To see the problem, try traveling through a long tunnel while using a web application on one of these devices. Odds are you'll get a nasty error page, and you'll have to start all over again when you get to the other side. But do the same with an *offline* web application, and you'll avoid interruption. Some of the features of the web application may become temporarily unavailable, but you won't get booted out. (Of course, some tunnels are longer than others. An ambitious offline web application can keep working through a three-hour plane flight—or a three-week trip to the Congo, if that's what you're after. There's really no limit to how long you can stay offline.)

By using HTML5's offline application feature, you can start to shift your ordinary web page into a web-based "mini-app." And if you combine the offline feature with plenty of JavaScript code, the data storage features described in Chapter 10, and the server communication features described in Chapter 12, your mini-app can be nearly as powerful and self-sufficient as the native applications designed for smartphones and tablets. The big advantage is that your HTML5-powered mini-app can run on *any* device, whereas a native app is locked into a specific platform.

In this chapter, you'll learn how to turn any web page (or group of web pages) into an offline application. You'll also learn how to tell when a website is available and when it's offline, and react accordingly.

FREQUENTLY ASKED QUESTION

When It Makes Sense to Go Offline

Should I make my web page offline-able?

Offline web applications don't suit every sort of web page. For example, there's really no point in turning a stock quote page into an offline web application, since the whole point of its existence is to fetch updated stock data from a web server. However, the offline feature might suit a more detailed stock analysis tool that downloads a bunch of data at once and then lets you choose how to chart it or analyze it. Using a page like this, you could download some data while you're online and then tweak options and fiddle with buttons until you reach the proverbial other side of the tunnel.

The offline feature also suits web pages that are interactive and *stateful*—ones that have piles of JavaScript code maintaining lots of information in memory. These pages do more on their own, so they make sense as offline applications. And the cost of losing your connection with one of these pages is also higher, because being kicked out in the middle of a complex task is seriously annoying. So while there's no point in making a simple page of content offline-able, it's immediately obvious that a word-processor-in-a-browser tool can benefit from offline support. In fact, an offline application like this might just be able to stand in for a more fully featured desktop program.

The other consideration is your audience. The offline application feature makes great sense if your visitors include people who don't have reliable Internet connections or are likely to need mobile access (for example, if you're creating a mapping tool for tablet devices). But if not, adding offline support might not be worth the trouble.

Caching Files with a Manifest

The basic technique that makes offline applications work is *caching*—the technique of downloading a file (like a web page) and keeping a copy of it on the web surfer's computer. That way, if the computer loses its web connection, the browser can still use the cached copy of the page. Of course, caching isn't limited to pages—it works with style sheets, JavaScript code files, pictures, fonts, and any other resource your web page needs to have on hand to do its work.

To create an offline application, you need to complete three steps. Here's the high-level overview:

1. **Create a *manifest* file.**

   A manifest is a special sort of file that tells browsers which files to store, which files not to store, and which files to substitute with something else. This package of cacheable content is called an *offline application*.

2. **Modify your web page so it refers to the manifest.**

That way, the browser knows to download the manifest file when someone requests the page.

3. **Configure the web server.**

Most importantly, the web server needs to serve manifest files with the proper MIME type. But as you'll see, there are a few more subtle issues that can also trip up caching.

You'll tackle all these tasks in the following sections.

Traditional Caching vs. Offline Applications

Caching is nothing new in the web world. Browsers use caching regularly to avoid repeatedly downloading the same files. After all, if you travel through several pages in a website, and each page uses the same style sheet, why download it more than once? However, the mechanism that controls this sort of caching isn't the same as the one that makes offline applications work.

Traditional caching happens when the web server sends extra information (called *cache-control headers*) along with some file that a web browser has requested. The headers tell the browser if the file should be cached and how long to keep the cached copy before asking the web server if the file has changes. Typically, caching is brief for web pages and much

longer for the resources that web pages use, like style sheets, pictures, and script files.

By comparison, an offline application is controlled by a separate file (called a manifest), and it doesn't use any time limit at all. Instead, it applies the following rule: "If a web page is part of an offline application, and if the browser has a cached copy of that application, and if the definition of that application hasn't changed, then use the cached copy." You, the web developer, can add certain exceptions—for example, telling the browser not to cache certain files or to substitute one file for another. But there's no need to worry about expiration dates and other potentially messy details.

Creating a Manifest

The manifest is the heart of HTML5's offline application feature. It's a text file that lists the files you want to cache.

The manifest always starts with the words CACHE MANIFEST (in uppercase), like this:

```
CACHE MANIFEST
```

After that, you list the files you want to cache. Here's an example that grabs two web pages (from the personality test example described on page 289):

```
CACHE MANIFEST

PersonalityTest.html
PersonalityTest_Score.html
```

Spaces (like the blank line in the manifest shown above) are optional, so you can add them wherever you want.

NOTE Watch for typos. If you attempt to cache a file that doesn't exist, the browser will ignore not just that file, but the entire manifest.

With an offline application, the browser must cache everything your application needs. That includes web pages and the resources these web pages use (like scripts, graphics, style sheets, and embedded fonts). Here's a more complete manifest that takes these details into account:

```
CACHE MANIFEST
# pages
PersonalityTest.html
PersonalityTest_Score.html

# styles & scripts
PersonalityTest.css
PersonalityTest.js

# pictures & fonts
Images/emotional_bear.jpg
Fonts/museo_slab_500-webfont.eot
Fonts/museo_slab_500-webfont.woff
Fonts/museo_slab_500-webfont.ttf
Fonts/museo_slab_500-webfont.svg
```

Here, you'll notice two new details. First, you'll see several lines that begin with a number sign (#). These are *comments*, which you can add to remind yourself what goes where. Second, you'll see some files that are in subfolders (for example, *emotional_bear.jpg* in the *Images* folder). As long as these files are on the web server and accessible to the browser, you can bundle them up as part of your offline application package.

Complex web pages will need a lot of supporting files, which can lead to long, complex manifest files. Worst of all, a single mistyped file name will prevent the offline application feature from working *at all*.

TIP You might decide to leave out some resources that are unimportant or overly large, like ad banners or huge pictures. That's quite all right, but if you think their absence might cause some trouble (like error messages, odd blank spaces, or scrambled layouts), consider using JavaScript to tweak your pages when the user is offline, by using the connection-checking trick described on page 370.

Once you've filled out the contents of your manifest file, you can save it in your site's root folder, alongside your web pages. You can use whatever file name you want, although you should add the file extension *.appcache* (as in *PersonalityTest.appcache*). Other file extensions may work (for example, in the early days of HTML5 some web developers used *.manifest*), but the latest versions of the HTML5 specification recommend *.appcache*. The important thing is that the web server is configured to recognize the file extension. If you're running your own web server, you can use the setup steps described on page 360. If not, you need to talk to your web hosting company and ask them what file extensions they use to support manifest files.

TROUBLESHOOTING MOMENT

Don't Cache Pages That Use the Query String

The query string is the extra bit of information that appears on the end of some URLs, separated by a question mark. Usually, you use the query string to pass information from one web page to another. For example, the original version of the personality test uses the query string to pass the personality scores from the *PersonalityTest.html* page to the *PersonalityTest_Score.html* page. If you fill out the multiple-choice questions on the first page and click Get Score, the browser redirects you using a URL like this:

> http://prosetech.com/html5/Personali-
> tyTest_Score.html**?e=-10&a=-5&c=10&n=5&o=20**

Here's the problem. In the eyes of the HTML5 caching system, a request for the page *PersonalityTest_Score.html* is not the same as a request for *PersonalityTest_Score.html?e=-10&a=-5&c=10&n=5&o=20*. The first page is cached, according to the manifest. But the second URL may as well point to a completely different page. Unless you add the page name and the complete query string in the manifest, it won't be cached. And because there's no way you want to add a separate manifest entry for every possible combination of personality scores, there's no way to properly cache the query-string-enabled version of the *PersonalityTest_Score.html* page.

To avoid this problem, don't use caching and query strings at the same time. For example, if you want to add caching to the personality test, use the version that puts personality scores in local storage. (That's the version used in the caching example on page 357.)

Using Your Manifest

Just creating a manifest isn't enough to get a browser to pay attention. To put your manifest into effect, you need to refer to it in your web pages. You do that by adding the manifest attribute to the root <html> element and supplying the manifest file name, like this:

```
<!DOCTYPE html>
<html lang="en" manifest="PersonalityTest.manifest">
...
```

You need to take this step for every page that's part of your offline application. In the previous example, that means you need to change two files: *PersonalityTest. html* and *PersonalityTest_Score.html*.

NOTE   A website can have as many offline applications as you want, as long as each one has its own manifest.

Putting Your Manifest on a Web Server

Testing manifest files can be a tricky process. Minor problems can cause silent failures and throw off the entire caching process. Still, at some point you'll need to give it a try to make sure your offline application is as self-sufficient as you expect.

It should come as no surprise that you can't test offline applications when you're launching files from your hard drive. Instead, you need to put your application on a web server (or use a test web server that runs on your computer, like the IIS web server that's built into Windows).

To test an offline application, follow these steps:

1. **Make sure the web server is configured to use the MIME type** *text/cache-manifest* **when serving manifest files (typically, those are files with the extension .appcache).**

   If the web server indicates that the file is any other type, including a plain text file, the browser will ignore the manifest completely.

> **NOTE** Every type of web server works differently. Depending on your skills, you may need the help of your web hosting company or your neighborhood webmaster to set MIME types (step 1) and change caching settings (step 2). Page 152 has more information about MIME types, and shows one example of how you might add a new MIME type through a web hosting account.

2. **Consider turning off traditional caching (page 357) for manifest files.**

   Here's the problem. Web servers may tell web browsers to cache manifest files for a short period of time, just as they tell them to cache other types of files. This behavior is reasonable enough, but it can cause king-sized testing headaches. That's because when you update the manifest file, some browsers will ignore it and carry on with the old, cached manifest file, and so they'll keep using the old, cached copies of your web pages. (Firefox has a particularly nasty habit of sticking with out-of-date manifest files.) To avoid this problem, you should configure the web server to tell browsers not to cache manifest files, ever.

   Once again, every web server software has its own configuration system, but the basic idea is to tell your server to send a no-cache header whenever someone requests an .appcache file.

3. **Request the page in a web browser that supports offline applications. Virtually every browser does, except old versions of Internet Explorer—you need IE 10 or better.**

   When a web browser discovers a web page that uses a manifest, it may ask for your permission before downloading the files. Mobile devices probably will, because they have limited space requirements. Desktop browsers may or may not—for example, Firefox does (see Figure 11-1), but Chrome, Internet Explorer, and Safari don't.

   If you give your browser permission (or if your browser doesn't ask for it), the caching process begins. The browser downloads the manifest and then downloads each of the files it references. This downloading process takes place in the background and doesn't freeze up the page. It's just the same as when a browser downloads a large image or video, while displaying the rest of the page.

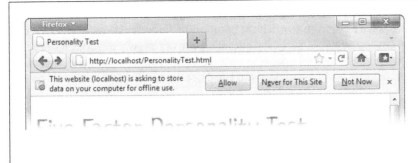

FIGURE 11-1

Firefox shows this message when it loads a web page that uses a manifest. Click Allow to grant permission to download and cache all the files that are listed in the manifest. On subsequent visits, when Firefox detects a changed manifest, it will download the new files without asking for permission again.

4. **Go offline.**

   If you're testing on a remote server, just disconnect your network connection. If you're testing on a local web server (one that's running on your computer), shut your website down (Figure 11-2).

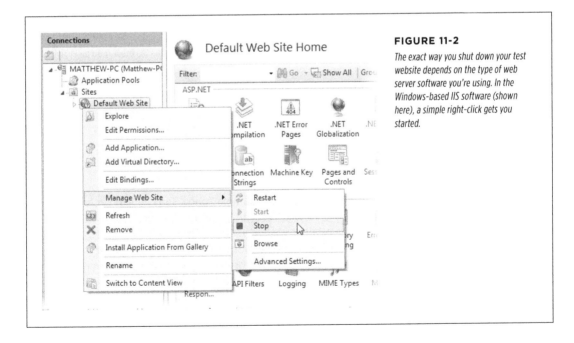

FIGURE 11-2

The exact way you shut down your test website depends on the type of web server software you're using. In the Windows-based IIS software (shown here), a simple right-click gets you started.

5. Browse to one of the pages in your offline application, and refresh it.

Ordinarily, when you click the Refresh or Reload button, your browser always tries to make contact with the web server. If you're requesting an ordinary page and you've lost your Internet connection, this request will fail. But if you're requesting a page from an offline application, the browser seamlessly substitutes the cached copy, without even informing you of the switch. You can even click links to jump from one page to another, but if you navigate to a page that's not part of the offline application, you'll get the familiar "no response" error.

TROUBLESHOOTING MOMENT

My Offline Application Doesn't Work Offline

The offline application feature is fragile and a bit quirky. A minor mistake can throw it all off. If you follow the steps described above, but you get a "no response" error when you attempt to access your offline pages, check for these common problems:

- **Problems downloading the manifest.** If the manifest isn't there, or isn't accessible to the browser, you'll have an obvious problem. But equally important is serving the manifest with the right MIME type (page 152).

- **Problems downloading the files that are listed in the manifest.** For example, imagine that your manifest includes a picture that no longer exists. Or it asks for a web font file, and that font file uses a file type that your web server doesn't allow. Either way, if the browser fails to download even a single file, it will give up completely (and throw away any cached information it already has).

To avoid this problem, start simple, with a manifest that lists just a single web page and no resources. Or, in more complex examples, look at the web server logs to find out exactly what resources the browser has requested (which may tell you the point at which it met an error and gave up).

- **An old manifest is still cached.** Browsers can cache the manifest file (according to the traditional caching rules of the Web) and ignore the fact that you've changed it. One of the signs that you've stumbled into this problem is when some pages are cached but other, more recently added pages are not. To solve this problem, consider manually clearing the browser cache (see the box on page 364).

Updating the Manifest File

Getting an application to work offline is the first challenge. The next is updating it with new content.

For example, consider the previous example (page 358), which caches two web pages. If you update *PersonalityTest.html*, fire up your browser, and reload the page, you'll still see the original, cached version of the page—regardless of whether your computer is currently online. The problem is that once a browser has a cached copy of an application, it uses that. The browser ignores the online versions of the associated web pages and doesn't bother to check whether they've changed. And because offline applications never expire, it doesn't matter how long you wait: Even months later, the browser will stubbornly ignore changed pages.

However, the browser *will* check for a new manifest file. So you can save a new copy of that, put it on the web server, and you've solved the problem, right?

Not necessarily. To trigger an update for a cached web application, you need to meet three criteria:

- **The manifest file can't be cached in the browser.** If the browser has a locally cached copy of the manifest file, it won't bother to check the web server at all. Browsers differ on how they handle manifest file caching, with some (like Chrome) always checking with the web server for new manifests. But Firefox follows the traditional rules of HTTP caching and holds onto its cached copy for some time. So if you want to save yourself development headaches, make sure your web server explicitly tells clients that they shouldn't cache manifests (page 360).

- **The manifest file needs a new date.** When a browser checks the server, the first thing it does is ask whether the last-updated timestamp has changed. If it hasn't, the web browser doesn't bother to download the manifest file.

- **The manifest file needs new content.** If a browser downloads a newly updated manifest file but discovers that the content hasn't changed, it stops the update process and keeps using the previously cached copy. This potentially frustrating step actually serves a valuable purpose. Re-downloading a cached application takes time and uses up network bandwidth, so browsers don't want to do it if it's really not necessary.

If you've been following along carefully, you'll notice a potential problem here. What if there's no reason to change the manifest file (because you haven't added any files), but you do need to force browsers to update their application cache (because some of the existing files have changed)? In this situation, you need to make a trivial change to the manifest file, so it appears to be new when it isn't. The best way to do so is with a comment, like this:

```
CACHE MANIFEST
# version 1.00.001
# pages
PersonalityTest.html
PersonalityTest_Score.html

# styles & scripts
PersonalityTest.css
PersonalityTest.js

# pictures & fonts
Images/emotional_bear.jpg
Fonts/museo_slab_500-webfont.eot
Fonts/museo_slab_500-webfont.woff
Fonts/museo_slab_500-webfont.ttf
Fonts/museo_slab_500-webfont.svg
```

The next time you need browsers to update their caches, simply change the version number in this example to 1.00.002, and so on. Presto—you now have a way to force updates and keep track of how many updates you've uploaded.

Updates aren't instantaneous. When the browser discovers a new manifest file, it quietly downloads all the files and uses them to replace the old cache content. The next time the user visits the page (or refreshes the page), the new content will appear. If you want to switch over to the newly downloaded application right away, you can use the JavaScript technique described on page 372.

> **NOTE** There is no incremental way to update an offline application. When the application has changed, the browser tosses out the old and downloads every file again, even if some files haven't changed.

GEM IN THE ROUGH

Clearing the Browser's Cache

When testing an offline application, it's often helpful to manually clear the cache. That way, you can test new updates without changing the manifest.

Every browser has a way to clear the cache, but every browser tucks it away somewhere different. The most useful browsers keep track of how much space each offline application uses (see Figure 11-3). This information lets you determine when caching has failed—for example, the application's website isn't listed or the cached size isn't as big as it should be. It also lets you remove the cached files for a single site without disturbing the others.

Browser Support for Offline Applications

By now, you've probably realized that all major browsers support offline applications, aside from the notable HTML5 laggard, Internet Explorer. Support stretches back several versions, which all but ensures that Firefox, Chrome, and Safari users will be able to run your applications offline. But Internet Explorer didn't get around to adding support until version IE 10, which means there's no caching in the still-popular IE 9 and IE 8.

However, the way that different browsers support offline applications isn't completely consistent. The most important difference is the amount of space they allow offline applications to fill. This variation is significant, because it sets the difference between websites that will be cached for offline access and ones that won't (see the box on page 366).

There's no worthwhile way to get offline application support on browsers that don't include it as a feature (like IE 9). However, this shouldn't stop you from using the offline application feature. After all, offline applications are really just a giant frill. Web browsers that don't support them will still work: They just require a live web connection. And people that need offline support—for example, frequent travelers—will discover the value of having a non-IE browser on hand for their disconnected times of need.

FIGURE 11-3

Top: In the Firefox menu, click Options, choose the Advanced icon, and then choose the Network tab to end up here. You can review the space usage of every website, or clear the cached resources of any one, by selecting it and clicking Remove. In this example, there's just one cached website, on the domain localhost (which represents a test server on the current computer).

Bottom: To get a similar display in Chrome, type chrome://appcache-internals into the address bar.

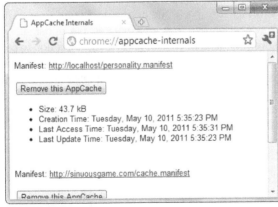

How Much Can You Cache?

Are there limits on how much information can be cached?

Different browsers impose wildly different size restrictions on offline applications.

Mobile browsers are the most obvious example. Because they run on space-limited devices, they tend to be stingy with their caching. Desktop browsers are more generous, but they're equally unpredictable. Browsers may assign a fixed space limit to each website domain, or they may calculate a suitable allotment based on the current amount of free space on your computer, along with other factors. Often, space is shared between several HTML5 features—for example, if you're using the File API or IndexedDB feature (see Chapter 10), your browser may use a single pool of space with these features and the application cache.

Unfortunately, the lack of consistency among browsers is a problem. If you create an offline application that attempts to stuff the cache beyond its limit, the browser quietly gives up and throws away all the downloaded data. Not only will you waste time and bytes, but your website users won't get any offline benefits. They'll be forced to use your application online.

The best rule of thumb is to assume you'll be limited to 50 MB on Apple devices (like the iPad and iPhone) and closer to 85 MB on Android devices. All mobile browsers will ask the user for permission before allowing a website to use the cache. On desktop browsers, you'll probably get a starting allotment of 250 or 350 MB. If your cache swells, some desktop browsers will offer to ratchet up the available space beyond the starting allotment, but there's no guarantee.

■ Practical Caching Techniques

So far, you've seen how to package up a group of pages and resources as an offline application. Along the way, you learned to write a manifest file, update it, and make sure browsers don't ignore your hard work. This knowledge is enough to put simple applications offline. However, more complex websites sometimes need more. For example, you may want to keep some content online, substitute different pages when offline, or determine (in code) whether the computer has a live Internet connection. In the following sections, you'll learn how to accomplish all these tasks with smarter manifest files and a dash of JavaScript.

Accessing Uncached Files

Earlier, you learned that once a page is cached, the web browser uses that cached copy and doesn't bother talking to any web servers. But what you may not realize is that the browser's reluctance to go online applies to *all* the resources an offline web page uses, whether they're cached or not.

For example, imagine you have a page that uses two pictures, using this markup:

```
<img src="Images/logo.png" alt="Personality quiz">
<img src="Images/emotional_bear.jpg" alt="Sad stuffed bear">
```

However, the manifest caches just one of the pictures:

```
CACHE MANIFEST
PersonalityTest.html
PersonalityTest_Score.html

PersonalityTest.css
PersonalityTest.js

Images/emotional_bear.jpg
```

You might assume that a browser will grab the *emotional_bear.png* picture from its cache, while requesting *logo.png* from the web server (as long as the computer is online). After all, that's the way it works in your browser when you step from a cached web page to an uncached page. But here, the reality is different. The browser grabs *emotional_bear.jpg* from the cache but ignores the uncached *logo.png* graphic, displaying a broken-image icon or just a blank space on the page, depending on the browser.

To solve this problem, you need to add a new section to your manifest. You title this section with a `NETWORK:` title, followed by a list of the pages that live online:

```
CACHE MANIFEST
PersonalityTest.html
PersonalityTest_Score.html

PersonalityTest.css
PersonalityTest.js
Images/emotional_bear.jpg

NETWORK:
Images/logo.png
```

Now the browser will attempt to get the *logo.png* file from the web server when the computer is online, but not do anything when it's offline.

At this point, you're probably wondering why you would bother to explicitly list files you don't want to cache. It could be for space considerations—for example, maybe you're leaving out large files to make sure your application can be cached on browsers that allow only small amounts of cache space (page 366).

But a more likely situation is that you have content that should be available when requested but never cached—for example, tracking scripts or dynamically generated ads. In this case, the easiest solution is to add an asterisk (*) in your network section. That's a wildcard character that tells the browser to go online to get every resource you haven't explicitly cached:

```
NETWORK:
*
```

You can also use the asterisk to target files of a specific type (for example, *.jpg refers to all JPEG images) or all the files on a specific server (for example, http:// www.google-analytics.com/* refers to all the resources on the Google Analytics web domain).

> **NOTE** It may occur to you that you could simplify your manifest by using the asterisk wildcard in the list of cached files. That way, you could cache bunches of files at once, rather than list each one individually. Unfortunately, the asterisk isn't supported for picking cached files, because the creators of HTML5 were concerned that careless web developers might try to cache entire mammoth websites.

Adding Fallbacks

Using a manifest, you tell the browser which files to cache and, using the network section, which files to always get from the Web and *never* cache. Manifests also support one more trick: a fallback section that lets you swap one file for another, depending on whether the computer is online or offline.

To create a fallback section, start with the FALLBACK: title, which you can place anywhere in your manifest. Then, list files in pairs on a single line. The first file name is the file to use when online; the second file name is the offline fallback:

```
FALLBACK:
PersonalityScore.html PersonalityScore_offline.html
```

The web browser will download the fallback file (in this case, that's *PersonalityScore_offline.html*) and add it to the cache. However, the browser won't use the fallback file unless the computer is offline. While it's online, the browser will request the other file (in this case, *PersonalityScore.html*) directly from the web server.

> **NOTE** Remember, you don't have to be disconnected from the Web to be "offline" with respect to a web application. The important detail is whether the web domain is accessible—if it doesn't respond, for any reason, that web application is considered to be offline.

There are plenty of reasons to use a fallback. For example, you might want to substitute a simpler page when offline, a page that doesn't use the same scripts, or smaller resources. You can put the fallback section wherever you want, so long as it's preceded by the section title:

```
CACHE MANIFEST
PersonalityTest.html
PersonalityTest_Score.html

PersonalityTest.css
```

```
FALLBACK:
PersonalityScore.html PersonalityScore_offline.html
Images/emotional_bear.jpg Images/emotional_bear_small.jpg
PersonalityTest.js PersonalityTest_offline.js

NETWORK:
*
```

NOTE Incidentally, the files that you want to cache are part of the CACHE : section in the manifest. You can add the section title if you want, but you don't need it unless you want to list files after one of the other sections.

The fallback section also supports wildcard matching. This feature lets you create a built-in error page, like this:

```
FALLBACK:
/ offline.html
```

This line tells the browser to use the fallback for *any* file that isn't in the cache.

Now imagine someone attempts to request a page that's in the same website as the offline application, but isn't in the cache. If the computer is online, the web browser tries to contact the web server and get the real page. But if the computer is offline, or if the website is unreachable, or if the requested page quite simply doesn't exist, the web browser shows the cached *offline.html* page instead (Figure 11-4).

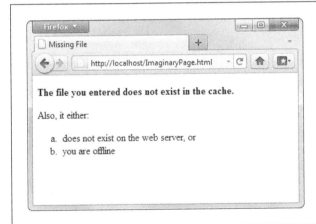

FIGURE 11-4

Here the page ImaginaryPage.html *doesn't exist. Interestingly, the browser doesn't update the address bar, so the visitor has no way of knowing the exact name of the error page.*

The previous example used the somewhat arbitrary convention of using a single forward slash character (/) to represent any page. That might strike you as a bit odd, considering that the network section uses the asterisk wildcard character for much the same purpose. (And some browsers, like Firefox, do allow you to substitute an asterisk for the slash.) You're simply looking at one more harmless HTML5 quirk.

Incidentally, you can write more targeted fallbacks that still use the slash to match all the files in a specific subfolder, like this:

```
FALLBACK:
/paint_app/ offline.html
```

How to Bypass the Cache When You're Online

When you load up a cached page, the browser expects to find everything in the cache. It doesn't matter whether you're online or offline. The browser prefers the cache and expects to use it for everything, aside from the files you've explicitly identified in the NETWORK: section.

This behavior is straightforward, but it's also frustratingly inflexible. The chief problem happens in situations where you would *prefer* to use the online version of a page, but you still want to have the cached copy ready if you can't connect to the network. For example, think of the front page of a news site. If you're online, it makes sense to grab the latest copy of the front page every time you visit it. But if you're offline, the most recently cached page would still be helpful. The standard caching system doesn't allow for this scenario, because it forces you to choose between caching *always* and caching *never*.

In the eleventh hour of the HTML5 standardization process, a new idea slipped in that offers the solution. The trick is to add a new section, called SETTINGS:, with the following information:

```
SETTINGS:
prefer-online
```

This tells the browser to try and get resources from the network if possible, but to use the cached version if that request fails.

Although this quick fix seems ideal, it raises several problems of its own. It's an all-or-nothing setting that applies to *every* page and resource (not just the files you choose). It guarantees that the cache won't be as fast in offline mode, because the browser will waste at least some time trying to contact the web server. But the biggest drawback is that, at the time of this writing, only Firefox respects the prefer-online setting. Other browsers simply ignore it and carry on using the cache in the normal way.

Checking the Connection

The fallback section is the secret to a handy JavaScript trick that lets you determine whether the browser is currently online. If you're an old-hand JavaScript developer, you probably know about the navigator.onLine property, which provides a slightly unreliable way to check whether the browser is currently online. The problem is that the onLine property really reflects the state of the browser's "work offline" setting, not the actual presence of an Internet connection. And even if the onLine property were a more reliable indicator of connectivity, it still wouldn't tell you whether the browser failed to contact the web server or whether it failed to download the web page for some other reason.

The solution is to use a fallback that loads different versions of the same JavaScript function, depending on whether the application is online or offline. Here's how you write the fallback section:

```
FALLBACK:
online.js offline.js
```

The original version of the web page refers to the *online.js* JavaScript file:

```
<!DOCTYPE html>
<html lang="en" manifest="personality.manifest">
<head>
  <meta charset="utf-8">
  <title>...</title>
  <script src="online.js"></script>
  ...
```

It contains this very simple function:

```
function isSiteOnline() {
  return true;

}
```

But if the *online.js* file can't be accessed, the browser substitutes the *offline.js* file, which contains a method with the same name but a different result:

```
function isSiteOnline() {
  return false;

}
```

In your original page, whenever you need to know the status of your application, check with the isSiteOnline() function:

```
var displayStatus = document.getElementById("displayStatus");
if (isSiteOnline()) {
  // (It's safe to run tasks that require network connectivity, like
  // contacting the web server through XMLHttpRequest.)
  displayStatus.innerHTML = "You are connected and the web server is online.";
}
else {
  // (The application is running offline. You may want to hide or
  // programmatically change some content, or disable certain features.)
  displayStatus.innerHTML = "You are running this application offline.";
}
```

Pointing Out Updates with JavaScript

You can interact with the offline application feature using a relatively limited JavaScript interface. It all revolves around an object called applicationCache.

The applicationCache object provides a status property that indicates whether the browser is checking for an updated manifest, downloading new files, or doing something else. This property changes frequently and is nearly as useful as the complementary events (listed in Table 11-2), which fire as the applicationCache switches from one status to another.

TABLE 11-1 *Caching events*

EVENT	DESCRIPTION
onChecking	When the browser spots the manifest attribute in a web page, it fires this event and checks the web server for the corresponding manifest file.
onNoUpdate	If the browser has already downloaded the manifest, and the manifest hasn't changed, it fires this event and doesn't do anything further.
onDownloading	Before the browser begins downloading a manifest (and the pages it references), it fires this event. This occurs the first time it downloads the manifest files and during updates.
onProgress	During a download, the browser fires this event to periodically report its progress.
onCached	Signals the end of a first-time download for a new offline application. No further events occur after that happens.
onUpdateReady	Signals the end of a download that retrieved updated content. At this point, the new content is ready to use, but it won't appear in the browser window until the page is reloaded. No further events occur after that happens.
onError	Something went wrong somewhere along the process. The web server might not be reachable (in which case the page will have switched into offline mode), the manifest might have invalid syntax, or a cached resource might not be available. If this event occurs, no more follow.
onObsolete	While checking for an update, the browser discovered that the manifest no longer exists. It then clears the cache. The next time the page is loaded, the browser will get the live, latest version from the web server.

Figure 11-5 shows how these events unfold when you request a cached page.

The most useful event is onUpdateReady, which signals that a new version of the application has been downloaded. Even though the new version is ready for use, the old version of the page has already been loaded into the browser. You may want to inform the visitor of the change, in much the same way that a desktop application does when it downloads a new update:

```
<script>
window.onload = function() {

  // Attach the function that handles the onUpdateReady event.
  applicationCache.onupdateready = function() {
    var displayStatus = document.getElementById("displayStatus");
    displayStatus.innerHTML = "There is a new version of this application. " +
      "To load it, refresh the page.";
  }
}
</script>
```

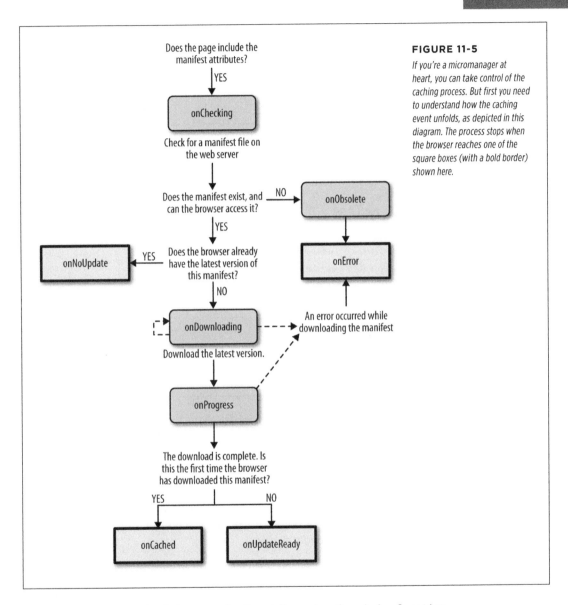

FIGURE 11-5

If you're a micromanager at heart, you can take control of the caching process. But first you need to understand how the caching event unfolds, as depicted in this diagram. The process stops when the browser reaches one of the square boxes (with a bold border) shown here.

Or, you can offer to reload the page *for* the visitor using the window.location. reload() method:

```
<script>
window.onload = function() {

  applicationCache.onupdateready = function() {
```

```
    if (confirm(
      "A new version of this application is available. Reload now?")) {
        window.location.reload();
      }
    }
  }
</script>
```

Figure 11-6 shows this code at work.

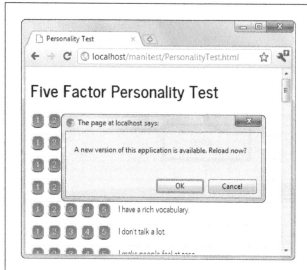

Five Factor Personality Test

The page at localhost says:

A new version of this application is available. Reload now?

OK   Cancel

I have a rich vocabulary.

I don't talk a lot.

FIGURE 11-6

Here, the application offers to reload itself with the newly downloaded content, if the visitor clicks OK. (Otherwise, the new content will appear the next time the page is loaded or refreshed.)

The applicationCache also provides two methods for more specialized scenarios. First is the confusingly named update() method, which simply checks for a new manifest. If one exists, it starts the download process in the background. Otherwise, it does nothing more.

Although browsers check for updates automatically, you can call update() if you think the manifest has changed since the user first loaded the page. This method might be important in a very long-lived web application—for example, one that users leave open on the same page, all day.

The second method is swapCache(), which tells the browser to start using the newly cached content, if it has just downloaded an update. However, swapCache() doesn't change the page that's currently on display—for that, you need a reload. So what good is swapCache()? Well, by changing over to the new cache, anything that you load from that point on—say, a dynamically loaded image—comes from the new cache, not the old one. If managed carefully, swapCache() could give your page a way to get access to new content without forcing a complete page reload (and potentially resetting the current application to its initial state). But in most applications, swapCache() is more trouble than it's worth, and it can cause subtle bugs by mixing old and new bits of the cache.

Communicating with the Web Server

W hen you started your journey with HTML5, you began with its markup-based features, like semantic elements, web forms, and video. But as you progressed through this book, you slowly shifted your focus to web page *programming* and the JavaScript-powered parts of HTML5. Now you're about to dip your toe into a few HTML5 features that take web page programming to the next level. They not only require JavaScript code but also some *server-side code*—code that runs on the web server, in whatever server-side programming language you want to use.

Adding a server-side language to the mix poses a bit of a problem. On one hand, it doesn't matter what server-side programming language you pick, as long as it can work with pure HTML5 pages (and they all can). On the other hand, there's not much point in getting knee-deep learning a technology that you don't plan to use or that your web host doesn't support. And there's no shortage of good choices for server-side programming, including PHP, ASP.NET, Ruby, Java, Python, and many more.

This chapter tackles the problem by using a small amount of very simple server-side code. It's just enough to round out each example and to let you test the HTML5 part of the equation (that's the JavaScript code in the web page). In your websites, you'll need to change and extend this server-side code, depending on what you're trying to accomplish and which server-side language you prefer.

So what are these features that require server-side interaction? HTML5 provides two new ways for your web pages to talk with a web server. The first feature is *server-sent events*, which lets the web server call up your page and pass it information at periodic intervals. The second feature is the much more ambitious *web sockets* framework, which lets browsers and web servers carry out a freewheeling back-and-forth conversation. But before you explore either of these, you'll start with a review of the current-day tool for web server communication: the XMLHttpRequest object.

NOTE Server-sent events and web sockets seem deceptively simple. It's easy enough to learn how they work and to create a very basic example (as in this chapter). But building on that to create something that will work securely and reliably on a professional website, and provide the sort of features you want, is an entirely different matter. The bottom line is this: To implement these features in your website, you'll probably need to get the help of someone with serious server-side programming experience.

■ Sending Messages to the Web Server

Before you can understand the new server communication features in HTML5, you need to understand the situation that web pages were in before. That means exploring XMLHttpRequest—the indispensable JavaScript object that lets a web page talk to its web server. If you already know about XMLHttpRequest (and are using it in your own pages), feel free to skip over this section. But if your web page design career so far consists of more traditional web pages, keep reading to get the essentials.

UP TO SPEED

The History of Web Server Involvement

In the early days of the Web, communicating with a web server was a straightforward and unexciting affair. A browser would simply ask for a web page, and the web server would send it back. That was that.

A little bit later, software companies began to get clever. They devised web server tools that could get in between the first step (requesting the page) and the second step (sending the page), by running some sort of code on the web server. The idea was to change the page dynamically—for example, by inserting a block of markup in the middle of it. Sometimes code would even create a new page from scratch—for example, by reading a record in a database and generating a tailor-made HTML page with product details.

And then web developers got even more ambitious, and wanted to build pages that were more interactive. The server-side programming tools could handle this, with a bit of juggling, as long as the web browser was willing to refresh the page. For example, if you wanted to add a product to your

ecommerce shopping cart, you would click a button that would submit the current page (using web forms; see Chapter 4) and ask for a new one. The web server could then send back the same page or a different page (for example, one that shows the contents of the shopping cart). This strategy was wildly successful, and just a bit clunky.

Then web developers got ambitious again. They wanted a way to build slick web applications (like email programs) without constantly posting back the page and regenerating everything from scratch. The solution was a set of techniques that are sometimes called Ajax, but almost always revolve around a special JavaScript object called XMLHttpRequest. This object lets web pages contact the web server, send some data, and get a response, without posting or refreshing anything. That clears the way for JavaScript to handle every aspect of the page experience, including updating content. It also makes web pages seem slicker and more responsive.

The XMLHttpRequest Object

The chief tool that lets a web page speak to a web server is the XMLHttpRequest object. The XMLHttpRequest object was originally created by Microsoft to improve the web version of its Outlook email program, but it steadily spread to every modern browser. Today, it's a fundamental part of most modern web applications.

The basic idea behind XMLHttpRequest is that it lets your JavaScript code make a web request on its own, whenever you need some more data. This web request takes place *asynchronously*, which means the web page stays responsive even while the request is under way. In fact, the visitor never knows that there's a web request taking place behind the scenes (unless you add a message or some sort of progress indicator to your page).

The XMLHttpRequest object is the perfect tool when you need to get some sort of data from the web server. Here are some examples:

- **Data that's stored on the web server.** This information might be in a file or, more commonly, a database. For example, you might want a product or customer record.

- **Data that only the web server can calculate.** For example, you might have a piece of server-side code that performs a complex calculation. You could try to perform the same calculation in JavaScript, but that might not be appropriate—for example, JavaScript might not have the mathematical smarts you need, or it might not have access to some of the data the calculation involves. Or your code might be super-sensitive, meaning you need to hide it from prying eyes or potential tamperers. Or the calculation might be so intensive that it's unlikely a desktop computer could calculate it as quickly as a high-powered web server. In all these cases, it makes sense to do the calculation on the web server.

- **Data that's on someone else's web server.** Your web page can't access someone else's web server directly. However, you can call a program on your web server (using XMLHttpRequest), and that program can then call the other web server, get the data, and return it to you.

The best way to really understand XMLHttpRequest is to start playing with it. In the following sections, you'll see two straightforward examples.

Asking the Web Server a Question

Figure 12-1 shows a web page that asks the web server to perform a straightforward mathematical calculation. The message is sent through the XMLHttpRequest object.

Before you can create this page, you need some sort of server-side script that will run, process the information you send it (in this case, that's the two typed-in numbers), and then send back a result. This trick is possible in every server-side programming language ever created (after all, sending back a single scrap of text is easier than sending a complete HTML document). This example uses a PHP script, largely because PHP is relatively simple and supported by almost all web hosting companies.

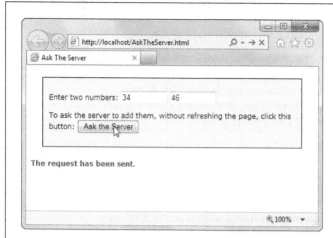

FIGURE 12-1

Click the "Ask the Server" button, and this web page creates an XMLHttpRequest object and sends the two numbers to the web server. The web server runs a simple script to calculate the answer and then returns the result (shown later, in Figure 12-2).

CREATING THE SCRIPT

To create a PHP script, you first create a new text file. Inside that text file, you start by adding the funny-looking codes shown here, which delineate the beginning and end of your script:

```php
<?php
  // (Code goes here.)
?>
```

In this example the code is straightforward. Here's the complete script:

```php
<?php
  $num1 = $_GET['number1'];
  $num2 = $_GET['number2'];
  $sum = $num1 + $num2
  echo($sum);
?>
```

Even if you aren't a PHP expert, you probably have a pretty good idea of what this code does just by looking over it. The first order of business is to retrieve the two numbers that the web page will have sent:

```php
  $num1 = $_GET['number1'];
  $num2 = $_GET['number2'];
```

The $ symbol indicates a variable, so this code creates a variable named $num1 and another named $num2. To set the variables, the code pulls a piece of information out of a built-in collection named $_GET. The $_GET collection holds all the information from the URL that was used to request the script.

For example, if you place the PHP script in a file named *WebCalculator.php*, a web request might look like this:

```
http://www.magicXMLHttpRequest.com/WebCalculator.php?number1=34&number2=46
```

Here, the URL holds two pieces of information tacked onto the end, in the URL section known as the *query string*. (The code is easier to interpret with a bit of extra spacing for illustrative purposes, as shown here. In real life, browsers don't let you use URLs with spaces.)

```
http://www.magicXMLHttpRequest.com/WebCalculator.php ? number1=34 & number2=46
```

First, the query string has a value named number1, which is set to 34. Next is a value named number2, which is set to 46. The question mark (?) denotes the start of the query string, and the ampersand symbol (&) separates each value from the one that precedes it (unless you have just a single value in your query string, in which case you don't need it). When the PHP engine fires up, it retrieves the query string values and stuffs them into the $_GET collection so your code can access them. (Most server-side programming platforms support a model like this. For example, in Microsoft's ASP.NET framework, you can access the same information through the Request.QueryString collection.)

NOTE HTML veterans know that there are two ways to send data to a web server—through the query string, or by posting it in the body of the request message. With either technique, the data is encoded in the same way, and it's accessed in the web server in a similar way as well. For example, PHP has a $_POST collection that provides access to any posted data.

Once the PHP script has the two numbers in hand, it simply needs to add them together and store the result in a new variable. Here, that new variable is named $sum:

```
$sum = $num1 + $num2
```

The last step is to send the result back to the web page that's making the request. You could package the result in a scrap of HTML markup or even some data-friendly XML. But that's overkill in this example, since plain text does just fine. But no matter what you choose, sending the data back is simply a matter of using PHP's echo command:

```
echo($sum);
```

Altogether, this script contains a mere four lines of PHP code. However, it's enough to establish the basic pattern: The web page asks a question, and the web server returns a result.

NOTE Could you write this page entirely in JavaScript, so that it performs its work in the browser, with no web server request? Of course. But the actual calculation isn't important. The PHP script shown here is an example that stands in for *any* server task you want to perform. You could make the PHP script as complex as you like, but the basic exchange of data will stay the same.

■ CALLING THE WEB SERVER

The second step is to build the page that uses the PHP script, with the help of XML-HttpRequest. It all starts out simply enough. At the beginning of the script code, an XMLHttpRequest object is created, so it will be available in all your functions:

```
var req = new XMLHttpRequest();
```

When the user clicks the "Ask the Server" button, it calls a function named askServer():

```
<div>
  <p>Enter two numbers:
    <input id="number1" type="number">
    <input id="number2" type="number">
  </p>
  <p>To ask the server to add them, without refreshing the page, click
  this button:<button onclick="askServer()">Ask the Server</button>
  </p>
</div>
<p id="result"></p>
```

Here's where the real work takes place. The askServer() function uses the XML-HttpRequest object to make its behind-the-scenes request. First, it gathers the data it needs—two numbers, which are in the text boxes in the form:

```
function askServer() {
  var number1 = document.getElementById("number1").value;
  var number2 = document.getElementById("number2").value;
```

Then it uses this data to build a proper query string, using the format you saw earlier:

```
var dataToSend = "?number1=" + number1 + "&number2=" + number2;
```

Now it's ready to prepare the request. The open() method of the XMLHttpRequest starts you out. It takes the type of HTTP operation (GET or POST), the URL you're using to make your request, and a true or false value that tells the browser whether to do its work asynchronously:

```
req.open("GET", "WebCalculator.php" + dataToSend, true);
```

> **NOTE** Web experts agree unanimously—the final argument of the open() method should *always* be true, which enables asynchronous use. That's because no website is completely reliable, and a synchronous request (a request that forces your code to stop and wait) could crash your whole web page while it's waiting for a response.

Before actually sending the request, you need to make sure you have a function wired up to the event of the XMLHttpRequest object's onReadyStateChange event. This event is triggered when the server sends back any information, including the final response when its work is done. Here, the code links the event to another function in the page, named handleServerResponse():

```
req.onreadystatechange = handleServerResponse;
```

Now you can start the process with the XMLHttpRequest object's send() method. Just remember, your code carries on without any delay. The only way to read the response is through the onReadyStateChange event, which may be triggered later on:

```
req.send();

document.getElementById("result").innerHTML = "The request has been sent.";
}
```

When the onReadyStateChange event occurs and you receive a response, you need to immediately check two XMLHttpRequest properties. First, you need to look at readyState, a number that travels from 0 to 4 as the request is initialized (1), sent (2), partially received (3), and then complete (4). Unless readyState is 4, there's no point continuing. Next, you need to look at status, which provides the HTTP status code. Here, you're looking for a result of 200, which indicates that everything is OK. You'll get a different value if you attempt to request a page that's not allowed (401), wasn't found (404), has moved (302), or is too busy (503), among many others. (See *www.addedbytes.com/for-beginners/http-status-codes* for a full list.)

Here's how the current example checks for these two details:

```
function handleServerResponse() {
    if ((req.readyState == 4) && (req.status == 200)) {
```

If those criteria are met, you can retrieve the result from the responseText property. In this case, the response is the new sum. The code then displays the answer on the page (Figure 12-2):

```
var result = req.responseText;
document.getElementById("result").innerHTML = "The answer is: " +
  result + ".";
    }
}
```

The XMLHttpRequest object doesn't make any assumptions about the type of data you're requesting. The name of the object has XML in it because it was originally designed with XML data in mind, simply because XML is a convenient, logical package for parceling up structured information. However, XMLHttpRequest is also used with requests for simple text (as in this example), JSON data (page 329), HTML (as in the next example), and XML. In fact, non-XML uses are now *more* common than XML uses, so don't let the object name fool you.

TIP You need to put your web pages on a test web server before you can use any server-side code, including PHP scripts. To run the example pages in this chapter without the frustration, visit the try-out site at *http://prosetech.com/html5*.

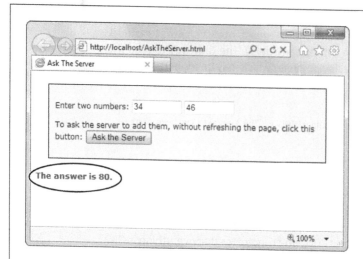

FIGURE 12-2

The web server has returned a response, triggering a JavaScript function, which changed the page.

Getting New Content

Another scenario where XMLHttpRequest comes in handy is loading new HTML content into a page. For example, a news article might contain multiple pictures but show just one at a time. You click a button, and some JavaScript fetches the content for the next picture and inserts it in the page. Or a page might use the same technique to show the slides in a top-five or top-10 list. Figure 12-3 shows a slideshow example that shows a series of captioned pictures that accompany an article.

There are a number of reasons to use a design like the one shown in Figure 12-3. Done skillfully, this technique can be a great way to tame huge amounts of content, so it's readily available but not immediately overwhelming. (In less capable hands, it's just a desperate attempt to boost page views by forcing readers to make multiple requests to get all the content they want.)

The best way to design this sort of page is with the XMLHttpRequest object. That way, the page can request new content and update the page without triggering a full refresh. And full refreshes are bad, because they download extra data, cause the page to flicker, and scroll the user back to the top. All of these details seem minor, but they make the difference between a website that feels slick and seamless, and one that seems hopelessly clunky and out of date.

FIGURE 12-3

This page splits its content into separate slides. Click the Previous or Next link to load in a new slide, with different text content and a new picture. To make this work, the page uses the XMLHttpRequest *object to request the new content as it's needed.*

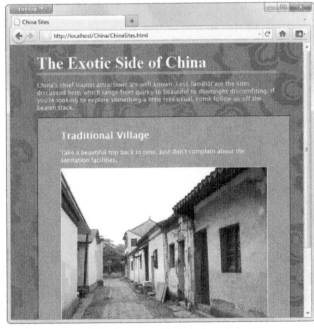

To build the example in Figure 12-3, you first need to carve out a spot for the dynamic content. Here it's a <div> element that creates a golden box and has two links underneath:

```
<div id="slide">Click Next to start the show.</div>
<a onclick="return previousSlide()" href="#">&lt; Previous</a> 
<a onclick="return nextSlide()" href="#">Next &gt;</a>
```

The links call previousSlide() or nextSlide(), depending on whether the visitor is traveling forward or backward in the list of sites. Both functions increment a counter that starts at 0, moves up to 5, and then loops back to 1. Here's the code for the nextSlide() function:

```
var slideNumber = 0;

function nextSlide() {
  // Move the slide index ahead.
  if (slideNumber == 5) {
    slideNumber = 1;
  } else {
    slideNumber += 1;
  }

  // Call another function that shows the slide.
  goToNewSlide();

  // Make sure the link doesn't actually do anything (like attempt
  // to navigate to a new page).
  return false;
}
```

And here's the very similar code for previousSlide():

```
function previousSlide() {
  if (slideNumber == 1) {
    slideNumber = 5;
  } else {
    slideNumber -= 1;
  }

  goToNewSlide();
  return false;
}
```

Both functions rely on another function, goToNewSlide(), which does the real work. It uses XMLHttpRequest to contact the web server and ask for the new chunk of data.

The real question: Where does the *ChinaSites.html* page get its data from? Sophisticated examples might call some sort of web service or PHP script. The new content could be generated on the fly or pulled out of a database. But this example uses a low-tech solution that works on any web server—it looks for a file with a specific name. For example, the file with the first slide is named *ChinaSites1_slide.html*, the file with the second is *ChinaSites2_slide.html*, and so on. Each file contains a scrap of HTML markup (not an entire page). For example, here's the content in *China-Sites5_slide.html*:

```
<figure>
  <h2>Wishing Tree</h2>
  <figcaption>Make a wish and toss a red ribbon up into the branches
  of this tree. If it sticks, good fortune may await.</figcaption>
  <img src="wishing_tree.jpg">
</figure>
```

Now that you know where the data is stored, it's easy enough to create an XMLHttpRequest that grabs the right file. A simple line of code can generate the right file name using the current counter value. Here's the goToNewSlide() function that does it:

```
var req = new XMLHttpRequest();

function goToNewSlide() {
  if (req != null) {
    // Prepare a request for the file with the slide data.
    req.open("GET", "ChinaSites" + slideNumber + "_slide" + ".html", true);
    // Set the function that will handle the slide data.
    req.onreadystatechange = newSlideReceived;

    // Send the request.
    req.send();
  }
}
```

The last step is to copy the retrieved data in the <div> that represents the current slide:

```
function newSlideReceived() {
  if ((req.readyState == 4) && (req.status == 200)) {
    document.getElementById("slide").innerHTML = req.responseText;
  }
}
```

> **TIP** To give this example a bit more pizzazz, you could create a transition effect. For example, the new picture could fade into view while the old one fades out of sight. All you need to do is alter the opacity property, either with a JavaScript timer (page 301) or a CSS3 transition (page 199). This is one of the advantages of dynamic pages that use XMLHttpRequest—they can control exactly how new content is presented.

This isn't the last you'll see of this example. In Chapter 13 (page 428), you'll use HTML5's history management to manage the web page's URL so that the URL changes to match the currently displayed slide. But for now, it's time to move on to two new ways to communicate with the web server.

> **NOTE** If you're using the popular jQuery JavaScript toolkit, you probably won't use XMLHttpRequest directly. Instead, you'll use jQuery methods, like jQuery.ajax(), which use XMLHttpRequest behind the scenes. The underlying technology remains the same, but jQuery streamlines the process.

■ Server-Sent Events

The XMLHttpRequest object lets your web page ask the web server a question and get an immediate answer. It's a one-for-one exchange—once the web server provides its response, the interaction is over. There's no way for the web server to wait a few minutes and send another message with an update.

However, there are some types of web pages that could use a longer-term web server relationship. For example, think of a stock quote on Google Finance (*www.google.com/finance*). When you leave that page open on your desktop, you'll see regular price updates appear automatically. Another example is a news ticker like the one at *www.bbc.co.uk/news*. Linger here, and you'll find that the list of headlines is updated throughout the day. You'll find similar magic bringing new messages into the inbox of any web-based mail program, like Microsoft Outlook.com (*www.outlook.com*).

In all these examples, the web page is using a technique called *polling*. Periodically (say, every few minutes), the page checks the web server for new data. To implement this sort of design, you use JavaScript's setInterval() or setTimeout() functions (see page 301), which trigger your code after a set amount of time.

Polling is a reasonable solution, but it's sometimes inefficient. In many cases, it means calling the web server and setting up a new connection, only to find out that there's no new data. Multiply this by hundreds or thousands of people using your website at once, and it can add up to an unnecessary strain on your web server.

One possible solution is *server-sent events*, which let a web page hold an open connection to the web server. The web server can send new messages at any time, and there's no need to continually disconnect, reconnect, and run the same server script from scratch. (Unless you want to, because server-sent events *also* support polling.) Best of all, the server-sent event system is simple to use, works on most web hosts, and is sturdily reliable. However, it's relatively new, as Table 12-1 attests, with no support in current versions of Internet Explorer.

> **NOTE** If you're looking for a polyfill that can fake server-sent event support using polling, there are several candidates worth checking out at *http://tinyurl.com/polyfills*.

TABLE 12-1 *Browser support for server-sent events*

	IE	FIREFOX	CHROME	SAFARI	OPERA	SAFARI IOS	CHROME FOR ANDROID
Minimum version	-	6	6	5	11	4	29

In the following sections, you'll put together a simple example that demonstrates server-sent events.

The Message Format

Unlike XMLHttpRequest, the server-sent events standard doesn't let you send just any data. Instead, you need to follow a simple but specific format. Every message must start with the text data: followed by the actual message text and the *new line* character sequence, which is represented as \n\n in many programming languages, including PHP.

Here's an example of what a line of message text looks like as it travels over the Internet:

data: The web server has sent you this message.**\n\n**

It's also acceptable to split a message over multiple lines. You use the end-of-line character sequence, which is often represented as a single \n. This makes it easier to send complex data:

data: The web server has sent you this message.**\n**
data: Hope you enjoy it.**\n\n**

You'll notice that you still need to start each line with data: and you still need to end the entire message with \n\n.

You could even use this technique to send JSON-encoded data (page 329), which would allow the web page to convert the text into an object in a single step:

data: {**\n**
data: "messageType": "statusUpdate",**\n**
data: "messageData": "Work in Progress"**\n**
data: }**\n\n**

Along with the message data, the web server can send a unique ID value (using the prefix id:) and a connection timeout (using retry:):

id: 495**\n**
retry: 15000**\n**
data: The web server has sent you this message.**\n\n**

Your web page pays attention to the message data, but it doesn't deal with the ID and connection timeout information. Instead, the *browser* uses these details. For example, after reading the above message, the browser knows that if it loses it connection to the web server, it should attempt to reconnect after 15,000 milliseconds (15 seconds). It should also send the ID number 495 to help the web server identify it.

> **NOTE** A web page can lose its connection to the web server for a variety of reasons, including a brief network outage or a proxy server that times out while waiting for data. If possible, the browser will attempt to reopen the connection automatically after waiting a default 3 seconds.

Sending Messages with a Server Script

Now that you know the message format, it's trivially easy to create some server-side code that spits it out. Once again, it makes sense to turn to PHP to build a straightforward example that virtually all web hosts will support. Figure 12-4 shows a page that gets regular messages from the server. In this case, the messages are simple—they contain the current time on the web server.

FIGURE 12-4

When this page is listening, it receives a steady stream of messages from the web server—approximately one every 2 seconds. Each message is added to the scrolling list at the top, and the time display at the bottom shows the time received from the most recent message.

> **NOTE** The web server time is a single piece of information that's continuously updated. That makes it a good candidate for creating a simple server-side event demonstration like this one. However, in a real example, you're more likely to send something more valuable, like the most up-to-date headlines for a news ticker.

The server-side part of this example simply reports the time, in regular intervals. Here's the complete script, at a glance:

```php
<?php
  header('Content-Type: text/event-stream');
  header('Cache-Control: no-cache');
  ob_end_clean();

  // Start a loop that goes forever.
  do {
    // Get the current time.
    $currentTime = date('h:i:s', time());

    // Send it in a message.
    echo 'data: ' . $currentTime . PHP_EOL;
    echo PHP_EOL;

    flush();

    // Wait 2 seconds before creating a new message.
    sleep(2);
  } while(true);
?>
```

The beginning of this script sets two important headers. First, it sets the MIME type to text/event-stream, which is required by the server-side event standard:

```php
header('Content-Type: text/event-stream');
```

Then, it tells the web server (and any proxy servers) to turn off web caching. Otherwise, it's possible that some of the time messages will arrive in uneven batches:

```php
header('Cache-Control: no-cache');
```

There's one more step needed to turn off PHP's built-in buffering system. This way, the data your PHP script returns is delivered to the browser immediately.

```php
ob_end_clean();
```

The rest of the code is wrapped in a loop that continues indefinitely (or at least until the client disappears). Each time the loop runs, it uses the built-in time() function to grab the current time (in the format *hours:minutes:seconds*), and it stuffs that into a variable:

```php
$currentTime = date('h:i:s', time());
```

Next, the loop uses this information to build a message in the proper format, which it sends using PHP's trusty echo command. In this example, the message is single line, starting with data: and followed by the time. It ends with the constant PHP_EOL (for PHP *end of line*), which is a shorthand way of referring to the \n character sequence described earlier:

```
echo 'data: ' . $currentTime . PHP_EOL;
echo PHP_EOL;
```

NOTE If this looks funny, it's probably because PHP uses the dot operator (.) to join strings. It works in the same way as the + operator with text in JavaScript, only there's no way to accidentally confuse it with numeric addition.

The flush() function makes sure the data is sent right away, rather than buffered until the PHP code is complete. Finally, the code uses the sleep() function to stall itself for 2 seconds before continuing with a new pass through the loop.

TIP If you wait a long time between messages, your connection might be cut off by a *proxy server* (a server that sits between your web server and the client's computer, directing traffic). To avoid this behavior, you can send a comment message every 15 seconds or so, which is simply a colon (:) with no text.

Processing Messages in a Web Page

The web page that listens to these messages is even simpler. Here's all the markup from the <body> section, which divides the pages into three <div> sections—one for the message list, one for the big time display, and one for the clickable buttons that start the whole process:

```
<div id="messageLog"></div>
<div id="timeDisplay"></div>
<div id="controls">
  <button onclick="startListening()">Start Listening</button><br>
  <button onclick="stopListening()">Stop Listening</button>
</div>
```

When the page loads, it looks up these messageLog and timeDisplay elements and stores them in global variables so they'll be easy to access in all your functions:

```
var messageLog;
var timeDisplay;

window.onload = function() {
  messageLog = document.getElementById("messageLog");
  timeDisplay = document.getElementById("timeDisplay");
};
```

The magic happens when someone clicks the Start Listening button. At this point, the code creates a new EventSource object, supplying the URL of the server-side resource that's going to send the messages. (In this example, that's a PHP script named *TimeEvents.php*.) It then attaches a function to the onMessage event, which fires whenever the page receives a message.

```
var source;

function startListening() {
  source = new EventSource("TimeEvents.php");
  source.onmessage = receiveMessage;
  messageLog.innerHTML += "<br>" + "Started listening for messages.";
}
```

TIP To check for server-side event support, you can test if the `window.EventSource` property exists. If it doesn't, you'll need to use your own fallback approach. For example, you could use the `XMLHttpRequest` object to make periodic calls to the web server to get data.

When `receiveMessage` is triggered, you can get the message from the `data` property of the event object. In this example, the data adds a new message in the message list and updates the large clock:

```
function receiveMessage(e) {
  messageLog.innerHTML += "<br>" + "New web server time received: " + e.data;
  timeDisplay.innerHTML = e.data;
}
```

You'll notice that once the message is delivered to your page, the pesky `data:` and `/n/n` details are stripped out, leaving you with just the content you want.

Finally, a page can choose to stop listening for server events at any time by calling the `close()` method of the `EventSource` object. It works like this:

```
function stopListening() {
  source.close();
  messageLog.innerHTML += "<br>" + "No longer listening for messages.";
}
```

Polling with Server-Side Events

The previous example used server-side events in the simplest way. The page makes a request, the connection stays open, and the server sends information periodically. The web browser may need to reconnect (which it will do automatically), but only if there's a problem with the connection or if it decides to temporarily stop the communication for other reasons (for example, low battery in a mobile device).

But what happens if the server script ends and the web server closes the connection? Interestingly, even though no accident occurred, and even though the server deliberately broke off communication, the web page still automatically reopens the connection (after waiting the default 3 seconds) and requests the script again, starting it over from scratch.

You can use this behavior to your advantage. For example, imagine that you create a relatively short server script that sends just one message. Now your web page acts like it's using polling (page 386), by periodically reestablishing the connection. The only difference is that the web server tells the browser how often it should check for new information. In a page that uses traditional polling, this detail is built into your JavaScript code.

The following script uses a hybrid approach. It stays connected (and sends periodic messages) for 1 minute. Then it recommends that the browser try again in 2 minutes and closes the connection:

```php
<?php
  header('Content-Type: text/event-stream');
  header('Cache-Control: no-cache');

  ob_end_clean();

  // Tell the browser to wait 2 minutes before reconnecting,
  // when the connection is closed.
  echo 'retry: 120000' . PHP_EOL;

  // Store the start time.
  $startTime = time();

  do {
    // Send a message.
    $currentTime = date('h:i:s', time());
    echo 'data: ' . $currentTime . PHP_EOL;
    echo PHP_EOL;
    flush();

    // If a minute has passed, end this script.
    if ((time() - $startTime) > 60) {
      die();
    }

    // Wait 5 seconds, and send a new message.
    sleep(5);
  } while(true);
?>
```

Now when you run the page, you'll get a minute's worth of regular updates, followed by a 2-minute pause (Figure 12-5). In a more sophisticated example, you might have the web server send a special message to the web browser that tells it there's no reason to wait for updated data (say, the stock markets have closed for the day). At this point, the web page could call the close() method of the EventSource object.

NOTE With complex server scripts, the web browser's automatic reconnection feature may not work out so well. For example, the connection may have been cut off while the web server was in the middle of a specific task. In this case, your web server code can send each client an ID (as described on page 387), which will be sent back to the server when the browser reconnects. However, it's up to your server-side code to generate a suitable ID, keep track of what task each ID is doing (for example, by storing some information in a database), and then attempt to pick up where you left off. All of these steps can be highly challenging if you lack super-black-belt coding skills.

FIGURE 12-5

This page uses a combination of streaming (for a batch of messages, over the course of a minute), followed by polling (for the next 2 minutes). This sort of design might make sense as a way to minimize web server traffic, depending on how often your data is updated and how important it is to have up-to-the-minute data.

Web Sockets

Server-sent events are a perfect tool if you want to receive a series of messages from the web server. But the communication is completely one-sided. There's no way for the browser to respond, or to enter into a more complex dialogue.

If you're creating a web application where the browser and the web server need to have a serious conversation, your best bet (without adopting Flash) is to use the XMLHttpRequest object. Depending on the sort of application you're building, this approach may work fine. However, there are stumbling blocks aplenty. First, the XMLHttpRequest object doesn't work well if you need to send multiple messages back and forth very quickly (like you might in a chat application, for example). Second, there's no way to associate one call with the next, so every time the web page makes a request, the web server needs to sort out who you are all over again. If your web page needs to make a chain of related requests, your web server code can become frightfully complicated.

There's a solution to these problems, but it's not for the faint of heart. That solution is *web sockets*, a standard that lets a browser hold open a connection to a web server and exchange back-and-forth messages for as long as it wants. The web sockets feature has generated plenty of excitement, and has gained reasonably good browser support (see Table 12-2), although Internet Explorer users need IE 10 or later to use it.

TABLE 12-2 *Browser support for web sockets*

	IE	FIREFOX	CHROME	SAFARI	OPERA	SAFARI IOS	CHROME FOR ANDROID
Minimum version	10	11	14	6	12.1	6	29

> **TIP** Web sockets are a bit finicky. For example, you could run a browser that supports them but still run into trouble because of restrictive computer network settings, a firewall, or the antivirus software on your computer. If you're in doubt about whether your computer can use web sockets, go to *http://websocketstest.com*. This site attempts to connect to a test server and provides a handy single-page report that tells you whether web sockets are working.

Before you use web sockets, you need to understand two important points. First, web sockets are a specialized tool. They make great sense in a chat application, a massive multiplayer game, or a peer-to-peer collaboration tool. They allow new types of applications, but they probably don't make sense in most of today's JavaScript-powered web applications (like ecommerce websites).

Second, web socket solutions can be fiendishly complex. The web page JavaScript is simple enough. But to build the server-side application, you'll need mad programming skills, including a good grasp of multithreading and networking concepts, which are beyond the scope of this book. However, if some other company, service, or hotshot programmer has already created a web socket server for you to use, you won't have too much trouble talking to it using a bit of HTML5-enhanced JavaScript. You'll learn how in the following sections.

The Web Socket Server

In order to use web sockets, you need to run a program (called a *web socket server*) on the web server for your website. This program has the responsibility of coordinating everyone's communication, and once it's launched it keeps running indefinitely.

> **NOTE** Many web hosts won't allow long-running programs, unless you pay for a *dedicated server* (a web server that's allocated to your website, and no one else's). If you're using ordinary shared hosting, you probably can't create web pages that use the web socket feature. Even if you can manage to launch a web socket server that keeps running, your web host will probably detect it and shut it down.

To give you an idea of the scope of a web socket server, consider some of the tasks a web socket server needs to manage:

- Set the message "vocabulary"—in other words, decide what types of messages are valid and what they mean.

- Keep a list of all the currently connected clients.

- Detect errors sending messages to clients, and stop trying to contact them if they don't seem to be there anymore.

- Deal with any in-memory data—that is, data that all web clients might access— safely. Subtle issues abound—for example, consider what happens if one client is trying to join the party while another is leaving, and the connection details for both are stored in the same in-memory object.

Most developers will never create a server-side program that uses sockets; it's simply not worth the considerable effort. The easiest approach is to install someone else's socket server and design custom web pages that use it. Because the JavaScript part of the web socket standard is easy to use, this method won't pose a problem. Another option is to pick up someone else's socket server code and then customize it to get the exact behavior you want. Right now, plenty of projects are developing usable web socket servers (many of them free and open source) for a variety of tasks, in a variety of server-side programming languages. You'll get the details on page 399.

A Simple Web Socket Client

From the web page's point of view, the web socket feature is easy to understand and use. The first step is to create the WebSocket object. When you do, you supply a URL that looks something like this:

```
var socket = new WebSocket("ws://localhost/socketServer.php");
```

The URL starts with *ws://*, which is the new system for identifying web socket connections. However, the URL still leads to a web application on a server (in this case, the script named socketServer.php). The web socket standard also supports URLs that start with wss://, which indicates that you want to use a secure, encrypted connection (just as you do when requesting a web page that starts with https:// instead of http://).

> **NOTE** Web sockets aren't limited to contacting their home web server. A web page can open a socket connection to a web socket server that's running on another web server, without any extra work.

Simply creating a new WebSocket object causes your page to attempt to connect to the server. You deal with what happens next using one of the WebSocket's four events: onOpen (when the connection is first established), onError (when there's a problem), onClose (when the connection is closed), and onMessage (when the page receives a message from the server):

```
socket.onopen = connectionOpen;
socket.onmessage = messageReceived;
socket.onerror = errorOccurred;
socket.onopen = connectionClosed;
```

For example, if the connection has succeeded, it makes sense to send a confirmation message. To deliver a message, you use the WebSocket object's send() method, which takes ordinary text. Here's a function that handles the onOpen event and sends a message:

```
function connectionOpen() {
  socket.send("UserName:jerryCradivo23@gmail.com");
}
```

Presumably, the web server will receive this and then send a new message back.

You can use the onError and onClose events to notify the web page user. However, the most important event (by far) is the onMessage event that fires every time the web server delivers new data. Once again, the JavaScript that's involved is perfectly understandable—you simply grab the text of the message from the data property:

```
function messageReceived(e) {
  alert("You received a message: " + e.data);
}
```

If the web page decides its work is done, it can easily close the connection with the close() method:

```
socket.close();
```

However, once the socket is closed, you can't send any more messages unless you recreate the socket object. Recreating the socket object is the same as creating it for the first time—you use the new keyword, supply the URL, and attach all your event handlers. If you plan to be connecting and disconnecting frequently, you'll want to move this code into separate functions so you can call on them when needed.

As you can see, the WebSocket object is surprisingly simple. In fact, you've now covered all the methods and events it offers. Based on this overview, you can see that using someone else's socket server is a breeze—you just need to know what messages to send and what messages to expect.

NOTE A lot of behind-the-scenes work takes place to make a web socket connection work. First, the web page makes contact using the well-worn HTTP standard. Then it needs to "upgrade" its connection to a web socket connection that allows unfettered back-and-forth communication. At this point, you could run into a problem if a proxy server sits between your computer and the web server (for example, on a typical company network). The proxy server may refuse to go along with the plan and drop the connection. You can deal with this problem by detecting the failed connection (through the WebSocket's onError event) and falling back on one of the socket polyfills described on GitHub at *http://tinyurl.com/polyfills*. They use tricks like polling to simulate a web socket connection as well as possible.

Web Socket Examples on the Web

Curious to try out web sockets for yourself? There are plenty of places on the web where you can fire up an example.

For starters, try *www.websocket.org/echo.html*, which features the most basic web socket server imaginable: You send a message, and it echoes the same message back to you (Figure 12-6). While this isn't very glamorous, it lets you exercise all the features of the WebSocket class. In fact, you can create your own pages that talk to the echo server, which is a good way to practice your web socket skills. As long as you use the correct socket server URL (in this case, that's *ws://echo.websocket. org*), the code works perfectly well. It doesn't matter whether the web page is on a different web domain or it's stored on your computer's hard drive.

It's easy to understand the JavaScript that powers a page like this. The first task is to create the socket when the page first loads and wire up all its events:

```
var socket;

window.onload = function () {
  connect();
}

function connect() {
  socket = new WebSocket("ws://echo.websocket.org")

  // Listen to all the web socket events.
  socket.onopen = connectionOpen;
  socket.onmessage = messageReceived;
  socket.onerror = errorOccurred;
  socket.onopen = connectionClosed;
}
```

Here, the socket-connection code is moved into its own dedicated function, named connect(), so you can call it whenever you need it. That way, you can connect and disconnect as you please. You've already seen the disconnection code:

```
function connect() {
  socket.close();
}
```

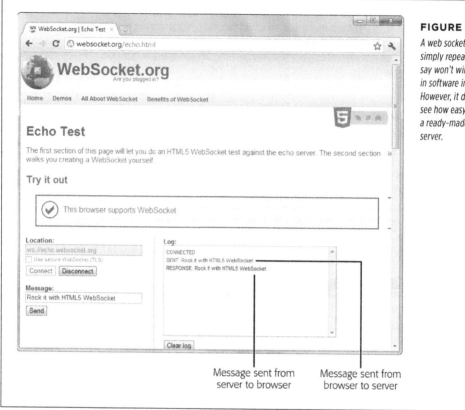

FIGURE 12-6

A web socket server that simply repeats what you say won't win any prizes in software innovation. However, it does let you see how easy it is to talk to a ready-made web socket server.

Message sent from server to browser

Message sent from browser to server

Incidentally, you can check the readyState property of your socket to determine whether it's open and ready to go (in which case readyState is 1), not yet established (0), in the process of closing (2), or closed (3).

The echo server has no real vocabulary to speak of. It treats all messages the same, as bits of text that it simply sends back to the page. Because of this simplicity, it's a simple job to send the current contents of a text box when the user clicks a button:

```
function sendMessage() {
  // Get the message data.
  var message = messageBox.value;

  // Send the message through the socket.
  socket.send(message);

  // Let the user know what just happened.
  messageLog.innerHTML += "<br>" + "Sent: " + message;
}
```

And it's just as easy to take the messages you receive and insert them into the page:

```
function messageReceived(e) {
  messageLog.innerHTML += "<br>" + "Message received: " + e.data;
}
```

> **NOTE** If you want to look at a slightly more exciting example, check out the chat free-for-all at *http://html5demos.com/web-socket*. Log in to this simple web socket server, send a message, and everyone gets it immediately.

Web Socket Servers

To actually run a practical example of your own, you need a web socket server that your web page can talk to. And although the server code that's required—which is several dozen lines at least—is beyond the scope of this chapter, there are plenty of places where you can find a test server. Here are some of your many options:

- **PHP.** This simple and slightly crude code project gives you a good starting point for building a web socket server with PHP. Get it at *http://code.google.com/p/phpwebsocket*.

- **Ruby.** There's more than one sample web socket server for Ruby, but this one that uses the Event-Machine model is popular. See *http://github.com/igrigorik/em-websocket*.

- **Python.** This Apache extension adds a socket server using Python. Get it at *http://code.google.com/p/pywebsocket*.

- **.NET.** Simple, it isn't. But this comprehensive project contains a complete web socket server that uses Microsoft's .NET platform and the C# language. Download it from *http://superwebsocket.codeplex.com*.

- **Java.** Similar in scope to the .NET project described above, this web socket server is pure Java. See *http://jwebsocket.org*.

- **node.JS.** Depending on who you ask, node.JS—a web server that runs JavaScript code—is either the next big thing in the making or an overgrown testing tool. Either way, you can get a web socket server that runs on it from *http://github.com/miksago/node-websocket-server*.

- **Kaazing.** Unlike the other items in this list, Kaazing doesn't provide the code for a web socket server. Instead, it provides a mature web socket server that you can license for your website. Adventurous developers who want to go it alone won't be interested. But it may make sense for less ambitious websites, especially considering the built-in fallback support in its client libraries (which try the HTML5 web socket standard first, then attempt to use Flash, or finally fall back to pure JavaScript polling). Learn more at *http://kaazing.com/products/html5-edition.html*.

Geolocation, Web Workers, and History Management

B y now, you know all about the key themes of HTML5. You've used it to write more meaningful and better-structured markup. You've seen its rich graphical features, like video and dynamic drawing. And you've used it to create self-sufficient, JavaScript-powered pages that can work even without a web connection.

In this chapter, you'll tackle three features that have escaped your attention so far. As with much of what you've already learned, these features extend the capabilities of what a web page can do—once you add a sprinkling of JavaScript code. Here's what awaits:

- **Geolocation.** Although it's often discussed as part of HTML5, geolocation is actually a separate standard that's never been in the hands of the WHATWG (page 5). Using geolocation, you can grab hold of a single piece of information: the geographic coordinates that pinpoint a web visitor's current location.

- **Web workers.** As web developers make smarter pages that run more JavaScript, it becomes more important to run certain tasks in the background, quietly, unobtrusively, and over long periods of time. You *could* use timers and other tricks. But the web workers feature provides a far more convenient solution for performing background work.

- **Session history.** In the old days of the Web, a page did one thing only: display stuff. As a result, people spent plenty of time clicking links to get from one document to another. But today, a JavaScript-fueled page can load content from another page without triggering a full page refresh. In this way, JavaScript creates a more seamless viewing experience. However, it also introduces a few wrinkles, like the challenge of keeping the browser URL synchronized with the current content. Web developers use plenty of advanced techniques to keep things in order, and now HTML5 adds a session history tool that can help.

> **NOTE** As you explore these last three features, you'll get a still better idea of the scope of what is now called HTML5. What started as a few good ideas wedged into an overly ambitious standard has grown to encompass a grab bag of new features that tackle a range of different problems, with just a few core concepts (like semantics, JavaScript, and CSS3) to hold it all together.

■ Geolocation

Geolocation is a feature that lets you find out where in the world your visitors are. And that doesn't just mean what country or city a person's in. The geolocation feature can often narrow someone's position down to a city block, or even determine the exact coordinates of someone who's strolling around with a smartphone.

> **NOTE** Most of the new JavaScript features you've seen in this book were part of the original HTML5 specification and were split off when it was handed over to the W3C. But geolocation isn't like that—it was never part of HTML5. Instead, it simply reached maturity around the same time. However, almost everyone now lumps them together as part of the wave of future web technologies.

How Geolocation Works

Geolocation raises quite a lot of questions in people who ordinarily aren't paranoid. Like, how does a piece of software know I'm hanging out at the local coffee shop? Is there some hidden code that's tracking my every move? And who's in that white van parked outside?

Fortunately, geolocation is a lot less Big Brotherish than it seems. That's because even if a browser can figure out your position, it won't tell a website unless you give it explicit permission (see Figure 13-1).

To figure out a person's location, the browser enlists the help of a *location provider*—for example, on Firefox that's Google Location Services. This location provider has the tough job of finding the location, and it can use several different strategies to do it.

For a desktop computer with a fixed (not wireless) Internet connection, the science is simple but imprecise. When someone goes online, her traffic is funneled from her computer or local network through a cable, telephone wire, or (horrors) dial-up connection, until it reaches a high-powered piece of network hardware that brings it onto the Internet. That piece of hardware has a unique *IP address*, a numeric code that establishes its public identity to other computers. It also has a postal address in the real world.

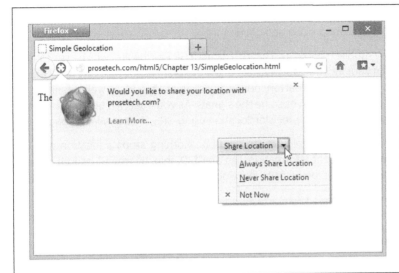

FIGURE 13-1

Here a web page wants location data, and Firefox asks whether you want to allow it just this once (click Share Location), to allow it every time (Always Share), or never to allow it (Never Share). This behavior isn't just Firefox being polite; the geolocation standard makes it an official rule to get user permission for every website that wants location data.

NOTE If you have some networking experience, you already know that your computer has its own IP address, like every computer on a network. However, this IP address is your own private one whose purpose is to separate your computer from any other devices that are sharing your connection (like the netbook in your kitchen or the tablet in your knapsack). Geolocation doesn't use that IP address.

The location provider combines these two features. First, it figures out the IP address you're connecting through, and then it pinpoints the home of the router that uses it. Because of this indirection, geolocation won't be spot-on when you're using a desktop computer. For example, if you surf from a computer on the west side of Chicago, you might find that your traffic is being funneled through a router that's several miles closer to downtown. Still, even an imprecise result like this is often useful. For example, if you're looking for nearby pizza stores in a mapping tool, you can quickly skip over to the area you're really interested in—your home neighborhood—even if you start a certain distance away.

NOTE The IP address technique is the roughest form of geolocation. If there's a better source of location data, the location provider will use that instead.

If you're using a laptop or a mobile device with a wireless connection, a location provider can look for nearby wireless access points. Ideally, the location provider consults a giant database to figure out the exact location of these access points and then uses that information to triangulate your location.

If you're using a web-enabled phone, the location provider provides a similar triangulation process, but it uses the signals from different cellphone towers. This quick, relatively effective procedure usually gets your position down to less than a kilometer. (More industrialized areas—like downtown city cores—have more cellphone towers, which results in more precise geolocation.)

Finally, many mobile devices also have dedicated GPS hardware, which uses satellite signals to pin your location down to just a few meters. The drawback is that GPS is a bit slower and draws more battery power. It also doesn't work as well in built-up cities, where tall buildings can obscure the signals. As you'll see, it's up to you whether you want to request a high-precision location using GPS, if it's available (page 409).

And of course, other techniques are possible. Nothing stops a location provider from relying on different information, like an RFID chip, nearby Bluetooth devices, a cookie set by a mapping website like Google Maps, and so on.

> **TIP** You may also be able to change your starting position by using another tool. For example, Chrome fans can use a browser plug-in named Manual Geolocation (*http://tinyurl.com/manual-geo*) to set the position that Chrome should report when you browse a website that uses geolocation. You can even use this technique to fake your address—for example, to pretend your computer in Iowa is actually surfing in from the Netherlands. This trick isn't for espionage only—it can also be a useful debugging trick when you're testing a location-aware web app.

The takeaway is this: No matter how you connect to the Internet—even if you're sitting at a desktop computer—geolocation can get somewhere near you. And if you're using a device that gets a cellphone signal or has a GPS chip, the geolocation coordinates will be scarily accurate.

How You Can Use Geolocation

Once you've answered the big question—how does geolocation work?—you need to resolve another one—namely, why should you use it?

The key point to understand is that geolocation tells your code the approximate geographic coordinates of a person—and that's it. You need to combine this simple but essential information with more detailed location data. This data could be provided by your web server (typically fetched out of a huge server-side database) or another geographic web service (like Google Maps).

For example, if you're a big business with a physical presence in the real world, you might compare the user's position with the coordinates of your different locations. You could then determine which location is closest. Or, if you're building some sort of social networking tool, you might plot the information of a group of people to show them how close they are to one another. Or you might take someone else's location data and use that to provide a service for your visitors, like hunting down the nearest chocolate store, or finding the closest clean toilet in Brooklyn. Either way, the geolocation coordinates of the visitor become important only when they're combined with more geographic data.

Although other businesses' mapping and geographic services are outside the scope of this chapter, you'll get the chance to try out an example with Google Maps on page 409.

Finding a Visitor's Coordinates

The geolocation feature is strikingly simple. It consists of three methods that are packed into the `navigator.geolocation` object: `getCurrentPosition()`, `watchPosition()`, and `clearWatch()`.

> **NOTE** If you aren't already familiar with the navigator object, it's a relatively minor part of JavaScript, with a few properties that tell you about the current browser and its capabilities. The most useful of these is `navigator.userAgent`, which provides an all-in-one string that details the browser, its version number, and the operating system on which it's running.

To get a web visitor's location, you call `getCurrentPosition()`. Of course, the location-finding process isn't instantaneous, and no browser wants to lock up a page while it's waiting for location data. For that reason, the `getCurrentPosition()` method is asynchronous—it carries on immediately, without stalling your code. When the geolocation process is finished, it triggers another piece of code to handle the results.

You might assume that geolocation uses an event to tell you when it's done, in much the same way that you react when an image has been loaded or a text file has been read. But JavaScript is nothing if not inconsistent. Instead, when you call `getCurrentPosition()` you supply the *completion function*.

Here's an example:

```
navigator.geolocation.getCurrentPosition(
  function(position) {
    alert("You were last spotted at (" + position.coords.latitude +
    "," + position.coords.longitude + ")");
  }
);
```

When this code runs, it calls `getCurrentPosition()` and passes in a function. Once the browser determines the location, it triggers that function, which shows a message box. Figure 13-2 shows the result in Internet Explorer.

To keep your code clear and organized, you probably won't define your completion function right inside the `getCurrentPosition()` call (as done in this example). Instead, you can put it in a separate, named function:

```
function geolocationSuccess(position) {
  alert("You were last spotted at (" + position.coords.latitude +
  "," + position.coords.longitude + ")");
}
```

Then you can point to it when you call `getCurrentLocation()`:

```
navigator.geolocation.getCurrentPosition(geolocationSuccess);
```

FIGURE 13-2

Top: First, you need to agree to let the browser tell the web server about your position.

Bottom: The results are in—your coordinates on the globe.

Remember, you need to use a browser that supports geolocation and let the web page track you. Also, it's a good idea to upload your page to a test server before trying it out. Otherwise, you'll see some quirks (for example, geolocation error-handling won't work) and some browsers will fail to detect your position altogether (like Chrome).

If you're wondering, "What good are geographic coordinates to me?" you've asked a good question. You'll explore how you can use the geolocation data shortly (page 409). But first, you should understand how to catch errors and configure a few geolocation settings.

Dealing with Errors

Geolocation doesn't run so smoothly if the visitor opts out and decides not to share the location data with your page. In the current example, the completion function won't be called at all, and your page won't have any way to tell whether the browser is still trying to dig up the data or has run into an error. To deal with this sort of situation, you supply two functions when you call getCurrentLocation(). The first function is called if your page meets with success, while the second is called if your geolocation attempt ends in failure.

Finding Out the Accuracy of a Geolocation Guess

When the getCurrentPosition() method meets with success, your code gets a position object that has two properties: timestamp (which records when the geolocation was performed) and coords (which indicates the geographic coordinates).

As you've seen, the coords object gives you the latitude and longitude—the coordinates that pin down your position on the globe. However, the coords object bundles up a bit more information that you haven't seen yet. For example, there are more specialized altitude, heading, and speed properties, none of which are currently supported by any browser.

More interesting is the accuracy property, which tells you how precise the geolocation information is, in meters. (Somewhat confusingly, that means the value of the accuracy property increases as the accuracy of the location data decreases.) For example, an accuracy of 2,135 meters converts to about 1.3 miles, meaning the geolocation coordinates have pinpointed the current visitor's position within that distance. To visualize this, imagine a circle with the center at the geolocation coordinates and a radius of 1.3 miles. Odds are the visitor is somewhere in that circle.

The accuracy property is useful for identifying bad geolocation results. For example, if you get an accuracy result that's tens of thousands of meters, then the location data isn't reliable:

```
if (position.coords.accuracy > 50000) {
  results.innerHTML =
    "This guess is all over the map.";
}
```

At this point, you might want to warn the user or offer him the chance to enter the right position information himself.

Here's an example that uses both a completion function and an error function:

```
// Store the element where the page displays the result.
var results;

window.onload = function() {
  results = document.getElementById("results");

  // If geolocation is available, try to get the visitor's position.
  if (navigator.geolocation) {
    navigator.geolocation.getCurrentPosition(
    geolocationSuccess, geolocationFailure
    );
    results.innerHTML = "The search has begun.";
  }
  else {
    results.innerHTML = "This browser doesn't support geolocation.";
  }
};
```

```
function geolocationSuccess(position) {
  results.innerHTML = "You were last spotted at (" +
   position.coords.latitude + "," + position.coords.longitude + ")";
}

function geolocationFailure(positionError) {
  results.innerHTML = "Geolocation failed.";
}
```

When the error function is called, the browser hands it an error object with two properties: code (a numeric code that classifies it as one of four types of problems) and message (which provides a short text message reporting the problem). Generally, the message is intended for testing, and your code will use the error code to decide how it should handle the issue.

Here's a revised error function that checks all possible error code values:

```
function geolocationFailure(positionError) {
  if (positionError.code == 1) {
    results.innerHTML =
      "You decided not to share, but that's OK. We won't ask again.";
  }
  else if (positionError.code == 2) {
    results.innerHTML =
      "The network is down or the positioning service can't be reached.";
  }
  else if (positionError.code == 3) {
    results.innerHTML =
      "The attempt timed out before it could get the location data.";
  }
  else {
    results.innerHTML =
      "This the mystery error. We don't know what happened.";
  }
}
```

> **NOTE** If you're running the test web page from your computer (not a real web server), the error function won't be triggered when you decline to share your location.

Setting Geolocation Options

So far, you've seen how to call getCurrentLocation() with two arguments: the success function and the failure function. You can also supply a third argument, which is an object that sets certain geolocation options.

Currently, there are three options you can set, and each one corresponds to a different property on the geolocation options object. You can set just one or any combination. Here's an example that sets one, named enableHighAccuracy:

```
navigator.geolocation.getCurrentPosition(geolocationSuccess,
    geolocationFailure, {enableHighAccuracy: true});
```

And here's an example that sets all three:

```
navigator.geolocation.getCurrentPosition(
    geolocationSuccess, geolocationFailure, {enableHighAccuracy: true,
    timeout: 10000,
    maximumAge: 60000}
);
```

Both of these examples supply the geolocation options using a JavaScript object literal. This technique works perfectly as long as you use the right property names, such as enableHighAccuracy and timeout, because these are the properties that the getCurrentPosition() method is expecting. (If this code still looks a bit weird to you, check out the more detailed object introduction on page 468 in Appendix B, "JavaScript: The Brains of Your Page.")

So what do these properties mean? The enableHighAccuracy property opts into high-precision GPS-based location detection, if the device supports it (and the user allows it). Don't choose this option unless you need exact coordinates, because it can draw serious battery juice and may take more time. The default for enableHighAccuracy, should you choose not to set it, is false.

The timeout property sets the amount of time your page is willing to wait for location data before throwing in the towel. The timeout is in milliseconds, so a value of 10,000 milliseconds means a maximum wait of 10 seconds. The countdown begins *after* the user agrees to share the location data. By default, timeout is 0, meaning the page will wait indefinitely, without ever triggering the timeout error.

The maximumAge property lets you use cached location data. For example, if you set maximumAge to 60,000 milliseconds, you'll accept a previous value that's up to a minute old. This saves the effort of repeated geolocation calls, but it also means your results will be less accurate for a person on the move. By default, maximumAge is 0, meaning cached location data is never used. (You can also use a special value of Infinity, which means use any cached location data, no matter how old it is.)

Showing a Map

Being able to grab someone's geographic coordinates is a neat trick. But the novelty wears off fast unless you have something useful to do with that information. Hardcore geo-junkies know that there's a treasure trove of location information out there. (Often, the problem is taking this information and converting it to a form that's useful to your web application.) There are also several web-based mapping services, the king of which is Google Maps. In fact, good estimates suggest that Google Maps is the most heavily used web application service, for *any* purpose.

Using Google Maps, you can create a map for any portion of the world, at any size you want. You can control how your visitors interact with that map, generate driving instructions, and—most usefully—overlay your own custom data points on that map. For example, a Google Maps–fortified page can show visitors your business locations or flag interesting sights in a Manhattan walking tour. To get started with Google Maps, check out the documentation at *http://tinyurl.com/maps-docs*.

NOTE Google Maps is free to use, even for commercial websites, provided you aren't charging people to access your site. (And if you are, Google has a premium mapping service you can pay to use.) Currently, Google Maps does not show ads, although the Google Maps license terms explicitly reserve the right to do that in the future.

Figure 13-3 shows a revised version of the geolocation page. Once it grabs the current user's coordinates, it shows that position in a map.

FIGURE 13-3

Geolocation and Google Maps make a potent combination. They let you generate a map for any position, with just a few extra lines of JavaScript.

Creating this page is easy. First, you need a link to the scripts that power the Google Maps API. Place this before any script blocks that use the mapping functionality:

```
<head>
  <meta charset="utf-8">
  <title>Geolocation Map</title>
  <script src="http://maps.google.com/maps/api/js?sensor=true"></script>
  ...
</head>
```

Next, you need a <div> element that will hold the dynamically generated map. Give it a unique ID for easy reference:

```
<body>
  <p id="results">Where do you live?</p>
  <div id="mapSurface"></div>
</body>
```

You can then use a style sheet rule to set the size of your map:

```
#mapSurface {
  width: 600px;
  height: 400px;
  border: solid 1px black;
}
```

Now you're ready to start using Google Maps. The first job is to create the map surface. This example creates the map when the page loads, so that you can use it in the success or failure function. (After all, failure doesn't mean the visitor can't use the mapping feature in your page; it just means that you can't determine that visitor's current location. You'll probably still want to show the map, but just default to a different starting point.)

Here's the code that runs when the page loads. It creates the map and then starts a geolocation attempt:

```
var results;
var map;

window.onload = function() {
  results = document.getElementById("results");

  // Set some map options. This example sets the starting zoom level and the
  // map type, but see the Google Maps documentation for all your options.
  var mapOptions = {
    zoom: 13,
    mapTypeId: google.maps.MapTypeId.ROADMAP };

  // Create the map, with these options.
  map = new google.maps.Map(document.getElementById("mapSurface"), mapOptions);

  // Try to find the visitor's position.
  if (navigator.geolocation) {
    navigator.geolocation.getCurrentPosition(geolocationSuccess,
     geolocationFailure);
    results.innerHTML = "The search has begun.";
  }
  else {
    results.innerHTML = "This browser doesn't support geolocation.";
```

```
        goToDefaultLocation();
    }
};
```

Even after you've created the map with this code, you still won't see it in the page. That's because you haven't set a geographic position. To do that, you need to create a specific global *point* using the LatLng object. You can then place that point on the map with the map's setCenter() method. Here's the code that does that with the visitor's coordinates:

```
function geolocationSuccess(position) {
    // Turn the geolocation position into a LatLng object.
    location = new google.maps.LatLng(
     position.coords.latitude, position.coords.longitude);

    // Map that point.
    map.setCenter(location);
```

This code is sufficient for displaying a map, like the one in Figure 13-3. But you can also add adornments to that map, like other places or an info bubble. For the latter, you need to create an InfoWindow object. Here's the code that creates the info bubble shown in Figure 13-3:

```
    // Create the info bubble and set its text content and map coordinates.
    var infowindow = new google.maps.InfoWindow();
    infowindow.setContent("You are here, or somewhere thereabouts.");
    infowindow.setPosition(location);

    // Make the info bubble appear.
    infowindow.open(map);

    results.innerHTML = "Now you're on the map.";
}
```

Finally, if geolocation fails or isn't supported, you can carry out essentially the same process. Just use the hard-coded coordinates of a place you know:

```
function geolocationFailure(positionError) {
    ...
    goToDefaultLocation();
}

function goToDefaultLocation() {
    // This is the location of New York.
    var newYork = new google.maps.LatLng(40.69847, -73.95144);

    map.setCenter(newYork);
}
```

Monitoring a Visitor's Moves

All the examples you've used so far have relied on the getCurrentPosition() method, which is the heart of geolocation. However, the geolocation object has two more methods that allow you to track a visitor's position, so your page receives notifications as the location changes.

It all starts with the watchPosition() method, which looks strikingly similar to getCurrentPosition(). Like getCurrentPosition(), watchPosition() accepts three arguments: a success function (which is the only required detail), a failure function, and an options object:

```
navigator.geolocation.watchPosition(geolocationSuccess, geolocationFailure);
```

The difference between getCurrentPosition() and watchPosition() is that watchPosition() may trigger the success function multiple times—when it gets the location for the first time, and again whenever it detects a new position. (It's not in your control to set how often the device checks for a new position. All you need to know is that the device won't bother you if the position hasn't changed, but it will trigger the success function again if it has.) On a desktop computer, which never moves, the getCurrentPosition() and watchPosition() methods have exactly the same effect.

Unlike getCurrentPosition(), watchPosition() returns a number. You can hold onto this number and pass it in to clearWatch() to stop paying attention to location changes. Or you can ignore this step and keep receiving notifications until the visitor surfs to another page:

```
var watch = navigator.geolocation.watchPosition(geolocationSuccess,
 geolocationFailure);
...

navigator.geolocation.clearWatch(watch);
```

Browser Compatibility for Geolocation

The geolocation feature has good support in every modern browser, including mobile browsers. The only exception is old versions of Internet Explorer. Sadly, geolocation isn't available in IE 8 or IE 7. If you expect your audience to include people using older versions of Internet Explorer, you can polyfill the gap. There are a number of simple JavaScript libraries that solve the problem. Usually, they use the IP lookup technique described on page 403, which is the crudest form of geolocation. For example, the geolocation polyfill at *http://github.com/inexorabletash/polyfill* grabs the router's IP address and looks up its physical location in the database at *http://freegeoip.net*.

Alternatively, you can choose to pick a default starting position without trying to get the user's current location. Or, if you're using Google Maps, you can let the user pick a point from a map and then use those coordinates. The documentation for the Google Maps API is filled with examples like these—start with *http://tinyurl.com/qbmqdsq* for one example that intercepts clicks on a map.

Web Workers

Way back when JavaScript was first created, no one worried too much about performance. JavaScript was built to be a straightforward language for running small bits of script in a web page. JavaScript was a frill—a simplified scripting language for amateur programmers. It certainly wasn't meant to run anyone's business.

Fast-forward nearly 20 years, and JavaScript has taken over the Web. Developers use it to add interactivity to almost every sort of page, from games and mapping tools to shopping carts and fancy forms. But in many ways, the JavaScript language is still scrambling to catch up to its high status.

One example is the way JavaScript deals with big jobs that require hefty calculations. In most modern programming systems, work like this would happen quietly in the *background*, while the person using the application carried on, undisturbed. But in JavaScript, code always runs in the *foreground*. So any time-consuming piece of code will interrupt the user and freeze up the page until the job is done. Ignore this problem, and you'll wind up with some seriously annoyed, never-to-return visitors.

> **NOTE** Crafty web developers have found some partial solutions to the JavaScript freeze-up problem. These involve splitting long-running tasks into small pieces and using setInterval() or setTimeout() to run one piece at a time. For certain types of tasks, this solution works well (for example, it's a practical way to animate a canvas, as demonstrated on page 301). But if you need to run a single, very long operation from start to finish, this technique adds complexity and confusion.

HTML5 introduces a better solution. It adds a dedicated object, called a *web worker*, that's designed to do background work. If you have a time-consuming job to polish off, you create a new web worker, supply it with your code, and start it on its way. While it works, you can communicate with it in a safe but limited way—by passing text messages.

A Time-Consuming Task

Before you can see the benefits of web workers, you need to find a suitable intensive piece of code. There's no point in using web workers for short tasks. But if you plan to run some CPU-taxing calculations that could tie up the web browser for more than a few seconds, web workers make all the difference. Consider, for example, the prime number searcher shown in Figure 13-4. Here, you can hunt for prime numbers that fall in a given range. The code is simple, but the task is *computationally difficult*, which means it could take some serious number-crunching time.

Clearly, this page can be improved with web workers. But before you get to that, you need to take a quick look through the existing markup and JavaScript code.

Web Worker Safety Measures

JavaScript's web worker lets your code work in the background while something else takes place in the foreground. This brings up a well-known theme of modern programming: If an application can do two things at once, one of them has the potential to mess up the other.

The problem occurs when two different pieces of code fight over the same data, at the same time. For example, one piece of code may attempt to read some data, while another attempts to set it. Or both may attempt to set a variable at the same time, causing one change to be overwritten. Or two pieces of code may attempt to manipulate the same object in different ways, pushing it into an inconsistent state. The possible issues are endless, and they're notoriously difficult to discover and solve. Often, a multithreaded application (that's an application

that uses several *threads* of independently executing code) works fine during testing. But when you start using it in the real world, maddeningly inconsistent errors appear.

Fortunately, you won't face these problems with JavaScript's web workers feature. That's because it doesn't let you share the same data between your web page and your web workers. You can *send* data from your web page to a web worker (or vice versa), but JavaScript automatically makes a copy of your data and sends that. That means there's no possible way for two threads to get hold of the same memory slot at the same time and cause subtle issues. Of course, this simplified model also restricts some of the things that web workers can do, but a minor reduction in capabilities is the cost of making sure ambitious programmers can't shoot themselves in the foot.

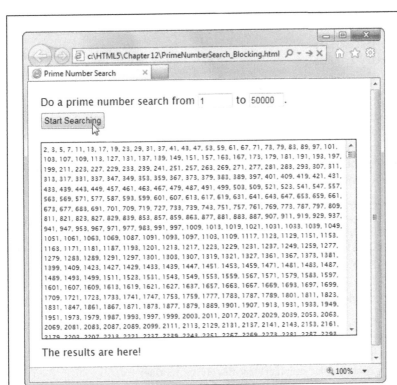

FIGURE 13-4

Pick your range and click the button to start the search. Pick a relatively narrow range (like this one, from 1 to 50,000), and the task completes in seconds, without inconveniencing anyone. But launch a broader search (say, from 1 to 500,000) and your page could become unresponsive for minutes or more. You won't be able to click, scroll, or interact with anything—and the browser may even give you a "long-running script" warning or gray out the entire page.

The markup is short and concise. The page uses two `<input>` controls, one for each text box. It also includes a button to start the search and two `<div>` elements, one to hold the results and another to hold the status message underneath. Here's the complete markup from inside the `<body>` element:

```html
<p>Do a prime number search from <input id="from" value="1"> to
 <input id="to" value="20000">.</p>
<button id="searchButton" onclick="doSearch()">Start Searching</button>

<div id="primeContainer">
</div>

<div id="status"></div>
```

One interesting detail is the styling of the `<div>` element that holds the prime number list. It's given a fixed height and a maximum width, and the `overflow` and `overflow-x` properties work together to add a vertical scroll bar (but not a horizontal one):

```css
#primeContainer {
  border: solid 1px black;
  margin-top: 20px;
  margin-bottom: 10px;
  padding: 3px;
  height: 300px;
  max-width: 500px;
  overflow: scroll;
  overflow-x: hidden;
  font-size: x-small;
}
```

The JavaScript code is a bit longer, but not much more complicated. It retrieves the numbers from the text boxes, starts the search, and then adds the prime number list to the page. It doesn't actually perform the mathematical operations that find the prime numbers—this is handled through a separate function, which is named `findPrimes()` and stored in a separate JavaScript file.

> **TIP** You don't need to see the `findPrimes()` function to understand this example or web workers—all you need is a suitably long task. However, if you're curious to see the math that makes this page work, or if you just want to run a few prime number searches yourself, check out the full code on the try-out site at *http://prosetech.com/html5*.

Here's the complete code for the `doSearch()` function:

```javascript
function doSearch() {
  // Get the numbers for the search range.
  var fromNumber = document.getElementById("from").value;
  var toNumber = document.getElementById("to").value;
```

```
// Perform the prime search. (This is the time-consuming step.)
var primes = findPrimes(fromNumber, toNumber);

// Loop over the array of prime numbers, and paste them together into
// one long piece of text.
var primeList = "";
for (var i=0; i<primes.length; i++) {
  primeList += primes[i];
  if (i != primes.length-1) primeList += ", ";
}

// Insert the prime number text into the page.
var displayList = document.getElementById("primeContainer");
displayList.innerHTML = primeList;

// Update the status text to tell the user what just happened.
var statusDisplay = document.getElementById("status");
if (primeList.length == 0) {
  statusDisplay.innerHTML = "Search failed to find any results.";
}
else {
  statusDisplay.innerHTML = "The results are here!";
}
}
```

As you can see, the markup and code is short, simple, and to the point. Unfortunately, if you plug in a large search you'll find that it's also as slow and clunky as riding a golf cart up a steep hill.

Doing Work in the Background

The web worker feature revolves around a new object called the Worker. When you want to run something in the background, you create a new Worker, give it some code, and send it some data.

Here's an example that creates a new web worker that runs the code in the file named *PrimeWorker.js*:

```
var worker = new Worker("PrimeWorker.js");
```

The code that a worker runs is *always* stored in a separate JavaScript file. This design discourages newbie programmers from writing web worker code that attempts to use global variables or directly access elements on the page. Neither of these operations is possible.

> **NOTE** Browsers enforce a strict separation between your web page and your web worker code. For example, there's no way for the code in *PrimeWorker.js* to write prime numbers into a `<div>` element. Instead, your worker code needs to send its data back to JavaScript code on the page, so the web page code can display the results.

Web pages and web workers communicate by exchanging messages. To send data to a worker, you call the worker's postMessage() method:

```
worker.postMessage(myData);
```

The worker then receives an onMessage event that provides a copy of the data. This is when it starts working.

Similarly, when your worker needs to talk back to the web page, it calls its own postMessage() method, along with some data, and the web page receives an onMessage event. Figure 13-5 shows this interaction close up.

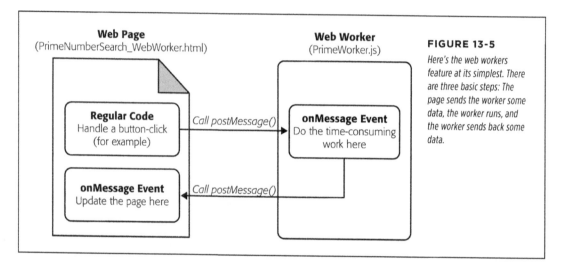

FIGURE 13-5

Here's the web workers feature at its simplest. There are three basic steps: The page sends the worker some data, the worker runs, and the worker sends back some data.

There's one more wrinkle to consider before you dive in. The postMessage() function allows only a single value. This fact is a stumbling block for the prime number cruncher, because it needs *two* pieces of data (the two numbers in the range). The solution is to package these two details into an object literal (see page 469). This code shows one example, which gives the object two properties (the first named from, and the second named to), and assigns values to both of them:

```
worker.postMessage(
  { from: 1,
    to: 20000 }
);
```

NOTE Incidentally, you can send virtually any object to a worker. Behind the scenes, the browser uses JSON (page 329) to convert your object to a harmless piece of text, duplicate it, and re-objectify it.

With these details in mind, you can revise the doSearch() function you saw earlier. Instead of performing the prime number search itself, the doSearch() function creates a worker and gets it to do the real job:

```
var worker;

function doSearch() {
  // Disable the button, so the user can't start more than one search
  // at the same time.
  searchButton.disabled = true;

  // Create the worker.
  worker = new Worker("PrimeWorker.js");

  // Hook up to the onMessage event, so you can receive messages
  // from the worker.
  worker.onmessage = receivedWorkerMessage;

  // Get the number range, and send it to the web worker.
  var fromNumber = document.getElementById("from").value;
  var toNumber = document.getElementById("to").value;

  worker.postMessage(
    { from: fromNumber,
      to: toNumber }
  );

  // Let the user know that things are on their way.
  statusDisplay.innerHTML = "A web worker is on the job ("+
    fromNumber + " to " + toNumber + ") ...";
}
```

Now the code in the *PrimeWorker.js* file springs into action. It receives the onMessage event, performs the search, and then posts a new message back to the page, with the prime list:

```
onmessage = function(event) {
  // The object that the web page sent is stored in the event.data property.
  var fromNumber = event.data.from;
  var toNumber = event.data.to;

  // Using that number range, perform the prime number search.
  var primes = findPrimes(fromNumber, toNumber);

  // Now the search is finished. Send back the results.
  postMessage(primes);
};

function findPrimes(fromNumber, toNumber) {
  // (The boring prime number calculations go in this function.)
}
```

When the worker calls postMessage(), it fires the onMessage event, which triggers this function in the web page:

```
function receivedWorkerMessage(event) {
  // Get the prime number list.
  var primes = event.data;

  // Copy the list to the page.
  ...

  // Allow more searches.
  searchButton.disabled = false;
}
```

You can now use the same code you saw earlier (page 417) to convert the array of prime numbers into a piece of text and insert that text into the web page.

Overall, the structure of the code has changed a bit, but the logic is mostly the same. The result, however, is dramatically different. Now, when a long prime number search is under way, the page remains responsive. You can scroll down, type in the text boxes, and select numbers in the list from the previous search. Other than the message at the bottom of the page, there's nothing to reveal that a web worker is plugging away in the background.

> **TIP** Does your web worker need access to the code in another JavaScript file? There's a simple solution with the importScripts() function. For example, if you want to call functions from the *FindPrimes.js* file in *PrimeWorker.js*, just add this line of code before you do:
>
> ```
> importScripts("FindPrimes.js");
> ```

GEM IN THE ROUGH

Running Web Workers Offline

If you take the time to prepare a complete web worker example and upload it to a web server, you can test your page complication-free. Of course, in the real world it's easier to try things out on your desktop and run them straight from your hard drive. This method works in Firefox and current versions of Internet Explorer, but not in Chrome—unless you take additional steps.

If you're running your web worker page from a local file, Chrome will fail unless you start it with the --allow-file-access-from-files parameter. In Windows, you accomplish this by changing your Chrome shortcut (right-click it and choose Properties) or by creating a new Chrome shortcut and customizing that. Either way, you need to look in the Target box and tack the parameter onto the end of the command line. For example, you would change a shortcut like this:

```
C:\Users\billcruft\ ... \chrome.exe
```

to this:

```
C:\Users\billcruft\ ... \chrome.exe
--allow-file-access-from-files
```

Now you can try out your web worker code in the comfort and privacy of your own computer, no uploads required.

Handling Worker Errors

As you've learned, the `postMessage()` method is the key to communicating with web workers. However, there's one more way that a web worker can notify your web page—with the `onerror` event that signals an error:

```
worker.onerror = workerError;
```

Now, if some dodgy script or invalid data causes an error in your background code, the error details are packaged up and sent back to the page. Here's some web page code that simply displays the text of the error message:

```
function workerError(error) {
  statusDisplay.innerHTML = error.message;
}
```

Along with the `message` property, the error object also includes a `lineno` and `file-name` property, which report the line number and file name where the error occurred.

Canceling a Background Task

Now that you've built a basic web worker example, it's time to add a few refinements. First is cancellation support, which lets your page shut down a worker in mid-calculation.

There are two ways to stop a worker. First, a worker can stop itself by calling `close()`. More commonly, the page that created the worker will shut it down by calling the worker's `terminate()` method. For example, here's the code you can use to power a straightforward cancel button:

```
function cancelSearch() {
  worker.terminate();
  statusDisplay.innerHTML = "";
  searchButton.disabled = false;
}
```

Click this button to stop the current search and re-enable the search button. Just remember that once a worker is stopped in this way, you can't send any more messages, and it can't be used to do any more operations. To perform a new search, you need to create a new worker object. (The current example does this already, so it works perfectly.)

Passing More Complex Messages

The last trick you'll learn to do with a web worker is return progress information. Figure 13-6 shows a revised version of the web worker page that adds this feature.

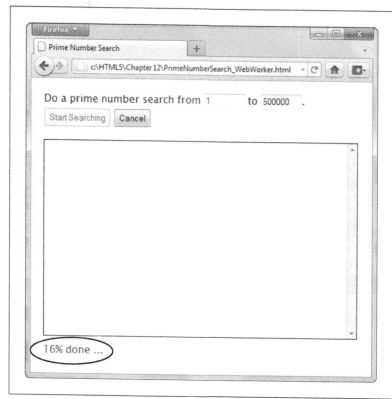

FIGURE 13-6

As the prime number search is under way, the search updates the status display to tell you how close the task is to completion. For a fancier display, you could use a color-filling progress bar like the one on page 165.

To build the progress display, the web worker needs to send the progress percentage to the page while it works. But as you already know, web workers have just one way to talk to the pages that own them—with the postMessage() method. So to create this example, the web worker needs to send *two* types of messages: progress notifications (while the work is under way) and the prime number list (when the work is finished). The trick is making the difference between these two messages clear, so the onMessage event handler in the page can easily distinguish between the two types.

The best approach is to add a bit of extra information to the message. For example, when the web worker sends progress information, it can slap the text label "Progress" on its message. And when the web worker sends the prime number list, it can add the label "PrimeList."

To bundle all the information you want together in one message, you need to create an object literal. This is the same technique the web page used to send the number range data to the web worker. The extra piece of information is the text that describes the type of message, which is placed in a property called messageType in this example. The actual data goes in a second property, named data.

Here's how you would rewrite the web worker code to add a message type to the prime number list:

```
onmessage = function(event) {
  // Perform the prime number search.
  var primes = findPrimes(event.data.from, event.data.to);

  // Send back the results.
  postMessage(
   {messageType: "PrimeList", data: primes}
  );
};
```

The code in the findPrimes() function also uses the postMessage() method to send a message back to the web page. It uses the same two properties—messageType and data. But now the messageType indicates that the message is a progress notification, and data holds the progress percentage:

```
function findPrimes(fromNumber, toNumber) {

  ...

  // Calculate the progress percentage.
  var progress = Math.round(i/list.length*100);

  // Only send a progress update if the progress has changed at least 1%.
  if (progress != previousProgress) {
    postMessage(
      {messageType: "Progress", data: progress}
    );
    previousProgress = progress;
  }
  ...
}
```

When the page receives a message, it needs to start by checking the messageType property to determine what sort of message it has just received. If it's a prime list, then the results are shown in the page. If it's a progress notification, then the progress text is updated:

```
function receivedWorkerMessage(event) {
  var message = event.data;

  if (message.messageType == "PrimeList") {
    var primes = message.data;

    // Display the prime list. This code is the same as before.
    ...
  }
```

```
else if (message.messageType == "Progress") {
  // Report the current progress.
  statusDisplay.innerHTML = message.data + "% done ...";
}
}
```

> **NOTE** There's another way to design this page. You could get the worker to call postMessage() every time it finds a prime number. The web page would then add each prime number to the list and show it in the page immediately. This approach has the advantage of showing results as they arrive. However, it also has the drawback of continually interrupting the page (because the web worker will find prime numbers quite quickly). The ideal design depends on the nature of your task—how long it takes to complete, whether partial results are useful, how quickly each partial result is calculated, and so on.

POWER USERS' CLINIC

More Ways to Use a Web Worker

The prime number search uses web workers in the most straightforward way possible—to perform one well-defined task. Every time the search is started, the page creates a new web worker. That web worker is responsible for a single task. It receives a single message and sends a single message back.

Your pages don't need to be this simple. Here are a few examples of how you can extend your web-worker designs to do more complicated things:

- **Reuse a web worker for multiple jobs.** When a worker finishes its work and reaches the end of the onMessage event handler, it doesn't die. It simply goes idle and waits quietly. If you send the worker another message, it springs back to life and does the work.

- **Create multiple web workers.** Your page doesn't need to stick to one worker. For example, imagine you want to let a visitor launch several prime number searches at a time. You could create a new web worker for each search and keep track of all your workers in an array. Each time a web worker responds with its list of prime numbers, you add that to the page, taking care not to overwrite

any other worker's result. (However, some words of caution are in order. Web workers have a relatively high overhead, and running a dozen at once could swamp the computer with work.)

- **Create web workers inside a web worker.** A web worker can start its own web workers, send them messages, and receive their messages back. This technique is useful for complex computational tasks that require recursion, like calculating the Fibonacci sequence.

- **Download data with a web worker.** Web workers can use the XMLHttpRequest object (page 377) to grab new pages or to send requests to a web service. When they get the information they need, they can call postMessage() to send it up to the page.

- **Do periodic tasks with a web worker.** Web workers can use the setTimeout() and setInterval() functions, just like ordinary web pages. For example, you might create a web worker that checks a website for new data every minute.

Browser Compatibility for Web Workers

The web worker feature isn't supported as broadly as the geolocation feature. Table 13-1 shows which browsers you can rely on.

TABLE 13-1 *Browser support for web workers*

	IE	FIREFOX	CHROME	SAFARI	OPERA	SAFARI IOS	CHROME FOR ANDROID
Minimum version	10	3.5	3	4	10.6	5	29

So what can you do if you face a browser that doesn't have web worker support? The easiest option is to simply do the same work in the foreground:

```
if (window.Worker) {
  // Web workers are supported.
  // So why not create a web worker
  // and start it?
} else {
  // Web workers aren't available.
  // You can just call the prime search
  // function, and wait.
}
```

This approach doesn't force you to write any extra code, because the prime-number-searching function is already written, and you can call it with or without a web worker. However, if you have a long task, this approach could lock up the browser for a bit. So if you use this strategy, it's wise to warn the user (for example, with a message on the page), that he's using a less-supported browser and the calculation process may temporarily freeze up the page.

An alternate (but more tedious) approach is to try to fake a background job using the setInterval() or setTimeout() methods. For example, you could write some code that tests just a few numbers every interval. Some polyfills even attempt to add this sort of system (see the Web Workers section on *http://tinyurl.com/polyfills*), but this approach gets messy quickly.

■ History Management

Session history is an HTML5 add-on that extends the capabilities of the JavaScript history object. This sounds simple, but the trick is knowing when and why you should use it.

If you've never noticed the history object before, don't be alarmed. Up until now, it's had very little to offer. In fact, the traditional history object has just one property and three basic methods. The property is *length*, and it tells you how many entries are in the browser's History list (the list of recently visited web pages that the browser maintains as you skip from page to page across the Web). Here's an example that uses it:

```
alert("You have " + history.length +
 " pages in your browser's history list.");
```

The most useful history method is back(). It lets you send a visitor one step back in the browsing history:

```
history.back();
```

This method has the same effect as if the visitor clicked the browser's Back button. Similarly, you can use the forward() method to step forward, or the go() method to move a specified number of steps backward or forward.

All this adds up to relatively little, unless you want to design your own custom Back and Forward buttons on a web page. But HTML5 adds a bit more functionality, which you can put to far more ambitious purposes. The centerpiece is the pushState() method, which lets you change the URL in the browser window without triggering a page refresh. This comes in handy in a specific scenario—namely, when you're building dynamic pages that quietly load new content and seamlessly update themselves. In this situation, the page's URL and the page's content can become out of sync. For example, if a page loads content from another page, the first page's URL stays in the browser's address box, which can cause all sorts of bookmarking confusion. Session history gives you a way to patch this hole.

If you're having a bit of trouble visualizing this scenario, hold on. In the next section, you'll see a page that's a perfect candidate for session history.

The URL Problem

In the previous chapter, you considered a page about Chinese tourism that had a built-in slideshow (page 382). Using the Previous and Next buttons on this page, the viewer could load different slides. But the best part about this example is that each slide was loaded quietly and unobtrusively and without reloading the page, thanks to the trusty XMLHttpRequest object.

Pages that include dynamic content and use this sort of design have a well-known limitation. Even though the page changes when it loads in new content, the URL stays the same in the browser's address bar (Figure 13-7).

To understand the problem, imagine that Joe reads the article shown in Figure 13-7, looks at the different sights, and is excited by the wishing tree in the fifth slide. Joe bookmarks the page, sends the URL to his friend Claire via email, and promotes it to the whole world with a Twitter message ("Throwing paper into a tree beats dropping coins in a fountain. Check it out at http://..."). The problem is that when Joe returns to his bookmark, or when Claire clicks the link in the email, or when any of Joe's followers visit the link in the tweet, they all end up at the first slide. They may not have the patience to click through to the fifth slide, or they may not even know where it is. And this problem grows worse if there are more than just five slides—for example, a Flickr photo stream could have dozens or hundreds of pictures.

Different content, same URL

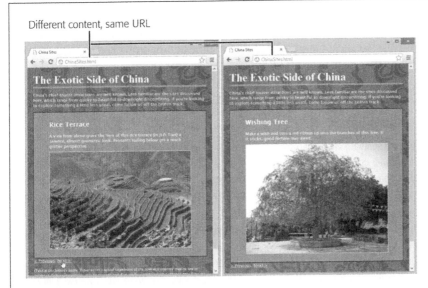

FIGURE 13-7

Here are two versions of the ChinaSites.html *page, with different slides loaded. In both pages, the URL stays the same (it's* ChinaSites.html*).*

The Old Solution: Hashbang URLs

To deal with this problem, some web pages tack extra information onto the end of the URL. Just a few years ago, leading sites like Facebook, Twitter, and Google fell over themselves in excitement to implement a controversial strategy called the *hashbang* technique. To use the hashbang technique, you add the characters #! at the end of any URL, followed by some additional information. Here's an example:

```
http://jjtraveltales.com/ChinaSites.html#!/Slide5
```

The reason the hashbang approach works is because browsers treat everything after the # character as the *fragment* portion of a URL. So in the example shown here, the web browser knows that you're still referring to the same *ChinaSites.html* page, just with an extra fragment added to the end.

On the other hand, consider what happens if your JavaScript code changes the URL without using the # character:

```
http://jjtraveltales.com/ChinaSites.html/Slide5
```

Now the web browser will immediately send this request to the web server and attempt to download a new page. This isn't what you want.

So how would you implement the hashbang technique? First, you need to change the URL that appears in the browser whenever your page loads a new slide. (You can do this by setting the location.href property in your JavaScript code.) Second, you need to check the URL when the page first loads, retrieve the fragment, and fetch the corresponding bit of dynamic content from the web server. All of this adds up to a fair bit of juggling, but you can use a JavaScript library like PathJS (*https://github.com/mtrpcic/pathjs*) to make life much easier.

Recently, the hashbang technique has fallen into disrepute, and many of its former supporters have dropped it altogether (for the reasons discussed in the box on this page). However, hashbangs still turn up in some heavily trafficked sites, like Google Groups.

UP TO SPEED

Why Nobody Likes Hashbangs

In recent Web history, the hashbang approach was widely used but deeply controversial. Today, web designers are backing away from it for a number of reasons:

- **Complex URLs.** Facebook is a good example of the problem. In the past, it wouldn't take much browsing before the browser's URL would be polluted with extra information, as in *http://www.facebook.com/profile.php?id=1586010043#!/pages/Haskell/401573824771*. Now designers use session history, if the browser supports it.

- **Inflexibility.** Hashbang pages store a lot of information in the URL. If you change the way a hashbanged page works, or the way it stores information, old URLs could stop working, which is a major website fail.

- **Search engine optimization.** Search engines may treat different hashbanged URLs as essentially the same page. In the *ChinaSites.html* page, that means you won't get a

separately indexed page for each tourist site—in fact, search engines might ignore this information altogether. This means that if someone searches for "china wishing tree," the *ChinaSites.html* page might not turn up as a match.

- **Cool URLs matter.** Cool URLs are web page addresses that are short, clear, and—most importantly—never change. Tim Berners-Lee, the creator of the Web, explains the philosophy at *www.w3.org/Provider/Style/URI.html*. And no matter how strongly you feel about keeping good web content alive, hashbang URLs are difficult to maintain and unlikely to survive the next stage in web evolution.

Although webmasters differ over how much they tolerate the hashbang approach, most agree that it's a short stage of web development that soon will be replaced by HTML5's session history feature.

The HTML5 Solution: Session History

HTML5's session history feature provides a different solution to the URL problem. It gives you a way to change the URL to whatever you want, without needing to stick in funny characters like the hashbang. For example, when the *ChinaSites.html* page loads the fourth slide, you could change the URL to look like this:

```
http://jjtraveltales.com/ChinaSites4.html
```

When you do this, the browser won't actually attempt to request a page named *ChinaSites4.html*. Instead, it keeps the current page, with the newly loaded slide, which is exactly what you want. The same is true if the visitor goes back through the browser history. For example, if a visitor moves to the next slide (and the URL changes to *ChinaSites5.html*) and then clicks the Back button (returning the URL to *ChinaSites4.html*), the browser sticks with the current page and raises an event that gives you the chance to load the matching slide and restore the right version of the page.

So far, this sounds like a perfect solution. However, there's a significant drawback. If you want this system to work the way it's intended, you actually need to create a page for every URL you use. In this example, that means you need to create *China-Sites1.html, ChinaSites2.html, ChinaSites3.html*, and so on. That's because surfers might go directly to those pages—for example, when returning through a bookmark, typing the link in by hand, clicking it in an email message, and so on. For big web outfits (like Facebook or Flickr), this is no big deal, because they can use a scrap of server-side code to serve up the same slide content in a different package. But if you're a small-scale web developer, it might be a bit more work. For some options on how to handle the challenge, see the box on page 431.

Now that you understand how session history fits into your pages (the hard part), actually using it is easy. In fact, session history consists of just two methods and a single event, all of which are added to the history object.

The most important of these is the pushState() method, which lets you change the web page portion of the URL to whatever you want. For security reasons, you can't change the rest of the URL. (If you could, hackers would have a powerful tool for faking other people's websites—including, say, the Gmail sign on a bank transaction form.)

Here's an example that changes the web page part of the URL to ChinaSites4.html:

```
history.pushState(null, null, "ChinaSites4.html");
```

The pushState() method accepts three arguments. The third one is the only essential detail—it's the URL that appears in the browser's address bar.

The first argument is any piece of data you want to store to represent the current state of this page. As you'll see, you can use this data to restore the page state if the user returns to this URL through the browser's History list. The second argument is the page title you want the browser to show. All browsers are currently unified in ignoring this detail. If you don't want to set either the state or the title, just supply a *null* value, as shown above.

Here's the code you'd add to the *ChinaSites.html* page to change the URL to match the currently displayed slide. You'll notice that the current slide number is used for the page state. That detail will become important in a moment, when you consider the onPopState event:

```
function nextSlide() {
  if (slideNumber == 5) {
    slideNumber = 1;
  } else {
    slideNumber += 1;
  }
  history.pushState(slideNumber, null, "ChinaSites" + slideNumber + ".html");
  goToNewSlide();
  return false;
}
```

```
function previousSlide() {
  if (slideNumber == 1) {
    slideNumber = 5;
  } else {
    slideNumber -= 1;
  }
  history.pushState(slideNumber, null, "ChinaSites" + slideNumber + ".html");
  goToNewSlide();
  return false;
}
```

The goToNewSlide() function hasn't changed from the first version of this example (page 385). It still uses the XMLHttpRequest object to fetch the data for the next slide, asynchronously.

Figure 13-8 shows the new URL management system at work.

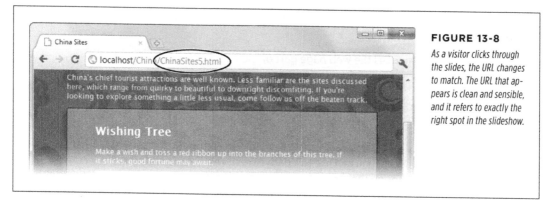

FIGURE 13-8

As a visitor clicks through the slides, the URL changes to match. The URL that appears is clean and sensible, and it refers to exactly the right spot in the slideshow.

If you use the pushState() method, you'll also need to think about the onPopState event, which is its natural counterpart. While the pushState() method puts a new entry into the browser's History list, the onPopState event gives you the chance to deal with it when the user returns.

To understand how it works, consider what happens if a visitor works through all the slides. As she clicks through, the URL in the address bar changes from *ChinaSites. html* to *ChinaSites1.html*, then *ChinaSites2.html*, *ChinaSites3.html*, and so on. Even though the page hasn't actually changed, all of these URLs are added to the browser's history. If the user clicks back to get to a previous slide (for example, moving from *ChinaSites3.html* to *ChinaSites2.html*), the onPopState event is triggered. It provides your code with the state information you stored earlier, with pushState(). Your job is to use that to restore the page to its proper version. In the current example, that means loading the corresponding slide:

```
window.onpopstate = function(e) {
  if (e.state != null) {
```

```
        // What's the slide number for this state?
        // (You could also snip it out of the URL, using the location.href
        // property, but that's more work.)
        slideNumber = e.state;

        // Request this slide from the web server.
        goToNewSlide();
    }
};
```

You'll notice that this example checks to see if there is any state object before it does its work. That's because some browsers (including Chrome) fire the onPopState event the first time a page is loaded, even if you haven't yet called pushState().

NOTE There's one more new history method, but it's used a lot less frequently—replaceState(). You can use replaceState() to change the state information that's associated with the current page, without adding anything to the History list.

UP TO SPEED

Creating Extra Pages to Satisfy Your URLs

Session history follows the original philosophy of the Web: Every piece of content should be identified with a unique, durable URL. Unfortunately, this means you'll need to make sure that these URLs lead visitors back to the content they want, which is a much stickier affair. For example, when someone types in a request for *ChinaSites3.html*, you need to grab the main content from *ChinaSites.html* and the slide content from *ChinaSites3_slide.html* and somehow stick it together.

If you're a hard-core web programmer, you can write code that runs on the web server, intercepts web requests, and carries out this assembly process on the fly. But if you don't have serious codemaster skills, you'll need to use a different approach.

The simplest option is to make a separate file for each URL—in other words, actually create the files *ChinaSites1.html*, *China-Sites2.html*, *ChinaSites3.html*, and so on. Of course, you don't want to duplicate the slide content in more than one place (for example, in both *ChinaSites3.html* and *ChinaSites3_slide.html*), because that would create a maintenance nightmare. Fortunately, there are two simple approaches that can simplify your life:

- **Use server-side includes.** If your web server supports this technique (and most do), you can use a special coded instruction like the following:

  `<!--#include file="footer.html" -->`

  Although it looks like a comment, this tells the web server to open the file and insert its contents at that position in the markup. Using this technique, you can insert the main content and the slide content into each slide-specific page. In fact, each slide-specific web page file (*ChinaSites1.html*, *ChinaSites2.html*, and so on) will need just a few lines of markup to create a basic shell of a page.

- **Use templates in a web design tool.** Some web design tools, like Adobe Dreamweaver, allow you to create web templates that can be copied to as many pages as you want. So if you create a template that has the main content and style details, you can reuse it to create all the slide-specific pages you need, quickly and easily.

Browser Compatibility for Session History

Session history has roughly the same level of support as the web workers feature. Once again, it's pre-IE 10 versions of Internet Explorer that are most likely to cause a problem (see Table 13-2).

TABLE 13-2 *Browser support for session history*

	IE	FIREFOX	CHROME	SAFARI	OPERA	SAFARI IOS	ANDROID
Minimum version	10	4	8	5	11.5	5	4.2

There are two ways you can handle a browser that doesn't support session history. If you do nothing at all, the fancy URLs just won't appear. This is what you get if you load the previous example in Internet Explorer—no matter what slide you load up, the URL stays fixed at *ChinaSites.html*. Flickr also uses this approach with its photo streams (to see an example, view *http://tinyurl.com/6hnvanw* with an old version of Internet Explorer).

Another choice is to trigger a full page refresh when the user loads new content on a browser that doesn't support session history. This makes sense if providing a good, meaningful URL is more important that providing the slick experience of dynamically loaded content. However, this approach also takes more work to implement.

One easy way to do it is to enhance your navigation logic so that it performs a page redirect if necessary. In the *ChinaSites.html* page, that involves enhancing the goToNextSlide() function, like this:

```
function goToNewSlide() {
  if (window.history) {
    // Session history support is available.
    if (req != null) {
      req.open("GET", "ChinaSites" + slideNumber + "_slide" + ".html", true);
      req.onreadystatechange = newSlideReceived;
      req.send();
    }
    else {
      // There was a problem. Ignore it.
    }
  }
  else {
    // There's no session history support, so direct the browser to a new page.
    window.location = "ChinaSites" + slideNumber + ".html"
  }
}
```

This code checks for session history using the window.history property. If support is there, the code downloads just the small chunk of slide data you need and loads it into the existing page. But if session support isn't available, the code abandons this fancy approach and performs an old-school redirect to the new page.

Appendixes

APPENDIX A:
Essential CSS

APPENDIX B:
JavaScript: The Brains of Your Page

Essential CSS

I t's no exaggeration to say that modern web design wouldn't be possible without *CSS*, the Cascading Style Sheet standard. CSS allows even the most richly format-ted, graphically complex web pages to outsource the formatting work to a separate document—a *style sheet*. This keeps the web page markup clean, clear, and readable.

To get the most out of HTML5 (and this book), you need to be familiar with the CSS standard. If you're a CSS pro, don't worry about this appendix—carry on with the material in the rest of the book, and pay special attention to Chapters 6 and 7, which introduce many of the new style features that CSS3 adds. But if your CSS skills are a bit rusty, this appendix will help to refresh your memory before you go any further.

NOTE This appendix gives a very quick (and not comprehensive) rundown of CSS. If you're still overwhelmed, consult a book that deals with CSS in more detail, like *CSS3: The Missing Manual* by David Sawyer McFarland.

■ Adding Styles to a Web Page

There are three ways to use styles in a web page.

The first approach is to embed style information directly into an element using the style attribute. Here's an example that changes the color of a heading:

```
<h1 style="color: green">Inline Styles are Sloppy Styles</h1>
```

This is convenient, but it clutters the markup terribly. You have to style every line, one by one.

The second approach is to embed an entire style sheet in a `<style>` element, which you must place in the page's `<head>` section:

```
<head>
  <title>Embedded Style Sheet Test</title>
  <style>
    ...
  </style>
</head>
```

This code separates the formatting from your web page markup but still keeps everything together in one file. This approach makes sense for one-off formatting tasks (when you don't want to reuse your formatting choices in another page), and it's a good choice for simple tests and examples, like the ones included with this book. However, it's not so great for a real-world, professional website, because it leads to long, bloated pages.

The third approach is to link to a separate style sheet file by adding a `<link>` element to the `<head>` section. Here's an example that tells a web browser to apply the styles from the style sheet named *SampleStyles.css*:

```
<head>
  <title>External Style Sheet Test</title>
  <link rel="stylesheet" href="SampleStyles.css">
</head>
```

This approach is the most common and the most powerful. It gives you the flexibility to reuse your styles in other pages. If you want, you can further divide your styles into multiple style sheets and link to as many as you need in any HTML page.

NOTE A simple philosophy underpins modern web development. HTML markup is for structuring a page into logical sections (paragraphs, headings, lists, images, links, and so on), while a CSS style sheet is for formatting it (by specifying fonts, colors, borders, backgrounds, and layout). Follow this rule, and your web pages will be easy to edit. You'll also be able to change the formatting and layout of your entire website simply by modifying its linked style sheet. (To see a truly impressive example of style sheet magic, check out *www.csszengarden.com*, where one website is given more than 200 different faces, simply by swapping in different style sheets.)

◼ The Anatomy of a Style Sheet

A style sheet is a text file, which you'll usually place on a web server alongside your HTML pages. It contains one or more *rules*. The order of these rules doesn't matter.

Each rule applies one or more formatting details to one or more HTML elements. Here's the structure of a simple rule:

```
selector {
  property: value;
  property: value;
}
```

And here's what each part means:

- The **selector** identifies the type of content you want to format. A browser hunts down all the elements in the web page that match your selector. There are many different ways to write a selector, but one of the simplest approaches (shown next) is to identify the elements you want to format by their element names. For example, you could write a selector that picks out all the level-one headings in your page.

- The **property** identifies the type of formatting you want to apply. Here's where you choose whether you want to change colors, fonts, alignment, or something else. You can have as many property settings as you want in a rule—this example has two.

- The **value** sets a value for the property. For example, if your property is color, the value could be light blue or a queasy green.

Now here's a real rule that does something:

```
h1 {
  text-align: center;
  color: green;
}
```

Pop this text into a style sheet and save it (for example, as *SampleStyles.css*). Then, take a sample web page (one that has at least one <h1> heading) and add a <link> element that refers to this style sheet. Finally, open this page in a browser. You'll see that the <h1> headings don't have their normal formatting—instead, they will be centered and green.

CSS Properties

The previous example introduces two formatting properties: text-align (which sets how text is positioned, horizontally) and color (which sets the text color).

There are many, many more formatting properties for you to play with. Table A-1 lists some of the most commonly used. In fact, this table lists almost all the style properties you'll encounter in the examples in this book (not including the newer CSS3 properties that are described in Chapters 6 and 7).

TABLE A-1 *Commonly used style sheet properties, by category*

	PROPERTIES
Colors	color background-color
Spacing	margin padding margin-left, margin-right, margin-top, margin-bottom padding-left, padding-right, padding-top, padding-bottom
Borders	border-width border-style border-color border (to set the width, style, and color in one step)
Text alignment	text-align text-indent word-spacing letter-spacing line-height white-space
Fonts	font-family font-size font-weight font-style font-variant text-decoration @font-face (for using fancy web fonts; see page 206)
Size	width height
Layout	position left, right float, clear
Graphics	background-image background-repeat background-position

TIP If you don't have a style sheet book on hand, you can get an at-a-glance overview of all the properties listed here (and more) at *www.htmldog.com/reference/cssproperties*. You can also get more information about each property, including a brief description of what it does and the values it allows.

Formatting the Right Elements with Classes

The previous style sheet rule formatted all the <h1> headings in a document. But in more complex documents, you need to pick out specific elements and give them distinct formatting.

To do this, you need to give these elements a name with the class attribute. Here's an example that creates a class named ArticleTitle:

```
<h1 class="ArticleTitle">HTML5 is Winning</h1>
```

Now you can write a style sheet rule that formats only this heading. The trick is to write a selector that starts with a period, followed by the class name, like this:

```
.ArticleTitle {
  font-family: Garamond, serif;
  font-size: 40px;
}
```

Now, the <h1> that represents the article title is sized up to be 40 pixels tall.

You can use the class attribute on as many elements as you want. In fact, that's the idea. A typical style sheet is filled with class rules, which take web page markup and neatly carve it into stylable units.

Finally, it's worth noting that you can create a selector that uses an element type and a class name, like this:

```
h1.ArticleTitle {
  font-size: 40px;
}
```

This selector matches any <h1> element that uses the ArticleTitle class. Sometimes, you may write this sort of style rule just to be clear. For example, you may decide to write your rule this way to make it clear that the ArticleTitle applies only to <h1> headings and shouldn't be used anywhere else. But most of the time, web designers just create straight classes with no element restrictions.

NOTE Different selectors can overlap. If more than one selector applies to the same element, they will both take effect, with the most general being applied first. For example, if you have a rule that applies to all headings and a rule that applies to the class named ArticleTitle, the all-headings rule is applied first, followed by the class rule. As a result, the class rule can override the properties that are set in the all-headings rule. If two rules are equally specific, the one that's defined last in the style sheet wins.

Style Sheet Comments

In a complicated style sheet, it's sometimes worth leaving little notes to remind yourself (or to let other people know) why a style sheet rule exists and what it's designed to do. Like HTML, CSS lets you add comments, which the web browser ignores. However, CSS comments don't look like HTML comments. They always start with the characters /* and end with the characters */. Here's an example of a somewhat pointless comment:

```
/* The heading of the main article on a page. */
.ArticleTitle {
  font-size: 40px;
}
```

Slightly More Advanced Style Sheets

You'll see an example of a practical style sheet in a moment. But first you need to consider a few of the finer points of style-sheet writing.

Structuring a Page with <div> Elements

When working with style sheets, you'll often use the <div> element to wrap up a section of content:

```
<div>
  <p>Here are two paragraphs of content.</p>
  <p>In a div container.</p>
</div>
```

On its own, the <div> does nothing. But it gives you a convenient place to apply some class-based style sheet formatting. Here are some examples:

- **Inherited values.** Some CSS properties are *inherited*, which means the value you set in one element is automatically applied to all the elements inside. One example is the set of font properties—set them on a <div>, and everything inside gets the same text formatting (unless you override it in places with more specific formatting rules).

- **Boxes.** A <div> is a natural container. Add a border, some spacing, and a different background color (or image), and you have a way to make select content stand out.

- **Columns.** Professional websites often carve their content up into two or three columns. One way to make this happen is to wrap the content for each column in a <div>, and then use CSS positioning properties to put them in their proper places.

TIP Now that HTML5 has introduced a new set of semantic elements, the <div> element doesn't play quite as central a role. If you can replace a <div> with another, more meaningful semantic element (like <header> or <figure>), you should do that. But when nothing else fits, the <div> remains the go-to tool. Chapter 2 has a detailed description of all the semantic elements.

The <div> element also has a smaller brother named <span>. Like the <div> element, the <span> element has no built-in formatting. The difference is that <div> is a block element, designed to wrap separate paragraphs or entire sections of content, while <span> is an inline element that's meant to wrap smaller portions of content inside a block element. For example, you can use <span> to apply custom formatting to a few words inside a paragraph.

NOTE CSS encourages good design. How? If you want to use CSS effectively, you need to properly plan your web page's structure. Thus, the need for CSS encourages even casual web-page writers to think seriously about how their content is organized.

Multiple Selectors

Sometimes, you might want to define some formatting that applies to more than one element or more than one class. The trick is to separate each selector with a comma.

For example, consider these two heading levels, which have different sizes but share the same title font:

```
h1 {
    font-family: Impact, Charcoal, sans-serif;
    font-size: 40px;
}

h2 {
    font-family: Impact, Charcoal, sans-serif;
    font-size: 20px;
}
```

You could pull the font-family setting into a separate rule that applies to both heading levels, like this:

```
h1, h2 {
    font-family: Impact, Charcoal, sans-serif;
}

h1 {
    font-size: 40px;
}

h2 {
    font-size: 20px;
}
```

It's important to understand that this isn't necessarily a better design. Often, it's better to duplicate settings because that gives you the most flexibility to change formatting later on. If you have too many shared properties, it's more awkward to modify one element type or class without affecting another.

Contextual Selectors

A contextual selector matches an element *inside* another element. Here's an example:

```
.Content h2 {
    color: #24486C;
    font-size: medium;
}
```

This selector looks for an element that uses the Content class. Then it looks for <h2> elements inside that element and formats them with a different text color and font size. Here's an example of an element it will format:

```
<div class="Content">
  ...
  <h2>Mayan Doomsday</h2>
  ...
</div>
```

In the first example, the first selector is a class selector, and the second selector (the contextual one) is an element type selector. However, you can change this up any way you want. Here's an example:

```
.Content .LeadIn {
  font-variant: small-caps;
}
```

This selector looks for an element in the LeadIn class, wrapped inside an element in the Content class. It matches this element:

```
<div class="Content">
  <p><span class="LeadIn">Right now</span>, you're probably feeling pretty
  good.  After all, life in the developed world is comfortable ...</p>
  ...
</div>
```

Once you get the hang of contextual selectors, you'll find that they're quite straight-forward and ridiculously useful.

ID Selectors

Class selectors have a closely related cousin called *ID selectors*. Like a class selector, the ID selector lets you format just the elements you choose. And like a class selector, the ID selector lets you pick a descriptive name. But instead of using a period, you use a number-sign character (#):

```
#Menu {
  border-width: 2px;
  border-style: solid;
}
```

As with class rules, browsers don't apply ID rules unless you specifically tell them to in your HTML. However, instead of switching on the rules with a class attribute, you do so with the id attribute. For example, here's a <div> element that uses the Menu style:

```
<div id="Menu">...</div>
```

At this point, you're probably wondering why you would use an ID selector—after all, the ID selector seems almost exactly the same as a class selector. But there's one difference: You can assign a given ID to just *one* element in a page. In the current example, that means only one <div> can be labeled as a Menu. This restriction doesn't apply to class names, which you can reuse as many times as you like.

That means the ID selector is a good choice if you want to format a single, never-repeated element on your page. The advantage is that the ID selector clearly indicates the special importance of that element. For example, if a page has an ID selector named Menu or NavigationBar, the web designer knows there's only one menu or navigation bar on that page. Of course, you never *need* to use an ID selector. Some web designers use class selectors for everything, whether the section is unique or not. It's a matter of personal preference.

NOTE The id attribute also plays an important role in JavaScript, letting web page designers identify a specific element so it can be manipulated in code. The examples in this book use ID rules whenever an element already uses the id attribute for JavaScript, which avoids setting both the id attribute and the class attribute. In every other case, the examples use class rules, regardless of whether or not the element is unique.

Pseudo-Class Selectors

So far, the selectors you've seen have been straightforward. They've taken a single, obvious piece of information into consideration, like the element type, class name, or ID name. *Pseudo-classes* are a bit more sophisticated. They take extra information into account—information that might not be set in the markup or might be based on user actions.

For most of CSS history, browsers have supported just a few pseudo-classes, which were mostly designed for formatting links. The :link pseudo-class formats any link that points to a new, unvisited location. The :visited pseudo-class applies to any link that points to a location the reader has already visited. The :hover pseudo-class formats a link when a visitor moves the mouse over it, and the :active pseudo-class formats a link as a reader clicks it, before releasing the mouse button. As you can see, pseudo-classes always start with a colon (:).

Here's a style rule that uses pseudo-classes to create a misleading page—one where visited links are blue and unvisited links are red:

```
a:link {
  color: red;
}
a:visited {
  color: blue;
}
```

You can also use pseudo-classes with a class name:

```
.BackwardLink:link {
  color: red;
}
.BackwardLink:visited {
  color: blue;
}
```

Now an anchor element needs to specify the class name to display your new style, as shown here:

```
<a class="BackwardLink" href="...">...</a>
```

Pseudo-classes aren't just a way to format links. The :hover pseudo-class is useful for applying animated effects and creating fancy buttons. It's used with CSS3 transitions, as explained in Chapter 6 (page 195).

> **NOTE** CSS3 also introduces some more advanced pseudo-classes that take other details into consideration, like the position of an element relative to other elements or the state of an input control in a web form. These pseudo-classes aren't described in this book, but you can learn about them from a Smashing Magazine article at *http://tinyurl.com/pc-css3*.

Attribute Selectors

Attribute selection is a feature offered by CSS3 that lets you format a specific type of element that also has a specific value set for one of its attributes. For example, consider the following style rule, which applies only to text boxes:

```
input[type="text"] {
  background-color:silver;
}
```

First, this selector grabs all the <input> elements. Then, it filters down its selection to include just those <input> elements that have a type attribute set to "text", which it then formats. In the following markup, that means the first <input> element gets the silver background but the second doesn't:

```
<label for="name">Name:</label><input id="name" type="text"><br>
<input type="submit" value="OK">
```

Technically, you don't need to include the type="text" attribute in the first <input> element, because that's the default value. If you leave it out, the attribute selector still works, because it pays attention to the current value of the attribute and doesn't care how that value is defined in your markup.

Similarly, you could create a rule that formats the caption for this text box but ignores all other labels:

```
label[for="name"] {
  width: 200px;
}
```

> **NOTE** You can still get a bit fancier with attribute selectors. For example, you can match a combination of attribute values, or match part of an attribute value. These techniques are awfully clever but inject too much complexity into the average style sheet. To get the lowdown, see the CSS3 standard for selectors at *http://tinyurl.com/s-css3*.

A Style Sheet Tour

Chapter 2 shows how you can learn to use HTML5's semantic elements by revising a straightforward, but nicely formatted page called *ApocalypsePage_Original.html* (Figure A-1). This page links to a style sheet named *ApocalypsePage_Original.css*:

```
<!DOCTYPE html>
<html lang="en">
<head>
  <title>Apocalypse Now</title>
  <link rel="stylesheet" href="ApocalypsePage_Original.css">
</head>
...
```

The style sheet is straightforward and relatively brief, weighing in somewhere over 50 lines. In this section, you'll dissect each one of its style rules.

FIGURE A-1

The styles in this page are simple, but they follow the basic organizational principles that you'll see put into practice throughout this book.

First, the style sheet begins with a selector that targets the `<body>` element, which is the root of the entire web page. This is the best place to set inherited values that you want to apply, by default, to the rest of the document. Examples include margins, padding, background color, the font, and the width:

```
body {
  font-family: "Lucida Sans Unicode", "Lucida Grande", Geneva, sans-serif;
  max-width: 800px;
}
```

When setting the `font-family` property in CSS, you should follow two rules. First, use a web-safe font—one of the small number of fonts that are known to work on virtually all web-connected computers (see *http://tinyurl.com/ws-fonts* for a list). Second, use a font list that starts with the specific variant you want, followed by other possible fallbacks, and ends with `serif` or `sans-serif` (two font instructions that all browsers understand). If you prefer to use a fancy font that the user must download from your web server, check out the CSS3 web font feature on page 206.

The body rule also sets a maximum width, capping it at 800 pixels. This rule prevents overly long, unreadable lines when the browser window is made very wide. There are other possible techniques for handling this situation, including splitting the text into columns (page 217), using CSS media queries (page 231), or creating a sidebar to soak up the additional space. However, although setting a fixed 800-pixel width isn't the most glamorous solution, it's a common approach.

Next in the style sheet is a class-specific rule that formats the header region at the top of the page:

```
.Header {
  background-color: #7695FE;
  border: thin #336699 solid;
  padding: 10px;
  margin: 10px;
  text-align: center;
}
```

> **NOTE** In this example, the header is simply a `<div>` with the class name Header. However, Chapter 2 explains how you might consider replacing that with HTML5's `<header>` element.

There's a lot of information packed into this rule. The `background-color` property can be set, like all CSS colors, using a color name (which provides relatively few choices), an HTML color code (as done here), or the `rgb()` function (which specifies the red, green, and blue components of the color). The examples in this book use all three approaches, with color names in simple examples and color codes and the `rgb()` function in more realistic examples.

Incidentally, every HTML color code can be written with the rgb() function, and vice versa. For example, you can write the color in the above example using the rgb() function, like this:

```
background-color: rgb(118,149,254);
```

TIP To actually get the RGB values for the color you want, try an online color picker, or look the numbers up in your favorite drawing or graphics program.

The header rule also draws a thin border around its edges. It uses the all-in-one border property to specify the border thickness, border color, and border style (for example, solid, dashed, dotted, double, groove, ridge, inset, or outset) in one property setting.

With the background color and border details out of the way, the header rule sets 10 pixels of padding (between the content inside and the border) and 10 pixels of margin space (between the border and the surrounding web page). Finally, the text inside the header is centered.

The following three rules use contextual selectors to control how elements are formatted inside the header. The first one formats <h1> elements in the header:

```
.Header h1 {
  margin: 0px;
  color: white;
  font-size: xx-large;
}
```

TIP When setting a font size, you can use keywords (like the xx-large value used here). Or, if you want precise control, you can supply an exact measurement using pixels or em units.

The next two rules format two classes, named Teaser and Byline, which are also inside the header:

```
.Header .Teaser {
  margin: 0px;
  font-weight: bold;
}

.Header .Byline {
  font-style: italic;
  font-size: small;
  margin: 0px;
}
```

This code works because the header contains two `<span>` elements. One `<span>` has the class name Teaser, and contains the subtitle. The second `<span>` has the author information, and uses the class name Byline. Here's the relevant portion of markup:

```html
<div class="Header">
  <h1>How the World Could End</h1>
  <p class="Teaser">Scenarios that spell the end of life as we know it</p>
  <p class="Byline">by Ray N. Carnation</p>
</div>
```

Next up is a rule that formats a `<div>` with the class name Content. It holds the main body of the page. The accompanying style sheet rule sets the font, padding, and line height:

```css
.Content {
  font-size: medium;
  font-family: Cambria, Cochin, Georgia, "Times New Roman", Times, serif;
  padding-top: 20px;
  padding-right: 50px;
  padding-bottom: 5px;
  padding-left: 50px;
  line-height: 120%;
}
```

Whereas the header rule set the padding to be the same on all sides, the content rule sets different padding on each side, adding more space above and the most space on the sides. One way to do that is to specify the expanded padding properties (like padding-top, padding-right, and so on), as done here. Another option is to use the padding property with a series of values in a particular order—top, right, bottom, left. Here's how you can replace the expanded padding properties with just one property:

```css
padding: 20px 50px 5px 50px;
```

Generally, you'll use this form when setting the padding on all sides, but you'll use the expanded padding properties if you want to change the padding on only certain sides. Of course, it's really a matter of taste.

The final line-height property sets the space between adjacent lines. The value of 120% gives some extra spacing, for a more readable feel.

Following the content rule are three contextual selectors that format elements inside. The first rule formats a span with the class name LeadIn. It's used to put the first two words in large, bold, small-cap lettering:

```css
.Content .LeadIn {
  font-weight: bold;
  font-size: large;
  font-variant: small-caps;
}
```

The next two rules change how the <h2> and <p> elements are formatted in the content region:

```
.Content h2 {
  color: #24486C;
  margin-bottom: 2px;
  font-size: medium;
}

.Content p {
  margin-top: 0px;
}
```

As you can see, as a style sheet grows longer it doesn't necessarily become more complex. Here, the style sheet simply repeats the same basic techniques (class selectors and contextual selectors), but uses them to format other parts of the document.

Finally, the style sheet ends with the rules that format the footer portion. By now, you can interpret these on your own:

```
.Footer {
  text-align: center;
  font-size: x-small;
}

.Footer .Disclaimer {
  font-style: italic;
}

.Footer p {
  margin: 3px;
}
```

This rounds out the *ApocalypsePage_Original.css* style sheet. Feel free to download it from the try-out site (*http://prosetech.com/html5*) and try tweaking it to see what happens. Or, check out Chapter 2, which revises this page and the accompanying style sheet to use the HTML5 semantic elements.

JavaScript: The Brains of Your Page

here was a time when the Web was all about markup. Pages held text and HTML tags, and not much more. Really advanced websites used server scripts that could tweak the HTML markup before it made its way to the browser, but the code stopped there.

Crack open a web page today and you're likely to find buckets of JavaScript code, powering everything from vital features to minor frills. Self-completing text boxes, pop-up menus, slideshows, real-time mapping, and webmail are just a few examples of the many ways crafty developers put JavaScript to work. In fact, it's nearly impossible to imagine a Web *without* JavaScript. While HTML is still the language of the Web, JavaScript is now the brains behind its most advanced pages.

In this appendix, you'll get a heavily condensed JavaScript crash course. This appendix won't provide a complete tutorial on JavaScript, nor does it have enough information to help you get started if you've never written a line of code in any programming language, ever. But if you have some rudimentary programming knowledge—say, you once learned a lick of Visual Basic, picked up the basics of Pascal, or took C out for spin—this appendix will help you transfer your skills to the JavaScript world. You'll get just enough information to identify familiar programming ingredients like variables, loops, and conditional logic. And you'll cover all the basic language elements that are used in the JavaScript-based examples in the rest of this book.

TIP If you need more help to get started with JavaScript, check out *JavaScript & jQuery: The Missing Manual* by David Sawyer McFarland, which also introduces jQuery, a popular JavaScript-enhancing toolkit. Or read Mozilla's detailed JavaScript guide at *http://developer.mozilla.org/JavaScript*.

How a Web Page Uses JavaScript

Before you can run a line of JavaScript, you need to know where to put it in your web page. It all starts with the `<script>` element. The following sections show you how to take a page from quick-and-dirty JavaScript injection to a properly structured example that you can put online without embarrassment.

Embedding Script in Your Markup

The simplest way to use the `<script>` element is to stick it somewhere in your HTML markup, like this:

```
<!DOCTYPE html>
<html lang="en">
<head>
  <meta charset="utf-8">
  <title>A Simple JavaScript Example</title>
</head>

<body>
  <p>At some point in the processing of this page, a script block
will run and show a message box.</p>

  <script>
alert("We interrupt this web page with a special JavaScript announcement.");
  </script>

  <p>If you get here, you've already seen it.</p>
</body>
</html>
```

This script block contains just one line of code, although you could just as easily pack it with a sequence of operations. In this case, the single line of code triggers JavaScript's built-in `alert()` function. The `alert()` function accepts a piece of text and shows that text in a message box (see Figure B-1). To move on, the user must click the OK button.

> **NOTE** This example introduces a JavaScript convention that you'll see throughout this book, and on good websites everywhere: the semicolon. In JavaScript, semicolons indicate the end of each programming statement. Strictly speaking, semicolons aren't necessary (unless you want to cram multiple statements on a single line). However, they're considered good style.

If you want to run some JavaScript right away (as in this example), you'll probably put the `<script>` section at the end of the `<body>` section, just before the final `</body>` tag. That way, it runs only after the browser has processed all the page markup.

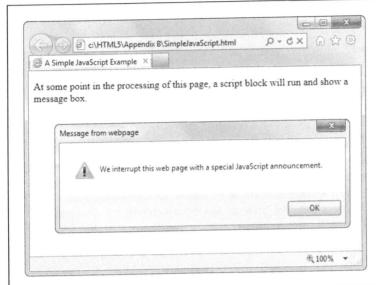

FIGURE B-1

When the web browser comes across JavaScript code, it runs it immediately. In fact, it even halts the page processing, temporarily. In this case, the code is held up until the web page user closes the message box by clicking OK. This allows the code to continue and the script block to end. The web browser then processes the rest of the markup.

GEM IN THE ROUGH

Dealing with Internet Explorer's Paranoia

If you run the alert example above in Firefox or Chrome, you'll find that everything works seamlessly. If you run it in Internet Explorer, you won't get the same satisfaction. Instead, you'll see a security warning in a yellow bar at the top or bottom of the page (depending on the version of IE). Until you go to that bar and click "Allow blocked content," your JavaScript code won't run.

At first glance, IE's security warning seems like a surefire way to scare off the bravest web visitor. But you don't need to worry; the message is just part of the quirky way Internet Explorer deals with web pages that you store on your hard drive. When you access the same page over the Web, Internet Explorer won't raise the slightest objection.

That said, the security warning is still an annoyance while you're testing your web page, because it forces you to keep explicitly telling the browser to allow the page to run JavaScript.

To avoid the security notice altogether, you can tell Internet Explorer to pretend you downloaded your page from a web server. You do this by adding a special comment called the *mark of the Web*. You place this comment in the <head> section of your page:

```
<head>
<meta charset="utf-8">
<!-- saved from url=(0014)about:internet
-->
   ...
</head>
```

When IE sees the mark of the Web, it treats the page as though it came from a web server, skipping the security warning and running your JavaScript code without hesitation. To all other browsers, the mark of the Web just looks like an ordinary HTML comment.

Using a Function

The problem with the previous example is that it encourages you to mingle code and markup in an unseemly mess. To keep things organized, you should wrap each code "task" in a *function*—a named unit of code that you can call into action whenever you need it.

When you create a function, you should give it a logical name. Here's a function named showMessage():

```
function showMessage() {
  // Code goes here ...
}
```

The function *body*—its guts—includes everything between the opening { bracket and the closing } bracket. Inside these delimiters, a function can hold as many lines of code as you need. Right now, the showMessage() function contains a single line, which is the "Code goes here" comment. (A JavaScript comment is a line that starts with two slash characters. The browser ignores all comments—you add them to remind yourself of important details or inform others about what the code is doing.)

To add some code to your function, just put all the statements you need between the curly brackets:

```
function showMessage() {
  alert("We interrupt this web page with a special JavaScript announcement.");
}
```

Of course, this whole shebang needs to go in a <script> block. The best place to put JavaScript functions is in the <head> section. This imposes some basic organization on your page, by moving the code out of the markup and into a separate section.

Here's a revamped version of the earlier example, which now uses a function:

```
<!DOCTYPE html>
<html lang="en">
<head>
  <meta charset="utf-8">
  <title>A Simple JavaScript Example</title>
  <script>
function showMessage() {
  alert("We interrupt this web page with a special JavaScript announcement.");
}
  </script>
</head>
...
```

Functions, on their own, don't do anything. To trigger a function, you need another piece of code that *calls* the function.

Calling a function is easy—in fact, you've already seen how to do it with the built-in alert() function. You simply write the function name, followed by a set of parentheses. Inside the parentheses, you put whatever data the function needs. Or, if the function doesn't accept any data, like showMessage(), you simply include parentheses with nothing inside them:

```
...
<body>
  <p>At some point in the processing of this page, a script block
will run and show a message box.</p>
 <script>
showMessage();
 </script>
  <p>If you get here, you've already seen it.</p>
</body>
</html>
```

In this example, the function and the code that calls the function are in separate <script> blocks. This design isn't necessary, but it's used here to emphasize the separation between these two pieces.

At first glance, adding a function seems to make this example more complicated than before. But it's actually a dramatic step forward in design, for several reasons:

- **The bulk of the code is out of the markup.** You need just one line of code to call a function. However, a realistic function will contain a pile of code, and a realistic page will contain a pile of functions. You definitely want to separate all those details from your markup.

- **You can reuse your code.** Once code is in a function, you can call that function at different times, from different places in your code. This isn't obvious in this simple example, but it becomes an important factor in more complex applications, like the painting application in Chapter 8.

- **You're ready to use external script files.** Moving your code out of the markup is a precursor to moving it right out of the HTML file, as you'll see in the next section, for even better organization.

- **You can add events.** An event is a way for you to tell the page to run a specific function when a specific occurrence takes place. Web pages are event-driven, which means most code is fired up when an event happens (rather than being launched through a script block). Events pair neatly with functions, as you'll see on page 457.

Moving the Code to a Script File

Pulling your JavaScript code together into a set of functions is the first step in good organization. The second step is to take that script code and put it in an entirely separate file. Do this with all your scripts, and you'll get smaller, simpler web pages—and the ability to reuse the same functions in different web pages. In fact, putting script code in an external file is analogous to putting CSS style rules in an external file. In both cases, you gain the ability to reuse your work and you leave simpler pages behind.

NOTE Virtually every well-designed web page that uses JavaScript puts the code in one or more script files. The only exceptions are if you have a few lines of very simple code that you're certain not to use anywhere else, or if you're creating a one-off example.

Script files are always plain text files. Usually, they have the extension *.js* (which stands for JavaScript). You put all your code inside a script file, but you don't include the <script> element. For example, here are the complete contents of a script file named *MessageScripts.js*:

```
function showMessage() {
  alert("We interrupt this web page with a special JavaScript announcement.");
}
```

Now save the file, and put it in the same folder as your web page. In your web page, define a script block, but don't supply any code. Instead, add the src attribute and indicate the script file you want to link to:

```
<!DOCTYPE html>
<html lang="en">
<head>
  <meta charset="utf-8">
  <title>A Simple JavaScript Example</title>
  <script src="MessageScripts.js"></script>
</head>

<body>
  <p>At some point in the processing of this page, a script block
will run and show a message box.</p>
  <script>
showMessage()
  </script>
  <p>If you get here, you've already seen it.</p>
</body>
</html>
```

When a browser comes across this script block, it requests the *MessageScripts.js* file and treats it as though the code were right inside the page. That means you can call the showMessage() function in exactly the same way you did before.

NOTE Even though the script block doesn't actually contain any code when you use external script files, you must still include the closing </script> tag. If you leave that out, the browser assumes everything that follows—the rest of the page—is part of your JavaScript code.

You can also link to JavaScript functions on another website—just remember that the `src` attribute in the `<script>` element needs to point to a full URL (like *http://SuperScriptSite.com/MessageScript.js*) instead of just a file name. This technique is necessary for plugging into other companies' web services, like Google Maps (page 410).

Responding to Events

So far, you've seen how to run script right away—by weaving a script block into your HTML markup. But it's far more common to trigger code after the page is finished processing, when the user takes a specific action—like clicking a button or moving the mouse pointer over an element.

To do so, you need to use JavaScript *events*, which are notifications that an HTML element sends out when specific things happen. For example, JavaScript gives every element an event named `onMouseOver` (a compressed version of "on mouse over"). As the name suggests, this event takes place (or *fires*, to use programmer-speak) when a visitor moves his mouse pointer over an HTML element like a paragraph, link, image, table cell, or text box. That action triggers the `onMouseOver` event and your code flies into action.

This discussion brings up one key question: How do you link your code to the event you want to use? The trick is to add an event attribute to the appropriate element. So if you want to handle the `onMouseOver` event of an `<img>` element, you need markup like this:

```
<img src="sunny.jpg" alt="A sunny day" onmouseover="showMessage()">
```

> **NOTE** In JavaScript, function, variable, and object names are case-sensitive, meaning `showMessage` is not the same as `showMESSAGE` (and the latter fails). However, the event attribute names are not case-sensitive, because they are technically a part of HTML markup, and HTML tolerates any combination of uppercase and lowercase letters. Even so, it's common to write event attributes with no capitals (as shown here) because this matches the old rules of XHTML, and most programmers are too lazy to reach for the Shift key anyway.

Now, when the mouse moves over the image, and the `onMouseOver` event fires, the browser automatically calls the `showMessage()` function. This function pops up a rather unremarkable message box (Figure B-2). When an event triggers a function in this way, that function is called an *event handler*.

To use events effectively, you need to know which events JavaScript supports. In addition, you need to know which events work on which HTML elements. Table B-1 provides a list of commonly used events and the HTML elements that they apply to. (You can find a more complete reference at *http://developer.mozilla.org/DOM/element*.)

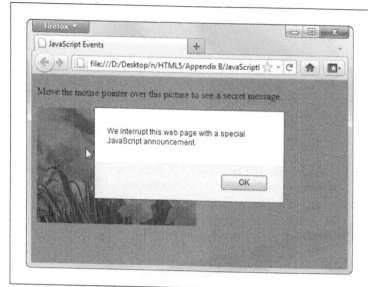

FIGURE B-2

In this example, the alert box doesn't pop up until you move your mouse pointer over the link.

TABLE B-1 *Common HTML object events*

EVENT NAME	DESCRIPTION	APPLIES TO
onClick	Triggered when you click an element.	Virtually all elements
onMouseOver	Triggered when you move your mouse pointer over an element.	Virtually all elements
onMouseOut	Triggered when you move your mouse pointer away from an element.	Virtually all elements
onKeyDown	Triggered when you press a key.	`<select>`, `<input>`, `<textarea>`, `<a>`, `<button>`
onKeyUp	Triggered when you release a pressed key.	`<select>`, `<input>`, `<textarea>`, `<a>`, `<button>`
onFocus	Triggered when a control receives *focus* (in other words, when you position the cursor on the control so you can type something in). Controls include text boxes, checkboxes, and so on—see page 108 to learn more.	`<select>`, `<input>`, `<textarea>`, `<a>`, `<button>`
onBlur	Triggered when focus leaves a control.	`<select>`, `<input>`, `<textarea>`, `<a>`, `<button>`

EVENT NAME	DESCRIPTION	APPLIES TO
onChange	Triggered when you change a value in an input control. In a text box, this event doesn't fire until you move to another control.	`<select>`, `<input type="text">`, `<textarea>`
onSelect	Triggered when you select a portion of text in an input control.	`<input type="text">`, `<textarea>`
onError	Triggered when the browser fails to download an image (usually due to an incorrect URL).	`<img>`
onLoad	Triggered when the browser finishes downloading a new page or finishes loading an object, like an image.	`<img>`, `<body>`
onUnload	Triggered when a browser unloads a page. (This typically happens after you enter a new URL or when you click a link. It fires just *before* the browser downloads the new page.)	`<body>`

■ A Few Language Essentials

A brief appendix isn't enough to cover any language, even one as straightforward as JavaScript. However, the following sections will fill you in on a few language essentials that you'll need to digest the examples elsewhere in this book.

Variables

Every programming language has the concept of *variables*—containers that you can use to store bits of information in memory. In JavaScript, every variable is created the same way, by declaring it with the var keyword followed by the variable name. This example creates a variable named myMessage:

```
var myMessage;
```

NOTE JavaScript variables are case-sensitive, which means a variable named myMessage differs from one named MyMessage. If you try to use them interchangeably, you'll wind up with an error message (if your browser is nice) or a bizarre mistake in the page (which is usually what happens).

To store information in a variable, you use the equal sign (=), which copies the data on the right side of the equal sign into the variable on the left. Here's a one-step example that defines a variable and puts a text value (which is known as a *string*) inside:

```
var myMessage = "Everybody loves variables";
```

You can then use your variable:

```
// Show the variable text in a message box.
alert(myMessage);
```

> **NOTE** JavaScript is a notoriously loose language, and it lets you use variables even if you don't specifically declare them with the var keyword. However, doing so is considered extremely bad form and is likely to lead to sloppy mistakes.

Null Values

One special value you may run into is null, which is programmer-speak for "nothing." If a variable is null, it indicates that a given object doesn't exist or is empty. Depending on the context, this may signal that a specific feature is unavailable. For example, Modernizr (page 31) uses null value tests to determine whether the browser supports certain HTML5 features. You may also check for null values in your scripts—for example, to determine whether you haven't yet created or stored an object:

```
if (myObject == null) {
  // There is no myObject in existence.
  // Now might be a good time to create one.
}
```

Variable Scope

There are two basic places you can create a variable—inside or outside a function. The following code snippet has one of both:

```
<script>
var outsideVariable;

function doSomething() {
  var insideVariable;
  ...
}
</script>
```

If you create a variable inside a function (called a *local variable*), that variable exists only while that function is running. Here, insideVariable is a local variable. As soon as the doSomething() method ends, the variable is tossed out of memory. That means the next time the page calls doSomething(), the insideVariable is created from scratch, with none of its previous data.

On the other hand, if you create a variable outside a function (called a *global variable*), its value lasts as long as the page is loaded in the browser. Furthermore, every function can use that variable. In the previous example, outsideVariable is a global variable.

> **TIP** The rule of thumb is to use a local variable, unless you specifically need to share your variable with multiple functions, or to retain its value after the function ends. That's because it's more trouble to keep track of global variables, and if you use too many, your code becomes messy.

Variable Data Types

In JavaScript, variables can store different data types, such as text, integers, floating point numbers, arrays, and objects. However, no matter what you want to store in your variable, you define it with the same var keyword. You do *not* set the data type of your variable.

That means you can take the myMessage variable, with its piece of text, and replace that with a numeric value, like this:

```
myMessage = 27.3;
```

This behavior makes JavaScript easy to use, because any variable can hold any type of content. It can also let JavaScript mistakes slip past undetected. For example, you might want to grab the text out of a text box and put that in a variable, like this:

```
var = inputElement.value;
```

But if you're not careful, you can accidentally end up putting the entire text box *object* into the variable, like this:

```
var = inputElement;
```

JavaScript allows both actions, so it won't complain. But a few lines into your code, this mistake will probably lead to some sort of unrecoverable problem. At that point, the browser simply stops running the rest of your code, without giving you any error message to explain what happened. In cases like these, you need the help of a Java-Script debugging tool (see the box on page 462), which can pause your code at any time and let you peer into your variables, so you can see what data they currently contain.

Operations

One of the most useful things you can do with numeric variables is perform *operations* on them to change your data. For example, you can use arithmetic operators to perform mathematical calculations:

```
var myNumber = (10 + 5) * 2 / 5;
```

These calculations follow the standard order of operations (parentheses first, then multiplication and division, then addition and subtraction). The result of this calculation is 6.

You can also use operations to join together multiple pieces of text into one long string. In this case, you use the plus (+) operator:

```
var firstName = "Sarah";
var lastName = "Smithers";
var fullName = firstName + " " + lastName;
```

Identifying Errors in JavaScript Code

In order to deal with problems (like the variable mistake shown on page 461), you need to master *debugging*—the fine art of hunting down the problems in your code and stamping them out. Unfortunately, the way you go about debugging depends on the browser you're using. Different browsers have different debugging tools (or support different debugging extensions). And while they all serve the same purpose, they don't work in exactly the same way.

Fortunately, all the information you need is on the Web. Here are some links that can explain how to debug JavaScript mistakes, based on your browser of choice:

- **Internet Explorer.** To sort out problems with IE, press F12 to pop up the Developer Tools window. To learn how to use it, visit *http://tinyurl.com/debug-ie*.

- **Firefox.** Serious Firefox developers use a Firefox add-in called Firebug to see what their code is doing at all times. Get it (and learn more) at *http://getfirebug.com/javascript*.

- **Google Chrome.** Chrome has a respectable built-in debugger. To get started, read Google's debugging tutorial at *http://tinyurl.com/c-debugger*.

- **Opera.** Opera's debugging tool of choice is Dragonfly. You can learn about it at *www.opera.com/dragonfly*.

- **Safari.** Safari has a powerful set of built-in debugging tools, although tracking down the documentation that explains them can be tricky. You can start with a fairly technical article from the Safari Developer Library at *http://tinyurl.com/safari-debug*.

Remember, it doesn't matter what browser and debugging tool you use to correct problems. Once they're fixed in one browser, they're fixed for everyone.

Now the `fullName` variable holds the text "Sarah Smithers." (The " " in the code above tells JavaScript to leave a space between the two names).

When making simple modifications to a variable, there's a shortcut you're likely to use. For example, if you have this basic addition operation:

```
var myNumber = 20;
myNumber = myNumber + 10;
// (Now myNumber is 30.)
```

You can rewrite it like this:

```
var myNumber = 20;
myNumber += 10;
// (Now myNumber is 30.)
```

This trick of moving the operator to the left side of the equal sign works with pretty much any operator. Here are some examples:

```
var myNumber = 20;
myNumber -= 10;
// (Now myNumber is 10.)
myNumber *= 10;
// (Now myNumber is 100.)
```

```
var myText = "Hello";
var myText += " there.";
// (Now myText is "Hello there.")
```

And if you want to add or subtract the number 1, there's an even more concise shortcut:

```
var myNumber = 20;
myNumber++;
// (Now myNumber is 21.)


myNumber--;
// (Now myNumber is 20.)
```

Conditional Logic

All conditional logic starts with a *condition*: an expression that is either true or false. Based on the result, you can decide to run some code or to skip over it.

To create a condition, you need to rely on JavaScript's *logical operators*, which are detailed in Table B-2.

TABLE B-2 *Logical operators*

OPERATOR	DESCRIPTION
==	Equal to.
!=	Not equal to.
===	Exactly equal to (in value *and* data type).
!==	Not exactly equal to.
!	Not. (This reverses the condition, so if it would ordinarily be true, it is now false, and vice versa.)
<	Less than.
>	Greater than.
<=	Less than or equal to.
>=	Greater than or equal to.
&&	Logical and (evaluates to true only if both expressions are true). If the first expression is false, the second expression is not evaluated.
||	Logical or (evaluates to true if either expression is true). If the first expression is true, the second expression is not evaluated.

Here's an example of a simple condition:

```
myNumber < 100
```

To use this condition to make decisions, you need to put it with an if statement. Here's an example:

```
if (myNumber < 100) {
  // (This code runs if myNumber is 20, but not if it's 147.)
}
```

> **NOTE** Technically, you don't need the curly brackets around your conditional code, unless you have more than one statement. However, including the brackets is always clearer and avoids potential errors if you do have multiple statements.

When testing equality, make sure you use two equal signs. A single equal sign sets a variable's value, rather than performing the comparison you want:

```
// Right:
if (myName == "Joe") {
}

// Wrong:
if (myName = "Sarah") {
}
```

Although two equal signs are good, it turns out that *three* may be even better. Many JavaScript pros prefer to test equality using the "exactly equal to" operator (that's ===) rather than the mere "equal to" operator (==). The difference is that the "equal to" operator will convert data types to try to make a match, while the more stringent "exactly equal to" operator insists on a perfect match of value and data type.

Here's an example that illustrates the difference:

```
var myNumberAsText = "45";

// This is true, because the "equal to" operator is willing to convert
// "45" the string to 45 the number.
if (myNumberAsText == 45) {
}

// This is false, because the data types don't match.
if (myNumberAsText === 45) {
}
```

In most cases, it doesn't matter whether you use the "equal to" or "exactly equal to" operator, but there are some rare type conversion mistakes that "exactly equal to" can prevent. For that reason, JavaScript experts generally prefer using three equal signs instead of two.

If you want to evaluate more than one condition, one after the other, you can use more than one if block (naturally). But if you want to look at a series of conditions and find the first one that matches (while ignoring the others), you need the else keyword. Here it is at work:

```
if (myNumber < 100) {
  // (This code runs if myNumber is less than 100.)
}
else if (myNumber < 200) {
  // (This code runs if myNumber is less than 200 but greater than or equal to
  // 100.)
}
else {
  // (In all other cases, meaning myNumber is 200 or more, this code runs.)
}
```

You can include as many or as few conditions as you like in an if block, and adding a final else without a condition is also optional.

Loops

A loop is a basic programming tool that lets you repeat a block of code. The king of JavaScript loops is the for loop. It's essentially a loop with a built-in counter. Most programming languages have their own version of this construct.

When creating a for loop, you set the starting value, the ending value, and the amount to increment the counter after each pass. Here's one example:

```
for (var i = 0; i < 5; i++){
  // (This code executes five times.)
  alert("This is message: " + i);
}
```

At the beginning of the for loop is a set of brackets with three important pieces of information. The first portion (in this example, var i = 0) creates the counter variable (i) and sets its initial value (0). The second portion (i < 5) sets a termination condition. If it's not true (for example, i is increased to 5), the loop ends and the code inside is not repeated again. The third portion (i++), increments the counter variable. In this example, the counter is incremented by 1 after each pass. That means i will be 0 for the first pass, 1 for the second pass, and so on. The end result is that the code runs five times and shows this series of messages:

```
This is message: 0
This is message: 1
This is message: 2
This is message: 3
This is message: 4
```

Arrays

The for loop pairs naturally with the *array*—a programming object that stores a list of values.

JavaScript arrays are remarkably flexible. Unlike in many other programming languages, you don't define the number of items you want an array to store in JavaScript. Instead, you simply begin by creating an empty array with square brackets, like this:

```
var colorList = [];
```

You can then add items using the array's push() method:

```
colorList.push("blue");
colorList.push("green");
colorList.push("red");
```

Or you can place an array item in a specific position. If this memory slot doesn't already exist, JavaScript creates if for you, happily:

```
colorList[3] = "magenta";
```

And you can pull it out yourself, also by position:

```
var color = colorList[3];
```

> **NOTE** Just remember that JavaScript arrays use zero-based counting: The first item in an array is in slot 0, the second is in slot 1, and so on.

Once you have an array stocked with items, you can process each of them using a for loop like this:

```
for (var i = 0; i < colorList.length; i++) {
  alert("Found color: " + colorList[i]);
}
```

This code moves from the first item (the item at position 0) to the last item (using the array's length property, which reports its total item count). It shows each item in a message box, although you could surely think of something more practical to do with your array items.

Using a for loop to process an array is a basic technique in JavaScript. You'll use it often in this book, with arrays that you create yourself and ones that are provided to you by other JavaScript functions.

Functions That Receive and Return Data

Earlier, you saw a simple function, showMessage(). When you called showMessage(), you didn't need to supply any data, and when it finished, it didn't provide you with any additional information.

Functions aren't always that simple. In many cases, you need to send specific information to a function, or take the results of a function and use them in another operation. For example, imagine you want to create a version of the showMessage() function that you can use to show different messages. To do so, you need to make the showMessage() function accept a single *parameter*. This parameter represents the customized text you want to incorporate into your greeting.

To add the parameter, you must first give it a name, say `customMessage`, and put it in parentheses after the function name, like so:

```
function showMessage(customMessage) {
  alert(customMessage);
}
```

Inside the function, it can work with the parameters just like normal variables. In this example, the function simply takes the supplied text and shows it in a message box.

Now, when calling the `showMessage()` function, you need to supply one value (called an *argument*) for each of the function's parameters:

```
showMessage("Nobody likes an argument.");
```

Parameters let you send information *to* a function. You can also create functions that send information *back* to the script code that called them. The key to doing this is the `return` command, which you put right at the end of your function. The `return` command ends the function immediately, and spits out whatever information your function generates.

Of course, a sophisticated function can accept *and* return information. For example, here's a function that multiplies two numbers (the `numberA` and `numberB` parameters) and returns the result to anyone who's interested:

```
function multiplyNumbers(numberA, numberB) {
  return numberA * numberB;
}
```

Here's how you use this function elsewhere on your web page:

```
// Pass in two numbers, and get the result.
var result = multiplyNumbers(3202, 23405);

// Use the result to create a message.
var message = "The product of 3202 and 23405 is " + result;

// Show the message.
showMessage(message);
```

Of course you don't really need a function to multiply numbers (an ordinary JavaScript calculation can do that), nor do you need a function to show a message box (because the built-in `alert()` function can handle that job). But both examples do a good job of showing you how functions tick, and you'll use parameters and return values in the same way in more complex functions.

Objects

Virtually all modern programming languages include the concept of an *object*, which is a package of related data and features that you can interact with in code. For example, every HTML element on a web page is an object in the eyes of your code. Using the different properties of this object, you can read or alter its content, change its style, and handle its events.

Programmers often need to create their own objects, too. For example, you'll create circle objects in the circle-drawing example in Chapter 9 (page 294) and ball objects for the bouncing ball example on page 304.

Objects make complex programming tasks easier, particularly when you need to manage multiple copies of the same data structure. For example, if you need to fill a page with bouncing balls, it would be a serious headache to create dozens and dozens of variables to hold the position and speed of each individual ball. But if you have a way to declare a *template* for your balls, you can reuse that single template to create as many live ball objects as you need, whether that's just one or eighty-four thousand.

Most languages have a specific syntax for creating object templates. Often, these templates are called *classes*. But JavaScript doesn't include an official class feature. This oversight is due to JavaScript's history—it started life as a simple, streamlined scripting language, not a serious tool for building online apps. Fortunately, clever JavaScript programmers have found ways to fill the object gaps. Although their tricks began as inventive-but-odd hacks, they're now considered standard practice.

For example, if you need to define an object in JavaScript, you write an object-definition function for it. This object-definition function is the template that takes the place of a true class in languages like C#, Java, and Visual Basic. Here's an object-definition function that lets you create Person objects:

```
function Person() {
  this.firstName = "Joe";
  this.lastName = "Grapta";
}
```

The object-definition function has a single task. It defines, one at a time, all the individual bits of data that constitute that object. In the case of the Person object shown above, this includes two details: a first and last name. (You could easily add additional details, like a date of birth, email address, and so on.) The this keyword is the magic touch—it makes sure that each property you create will become part of the object.

As long as you start the line with this followed by a dot, you can name the property variable whatever you want. So the following example is an equally valid person that stores the same data, but with different property names:

```
function Person() {
  this.F_name = "Joe";
```



```
      this.L_name = "Grapta";
  }
```

Now you can use the `Person()` function to create a new person object. The trick is that you don't want to call the function and trigger its code. Instead, you want to create a new copy of the function by using the `new` keyword. Here's how that works:

```
// Create a new Person, and store it in a variable named joePerson.
var joePerson = new Person();
```

Once you have a live object, you can access all its details through the property names that you used in the object-definition function:

```
// Read the firstName property.
alert("His name is " + joePerson.firstName);

// Change the firstName property.
joePerson.FirstName = "Joseph";
```

You can improve your object-definition function so your code specifies some or all the data details through arguments. This saves you the trouble of creating your object and then customizing it with additional lines of code. It also makes sure your object starts out in the correct state, avoiding potential mistakes. Here's an example that updates the `Person()` function in this way:

```
function Person(fname, lname) {
  this.firstName = fname;
  this.lastName = lname;
}
```

And here's how you use the new `Person()` function to create two objects:

```
var newCustomer1 = new Person("Christy", "Shanks");
var newCustomer2 = new Person("Emilio", "Taginelle");
```

Page 294 has a full walkthrough of an example that uses basic object creation, and you'll see the same technique at work throughout this book.

Object Literals

In the previous section, you saw how to create objects in JavaScript using a function, which acts as a template. When you want to formally define the ingredients that make up an object, using a function is the best approach. It leads to well-organized code and makes complex coding tasks easier. It's the best choice when you want to work with your objects in different ways and in different places in your code. But sometimes you just need a quick way to create an object for a one-off task. In this case, an *object literal* makes sense, because it requires nothing more advanced than a pair of curly braces.

To create an object literal, you use an opening curly brace, supply a comma-separated list of properties, and then end with a closing curly brace. You can use spacing and line breaks to make your code more readable, but that's not required. Here's an example:

```
var personObject = {
  firstName="Joe",
  lastName="Grapta"
};
```

For each property, you specify the property name and its starting value. Thus, the above code sets personObject.firstName to the text "Joe" and personObject.lastName to "Grapta."

The example on page 408 uses object literals to send information to the geolocation system. As long as you use the right property names (the ones the getCurrentPosition() method is expecting), an object literal works perfectly.

> **TIP** If you want to learn more about object literals, object functions, and everything else to do with custom objects in JavaScript, check out the detailed information at *www.javascriptkit.com/javatutors/oopjs.shtml*.

Interacting with the Page

So far, you've seen the right way to put JavaScript in a page, but you haven't done anything impressive (in fact, you haven't done anything but pop up a message box). Before going ahead, you need to know a bit more about the role JavaScript typically plays.

First, it's important to understand that JavaScript code is *sandboxed*, which means its capabilities are carefully limited. Your page can't perform any potentially risky tasks on your visitor's computer, like sending orders to a printer, accessing files, running other programs, reformatting a hard drive, and so on. This design ensures good security, even for careless visitors.

Instead, JavaScript spends most of its time doing one of these tasks:

- **Updating the page.** Your script code can change elements, remove them, or add new ones. In fact, JavaScript has complete flexibility to change every detail about the currently displayed HTML, and can even replace the whole document.

- **Retrieving data from the server.** JavaScript can make new web requests from the same web server that sent the original page. By combining this technique with the one above, you can create web pages that seamlessly update important information, like a list of news stories or a stock quote.

- **Sending data to the server.** HTML already has a way to send data to a web server, called web forms (Chapter 4). But JavaScript can take a much more subtle approach. It can grab bits of information out of your form controls, validate them, and even transmit them to the web server, all without forcing the browser to refresh the page.

The last two techniques require the XMLHttpRequest object, a JavaScript extension that's described on page 377. In the following sections, you'll take a look at the first of these, which is a fundamental part of almost every JavaScript-powered page.

Manipulating an Element

In the eyes of JavaScript, your page is much more than a static block of HTML. Instead, each element is a live object that you can examine and modify with JavaScript code.

The easiest way to get hold of an object is to identify it with a unique name, which you apply through the id attribute. Here's an example:

```
<h1 id="pageTitle">Welcome to My Page</h1>
```

Once you give your element a unique ID, you can easily locate that object in your code and have JavaScript act on it.

JavaScript includes a handy trick for locating an object: the document.getElementById() method. Basically, document is an object that represents your whole HTML document. It's always available, and you can use it anytime you want. This document object, like any object worthy of the name, gives you some handy properties and methods. The getElementById() method is one of the coolest—it scans a page looking for a specific HTML element.

> **NOTE** If you're familiar with the basics of object-oriented programming, properties and methods are old hat. If not, you can think of *properties* as data attached to an object, and you can think of *methods* as functions built into an object.

When you call the document.getElementById() method, you supply the ID of the HTML element you're looking for. Here's an example that digs up the object for an HTML element with the ID pageTitle:

```
var titleObject = document.getElementById("pageTitle");
```

This code gets the object for the <h1> element shown earlier and stores it in a variable named titleObject. By storing the object in a variable, you can perform a series of operations on it without having to look it up more than once.

So what, exactly, can you do with HTML objects? To a certain extent, the answer depends on the type of element you're working with. For example, if you have a hyperlink, you can change its URL. If you have an image, you can change its source. And there are some actions you can take with almost all HTML elements, like changing their style or modifying the text that appears between the beginning and ending tags. As you'll see, you'll find these tricks useful in making your pages more dynamic—for example, you can change a page when a visitor takes an action, like clicking a link. Interactions like these make visitors feel as though they're using an intelligent, responsive program instead of a plain, inert web page.

Here's how you modify the text inside the just-mentioned <h1> element, for example:

```
titleObject.innerHTML = "This Page Is Dynamic";
```

This script works because it uses the *property* named `innerHTML`, which sets the content that's nested inside an element (in this case, an `<h1>` element with the page title). Like all properties, `innerHTML` is just one aspect of an HTML object you can alter. To write code statements like this, you need to know what properties JavaScript lets you play with.

Obviously, some properties apply to specific HTML elements only, like the `src` attribute that's used to load a new picture into this `<img>` element:

```
var imgObject = document.getElementById("dayImage");
dayImage.src = "cloudy.jpg";
```

You can also tweak CSS properties through the style object:

```
titleObject.style.color = "rgb(0,191,255)";
```

Modern browsers boast a huge catalog of DOM properties you can use with just about any HTML element. Table B-3 lists some of the most useful.

TABLE B-3 *Common HTML object properties*

PROPERTY	DESCRIPTION
className	Lets you retrieve or set the `class` attribute (see page 438). In other words, this property determines what style (if any) this element uses. Of course, you need to define this style in an embedded or linked style sheet, or you'll end up with the plain-Jane default formatting.
innerHTML	Lets you read or change the HTML inside an element. The `innerHTML` property is insanely useful, but it has two quirks. First, you can use it on all HTML content, including text and tags. So if you want to put bold text inside a paragraph, you can set `innerHTML` to `<b>Hi</b>`. Second, when you set `innerHTML`, you replace all the content inside this element, including any other HTML elements. So if you set the `innerHTML` of a `<div>` element that contains several paragraphs and images, all of these items disappear, to be replaced by your new content.
parentElement	Provides the HTML object for the element that contains this element. For example, if the current element is a `<b>` element in a paragraph, this gets the object for the `<p>` element. Once you have this element, you can modify it too.
style	Bundles together all the CSS attributes that determine the appearance of the HTML element. Technically, the `style` property returns a full-fledged style object, and you need to add another dot (.) and the name of the `style` attribute you want to change, as in `myElement.style.fontSize`. You can use the `style` object to dictate colors, borders, fonts, and even positioning.
tagName	Provides the name of the HTML element for this object, without the angle brackets. For example, if the current object represents an `<img>` element, this returns the text "img."

TIP HTML elements also provide a smaller set of useful methods, including some for modifying attributes, like getAttribute() and setAttribute(); and some for adding or removing elements, like insert-Child(), appendChild(), and removeChild(). To learn more about the properties and methods that a specific HTML element supports, check out the reference at *http://developer.mozilla.org/DOM/element.*

Connecting to an Event Dynamically

On page 457, you saw how to wire up a function using an event attribute. However, it's also possible to connect an event to a function using JavaScript code.

Most of the time, you'll probably stick to event attributes. However, there are cases where that isn't possible or convenient. One of the most common examples is when you create an HTML object in your code and then add it to the page dynamically. In this situation, there's no markup for the new element, so there's no way to use an event attribute. (You'll see this technique in the canvas-drawing example in Chapter 8.) Another case is when you're attaching an event to a built-in object rather than an element. (You'll see this example when you handle storage events in Chapter 10.) For all these reasons, it's important to understand how to wire up events with code.

NOTE There are several different ways to attach events, but they aren't all supported by all browsers. This section uses the *event property* approach, which is supported by all. Incidentally, if you decide to use a JavaScript toolkit like jQuery, you'll probably find that it adds yet another event-attaching system, which will work on all browsers and may provide a few extra features.

Fortunately, attaching events is easy. You simply set an event property that has the same name as the event attribute you would normally use. For example, say you have an <img> element like this somewhere on your page:

```
<img id="dayImage" src="sunny.jpg" alt="The weather">
```

Here's how you tell the browser to call the swapImage() method when that image is clicked:

```
var imgObject = document.getElementById("dayImage");
imgObject.onclick = swapImage;
```

However, don't make this mistake:

```
imgObject.onclick = swapImage();
```

This runs the swapImage() function, takes the result (if it returns one), and uses that to set the event handler. This is almost certainly not what you want.

To understand what really happens when the <img> element is clicked, you need to look at the code in the swapImage() function. It grabs the <img> element and modifies the src attribute to point to a new picture (see Figure B-3):

```
// Keep track of whether the picture has been swapped from day to night.
var dayTime = true;
```

```
// This function runs when the onClick event happens.
function swapImage() {
  var imgObject = document.getElementById("dayImage");

  // Flip from day to night or night to day, and update the picture to match.
  if (dayTime === true) {
    dayTime = false;
    imgObject.src = "cloudy.jpg";
  }
  else {
    dayTime = true;
    imgObject.src = "sunny.jpg";
  }
}
```

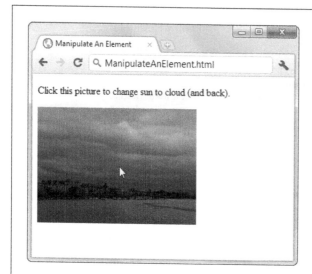

FIGURE B-3

Click this picture, and the page fires an event. That event triggers a function, and that function loads a new image.

Sometimes, an event passes valuable information to your event-handling function. To capture this information, you need to add a single parameter to your function. By convention, this parameter is usually named event or just e:

```
function swapImage(e) {
  ...
}
```

The properties of the event object depend on the event. For example, the onMouse-Move event supplies the current mouse coordinates (which you'll use when creating the painting program on page 263).

There's one more fine point to note. When you use code to connect an event, you *must* put the entire event name in lowercase letters. This is different from when you wire up an event using an attribute in HTML. Unlike JavaScript, HTML doesn't care one whit about case.

> **NOTE** This book refers to events using an easy-to-read convention called Pascal case, which uses uppercase letters to indicate each new word (for example, onLoad and onMouseOver). However, the code listings use all lowercase letters (for example, onload and onmouseover) because JavaScript requires it.

Inline Events

In order for the previous example to work, the swapImage() function must be defined somewhere else in your code. Sometimes, you may want to skip this step and define the function code in the same place where you attach the function to the event. This slick technique is called an *inline function*.

Here's an example that connects an inline function to the onClick event:

```
var imgObject = document.getElementById("dayImage");
imgObject.onclick = function() {
  // The code that went in the swapImage() function
  // now goes here.
  if (dayTime === true) {
    dayTime = false;
    imgObject.src = "cloudy.jpg";
  }
  else {
    dayTime = true;
    imgObject.src = "sunny.jpg";
  }
};
```

This shortcut approach to event handling is less common than using a separate, named function to handle the event. However, it's still a useful convenience, and the examples in this book use it occasionally.

> **NOTE** Inline functions are sometimes useful when you're dealing with an *asynchronous task*—a task that the browser handles in the background. When an asynchronous task is finished, the browser fires an event to notify your code. Sometimes, the clearest way to deal with this situation is to put the code that handles the *completion* of a task right next to the code that triggered the *start* of the task. (Page 277 shows an example with a picture that's loaded asynchronously and then processed.)

Finally, there's one sort of inline function that's used in many of the examples in this book. It's the event handler for the window's onLoad event, which fires after the entire page is rendered, displayed, and ready to go. This makes it a logical point for your code to take over. If you try to run code before this point, you might run into trouble if an object hasn't been created yet for the element you want to use:

```
<script>
window.onload = function() {
  alert("The page has just finished loading.);
}
</script>
```

This approach frees you from worrying about the position of your script block. It lets you place the initialization code in the <head> section, where it belongs, with the rest of your JavaScript functions.

Index

Symbols

3-D transforms, 204
3D Walker website, 315
$_GET collection (PHP), 378–379
$_POST collection (PHP), 379
: (colon) and pseudo-classes, 443
{} (curly brackets), 464
== (equal to), 463
=== (exactly equal to), 463
@font-face, 206–208, 213–216
@font-face property, 438
> (greater than), 463
>= (greater than or equal to), 463
< (less than), 463
<= (less than or equal to), 463
&& (logical and), 463
|| (logical or), 463
@media block, 239–241
! (not), 463
!= (not equal to), 463
!== (not exactly equal to), 463
-prefix-free JavaScript tool, 185, 201
: (semicolon)
    JavaScript, 452
-webkit- vendor prefix, 183–184,
    193–194, 197, 201

A

<abbr> element, 22
"About Me" page, retrofitting, 88–93

accessibility, 39
    best practices, 39
    canvas and, 274
    video captions, 169–176
<acronym> element, 22
<address> element, 24
<a> element, 24
Android
    animation performance, 303
    browser support for
        File API, 340
        forms, 119
        HTML5 audio formats, 153
        HTML5 video formats, 153
        IndexedDB, 353
        server-sent events, 387
        session history, 432
        <track> element, 174
        validation, 119
        web sockets, 394
        web workers, 425
    cache, 366
    calc() function, 226
    embedded font formats, 208
    H.264 Baseline Profile, 154
    linear-gradient() function, 193
    Miro Video Converter and, 156
    mobile-optimized video, 154
    simulators, 231
<applet> element, 22
applicationCache objects, 371–374
    swapCache() method, 374
    update() method, 374

ARIA (Accessible Rich Internet Applications), 82–83
<article> element, 21, 45–46, 76
  outlines and, 68–70
Arvidsson, Erik, 271
<aside> element, 21, 49–51, 56, 76
  <footer> element inside of, 63
  outlines and, 68–70
    solving problems with, 72–74
asynchronous tasks, 475
attribute values, 16
  quotation marks around, 17
Audacity, 156
audio
  Audacity, 156
  <audio>. *See* <audio> element
  automatic playback, 147
  browser support for, 150, 153–154
  codec, 151
  container format, 151
  controlling players with
    JavaScript, 160–169
  dynamically created or edited, 145
  editors, 156
  encoding media, 156
  fallbacks, 154–160
    Flash, 157–160
    supporting multiple formats, 155–156
  file formats
    MP3, 149–156
    Ogg Vorbis, 150, 153–154
    using multiple, 155–156, 163
    WAV, 147, 150, 153, 156
  Flash players, 157
  JavaScript and media players, 167–175
  licensed content, 145
  linking multiple media files
    together, 149
  looping playback, 147
  low-latency, high-performance, 145
  MIME type, 151
    why to use them, 152
  mobile browser support for, 153
  mute button, 147
  overview, 145–149
  paired with video, 147–149
  playback controls, 146
  preloading media files, 146–147

  recording, 145
  Web Audio API, 145
<audio> element, 21, 143
  adding sound effects, 161–164
  autoplay attribute, 147
  browser support for, 29
  controlling players with
    JavaScript, 160–169
    adding sound effects, 161–164
  controls attribute, 146
  empty syntax tags, 146
  example of, 145–146
  format fallbacks, 155–156
  hidden, 164
  loop attribute, 147
  mediagroup attribute, 149
  metadata, 146
  MIME type, 155
  multiple instances, 147, 163
  mute button, 147
  nested <source> elements, 155–156
  paired with <video> element, 147–149
  preload attribute, 146–147
  src attribute, 145–146
autocapitalize attribute, 122
autocomplete attribute, 122
autocorrect attribute, 122

B

background-color property, 438, 446
background-image property, 438
background-position property, 438
background-repeat property, 438
base-64 encoding, 269
<bdo> element, 21
<b> element, 23
Berners-Lee, Tim, 428
<big> element, 22
bitmap images, 258
**Blackberry mobile-optimized
  video,** 154
blank values and validation, 117
block elements, 51–52
Blu-ray players, 151, 153
<body> element, 11, 446
bold formatting, 23
bookmarklet, 66
border-color property, 438
border property, 438, 447

border-style property, 438
border-width property, 438
box shadows, 190–191
box-sizing, 226
browsers
blank values and validation, 117
browser-specific styles with
CSS3, 183–184
clearing browser cache, 364
complex scripts and browser's
automatic reconnection
feature, 393
dealing with old, 27
differences in way rich HTML editing
works in different, 138
extracting semantic data in, 92–93
feature detection, 32–34
finding requirements for HTML5, 27–
29
GlobalStats, 30–31
Google Chrome. *See* Chrome
HTML5 and, 26–35
IE. *See* Internet Explorer
mobile. *See* Android; mobile
browsers
Modernizr and, 32–34
Mozilla Firefox. *See* Firefox
old browsers and HTML5, 27
Opera. *See* Opera
placeholder text and, 110
plug-ins, 9
Safari. *See* Safari
single page for desktop browsers and
mobile devices, 156
support for form validation, 119–122
Modernizr and, 120–121
polyfills and, 121–122
tricking into switching into XHTML
mode, 21
turning into HTML editors, 136–140
used by audience, 30–31
using polyfills to fill HTML5 gaps, 35–
36
web storage
communicating between different
browser windows, 330–332
browser support for
Android
forms, 119

<audio> element, 29
canvas and, 271–274
File API, 340
foreign elements in Internet
Explorer, 52
geolocation feature, 413
HTML5 audio formats, 150, 153
HTML5 video formats, 151, 153
IndexedDB, 353
new input types in forms, 124–125
offline applications, 364–366
semantic elements, 51–53
server-sent events, 387
session history, 432
<track> element, 174
validation, 119
video captions, 174–175
web sockets, 394
web storage, 325
web workers, 425

C

caching
bypassing cache when online, 370
clearing browser cache, 364
events, 372
practical techniques, 366–374
accessing uncached files, 366–
368
adding fallbacks for cached
files, 368–370
checking the connection, 370–371
updates with JavaScript, 371–374
query string and, 359
size, 366
tradition vs. offline applications, 357
triggering update for cached
application, 363
with manifest files, 356–366
creating, 357–359
putting on web server, 359–362
updating, 362–364
using, 359
calc() function, 226
canvas, 245–274
accessibility, 274
animation, 300–307
basic, 301–302
for lazy people, 307
hit testing, 313–316

maze game, 307–316
multiple objects, 302-307
performance, 303
arc() method, 254–255
arcTo() method, 254–255
base-64 encoding, 269
beginPath() method, 251
bezierCurveTo() method, 254–255
bitmap images, 258
browser compatibility, 271–274
building a basic paint program, 263–271
   drawing on the canvas, 266–268
   preparing to draw, 264–266
   saving the picture in canvas, 268–271
<canvas>. *See* <canvas> element
Canvas plug-in for Adobe Illustrator, 258
changeColor() function, 265
changeThickness() function, 266
chess simulator, 315
clearCanvas() function, 267
clearRect() method, 267, 298
closePath() medthod, 252–253, 255–256, 261
composite operations, 262–263
control points, 255–257
Core HTML5 Canvas, 315
createImageData() method, 276, 313
createLinearGradient() function, 285
createRadialGradient() function, 285
creating image object, 276
curved lines, 254–256
custom objects, 294–298
data URLs, 268–271
drawFrame() function, 302, 304, 305, 312
draw() function, 267
drawImage() function, 276–277
   slicing, dicing, and resizing images, 278–279
drawing
   for math-phobes, 258
   graphs, 288–293
   images, 276–277. *See* canvas, images
   library, 258
   text, 279–280

ExplorerCanvas library, 271–272
Fabric.js, 258
fillEllipse() method, 258
filling shapes with patterns, 283–284
fill() method, 252–253
fillRect() method, 253, 256–257
fillStyle property, 252–253, 283
getContext() method, 247
getElementById() method, 246
getElementById() method and, 246
getting started, 246–263
globalAlpha property, 261
gradients, 281, 284–288
   addColorStop() method, 287
   creating gradient object, 285
   setting colors in, 287
graphs, 288–293
   plotScore() function, 292
hit testing, 298–301, 313–316
HTML Canvas, 315
images
   drawing, 276–277
   slicing, dicing, and resizing, 278–279
   squashed, 277
<img> element
   creating image object, 276
   handing data URL to, 269
   onclick attribute, 265
iPaint, 271
isDrawing variable, 266–267
KineticJS, 258
lineTo() method, 249, 253, 267
making shapes interactive, 293–300
   animation, 300–307
   hit testing, 298–301
   keeping track of what you've done, 294–298
matrix transform, 259
maze game, 307–316
   animating the face, 311–313
   drawMaze(), 309
   hit testing, 313–316
   processKey() function, 309–312
   setting up, 309–310
Modernizr and, 273
moveTo() method, 249, 253
online examples, 315
onMouseDown event, 266, 267
onMouseMove event, 267

onMouseUp event, 264, 267
paint programs, 271
paths and shapes, 251–253
polyfilling
    with ExplorerCanvas, 271–272
    with FlashCanvas library, 272–273
processKey() function, 309–312
quadraticCurveTo() method, 254–
    255
requiring JavaScript, 245
restore() method, 260
rgba() function, 260
rgb() function, 250, 260
rotate transform, 259
save() method, 260
saving content in Firefox, 270
scale transform, 258
setTimeout() method, 302
shadowBlur property, 282
shadowColor property, 282
shadowOffsetX and shadowOffsetY
    properties, 282
shadows, 281–283
    properties for creating, 282
Sketchpad, 271
Stack Overflow site, 258
startDrawing() function, 266
stopDrawing() function, 267
straight lines, 248–251
    capping off ends, 250
    lineTo() method, 249
    moveTo() method, 249
    setting color of, 250
    stroke() method, 249
stroke() method, 251–263
strokeRect() method, 253
transforms, 256–260
    documentation and
        examples, 260
translate transform, 258
transparency, 260–262
triangle-drawing code, 252
<video> element, 279
VML (Vector Markup
    Language), 271–272
Canvas Demos website, 315
<canvas> element, 21, 246, 248
    fallback content, 273–274
    squashed images, 277
Canvas-text JavaScript library, 272

capitalization, 16
Captionator.js, 175
<center> element, 22
character encoding, 12–13
chess simulator, 315
Chrome
    audio/video playback controls, 146
    browser support for
        File API, 340
        HTML5 audio formats, 153
        HTML5 video formats, 153
        IndexedDB, 353
        server-sent events, 387
        session history, 432
        <track> element, 174
        validation, 119
        web sockets, 394
        web workers, 425
    debugging JavaScript code, 462
    extensions
        h5o, 66
        outline that lets visitors jump to
            the appropriate section in a
            page, 39, 65
        Semantic Inspector, 93
    HTML5 and, 26
    Manual Geolocation plug-in, 404
    transform property, 184
    transforms, 201
    vendor prefix, 183
    WebVTT files and, 174
<cite> element, 24
CKEditor, 136
className property, 472
clear property, 438
client-side validation, 113
collapsible boxes, 60
colon (:) and pseudo-classes, 443
color
    data type, 125, 129
    gradients, 191–195, 250, 272
        linear, 192–193
        online gradient-generating
            tool, 195
        radial, 193–194
        repeating, 194–195
        transitions, 198
    property, 438
<command> element, 21, 135
composite operations, 262–263

conditional logic, 463–465
contenteditable attribute, 136–140
  using to edit element, 136–138
contextual selectors, 43, 442, 447–449
cookies, 319, 320, 325
coords object, 407–408
Core HTML5 Canvas, 315
createImageData() method, 276
**Creating a Website: The Missing
  Manual,** xiii, 196
CSS3
  background images, 188–190
  backwards compatibility, 179
  border-radius property, 179, 187
  box and text shadows, 190–191
  box-sizing, 226
  browser-specific styles, 183–184
  calc() function, 226
  creating fallbacks with
    Modernizr, 180–182
  current features, 178–184
  fonts. See web fonts
  gradients, 191–195
    linear, 192–193
    online gradient-generating
      tool, 195
    radial, 193–194
    repeating, 194–195
    transitions, 198
  matrix(n1, n2, n3, n4, n5, n6)
    function, 203
  modules, 177
  multicolumn text, 217–220
  responsive design. See responsive
    web design with CSS3
  rotate(angle) function, 203
  rounded corners, 187
  scaleX(x) function, 203
  scale(x, y) function, 203
  scaleY(y) function, 203
  shadows
    transitions, 198
  skewX(angle) function, 203
  skew(x-angle, y-angle) function, 203
  skewY(angle) function, 203
  specifications, 178
  transforms, 201–206
    3-D, 204
    shifting starting point, 204

    transform functions, 203
    transitions that use, 198, 204–206
  transitions, 195–206, 385
    basic, 196–198
    gradients, 198
    making more natural, 202
    shadows, 198
    that use transforms, 198, 204–206
    transparency, 198
  translateX(x) function, 203
  translate(x, y) function, 203
  translateY(y) function, 203
  transparency, 185–187
  vendor prefixes, 183–184
  when an em becomes a rem, 230
CSS3: The Missing Manual, xiii, 435
CSS (Cascading Style Sheets), 435–450
  <body> element, 446
  body rule, 446
  boxes, 440
  class attribute, 439
  class-specific rule, 446
  columns, 440
  comments, 439
  <div> element, 440, 448
  elements
    naming, 439
  embedding style information directly
    into element, 435
  embedding style sheet in <style>
    element, 436
  example of style sheet magic, 436
  formatting right elements, 438–439
  header rule, 447
  ID selectors, 442–443
  linking separate style sheet file, 436
  media types, 234
  properties, 437, 437–438
    borders, 438
    colors, 438
    common, 438
    fonts, 438
    graphics, 438
    inherited, 440
    layout, 438
    overview of all, 438
    padding, 448
    size, 438
    spacing, 438
    text alignment, 438

selectors, 437, 446
  attribute, 444
  contextual, 441–442, 447, 448
  creating, 439
  ID, 442–443
  multiple, 441
  overlapping, 439
  pseudo-class, 443–444
  <span> element, 440, 448
styles, adding to page, 435–436
style sheets, 436–439
  adding, 14–35
  overview, 445–450
values, 437
  inherited, 440
csszengarden.com, 436
curly brackets ({}), 464

D

databases. *See also* IndexedDB
  difference between server-side and
    client-side, 341
  primary keys, 346
<datalist> element, 21, 130–133
  with <option> element, 131–133
data storage. *See* web storage
data URLs, 268–271
date data type, 125, 128–129
dates. *See* <time> element
datetime data type, 129
datetime-local data type, 129
debugging JavaScript code, 462
  logical operators, 463
dedicated web servers, 395
designMode attribute, 136–140
  editing pages, 138–140
<details> element, 21, 60
<div> element, 37, 440, 448
  in HTML, 40–43
  in HTML5, 43
  itemprop, itemscope, or itemtype
    attribute, 90–95
doctype, 11–12
  standards mode, 12
document outlines. *See* outlines
drawing. *See* canvas
drawing library, 258

E

easier editing and maintenance, 38
echo server, 397–398
elements
  adapted, 22–24
  added, 21
  removed, 22
  standardized, 25–26
  tweaked, 24–25
ellipsis in book examples, 41
email data type, 124–125
<embed> element, 21, 25
<em> element, 23
em unit, 228
  when an em becomes a rem, 230
enhanced search results, 94–98
EOT (Embedded Open Type), 207–
  208, 213
equal to (==), 463
events
  caching, 372
exactly equal to (===), 463
ExplorerCanvas library, 271–272

F

Fabric.js, 258, 307
fallbacks
  adding for cached files, 368–370
  creating with Modernizr
    CSS3, 180–182
    JavaScript, 182
  multiple background images, 190
feeds, 93
<fieldset> element, 107
<figcaption> element, 21, 48, 76
<figure> element, 21, 46–49, 76
File API, 332–340. *See also* FileReader
  object
  browser support for, 340
  getting hold of a file, 333
  <input> element, 333
    reading multiple files at
      once, 336–337
    reading text file with, 333–336
  reading image file wth drag-and-
    drop, 337–340
  replacing standard upload
    control, 336

FileReader object, 334–340
  abort() method, 340
  drop() function, 339
  ignoreDrag() function, 338
  processFiles() function, 339
  readAsArrayBuffer() method, 335
  readAsBinaryString() method, 335
  readAsDataUrl() method, 335
  readAsDataURL() method, 337–340
  readAsText() method, 335
Firefogg plug-in, 156
Firefox
  audio/video playback controls, 146
  browser support for
    File API, 340
    HTML5 audio formats, 153
    HTML5 video formats, 153
    IndexedDB, 353
    server-sent events, 387
    session history, 432
    <track> element, 174
    validation, 119
    web sockets, 394
    web workers, 425
  calc() function, 226
  debugging JavaScript code, 462
  Firefogg plug-in, 156
  HTML5 and, 26
  metadata and <audio> element, 147
  saving canvas content in, 270
  transform property, 184
  transforms, 201
  vendor prefix, 183
Flash
  fallbacks, 157–160
    JavaScript media players, 168
  Flowplayer Flash, 158
  Flowplayer HTML5, 160
  H.264 video file format, 151
  players, 157
    with HTML fallback, 160
FlashCanvas library, 272–273
Flash plug-ins, 9
float property, 438
Flowplayer Flash, 158
Flowplayer HTML5, 160
fluid design and media queries, 234–235
fluid images, 226–228

fluid layouts, 222–226. *See also* media queries
  adapting with media queries, 231–244
  max-width and min-width properties, 232
fluid typography, 228–230
<font> element, 22
font-family property, 438, 446
fonts
  creating font collections, 216
  embedded font formats, 208
  licensing, 211
  subscription sites, 216
  web. *See* web fonts
font-size property, 438
Font Squirrel, 209–211
  preparing fonts for web, 211–214
font-style property, 438
font-variant property, 438
font-weight property, 438
<footer> element, 21, 43–46, 50, 61–63, 76
  animation, 62
  close button, 61
  fixed positioning, 61
  in an <aside> element, 63
  partially transparent background, 62
<form> element, 105–106, 114
forms, 103–140
  autocapitalize attribute, 122
  autocomplete attribute, 122
  autocorrect attribute, 122
  autofocus attribute, 111–112
  bypassing form submission with JavaScript, 105
  <command> element, 135
  controls, 108
    how browser draws, 109
  <datalist> element, 130–133
    with <option> element, 131–133
  error-prevention and error-checking features, 124
  <fieldset> element, 107
  Google Instant feature, 105
  HTML5Forms library, 122
  <input> element, 107, 111, 115, 118
    browser compatibility for new input types, 124–125
    color data type, 129

date-related types, 128–129
email data type, 124–125
new data types, 123–130
number type, 126
range data type, 127–128
search data type, 126
tel data type, 126
url data type, 126
limit of, 109
<menu> element, 135
<meter> element, 133–135
mobile devices and, 124
multiple attribute, 122
overview, 104–105
placeholders, 109–111
browsers not supporting, 110
special characters and, 111
writing good, 111
placing controls outside of, 107
<progress> element, 133–135
revamping traditional forms, 105–112
spellcheck attribute, 122
starting in right place, 111–112
<textarea> element, 107, 111, 113, 117
validation, 112–119
browser support for, 119–122
client-side validation, 113
how HTML5 form validation
works, 112–114
Modernizr, 120–121
polyfills and, 121–122
regular expression, 116–119
server-side validation, 113
styling hooks, 115–116
turning off, 114–115
XForms, 103
XMLHttpRequest object, 105, 133,
138, 140
frames feature, 22
Friedl, Jeffrey, 117
Fulton, Jeff, 315
Fulton, Steve, 315

G

Geary, David, 315
geolocation, 401, 402–413. *See
also* Geolocation object
assessing accuracy of guess, 407
finding visitor coordinates, 405–406

how it works, 402–404
IP addresses, 402–403, 413
Manual Geolocation plug-in, 404
monitoring visitor's moves, 413
showing a map, 409–412
why you should use it, 404
Geolocation object
accuracy property, 407
browser compatibility and, 413
clearWatch() method
(geolocation), 405, 413
coords object and, 405, 407–408,
412
enableHighAccuracy property, 409
errors, 406–408
getCurrentLocation() method, 405,
406, 408
getCurrentPosition() medthod, 405,
407, 409, 413
maximumAge property, 409
methods, 405
setting options, 408–409
timeout property, 409
watchPosition() method, 405, 413
GlobalStats, 30–31
global variables, 460
Goldwave, 156
Google
ignoring semantic data, 99
job search technology for
veterans, 99
product searches, 99
Recipe View, 98–102
rich snippets, 94
Structured Data Testing Tool, 94–98
Google Analytics, 31, 368
Google Chrome. *See* Chrome
Google Fonts, 214–216
Google Instant feature, 105
Google Maps, 409–412
gradients, 191–195
linear, 192–193
online gradient-generating tool, 195
radial, 193–194
repeating, 194–195
transitions, 198
greater than (>), 463
greater than or equal to (>=), 463

H

h5o plug-in, 65
H.264 Baseline Profile, 154
H.264 video format, 149–160
   converting to, 156
   in Opera browser, 150
   licensing, 154
HandBrake, 156
hardware acceleration, 303
hashbang URLs, 427–428
hCalendar microformat, 85
hCard microformat, 84
<head> element, 11
<header> element, 21, 43–46, 50, 76
   adding headings you can't see, 55
   getting IE to recognize, 52
   multiple inclusions, 54
heading structure of a site, 56
height property, 438
highlighted text, 80–82
hit testing, 298–301, 313–316
<hr> element, 23
HTML
   <div> element, 41–43
   frames feature, 22
   page structure the old way, 40–43
   retrofitting traditional page, 39–50
HTML5
   a living language, 6–7
   availability, xiv–xv
   back from the dead, 5
   browser plug-ins, 9
   browsers
      finding requirements for, 27–29
      used by audience, 30–31
   Chrome and, 26
   current, evolving draft of, 7
   <div> element, 440
   <div> element, 43
   example, 15
   Firefox and, 26
   included features, 6
   Internet Explorer and, 26
   loosened rules, 16–17
   number 5 in the name, 5
   obsolete elements, 8
   old browsers and, 27
   Opera and, 26
   Safari and, 26
   smartphones and, 26
   standard, 10
   story of, 3–7
   syntax, 16–21
   tablet computers and, 26
   three key principles of, 7–9
      being practical, 9
      "Don't break the Web", 7–8
      "pave the cowpaths"
         approach, 8–9
   using polyfills to fill HTML5 gaps, 35–36
   viewing, xiii–xiv
   vs. HTML, xv
   writing, xiii
HTML5Forms library, 122
HTML Canvas, 315
HTML color code, 250, 446–447
HTML editors
   browser differences, 138
   turning browsers into, 136–140
<html> element, 11

I

<i> element, 23
<iframe> element, 22
image-based patterns, 250
images. See also <figure> element;
   <figcaption> element
   background images with CSS3, 188–190
   <img> element
      handing data URL to, 269
      onclick attribute, 265
   reading image file wth drag-and-drop, 337–340
   transparency, 185–187
   transitions, 198
<img> element, 16
   creating image object, 276
   handing data URL to, 269
   onclick attribute, 265
IndexedDB, 340–354
   browser support for, 353
   calling open() method, 344
   creating and connecting to a database, 343–346
   difference between server-side and client-side databases, 341
   enhancing performance, 341

improving local storage, 341
key path, 345
LinkRecord object, 342–343, 347–348
making self-sufficient offline application, 341
naming database, 344
onError event handler, 344–345
onSuccess event handler, 344
onUpgradeNeeded event handler, 344–345
primary keys, 346
querying
 all records in a table, 349–351
 single record, 351–352
records
 deleting, 352–353
 querying all, 349–351
 querying single, 351–352
similarities with local storage, 342
storing records in the database, 346–348
 calling object store method, 347
 creating transaction, 346
 handling success and error events, 347
 retrieving object store, 347
tables
 creating, 345
 querying all records in, 349–351
InfoWindow object, 412
inline functions, 475
innerHTML property, 472
<input> element, 21
File API, 333
 reading text file with, 333–336
forms, 107, 111, 115, 118
 browser compatibility for new input types, 124–125
 color data type, 129
 date-related types, 128–129
 email data type, 124–125
 new data types, 123–130
 number type, 126
 range data type, 127–128
 search data type, 126
 tel data type, 126
 url data type, 126
multiple attribute, 122
reading multiple files at once, 336–337

"Insufficient data to generate the preview" error message, 96
interactivity elements, 21
Internet Explorer
alert( ) function, 453
audio/video playback controls, 146
browser support for
 File API, 340
 HTML5 audio formats, 153
 HTML5 video formats, 153
 IndexedDB, 353
 server-sent events, 387
 session history, 432
 <track> element, 174
 validation, 119
 web sockets, 394
 web workers, 425
calc() function, 226
debugging JavaScript code, 462
HTML5 and, 26
JavaScript patches that can bring IE up to speed, 110
radial-gradient() function, 184
storage events, 331
transform property, 184
transforms, 201
tricking into recognizing a foreign element, 52
vendor prefix, 183
workaround for <output> element, 79
iPad
cache, 366
Miro Video Converter and, 156
simulators, 231
IP addresses, 402–403, 413
iPaint, 271
iPhone
animation performance, 303
cache, 366
H.264 Baseline Profile, 154
Miro Video Converter and, 156
mobile-optimized video, 154
simulators, 231
italic formatting, 23
itemprop, itemscope, or itemtype attribute, 90–95
generating properly formatted microdata-enriched markup, 91
itemReviewed property, 96–97

J

JavaScript, 451–476. *See also* objects
abort() method, 340
adding, 14
appendChild() method, 473
arrays, 465–466
asynchronous tasks, 475
audio/video players, 160–169
adding sound effects, 161–164
creating custom video
player, 164–167
beginPath() method, 251
bookmarklet, 66
buttons and, 108
bypassing form submission with, 105
calculations, 78–80
Canvas-text library, 272
Captionator.js, 175
checking whether browser is
online, 370–371
clearWatch() method, 405, 413
client-side code, 106
closing </script> tag, 14
collapsible boxes, 60
conditional logic, 463–465
connecting to event
dynamically, 473–475
contenteditable, 137
datalist and, 133
dealing with old browsers, 27
debugging code, 462
defining data structure in, 342
drawing. *See* canvas
dynamically connecting to
events, 470–471
embedding script in markup, 452–453
events. *See* JavaScript events
extending history object, 425–432
Fabric.js, 258, 307
fallbacks, 180–182
multiple background images, 190
transparency, 186
focus() method, 111
freeze-up problem, 414
functions. *See* JavaScript functions
geolocation, 405–413
getAttribute() method, 473
getCurrentLocation() method, 405–408

getCurrentPosition() method, 405, 407, 409, 413, 470
getElementById() method, 471
hiding element that wraps footer, 61
how web pages use, 452–459
HTML5 features that require, 375
inline events, 475–476
insertChild() method, 473
interacting with offline
applications, 371–374
interacting with pages, 470–476
jQuery UI, 201
JS API group, 28
KineticJS, 258, 298, 307
language="JavaScript" attribute, 14
logical operators, 463
loops, 465
manipulating elements, 471–473
media players, 167–169
controlling with JavaScript, 160–169
creating custom, 164–167
Flash fallbacks, 168
Microdata Tool, 92
Modernizr tool. *See* Modernizr
MooTools, 201
moving code to script file, 455–457
null values, 460
Paper.js, 307
patches that can bring IE up to
speed, 110
peeking at the DOM, 11
polyfill that adds autofocus
support, 112
postMessage() method, 418, 421–423
web workers and, 418
-prefix-free, 185, 201
processFiles() function, 339
properties and HTML5
specification, 117
pushState() method, 426, 429–430
readAsArrayBuffer() method, 335
readAsBinaryString() method, 335
readAsDataUrl() method, 335
readAsText() method, 335
reading text files, 333–336
regular expressions, 116
removeChild() method, 473
replaceState() method, 431
responding to events, 457–459

retrieving data from server, 470
RGraph, 293
<script> block, 452
    </script> tag and, 456
semicolon (:), 452
sending data to the server, 470
setAttribute() method, 473
setCustomValidity() method, 117–119
terminate() method, 421
transitions, 198–220
    adding, 385
tricking IE into recognizing a foreign
    element, 52
updating pages, 470
variables, 459–460
    data types, 461
    global, 460
    local, 460
    naming, 457, 459
    null values, 460
    operations, 461–463
    scope, 460
VideoJS player, 167–169
watchPosition() method, 405, 413
web storage. *See* web storage
XMLHttpRequest
    objects. *See* XMLHttpRequest
    objects
XML parser, 335
ZingChart, 293
JavaScript events, 455
    common object events, 458–459
    connecting dynamically to, 473–475
    event handlers, 457, 473, 476
    event property approach, 473
    responding to, 457–459
    server-sent, 387
JavaScript functions, 454–455
    adding code to, 454
    adding events, 455
    advantages of using, 455
    alert(), 452, 454, 467
    arguments, 467
    boing(), 163
    calling, 454–455
    doSearch(), 416–432
    drop(), 339
    findPrimes(), 416, 423
    goToNewSlide(), 384, 430
    goToNextSlide(), 432

ignoreDrag(), 338
importScripts(), 420
inline, 475, 475–476
linear-gradient(), 193
LinkRecord(), 347
naming, 457
Number(), 325, 328–329
object-definition, 468–469
processFiles(), 334, 336, 339
receiving and returning data, 466–
    467
rgb(), 446–447
    canvas, 250, 260
rgba(), 260
setInterval(), 386
    animation, 301
    web workers and, 414, 424–425
setTimeout(), 386
    animation, 301
    web workers and, 414, 424–425
showFileInput(), 336
showMessage(), 454–457
    parameters, 466–467
swapImage(), 473, 475
that receive and return data, 466–
    467
triggering, 454
using, 454–455
**JavaScript & jQuery: The Missing
    Manual,** xiii, 451
Java web socket server, 399
**job search technology for
    veterans,** 99
jPlayer, 167
jQuery UI, 201
**JSON (JavaScript Object
    Notation),** 329–330

K

Kaazing web socket server, 399
<keygen> element, 21
KineticJS, 258, 298, 307

L

LAME MP3 encoder, 156
lang attribute, 13
LatLng object, 412
left property, 438
less than (<), 463
less than or equal to (<=), 463

letter-spacing property, 438
licensed content, 145
line caps, 250
line-height property, 438
<link> element, 436
LinkRecord object, 342–343, 347–348
local variables, 460
logical and (&&), 463
logical operators, 463
logical or (||), 463
loops, 465

M

<main> element, 63–65, 76
manifest files, 356–366
  adding fallbacks for cached
    files, 368–370
  browser support for offline
    applications, 364–366
  caching and query string, 359
  clearing browser cache, 364
  creating, 357–359
  putting on web server, 359–362
  triggering update for cached
    application, 363
  updating, 362–364
  using, 359
Manual Geolocation plug-in, 404
margin-bottom property, 438
margin-left property, 438
margin property, 438
margin-right property, 438
margin-top property, 438
<mark> element, 21, 80–82
mark of the Web comment, 14
Mastering Regular Expressions, 117
max-device-width media feature, 233,
    235, 238, 242–244
max-width media feature, 233–242
McFarland, David Sawyer, xiii, 435, 451
media. *See* audio; video
media queries, 221
  adapting layout with, 231–244
  anatomy of, 233–234
  building mobile-friendly layout, 236–
    239
  creating simple, 234–235
  for video, 244
  max-device-width media
    feature, 233, 235, 238, 242–244

  max-width media feature, 233–242
  @media block, 239–241
  more advanced query
    conditions, 239–241
  most useful features for
    building, 233–234
  orientation media feature, 234–235,
    238, 242–244
  recognizing specific mobile
    devices, 242–244
  replacing entire style sheet, 241–242
<menu> element, 21, 135
metadata
  <audio> element, 146
  enhanced search results, 94–98
  how search engines use, 93–102
    enhanced search results, 94–98
    rich snippets, 94
  plug-ins that can spot different types
    of, 92
<meta> element, 231, 236
<meter> element, 21, 133–135
microdata, 75, 85–88
  formats, 98
  generating properly formatted
    microdata-enriched markup, 91
  namespaces, 86
  nested structure, 90
  Recipe data format, 98–102
  vs. micro formats, 87
  when to define new section, 91
Microdata Tool, 92
microformats, 84–85
  Recipe data format, 98–102
  vs. microdata, 87
MIME type, why to use them, 152
Miro Video Converter, 156
mobile browsers. *See also* Android
  audio and video support, 153
  H.264 Baseline Profile, 154
  mobile-optimized video, 154
  single page for desktop browsers and
    mobile devices, 156
mobile devices. *See also* Android; iPad;
    iPhone; mobile browsers
  common device widths, 243
  forms and, 124
  recognizing specific, 242–244

Modernizr, 32–34, 51, 53
  canvas and, 273
  creating fallbacks with
    CSS3, 180–182
    JavaScript, 182
  form validation and, 120–121
  full list of features, 32
  hiding and replacing sections, 240
month data type, 125, 129
MooTools, 201
MP3 file format, 149–156
  LAME MP3 encoder, 156
multicolumn text, 217–220
multiple attribute, 122

N

natural language, 13
navigator object, 405
<nav> section, 21, 39, 50, 56–59, 76
  multiple, 58
  outlines and, 68–70
  within <aside> or <header>, 59
nested structure and microdata, 90
.NET web socket server, 399
<nobr> element, 26
node.JS web socket server, 399
not (!), 463
not equal to (!=), 463
not exactly equal to (!==), 463
null values, 460
number data type, 125, 126
numeric variables, 461–476

O

<object> element, 22
objects, 468–469. *See also* FileReader
  object; Geolocation object;
  XMLHttpRequest objects
  applicationCache, 371–374
    swapCache() method, 374
    update() method, 374
  common events, 458–459
  common properties, 472
  coords, 407–408
  custom objects in canvas, 294–298
  defining, 468
  InfoWindow, 412
  JSON (JavaScript Object
    Notation), 329–330
  LatLng, 412

LinkRecord, 342–343, 347–348
literals, 469–470
naming, 457
navigator, 405
storing, 329–330
WebSocket
  creating, 395–397
  detecting failed connection, 397
  socket-connection code, 397
offline application feature, 355–374
  browser support for, 364–366
  browser support for offline
    applications, 364–366
  bypassing cache when online, 370
  caching and query string, 359
  caching events, 372
  manifest files, 356–366
    clearing browser cache, 364
    creating, 357–359
    putting on web server, 359–362
    updating, 362–364
    using, 359
  practical caching techniques, 366–
    374
    accessing uncached files, 366–
      368
    adding fallbacks for cached
      files, 368–370
    checking the connection, 370–371
    updates with JavaScript, 371–374
  triggering update for cached
    application, 363
  troubleshooting, 362
  when to work offline, 356
Ogg Theora video file format, 151, 153
  converting to, 156
Ogg Vorbis audio file format, 150,
  153–154
<ol> element, 25
onBlur event, 458
onCached event, 372
onChange event, 459
onChecking event, 372
onClick event, 458
onDownloading event, 372
onError event, 372, 459
onFocus event, 458
onKeyDown event, 458
onKeyUp event, 458
Online HTML outliner, 65

onLoad event, 459
onMouseDown event, 266–267
onMouseMove event, 267
onMouseOut event, 458
onMouseOver event, 457–458, 475
onMouseUp event, 264, 267
onNoUpdate event, 372
onObsolete event, 372
onPopState event, 429, 430, 431
onProgress event, 372
onSelect event, 459
onUnload event, 459
onUpdateReady event, 372
Opera
   browser support for
      File API, 340
      HTML5 audio formats, 153
      HTML5 video formats, 153
      IndexedDB, 353
      server-sent events, 387
      session history, 432
      <track> element, 174
      validation, 119
      web sockets, 394
      web workers, 425
   debugging JavaScript code, 462
   extension for outlines, 66
   H.264 video, 150
   HTML5 and, 26
   transform property, 184
   transforms, 201
   vendor prefix, 183
operations, 461–463
optional word break, 25
<option> element with <datalist>
   element, 131–140
orientation media feature, 234–235,
   238, 242–244
OTF (OpenType PostScript), 207–208,
   210
outlines, 65–74
   basic, 66–68
   sectioning elements, 68–70
   solving an outline problem, 70–74
   viewing, 65–66
<output> element, 21, 78–80
   Internet Explorer workaround, 79

P

padding-bottom property, 438
padding-left property, 438
padding properties, 448
padding property, 438
padding-right property, 438
padding-top property, 438
page redirect, 432
page structure, 37–74, 75
   elements, 76
   nested structure and microdata, 90
   the old way, 40–43
page structuring elements, 21
Paper.js, 307
parentElement property, 472
Person data format, 98
PHP scripts
   $_GET collection, 378–379
   $_POST collection, 379
   asking the web server a
      question, 377–382
   calling the web server with, 380–382
   close() method of the EventSource
      object, 391
   complex scripts and browser's
      automatic reconnection
      feature, 393
   creating, 378–379
   dot operator (.), 390
   final argument of the open()
      method, 380
   flush() function, 390
   onMessage event, 390
   polling with server-side events, 392
   sending messages with a server
      script, 388–390
   time() function, 389
PHP web socket server, 399
polling with server-side events, 386,
   391–393
polyfills, 35–36
   canvas
      with ExplorerCanvas library, 271–
      272
      with FlashCanvas library, 272–273
   form validation and, 121–122
position property, 438
primary keys, 346

prime numbers that fit in certain range, 414–432
<progress> element, 21, 133–135
  playback progress bar, 166
pseudo-classes
  for transitions, 195, 196, 198
  validation styling hooks, 115
pull-quotes, 49–50, 56, 70, 74
Python web socket server, 399

Q

query string, 379–380
quotation marks around attribute values, 17

R

range data type, 125, 127–128
Rating data format, 98
RDFa (Resource Description Framework), 83
Recipe data format, 99–102
Recipe View (Google), 98–102
recording audio or video, 145
regular expression and form validation, 116–140
rems, 230
responsive web design with CSS3, 221–244. *See also* media queries
  basics, 222–231
  box-sizing, 226
  calc() function, 226
  fluid images, 226–228
  fluid layouts, 222–226
  fluid typography, 228–230
  making layouts work on smartphones, 230–231
  max-width and min-width properties, 232
  when an em becomes a rem, 230
retrofitting an "About Me" page, 88–93
reviewBody property, 96–97
Review data format, 98
rgba() function and transparency, 186
rgb() function, 250, 446–447
RGraph, 293
rich snippets, 94
right property, 438
rounded corners, 187

<rp> element, 21
RSS feeds, 93
<rt> element, 21
<ruby> element, 21
Ruby web socket server, 399
running applications
  offline. *See* offline application feature

S

Safari
  browser support for
    File API, 340
    HTML5 audio formats, 153
    HTML5 video formats, 153
    IndexedDB, 353
    server-sent events, 387
    session history, 432
    <track> element, 174
    validation, 119
    web sockets, 394
    web workers, 425
  debugging JavaScript code, 462
  HTML5 and, 26
  linear-gradient() function, 193
  transform property, 184
  transforms, 201
  vendor prefix, 183
screen reader, 39
<script> block, 452
  </script> tag and, 456
script files, moving code to, 455–476
search data type, 124, 126
search engine optimization (SEO), 39, 93
  hashbang URLs and, 428
search engines
  enhanced search results, 94–98
  Recipe View (Google), 98–102
  smarter search filtering, 98
  Structured Data Testing Tool, 94–95
  using metadata, 93–102
  video subtitles and, 173
<section> element, 21, 59–60, 76
  outlines and, 68–70
sectioning elements, 68–70
  complex pages and, 71
sections, hiding and placing, 240
<select> element, 122

selectors, contextual, 43, 442,
 447–449
<s> element, 23
semantic data. *See also* metadata;
 microdata; microformats
 extracting in browser, 92–93
 Google ignoring, 99
 hidden, 99
 structuring pages with. *See* page
  structure
 text-level information, 75–102
semantic elements, 38–39
 browser compatibility for, 51–53
 designing a site with, 53–65
 how they were chosen, 50
 styling, 51
Semantic Inspector, 93
semicolon (:) in JavaScript, 452
server-side programming. *See
  also* PHP scripts; web servers; web
  sockets; XMLHttpRequest objects
 checking for server-side event
  support, 391
 complex scripts and browser's
  automatic reconnection
  feature, 393
 final argument of the open()
  method, 380
 frameworks, 55
 processing messages in web
  page, 390–391
 sending messages with a server
  script, 388–390
 server-sent events, 375, 386–393
  browser support for, 387
  message format, 387
 server-side events
  polling with, 391–393
 server-side includes
  session history and, 431
 validation, 113
 XMLHttpRequest objects, 105, 133,
  138, 140, 430
  web workers and, 424
session history, 401, 425–432
 back() method, 426
 browser compatibility and, 432
 browser support for, 432
 forward() method, 426
 go() method, 426

goToNewSlide() function, 430
hashbang URLs, 427–428
onPopState event, 429, 430, 431
pushState() method, 426, 429–430
replaceState() method, 431
server-side includes and, 431
templates and, 431
three basic methods, 425
URL problem, 426
sidebars, 56–59. *See also* <aside>
 element
 complex, 58
 shaping into three sections, 57
Silverlight, 151
simulators, 231
Sketchpad, 271
<small> element, 22
smartphones
 HTML5 and, 26
 making layouts work on, 230–231
<source> element, 21
 media attribute, 244
<span> element, 41, 440, 448
 itemprop, itemscope, or itemtype
  attribute, 90–95
special characters, 111
spellcheck attribute, 122
Stack Overflow site, 258
standards that boost semantics, 82–
 88
 ARIA (Accessible Rich Internet
  Applications), 82–83
 microdata, 85–88
  namespaces, 86
  vs. microformats, 87
 microformats, 84–85
 RDFa (Resource Description
  Framework), 83
streaming video, 145
<strike> element, 22
<strong> element, 23
Structured Data Testing Tool, 94–98
 HTML tab, 95
 URL tab, 95
<style> element, 436
style property, 472
<summary> element, 21, 60
SVG (Scalable Vector Graphics), 207–
 208, 213

T

tablet computers and HTML5, 26
tagName property, 472
tel data type, 124, 126
templates, 55
  session history and, 431
text
  drawing in canvas, 279–280
  highlighted, 80–82
  multicolumn, 217–220
  optional word break, 25
text-align property, 438
<textarea> element, 107, 111, 113, 117
text-decoration property, 438
text elements, 21
text-indent property, 438
text-level information, 75–102
text shadows, 190–191
Thing data format, 98
Third Edition, xiii
time-consuming tasks, 414–417
time data type, 125, 129
<time> element, 21, 38, 77–78
TinyMCE, 136
<track> element, 172–173
  browser support for, 174
transforms, 201–206
  3-D, 204
  shifting starting point, 204
  transform functions, 203
  transitions, 198, 204–206
transitions
  CSS3, 195–206, 385
    basic transition, 196–198
  gradients, 198
  JavaScript, 385
  making more natural, 202
  pseudo-classes for, 195, 196, 198
  shadows, 198
  transforms, 198, 204–206
  transparency, 198
  triggering with JavaScript, 198–220
transparency, 185–187, 260–262
  fallbacks, 186
  rgba() function, 186
  transitions, 198
troubleshooting
  debugging JavaScript code, 462
  "Insufficient data to generate the
    preview" error message, 96

  offline application feature, 362
<tt> element, 22
TTF (TrueType), 207–208, 210

U

url data type, 124, 126
URLs
  changing to anything you
    like. *See* session history
  creating extra pages to satisfy, 431
  data URLs, 268–271
  hashbang, 427–428
UTF-8 encoding, 13

V

validation, 17–19
  blank values and, 117
  browser support for, 119
  forms, 112–119
    browser support for, 119–122
    client-side validation, 113
    how HTML5 form validation
      works, 112–114
    Modernizr, 120–121
    polyfills and, 121–122
    regular expression, 116–119
    server-side validation, 113
    styling hooks, 115–116
    turning off, 114–115
  JavaScript setCustomValidity()
    method, 117–119
  potential problems that a validator
    can catch, 17
  validator provided by the W3C
    standards organization, 17–19
  XHTML5 validator, 20
vendor prefixes, 183–184
  -prefix-free, 185
  -webkit-, 183–184, 193–194, 197, 201
**veterans, job search technology
  for,** 99
video. *See also* <video> element
  accessibility. *See* video, subtitles
  adaptive streaming, 145
  automatic playback, 147
  browser support for, 153–154
    captions, 174–175
    HTML5 formats, 151, 153
  captions. *See* video, subtitles
  codec, 149, 151
  container format, 151

drawing video frame, 279
encoding media, 156
fallbacks, 154–160
  Flash, 157–160
  Flash player with HTML
    fallback, 160
  format, 154
  supporting multiple formats, 155–
    156
  technology, 154
file formats
  encoding media, 156
  H.264, 149–160
  Ogg Theora, 151, 153
  using multiple, 155–156
  WebM, 151, 153–156, 158, 160
Firefogg plug-in, 156
Flash players, 157
  with HTML fallback, 160
Flowplayer Flash, 158
Flowplayer HTML5, 160
frame, 148
H.264 Baseline Profile, 154
H.264 licensing, 154
HandBrake, 156
JavaScript
  Captionator.js, 175
  controlling players with, 160–169
  creating custom player with, 164–
    167
  media players, 167–169
jPlayer media player, 167
licensed content, 145
linking multiple media files
  together, 149
link to download file and open it in an
  external program, 158
looping playback, 147
media queries for, 244
MIME type, 151
  why to use them, 152
Miro Video Converter, 156
mobile browser support for, 153
mobile-optimized, 154
overview, 145–149
paired with audio, 147–149
playback controls, 146
  H.264 video in Opera, 150
playback progress bar, 166

preloading, 146–147
recording, 145
single page for desktop browsers and
  mobile devices, 156
subtitles, 169–175
  adding, 172–173
  search engines and, 173
  timed text tracks, 170
  versus captions, 173
  WebVTT file, 170–176
VideoJS player, 167–169
YouTube, 157
Zencoder, 156
<video> element, 21, 38
  adding subtitles with <track>
    element, 172–173
  autoplay attribute, 147, 148
  controlling players with
    JavaScript, 160–169
  controls attribute, 146, 148
  drawing video frame, 279
  empty syntax tags, 146
  format fallbacks, 155–156
  height attribute, 148
  inserting Flowplayer Flash, 158
  loop attribute, 147, 148
  mediagroup attribute, 149
  metadata, 146
  MIME type, 155
  muted attribute, 148
  nested <source> elements, 155–156
  paired with <audio> element, 147–
    149
  poster attribute, 148–149
  preload attribute, 146, 148
  <progress> element
    playback progress bar, 166
  src attribute, 146, 148
  width attribute, 148
VideoJS, 167–169
Vimeo, 151
VML (Vector Markup Language), 271–
  272
void element, omitting final slash, 16

W

W3C validator, 18–19
WAI-ARIA, 83
WAI (Web Accessibility Initiative)
  website, 39

watchPosition() method (geolocation), 405, 413
watermark, 109
WAV audio file format, 147, 150, 153, 156
<wbr> element, 21, 25
Web Audio API, 145
web fonts, 206–220
  converting desktop fonts to, 209
  creating font collections, 216
  embedded font formats, 208
  finding, 208–209
  @font-face, 206–208, 213–216
  Font Squirrel, 209–211
    preparing fonts for web, 211–214
  formats, 207–208
  free, 209–211
  Google Fonts, 214–216
  licensing, 211
  preparing fonts for web, 211–214
  some problems with, 209
  subscription sites, 216
  using on computer, 211
web forms, 21
WebM video file format, 151, 153–156, 158, 160
  converting to, 156
web pages
  heading structure, 56
  JavaScript and, 452–459
  retrofitting an "About Me" page, 88–93
  sections, hiding and placing, 240
  turning into websites, 55
web servers, 375–400. *See also* server-side programming; web sockets
  asking a question, 377–382
    calling the web server, 380–382
    creating PHP script, 378–379
  dedicated, 395
  history of, 376
  polling, 386
  sending messages to, 376–386
  time, 388
  XMLHttpRequest objects, 105, 133, 138, 140, 430
    web workers and, 424

WebSocket objects
  creating, 395–397, 397
  detecting failed connection, 397
  socket-connection code, 397
web sockets, 375, 393
  browser support for, 394
  checking support for, 394
  echo server, 397–398
  examples on the web, 397–400
  simple client, 395–397
  web socket server, 394–395
  web socket servers, 399
Web SQL Database, 353
web storage, 319–354. *See also* File API; IndexedDB
  application preferences, 325
  application state, 319, 325
  basics, 320–325
  browser support for, 325
  communicating between different browser windows, 330–332
  cookies, 319–320, 325
  finding all stored items, 326–327
  JSON (JavaScript Object Notation), 329–330
  local storage, 319–321
    improving, 341
    storing data, 321–323
  session storage, 320–321
    storing data, 321–323
  storage events, 331
  storage space limits, 321
  storing last position in a game, 323–325
  storing numbers and dates, 327–328
  storing objects, 329–330
  user preferences, 319
  without web server, 323
WebVTT file, 171–176
  Chrome and, 174
web workers, 401
  accessing code in another JavaScript file, 420
  browser support for, 425
  cancelling background task, 421
  communicating with web pages, 418
  creating multiple, 424
  doing periodic tasks with, 424
  downloading data with, 424
  error handling, 421

nested, 424
passing complex messages, 421–424
postMessage() method, 418, 421–423
prime numbers that fit in certain
    range, 414–425
reusing for multiple jobs, 424
running offline, 420
safety measures, 415
sending progress percentage to
    page, 422
setInterval() function and, 414,
    424–425
setTimeout() function and, 414,
    424–425
time-consuming tasks and, 414–417
Worker object, 417–420
XMLHttpRequest object, 424
week data type, 125, 129
**WHATWG (Web Hypertext Application
    Technology Working Group),** 5–6
white-space property, 438
width property, 438
**Wikipedia knowledge map
    website,** 315
WOFF (Web Open Font Format), 208
word-spacing property, 438
Worker object, 417–420

X

XForms, 103
XHTML
    enforcing syntax rules, 20
    return of, 19–21
    tricking browser into switching into
        XHTML mode, 21
    version 1.0, 4
    version 2, 4–5

XHTML5 validator, 20
XMLHttpRequest objects, 105, 133,
    138, 140, 377, 430
    asking the web server a
        question, 377–382
    calling the web server, 380–382
    getting new content, 382–386
    goToNewSlide() function, 384
    onReadyStateChange event, 380–
        381
    query string, 379
    sending messages to web
        server, 376
    send() method, 381, 396
    web workers and, 424

Y

Your Brain: The Missing Manual, 290
YouTube
    H.264 video file format, 151
    re-encoding videos, 157
    screen reader video on, 39
    trial HTML5 player, 144

Z

Zencoder, 156
ZingChart, 293

HTML5

THE MISSING CD

There's no
CD with this book;
you just saved $5.00.

Instead, every single Web address, practice file, and
piece of downloadable software mentioned in this
book is available at *missingmanuals.com*
(click the Missing CD icon).
There you'll find a tidy list of links,
organized by chapter.

Don't miss a thing!
Sign up for the free Missing
Manual email announcement
list at missingmanuals.com.
We'll let you know when we
release new titles, make
free sample chapters available,
and update the features and
articles on the Missing Manual
website.